SAUNDERS BOOKS IN PSYCHOLOGY

LEWIS F. PETRINOVICH AND ROBERT D. SINGER, *Editors*

Psychology: a social science

JOHN WALLACE

UNIVERSITY OF CALIFORNIA, IRVINE

1971   W. B. Saunders Company
Philadelphia/London/Toronto

W. B. Saunders Company: West Washington Square
Philadelphia, Pa. 19105

12 Dyott Street
London, WC1A 1DB

1835 Yonge Street
Toronto 7, Ontario

Psychology: A Social Science

SBN 0-7216-9115-3

© 1971 by W. B. Saunders Company. Copyright under the International Copyright Union. All rights reserved. This book is protected by copyright. No part of it may be reproduced, stored in a retrieval system, or transmitted in any form or by any means, electronic, mechanical, photocopying, recording, or otherwise, without written permission from the publisher. Made in the United States of America. Press of W. B. Saunders Company. Library of Congress catalog number 70-108374.

Print No.:   9   8   7   6   5   4   3   2   1

To Ruth, Andrea, and Tracy

PREFACE

My book *Psychology: A Social Science*, had its beginnings at Northwestern University in 1962. I was a graduate student at the time and when a chance came my way to teach the introductory course, I grabbed it. I remembered the distasteful introduction to the field I had received many years before and was determined that my students would not receive the same treatment. For the length of a quarter, I worried over lectures as only a graduate student teaching his first course can. I remember spending long afternoons in the physiology laboratory being reassured by my wonderful friend, Bernie Schiff (now on the faculty of Toronto University), that my course was not a complete and utter failure, that the kids were learning a lot of psychology, that my lectures were stimulating, and so forth—all the things that a good friend is supposed to say whether they are true or not. I only realized later that Bernie said all those things simply because he wanted me to keep coming back to the lab. Steve Glickman, the only other physiological psychologist around at the time, had departed on a leave of absence leaving Bernie alone with a sloth named "Fast Eddie."

Barry Collins, another good friend and graduate student colleague, taught the undergraduate social psychology course which met immediately after my class in the same lecture hall. I was surprised to discover that Barry made a practice of taking whatever I had left on the blackboard and building a lecture around it. It was only inadvertently that I discovered this peculiar practice of Barry's. News had reached me that Collins was a very good lecturer, and I decided to stay for his class. Pacing about the stage, concentrating intently on his subject matter,

Collins was indeed a fine lecturer. The highlight of the lecture came when, deep in thought, Collins stepped right off the stage, and after striking the floor with some force, he bounced right back to continue his line of argument without a whimper. The assembled undergraduates and I were deeply impressed and we whistled and cheered loudly at such a display of courage, strength, determination, and tenacity of purpose. However, when he managed to do the same number a *second* time within ten minutes, I began to wonder if he hadn't suffered a bit of brain damage in the first fall. The undergraduates, of course, enjoyed the whole show.

Although I didn't fall off the stage that quarter, I did just about everything else to make introduction to psychology an interesting course. Despite all of my efforts, I didn't like the course I presented. I had begun to wonder why the introductory course was traditionally treated as a survey course. The more I questioned this approach to the introductory course, the more dissatisfied I became. The never ending series of survey textbooks that appeared over the years prompted me to loudly harangue anybody who would listen that somebody simply had to write an introductory textbook that departed from the tradition of the survey text.

In the meantime, I played with alternative ways to teach the course. At Stanford University, I tried to build a course around several very large ideas that I thought I saw lurking behind all the minutiae of contemporary psychology. In their year-end evaluations, students described the course as rather a "nightmare." They found the instructor one of the most cognitively disorganized, diffuse, and complex teachers they had encountered. Secretly I was pleased. Anybody who could confound Stanford undergraduates surely had to be onto something good. After the initial sting wore off, however, I found that I really didn't need that rationalization either. And so I continued experimenting with alternative approaches. I tried methodological approaches, personality approaches, and even went so far as to attempt to build a course around the idea that psychological thought was a fascinating collection of "exotic beliefs" which are interesting in and of themselves. I was pleased to discover that students, given the latter perspective, found Skinner as fascinating as Freud.

In any case, I had been teaching at Irvine during this period, holding a joint appointment in the Division of Social Sciences and the Graduate School of Administration. From my many contacts with much too sane political scientists, insane sociologists, and bizzare anthropologists, a new idea for the introductory course began to glimmer in the depths. It was not until Paul Streeter of the W. B. Saunders Company approached me with the idea of writing an introductory text entirely from the perspective of psychology as a social science did I fully realize that this was the organizing principle that I had been searching for.

This book is not a survey textbook. In writing it, I have firmly resisted the temptation to "touch all bases." Instead, I have tried to give the introductory student a beginning course in social thought and behavior that gives him some understanding of the ways in which an inquisitive psychologist inquires into the nature of things. I have tried to show the student that psychology is much more than the study of the individual, and that if we are ever to understand human behavior, we shall have to consider the person in the many social contexts in which we find him. My approach is *selective*. In most cases, I have tried to include content that gives the student mileage; that is, content which imparts something beyond itself — an illustration of a principle, of an epistemological quandary, of a larger generalization, and so forth. Finally, I have tried to include, wherever appropriate, content that I feel is relevant to the current interests and needs of students. As a consequence, the reader will find extended treatments of such topics as racism in America, alienation, power and manipulation motivation, interpersonal dynamics, violence, and the ecological catastrophe. I have tried to show the student that intellectual integrity and relevance are not mutually exclusive.

In short, I have not regarded the introductory course as the occasion to impart so-called "facts" drawn willy-nilly from the entire field of psychology, and I feel that there are good reasons not to do so. First, and most important, the "facts" of contemporary psychology have an undeniable way of slipping rather rapidly into the markedly "uncertain" column and then quietly disappearing as more recent novelties burst upon the scene. Secondly, as psychologists well aware of the results of research on memory, we should know better than to build courses around a hodgepodge of information that nobody really remembers for any appreciable length of time after the course is over. Third, only the most convergent intellects among undergraduates can remain fascinated with a content that veers wildly from the way cockroaches learn to the way schizophrenics mix up their syntax. That kind of curiosity seems more often in the service of conformity and grade getting than in any real wonderment at the behavior of human beings. Finally, I can't help feeling that survey books give the student the very undesirable feeling that the majority of psychological findings and theories are part of a highly certain body of factual information rather than the tentative, uncertain, and, at times, incoherent bits of information that they really are.

In essence, I have tried to write a book about social thought and behavior that lets the student in on the processes through which inquisitive psychologists attempt to understand the many puzzles and complexities that characterize inquiry into the behavior of human beings. I have tried to write a relevant book, one that will grasp the attentions of the introductory student without sacrificing the integrity of the discipline of psychology. At times I have permitted my values and beliefs to show clearly in my writing. At other times, I have drawn upon my own experiences to illustrate a point that I wish to make. And at times I frankly speculate about the nature of things. I don't regard any of this as out of place in an introductory psychology book. At least half of the fun of being a psychologist is getting one's own values into perspective, getting one's own experiences together, and speculating about the way many complex events combine to produce the behavior of human beings.

The book is sufficient to stand alone as an introductory text in a course in which the teacher wishes to follow an exclusively social approach. It could also be effectively combined with a text in which social psychology is not given the relevant emphasis desired for the course. The instructor who wishes to stay with a survey text in a course of longer duration might find it profitable supplementary reading for his class. While entirely suitable for undergraduate majors, the text should have very high appeal to nonmajors in psychology as well.

In closing, I wish to thank those many friends, students, and colleagues—from Aliquippa, Pennsylvania, to Laguna Beach, California, and from Evanston, Illinois, to Sydney, Australia—who made this work possible. Many are undoubtedly unaware that they even had a hand in it.

J.W.

Laguna Beach, California

CONTENTS

CHAPTER 1

PSYCHOLOGY AS A SOCIAL SCIENCE: METHODS OF INQUIRY... 1

Methods of Inquiry in the Study of Social Thought and
    Behavior, 4
        The Clinical Method, 4
        Correlational Methods, 7
        Laboratory Experiments, 8
        The Field Study, 14
        Quasi-experimental Methods, 19
        Simulation and Gaming Methods, 21
Formal Mathematical Models, 26
Methodological Controversy, 28

CHAPTER 2

SPECIAL PROBLEMS IN PSYCHOLOGICAL INQUIRY................. 32

Observation, Inference, and Prediction, 35
Scientific Inquiry as Choice Among Plausible Alternative
    Hypotheses, 38
Sources of Uncertainty in Psychological Inquiry, 39
        The Subject, 42
        The Inquirer, 44
        Sampling Procedures, 47
The Search for Generality in Psychological Inquiry, 49
Generality and Truth, 51
The Deeper Meaning of Uncertainty in Psychological Inquiry, 53

CHAPTER 3

LEVELS OF ANALYSIS... 56

Within Levels of Analysis, 59
        Individual Level: Self-esteem and Creative
            Performance, 59

xiii

Interpersonal Level: Obedience and Disobedience
to Authority, 63
Group Interactional Level: Communication
Structures, 66
Interactions Between Levels of Analysis, 69
Interaction Between the Individual and Societal Levels:
Need for Achievement and Economic Growth, 70
Interactions Among Levels of Analysis, 82
Psychological Stress, Interpersonal Conflict, and
Organizational Structure, 83

CHAPTER 4
CONCEPTUALIZING THE PERSON 90

Energy Theories, 90
  The Instinct Doctrine, 91
  The Drive Doctrine, 100
    Arousal Theory, 106
    Need Theories, 106
Cognitive-Informational Theories, 109
    The Psychology of Personal Constructs, 110
    Cognitive-Consistency Theories, 112
    Theories Emphasizing Choice, 118
    The Self Concept, 123
Social Role Conceptions, 127
Conditioned Response Theory, 132

CHAPTER 5
THE PSYCHOLOGICAL STUDY OF THE PERSON 139

Social Motives and Their Measurement, 140
  Achievement Motivation, 141
    Motive, Expectancy, and Incentive: Need
    Achievement and Risk-taking, 147
  Power, Manipulation, and Machiavellianism, 150
    Personality and Politics, 152
    Machiavellianism, 156
  Hostility and Aggression, 158
Anxiety Conflict and Defense, 167
  Anxiety, 167
  Conflict, 174
  Defense, 176
The Self Concept, 181

CHAPTER 6
INTERPERSONAL KNOWING 188

The Human Being as a Complex Information
  Processing System, 190
Properties of the Observer, 195
  Inferential Sets and Interpersonal Knowledge, 196

Language and Interpersonal Knowing, 198
Naive Personality Theories, 202
Cognitive Complexity-Simplicity, 204
Temporal Focusing and Interpersonal Knowing, 206
Strategies in Coming to Know Others, 208
Affective States, Attention, and Social Perception, 216
Individual Differences in Ability to Judge Others, 217
Properties of the Observed, 218
Physical Characteristics, 218
Eye Contact, 219
Distance, 220
Postural Cues, 221
Verbalizations and Vocalizations, 222
Properties of the Context, 223
Locus of Causality, 224
Intentionality and Social Contexts, 225
Perceived Justifiability, 226

CHAPTER 7

INTERPERSONAL INTERACTION 230

The Purposeful Nature of Human Interaction, 231
Social Comparisons and Information Seeking, 232
Uncertainty, Social Comparisons, and Affiliation, 233
Expected Gain and Social Interaction, 237
Interpersonal Tactics, 238
Interpersonal Influence, 243
Bases of Power, 244
Social Learning, 252
Communication and Interpersonal Interaction, 257
Development of Communication Skills, 258
Communication of Expectancies, 261
Communication and Interpersonal Influence, 263
Properties of the Message, 264
Attributes of Communicators, 267
Properties of Receivers, 268
Personality Change and Interpersonal Communication, 269

CHAPTER 8

GROUPS AND ORGANIZATIONS 275

The Psychological Study of Groups, 279
Normative and Informational Influence in Groups, 280
Conditions That Increase Susceptibility to Group Influence, 283
The Significance of Career Choice, 291
Groups and Deviant Behavior, 293
Group Conflict and its Resolution, 295
Some Generalizations Emerging from Group Research, 299
The Person in the Complex Organization, 303
Approaches to the Study of Organizations, 305

Scientific Management, 305
Classic Organization Theory, 306
The Human Relations School, 311
Human Potentialities Theory, 313
Assumptions About the Individual and Organizational Theory, 316
Psychology and the Physical Design of Organizations, 317
The Relevance of the Psychological Study of Organizations, 318

CHAPTER 9
THE PSYCHOLOGICAL STUDY OF SOCIETY 322

Riots in Anytown, U.S.A., 322
Racism in American Society, 328
    Blacks and the Opportunity Structure, 330
    Ghetto Social Structure and the Opportunity Structure, 332
    Education, Unemployment, and the Opportunity Structure, 333
    Psychological Consequences of Racism, 334
    Prescriptions for Change, 343
Alienation in American Society, 348
    Rejection of American Social Structure and Alienation, 351
    The Psychology of Alienation, 353
    Life in the Kibbutz: An Interesting Contrast to American Society, 358
Psychology and the Ecological Crisis, 360
    Human Values and Ecological Catastrophe, 361
  The Multi-dimensional Nature of Ecological Problems, 366
    Population and the Necessity for Changes in Human Values, 368
    The Scientific-technological Information Environment, 371

CHAPTER 10
CULTURE AND THE PERSON... 375

    Some Generalizations in the Study of Culture and the Person, 384
Human Personality in Culture, 390
    Group Character Versus Modal Personality, 392
    Cross-cultural Studies of Child-rearing Practices, 394
    Factors Affecting Child-rearing, 402
    Language, Thought, and Personality, 404
    Culture and Deviant Behavior, 407
    Culture and Mental Disorder, 409

INDEX OF NAMES... 417
INDEX OF SUBJECTS.. 421

CHAPTER 1

Psychology as a Social Science: Methods of Inquiry

We who live in the latter part of the twentieth century are witnesses to truly radical change. Even the most casual observer of the times senses that revolutionary change is in progress. The rapid and remarkable growth of information, the bold advances of modern technology, and the striking questioning of accepted patterns of social thought and values are characteristic. Psychology cannot and will not remain unaffected by these revolutionary currents of change. Much of traditional psychology, while still of value in and of itself, seems largely irrelevant to the complex problems confronting human beings today. The crises of urban societies, world wide social and political unrest, and continuing international tensions and turbulence, pose new and complex problems for the inquiring psychologist. Moreover, it has become increasingly evident that rigorous and sensitive analyses of the isolated individual will prove insufficient for understanding human behavior. The behavior of persons does not originate nor is it maintained in a social vacuum. If we are ever to arrive at a complete understanding of human behavior, it is imperative that we consider persons in the important *social contexts* in which we find them. Thus, for example, the child's behavior can only be grasped fully in terms of the *interaction* between child and parent, child and teacher, child and child, and so on. The behavior of the worker in an industrial corporation must be seen as imbedded in a complex *organizational system*. The protests of minority group members can be understood properly only in the *cultural* and *social* surroundings in which they occur. It is for these reasons that psychology as a social science has come of age.

The study of social thought and behavior

For our purposes, we shall define psychology as the study of social thought and behavior; we will focus upon the behavior of the individual in given social contexts. At the conclusion of our study, we will have examined interpersonal interaction, group interaction, behavior within complex organizations, the individual and society, and the cultural influences over behavior.

Given this definition of psychology, one might object that it is both far too broad and far too narrow. On the one hand, it fails to differentiate psychology from disciplines such as anthropology, sociology, political science, and even some aspects of philosophy, and in a sense, this possible objection has some basis. However, as we shall see, psychology either implicitly or explicitly serves as the foundation for much of the theory in these related disciplines. Moreover, as the necessity for interdisciplinary collaboration in the social sciences is increasingly recognized, the boundaries that separate one discipline from another have become increasingly difficult to specify.

On the other hand, our definition fails to include the biological aspects of psychological study. Let us consider this possible objection in greater detail.

Psychology: a social or biological science?

Although we have defined psychology as the study of social thought and behavior, it is imperative that the student realize that this is a definition of convenience. Much of modern psychology owes its intellectual heritage to the biological sciences rather than to the social sciences. Indeed, the roots of modern experimental psychology can be traced to physiology in Germany during the latter half of the nineteenth century. Moreover, numerous psychologists continue to search for the underlying biological determinants of human motivation, learning, memory, mental disorders, and so forth. Clearly, modern psychology is both a biological and social science, and it seems almost fruitless to argue that it is primarily one or the other. Certainly we can expect continued research to reveal much about the biological determinants of behavior, but it is equally likely that much of the behavior of human beings will be understood in terms of social processes as well.

It is interesting to note that the man generally accepted as

Figure 1. The behavior of human beings cannot be understood in a social vacuum. (Photo by Gordon Cole.)

the "father of modern experimental psychology," Wilhelm Wundt, thought of his life work in terms of two separate grand endeavors. Wundt wished to create an experimental psychology, and toward this effort, he contributed an enormous number of words on both the theory of sensory perception and the methodology of scientific experimental psychology. However, Wundt envisioned a "social psychology" as well. Although he correctly perceived the need for the study of social behavior, he incorrectly maintained that it was impossible to study these aspects of human beings scientifically. As we shall see, thousands of subsequent scientific studies of social behavior have proved Wundt wrong on this score.

In short, then, while psychology is best thought of as both a biological and a social science, we shall restrict our study to psychology as a social science. In doing so, we do not deny the value of a biological approach to the study of human behavior; however, we are content to leave such matters in more competent hands. The student who wishes a good introduction to psychology as a biological science is encouraged to read Donald Hebb's excellent book, *A Textbook of Psychology*.

METHODS OF INQUIRY IN THE STUDY OF SOCIAL THOUGHT AND BEHAVIOR

Most people recognize that the psychologist has available to him tools and techniques of study that the layman does not possess. These methods of inquiry are the clinical or case method, correlational methods, the laboratory experiment, the field study, quasi-experimental methods, and simulation, gaming, and mathematical models. Let us discuss and illustrate each method briefly.

The clinical method

Intensive study of the single person or a given group of persons is characteristic of the clinical method. Although the clinical method may involve the use of psychological tests of various kinds, the sensitive and well-trained psychologist following his hunches and speculations, interpreting complex bits and pieces of information, and arriving at a reasonable account of things remains as the critical ingredient.

The clinical method is illustrated in the following dramatic report of a case of "multiple personality,"

Case 27. Eve White was (at time of examination) a twenty-five year old married woman faced with serious marital and personality problems. A demure, retiring individual, Eve White was quiet, industrious, and, as the authors put it, "in some degrees almost saintly." During the course of therapy the authors were led to suspect the existence of another personality. Eve White could not remember a previous therapy session. Later she wrote a letter to one of the authors expressing concern over this lapse of memory. In the middle of the letter the handwriting changed and a new line of discourse was established. On the succeeding therapy day, the suspicions of the authors were startlingly confirmed when a second personality became dominant for the first time.

This new personality, Eve Black, had been co-existing with Eve White since childhood. . . . Eve Black's behavior was the opposite of White. Black was shrewd, rowdy, and provocative; she enjoyed joking and pranks. Uninhibited and frank, Black lived for the moment. Furthermore, Black was aware of the existence of White while Eve White knew nothing of her other personality. Black delighted in placing Eve White in embarrassing positions: "When I go out and get drunk," Eve Black once said with an easy wink to her therapists, "*she* wakes up with the hangover."*

In this example, the sensitive and inquiring attitudes of the well-trained clinician are evident. Eve White's therapists were alert to the importance of attending to all of the information about their patient. When Eve White reported her inability to remember a previous therapy session, the therapists considered this memory lapse significant. In the letter Eve White wrote to them, they detected the abrupt change in her handwriting as well as the altered nature of the discourse. This led the therapists to hypothesize the existence of a second personality, Eve Black, and as the following day's therapy session unfolded, this prediction was confirmed.

That the clinical method need not be restricted to intensive study of the single case is amply demonstrated by Sudnow's recent work on the management of death in private and public hospitals (Sudnow, 1967). Sudnow's book, wryly entitled *Passing On,* is a rich mine of direct observations on this important medical, social, and psychological topic. Obtaining work as a hospital aide, Sudnow simply used his considerable abilities as a sen-

---

*From Thigpen, C. H., and Cleckley, H. M.: *The Three Faces of Eve.* New York, McGraw-Hill Book Co., 1957, p. 141.

sitive observer and interpreter of behavior in real life settings to arrive at some remarkable conclusions. In addition to the well-known states of biological and clinical death, Sudnow hypothesized the existence of a state of *sociopsychological* death. In this state, the patient may very well be biologically alive, but he is treated by those concerned with his care and management *as though he were already dead.* For example, physicians discussed autopsy plans in the presence of a patient thought to be in coma and who was not expected to live. As Sudnow points out, the physicians made the questionable assumption that simply because the patient was incapable of *transmitting* information, his abilities to *receive* information were inoperative as well. In essence, the physicians were treating the patient as if he were dead when, in fact, the patient was still very much alive.

Another incident enabled Sudnow to recognize the existence and importance of certain temporal expectations in the passage of a person from the state of living through sociopsychological death into biological death. A young man was admitted to an emergency ward suffering from relatively minor gun shot wounds. Although surgery was required, the attending physicians anticipated no difficulties and so informed relatives who had come to the hospital. Unfortunately, for no apparent reason, the young man died suddenly and unexpectedly on the operating table. Since the relatives had not been prepared for the death of the patient, the attending physicians feared that the sudden passage from life to biological death would arouse suspicions of the competence of the physicians and that such suspicions might lead to a serious medical malpractice suit. As a consequence, even though the patient had in fact died, information concerning the "growing complexities" of the case were sent from the operating room to the relatives. After a lengthy period had elapsed in which communications such as "he seems to have more serious problems than we realize," "the situation is getting worse," "the situation is critical," and so forth, had been released from the operating room, the relatives were informed that the patient had "finally died." In short, the physicians intuitively recognized that passage from life into sociopsychological death and finally into biological death required given amounts of time. Otherwise, the patient's relatives might have assumed, correctly or incorrectly, that the case had been handled incompetently.

Correlational methods

When the observations of the psychologist can be expressed quantitatively, the search for systematic relationships among *variables* can be undertaken. For example, consider the following hypothesis: *Creative people, if given a choice, will prefer complexity to simplicity.* How might the psychologist proceed to inquire about this hypothesis using correlational methods? First, the psychologist must find a way to *measure* creativity. He might do this by devising a test of "creative ability." Or he might ask members of a specialized group of persons, such as an architects' association, a university faculty, or a research team in an aerospace laboratory, to make *ratings* of one another's creative abilities.

If the psychologist manages to develop a valid and reliable means of measuring creative ability, he must still devise a way of measuring "preference for complexity" if he is to test the aforementioned hypothesis. Since the hypothesis is stated quite generally, there are numerous ways in which the psychologist could attempt to measure preference for complexity. He might, for example, construct a series of visual designs varying in complexity from exceedingly simple, symmetrical line drawings to intricate and asymmetrical configurations. The ratio of complex designs preferred to simple designs preferred might then serve as a quantitative measure of preference for complexity.

Once the psychologist has devised the means by which "creative ability" and "preference for complexity" can be measured, he can then proceed to test the hypothesis that creative people, if given a choice, will prefer complexity to simplicity. Quite typically, he would select a *sample* of persons and administer both the measures of "creative ability" and "preference for complexity" to them. The hypothesis would be supported to the extent that the two sets of measurements are related to one another; that is, a *positive relationship* would be evident if persons scoring high on one measure also scored high on the other, if persons scoring moderately on one measure also scored moderately on the other, and if persons scoring low on one measure also scored low on the other. Most frequently the relationship between sets of scores is expressed in terms of a single, numerical index called the *correlation coefficient.*

Research much like that just discussed has, in fact, already been accomplished. A preference for complexity has been found in creative persons in research by Barron and Welsh (1952).

Correlational studies have proved invaluable in the study of the many ways in which human beings differ from one another. Psychologists interested in such *individual differences* have conducted thousands of studies of personalities, aptitudes, beliefs, values, abilities, and motives. The questions for which psychologists have sought answers through the use of correlational methods are numerous and varied, and it would very likely require several chapters simply to list such questions. However, some examples might prove illustrative: Is intelligence a single, unitary, general human capability, or does it consist of relatively independent specific abilities? That is, would we expect to find a general factor of intelligence that entered into human performance across a wide variety of intellectual tasks, or would we expect to find numerous independent factors? Do the symptoms of mental hospital patients cluster together in such a way as to permit the construction of clear cut *types* of mental disorder? Do measures of childhood personality attributes predict subsequent adult characteristics? Are highly anxious persons good or poor performers on complex intellectual tasks? Do measures of intelligence relate to school achievement? Do measures of the "psychological needs" of individuals relate to such things as marital success, job satisfaction, reactions to failure, and so on? These are but a mere handful of the enormous number of questions that have been explored through use of correlational methods.

Laboratory experiments

For certain types of problems in the study of social behavior, the laboratory experiment remains a very powerful method of inquiry. In theory, by means of rigorous procedures, the experimenter can exercise considerable control over his subjects as well as over the situation in which his research is conducted. In practice, experimentation in the study of social behavior frequently proves more complex than one would anticipate. Considering the large number of variables that can affect the behavior of persons, this is not surprising. However, in the past several decades important and significant improvements in experimental designs and research methodology have provided encouraging signs that a rigorous experimental approach to the study of social behavior is entirely possible.

The central idea of the experimental method is elegantly simple; in actual practice it is enormously difficult to achieve. For the experimenter, the principal task is *to hold all variables constant except one* and to study the effects of systematic variation of this single variable. While this may sound complex, the idea really is very simple. Suppose that one wished to determine the effects of subordinate participation in organizational decision-making upon member morale. Are workers who are given the opportunity to affect the decisions made concerning their jobs happier than those who are not? Would the college student who is permitted to influence the nature of his curriculum be a more satisfied student than the one who is not? It is possible to study such questions in the laboratory in various group interactions. However, when one has completed the experiment, one must be in a position to say that any differences in morale that are found are attributable to the single variable studied, member participation in decision-making, and not to any one of a host of other possible variables, e.g., possible differences among experimenters, times of day, varying temperature of the laboratory, different interest value of the tasks used, differences in group composition, and so forth. Although many of the variables that can influence results are essentially trivial and uninteresting in and of themselves, they must be controlled for their potential effects upon the behavior of the subject. Experience has shown time and time again that even the most "trivial" variables, if left uncontrolled, can produce important effects upon subjects' behavior. For example, the fact that patients' diets were left uncontrolled in one series of studies, led investigators to an erroneous theory of the cause of the serious mental disorder, schizophrenia. Although the experimenters were led to believe that schizophrenia is caused by a dysfunction in the metabolism of the hormone adrenaline, their results were in fact attributable to a vitamin C deficiency in the patients studied. In subsequent studies, when patients were given appropriate doses of vitamin C, their adrenaline metabolism proved entirely normal. However, they remained schizophrenic. In short, these investigators failed to control all variables but the one they were interested in, e.g., metabolism of adrenaline. As a consequence, they were led to a completely erroneous conclusion.

Throughout this course of study, the student will encounter numerous reports of experimental findings. The student should constantly ask himself the following questions: (1) Has the experimenter exercised complete control over his experiment, and (2) can the results be explained in some plausible, alternative way other than the experimenter's?

Laboratory experiments on social behavior are as numerous and varied as correlational methods. In the course of our study, we will consider experiments on communication, motivation, group interaction, conformity, social learning, attitude change, persuasion, decision-making, and conflict. Let us examine one representative experiment in some detail. In this manner, it is possible to gain a more detailed picture of the ingredients of an experiment on social behavior.

In 1952, Carl Hovland and Walter Weiss performed an important experiment published under the title The Influence of Source Credibility on Communication Effectiveness. In this particular experiment, Hovland and Weiss were concerned with the general question of the *attitudes* of an audience toward a communicator and the effects such attitudes would have upon changes in opinion in audience members. In particular, the experimenters wished to study opinion change when a communicator was considered "trustworthy" and when he was considered generally "untrustworthy." In light of recent concern with the "credibility" of certain governmental figures, this early experiment seems to have enduring relevance.

Subjects in the experiment were college students enrolled in a history course at Yale University. They were pretested on their opinions concerning a number of issues, four of which were as follows:

1. "Should the antihistamine drugs continue to be sold without a doctor's prescription?"
2. "Can a practicable atomic-powered submarine be built at the present time?"
3. "Is the steel industry to blame for the current shortage of steel?"
4. "As a result of TV, will there be a decrease in the number of movie theaters in operation by 1955?"

At the same time, the students were asked to rate the "credibility" of a number of sources of information, e.g., various scholarly journals, popular magazines, particular writers, national figures, and so on. From these ratings it was possible to select four sources of information with high credibility and four with low credibility in the eyes of this particular group of subjects. The high credibility sources were *New England Journal of Biology and Medicine,* J. Robert Oppenheimer (the distinguished atomic scientist now deceased), *Bulletin of National Resources Planning Board,* and *Fortune* magazine. The low credibility sources were a mass circulation monthly pictorial magazine, *Pravda* (the official newspaper of the Russian Communist Party), a syndicated woman movie-gossip columnist, and an extremely conservative syndicated newspaper columnist.

Articles either affirming or negating the four questions concerning antihistamine drugs, atomic submarines, the steel shortage, and the future of movie theaters were carefully prepared and assembled into booklets, with the names of the high credibility or low credibility authors and sources clearly marked at the close of the articles. These booklets comprised the communications received by the subjects. For example, a student might receive a booklet containing an article attributed to *For-*

Figure 2. A crisis in credibility. Large numbers of Americans questioned the credibility of the Nixon administration as United States forces moved into Cambodia. (Photo by Cathy L. Jones.)

tune magazine affirming that movie attendance would decrease because of TV or another article in which *Pravda* holds that it would be impossible to build a nuclear submarine, and so forth. Given the many possible combinations of topics, versions, and sources of communication, it was necessary to construct 24 different booklets. An example of one of these, a booklet combination in the Hovland-Weiss experiment, is given below:*

Topic	Version	Source
Future of movie theaters	Affirmative	*Fortune*
Atomic submarines	Negative	*Pravda*
Steel shortage	Affirmative	Extremely conservative columnist
Antihistamine drugs	Negative	*New England Journal of Biology and Medicine*

The students were requested to read the articles contained in the booklets. Their opinions were measured immediately after reading and again after a lapse of four weeks.

Since this experiment, like many in the study of social behavior, may seem quite complicated, let us review it in the form of an outline.

Hypothesis: The amount of opinion change will vary as a function of the degree of credibility of a communicator.

Subjects: Yale University undergraduates.

Materials: Specially prepared booklets containing articles presumably appearing in either high or low credibility sources or written by either high or low credibility authors.

Procedure: 1. Determination of initial opinions and ratings of credibility.
2. Exposure to high and low credibility communications in the form of the specially prepared booklets.
3. Immediate retesting of opinion.
4. Final testing of opinion after lapse of four weeks.

---

*Adapted from Hovland, C. I., and Weiss, W.: The influence of source credibility on communication effectiveness. Public Opinion Quarterly, 15: 635, 1952.

The results of the Hovland and Weiss experiment are very interesting indeed. When the amount of opinion change is measured immediately, exposure to a high credibility source of information results in far greater opinion change than does exposure to a low credibility source. While these results would seem to be in accord with common sense and might even prompt the student to say that he could easily have predicted them, the findings for opinion change following the four-week delay are not nearly so obvious. As time progressed, a striking reversal in the trend of the data was apparent, i.e., opinion change in subjects exposed to highly credible sources *decreased* while opinion change in subjects exposed to low credibility sources *increased*! Figure 1 presents a graph of these data.

How might we interpret this dramatic reversal in the data with the passage of time? Why should time alone produce such an effect? Terming the phenomenon the "sleeper effect," Hovland and Weiss argue that with the passage of time, the *source* of the communication and the *content* of the communication tend to become disassociated. That is, while the subject may be able to recall both what was said and who was doing the saying, the precise association between who said what and where it was said may be weakened. Moreover, in some cases, while subjects may retain the content of the communication, they may forget

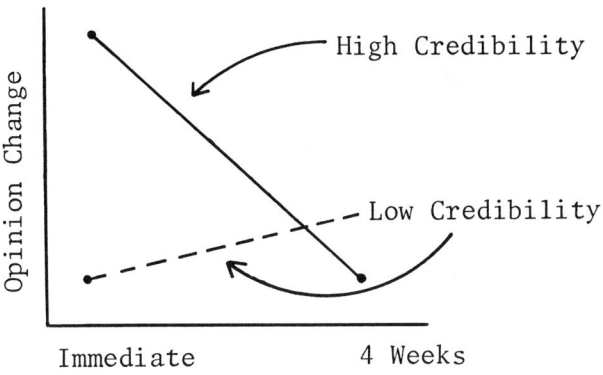

Figure 3. "Retention" of opinion. Changes in extent of agreement with position advocated by "high credibility" and "low credibility" sources. *Adapted from* Hovland, C. I., and Weiss. W.: The influence of source credibility on communication effectiveness. Public Opinion Quarterly, *15:*635, 1952.

the source entirely. As a consequence, the initial resistance to a communication from a low credibility source might very well weaken as the content increases in credibility. Subjects would then show a delayed influence effect even from a source they regarded as low in credibility—hence, the term "sleeper effect." If Hovland and Weiss are taken seriously, one might very well reconsider his or her reading habits. It is a bit disconcerting to think that one might vigorously defend an opinion that was shaped from the casual reading of a third-rate magazine several weeks before!

In any case, the experiment by Hovland and Weiss is an excellent example of a carefully conducted experiment on social behavior.

The field study

While the laboratory experiment has made significant contributions to the study of social behavior, numerous psychologists prefer to make their observations in natural settings rather than in the restricted situation of the laboratory. The decision to use either the laboratory experiment or the field study is often based upon the choice by the researcher between maximizing *control* over his variables or maximizing the *generalizability* of his findings. In the laboratory fairly precise control over variables can frequently be achieved. However, the laboratory setting is in many respects atypical and unique, and consequently it is difficult to apply results to situations outside the laboratory. On the other hand, the richness of the field situation coupled with the fact that the researcher cannot exercise experimental control over his variables creates difficulties. The lesson here is very simple: there is *no perfect* method of inquiry in the study of social behavior. All methods have their advantages and disadvantages.

A very recent study by Richard Jessor, Theodore Graves, Robert Hanson, and Shirley Jessor (1968) is an excellent example of well-designed and well-executed field study. Through intensive study of a southwestern Colorado community, Jessor and his colleagues were able to develop interesting hypotheses concerning the occurrence of deviant behavior, particularly excessive alcohol usage. The study focused upon the fact that various measures of deviance showed strikingly different rates among the three ethnic groups of the community, Anglos, Spanish, and Indians. Table 1 illustrates these differences.

As Table 1 indicates, the Indian population of the community far exceeded the Anglos in deviance rates. The deviance rates for the Spanish, although not different from the Anglos for certain measures, showed moderate increases for the others. How might these differences by explained?

According to Jessor and his colleagues, deviant behavior does not require explanations that are radically different from those used to explain conformity. Both forms of behavior are seen as adaptive or adjustive. Although deviant acts may seem purposeless or aimless, they are essentially goal-oriented behaviors just as many socially acceptable behaviors of the individual are also goal-oriented. In a socially disadvantaged group such as the Indian community, individuals may resort to socially unacceptable means of achieving satisfaction when the social structure does not permit socially acceptable means of achieving goal satisfaction.

Given this general theoretical view of deviance, the authors attempted to clarify aspects of the *social-cultural* system which characterized the community as well as certain differences in the *personality* systems among the various ethnic groups. By careful measurements of variables describing the social-cultural system and of the personality structure of the members of the

TABLE 1. Ethnic Group Percentages for Various Measures of Deviance and Alcohol Use*

Measure	Anglo (N = 92)†	Spanish (N = 60)	Indian (N = 66)
Court convictions over 10 years	1	12	54
Self-report of deviance (for example, child neglect)	25	29	60
Frequent drinking in the morning	9	22	33
Reports of drunkenness 3 or more times in the past year	3	15	38
Reports of 5 or more occurrences of deviant behavior related to drinking (for example, fights while drinking)	14	15	53

*Adapted from Jessor, R., Graves, T., Hanson, R., and Jessor, S.: *Society, Personality, and Deviant Behavior: A Study of a Tri-ethnic Community.* New York, Holt, Rinehart and Winston, 1968, p. 17.

†N indicates the number of subjects studied in each ethnic group.

ethnic groups, they were able to show relationships between these and the differing rates for deviant behavior among the three ethnic groups.

Although the results for both the social-cultural system and the personality structure are of equal interest, it would prove too complex for our purposes to discuss them here. Let us consider the manner in which Jessor and his colleagues using field methods studied the social-cultural system of the community.

The social-cultural system was broken down into the following components:

1. *The Opportunity Structure.* This comprises the socially approved, legitimate channels of access to culturally valued goals. The location of any individual in the opportunity structure of a social system can be determined by the degree of access he has to culturally valued goals.

    Consider the lower-class ghetto black man in American society. By no stretch of the imagination can his degree of access to culturally valued goals be considered equivalent to that of the suburban middle-class white. The same condition prevailed for the Indian and the Spanish in the present study. Objective measurements of the community studied by Jessor and his colleagues indicated that the various ethnic groups occupied differing positions in its opportunity structure. The Anglos occupied positions of greatest access to opportunity, and the Spanish and Indian positions of least access. These results are, of course, in accord with the theoretical expectation that greater pressure toward socially disapproved means of goal satisfaction will take place in groups with limited access to socially approved goals.

    The measurement of the opportunity structure was developed in two ways. First, a *socioeconomic status index* was developed from information concerning occupation and education. Second, an *objective access index* was developed consisting of the following eight variables: age, age combined with marital status, language spoken in the home, occupation, education, occupational status relative to father, religion, and participation in both formal and informal social groups.

2. *The Normative Structure.* Social norms can be thought of as standards guiding the conduct of members of a given

social group. In essence, interacting groups of individuals come to share expectations that concern the appropriateness of given behaviors in particular social situations. When there is *consensus* concerning most aspects of behavior within social situations, groups tend toward stability and cohesion. When consensus is lacking, a sociopsychological state of anomie exists. The term *anomie* describes social systems in which agreement concerning the appropriateness of given behaviors does not exist. All members of such a social system do not share the same expectations concerning the legitimacy of various standards for behavior.

When a substantial degree of anomie is present in a social group, individual members of that group are confronted with considerable uncertainty and insecurity in social relations. Given the lack of consensus regarding appropriate behavior, in addition to the associated uncertainty and insecurity in social relations, problematic individual behaviors of all types may appear.

Efforts were made in the community study by Jessor and his colleagues to measure the degree of anomie in the Anglo, Spanish, and Indian subcultures. As might be expected, the greatest degree of consensus concerning standards for behavior was obtained in the Anglo subculture. The Spanish showed substantial agreement on certain norms for behavior and considerable conflict on others. The Indian subculture displayed a general pattern of low consensus on norms for behavior. This pervasive *normlessness* of the Indian subculture is thought to be related to the high degree of deviant behavior, particularly excessive drinking, which characterizes that group.

Measurement of the normative structure was accomplished by means of a community survey questionnaire and interview procedure. Members of the Anglo, Spanish, and Indian subcultures were asked their opinions on items such as the following:

(a) A teenage daughter obeys her parents without question.
(b) The husband by himself makes all important money decisions for the family.
(c) A policeman ignores a drunk person unless some actual damage has been done.

From the various responses to items such as these, it was possible for the researchers to establish the degree of consensus in each of the three subcultures regarding norms for particular behaviors.

3. *The Social Control Structure.* All social systems develop means of controlling the behavior of individuals within them. Through both formal and informal structures, efforts are made to reduce or eliminate "illegitimate means" of goal attainment. The example of the police patrol car readily comes to mind. The person of criminal intent is less likely to engage in stealing as a means of achieving his material wants if he expects the frequent inspection of his area of operations by police officers. While this example of social structural controls over behavior is quite obvious, other less obvious controls do exist. In the field study presently being considered, efforts were made to measure three important aspects of the social control structure: (1) the opportunity to learn deviant behavior by witnessing deviant acts in others, particularly deviant adult role models, (2) the extent to which the person is imbedded in a social system in which other members monitor his behavior and administer rewards for conformity and punishment for deviance, and (3) the opportunity to engage in deviant behavior as a consequence of access to the materials, instruments, and situations necessary to perform deviant acts.

Although we frequently fail to take them into account, variables such as these are of great importance in predicting deviant behavior. The exposure of a child throughout his formative years to parents who are antagonistic to one another, parents with alcoholic drinking problems, and so forth, may exert profound influences over his behavior. The opportunity to engage in deviant acts is another variable often overlooked but clearly of great significance in understanding their occurrence.

Once again, differences among the three ethnic groups were discovered. The Anglos occupied social positions in the social control structure with the least access to illegitimate means, the Spanish were intermediate, and the Indian occupied the position in the social control structure with the greatest access to illegitimate means.

From the results of this excellently conducted field study, then, a portrait of the Indian subculture in this southwestern Colorado community is possible. (1) The Indian has low access to the opportunity structure of the community. (2) Normative consensus among the Indian community does not exist; there is considerable uncertainty and insecurity in social relations as a result. (3) The Indian child is more frequently exposed to deviant adult role models than are the Anglo or Spanish children. (4) The lack of a cohesive social structure in the Indian subculture does not permit consistent control over behavior within the subculture through the administration of rewards and punishments. (5) Finally, the Indian possesses greater access to "illegitimate" means of goal satisfaction than either the Anglo or the Spanish. The occurrence of greater deviance rates among the Indian subculture is partially explained as a consequence of these social-cultural variables.

Quasi-experimental methods

An inventive and imaginative experimenter can often develop methods of study that combine the advantages of the laboratory and the field study. Various combinations of laboratory and field methods have led to interesting *quasi-experimental designs*. For example, Merritt and Fowler (1948) developed an ingenious method for the study of honesty. They prepared two types of stamped, addressed envelopes, one containing a bland message, the other containing a metal disc the weight and size of a fifty-cent piece. These specially prepared envelopes were deliberately "lost" in a number of different locations on different days. The experimenters then sat back and waited for the return of the "lost" letters. Although 85 per cent of the letters containing the message were returned, only 54 per cent of those containing the metal disc were returned. In some cases Merritt and Fowler arranged conditions so that they could observe unsuspecting subjects who had found the letters:

Watching the pickup of the letters proved to be a most entertaining pastime. Some were picked up and immediately posted at the nearest mailbox. Others were examined minutely, evidently precipitating quite a struggle between the finder and his conscience, before being pocketed or mailed. Some were carried a number of blocks before being posted, one person carrying a letter openly for nine blocks before mailing it. A lady in Ann Arbor, Michigan found a letter and carried it six miles in her car to deliver it personally, although she was not acquainted with the addressee.... Two of five letters left on church steps during Sunday services failed to return.*

A study by Lefkowitz, Blacke, and Mouton (1955) conducted on the streets of Austin, Texas, concerned itself with the effects of status. The investigators enlisted the aid of "confederates" dressed in either a high-status fashion (suit, white shirt, tie, etc.) or a low-status fashion (levis, workshirt, etc.). At various intersections of the city the confederates either conformed to or disobeyed a flashing "don't walk" signal. Hidden observers counted the number of people in each case who followed the behavior of the two types of confederates. There proved to be a greater tendency for people to violate the signal after having observed a high-status person do so than after having observed the low-status person.

In the two examples given above, the variables under investigation were manipulated by the experimenters. It is possible in other types of quasi-experimental designs to allow conditions to vary naturally and to simply record the outcomes of such naturally occurring variations. For example, Bain and Hecock (1957) dealt with the question, "Does the position in which a candidate's name appears on the ballot affect the number of votes he receives?" Most veteran politicians argue that it does indeed. Some have estimated that the initial position on the ballot may give a candidate as much as a 20 per cent edge on his opponents. By means of appropriate statistical techniques, Bain and Hecock were able to establish quite convincingly that the position does, in fact, have an effect on voter choice.

Sechrest (1965) in a clever study of restroom graffiti was able to establish cross-cultural differences in sexual preoccupations between Filipinos and Americans. Inscriptions on the walls of public toilets in the United States showed a far greater preoccupation with heterosexual and homosexual activities than did inscriptions on the walls of Filipino public toilets. One investigator (Sawyer, 1961), interested in the problem of measuring alcohol consumption in a supposedly "dry" city, actually went so far as to inspect the trash removed from homes in order to count empty liquor bottles.

---

*From Merritt, C. B., and Fowler, R. G.: The pecuniary honesty of the public at large. J. Abnorm. Soc. Psychol., *43:* 93, 1948.

We will have more to say about unusual methods of measurement under natural circumstances at a later point. For the moment, the student should see that psychological research on social behavior can proceed in a number of ingenious ways. Through use of quasi-experimental methods, the psychological researcher can retain much of the rigor and control of the laboratory and still enjoy the complexity and representativeness of the real life situation.

Simulation and gaming methods

With the development of electronic digital computers, new methods of inquiry have become available to the psychologist. It is now possible to "simulate" complex social events through the construction of a *model*. A model is, in essence, a formal theoretical representation of some aspect of reality. It consists of a particular theoretical language, sets of assumptions, and deductions. Through use of the model, an effort is made to "simulate" some real life process.

As virtually everyone knows, the behavior of the computer is controlled by a *program*. Programs may be written in any one of a number of available languages especially designed for computer usage. The central task in computer simulation is to write a program that will cause the computer to behave in much the same way as a person or a group of persons. The statements that make up the program are in essence a theory of the particular behavior being simulated. Once a program has been conceived, the "fit" between the model and reality as well as the implications of the model can be determined by running the program on the computer and observing the results.

In one sense, all psychological theories are models. Each attempts to represent some aspect of reality, and each, while never capturing completely the essence of reality, achieves varying degrees of success in approximating reality. The theory builder in psychology has available to him three different languages. First, he can express his theory in ordinary prose. Thus far, the vast majority of psychological theories have been expressed in this manner and as such can be comprehended by the intelligent layman. More recently, however, efforts have been underway to develop alternative languages for theory building. One of these is the language of the electronic digital computer. As we have already indicated, the program is the form in which the definitions, assumptions, and deductions of the theory are expressed. In addition to ordinary prose and computer languages, the theory builder can also make use of the language of formal mathematics. We will have more to say about formal mathematical models later in this chapter. For the moment, the student should see that simulation procedures have much in common with other efforts directed toward theory building in psychology.

Perhaps the greatest advantage in employing computer languages in theory construction lies in the fact that computers do not tolerate ambiguous statements! Ordinary prose, on the other hand, is characterized by considerable uncertainty as to the exact meanings of terms. Consider the following amusing passage from Charlton Laird's delightful book, *The Miracle of Language*. What might happen when a speaker utters the word *wrist* to a listener?

> Exact communication is impossible among men. Gertrude Stein may have felt that a "rose is a rose is a rose," but our speaker, if he considers the matter carefully, must know that a wrist is not necessarily a wrist. It may be some bones hung together by ligaments. It may be the skin outside these bones. It may be the point which marks the end of the sleeve. If the speaker is a tailor, *wrist* may be a command to hem a glove. But even granted that both speaker and hearer agree that *wrist* is here associated with the bones, flesh, and skin at the juncture of the human hand and arm, they may still associate highly varied feelings with this part of the body. The speaker may have big, bony wrists, and have hated them all her life. The hearer may have been forced out of an Olympic skiing contest when he fell and broke a wrist. There is no one thing which *wrist* calls up in exactly the same form to everyone; there are not even areas of meaning which are the same for everybody.*

If the simple word *wrist* can call forth such remarkable ambiguity in meaning, one wonders about such complex psychological terms as "social power," "defensiveness," "hostility," "needs," and so on. Viewed in this light, it is not at all surprising that psychological theorists have begun examining the usefulness of languages other than ordinary prose for theory building.

As Cohen and Cyert (1965) have pointed out, four classes of simulations exist. These are as follows:

---

*From Laird, C.: *The Miracle of Language*. Greenwich, Conn., Fawcett Publications, Inc. 1967, p. 15.

1. *Descriptive simulations.* These are simulations which are designed to describe an existing behavioral process. For example, Cyert, March, and Moore (*in* Cyert and March, 1963) developed a computer simulation which described in great detail the behavior of a *single person,* a buyer for a large department store. Predictions of the actual behavior of the buyer from the model proved remarkably precise. For example, predictions were made as to the buyer's price decisions on new merchandise. Unless the predicted price matched the actual price to the exact penny, the prediction was counted as incorrect. Under these unusually rigorous criteria, the model achieved a 95.4 per cent level of accuracy!

    Descriptive simulations involving widely different situations have been developed, e.g., simulations of the behavior of particular chess players, persons solving logical problems, and decision-making by an investment trust officer. The neurotic decision processes of a patient in psychotherapy have even been subjected to computer simulation! In all of these cases, the intent of the computer model builders has been the same, i.e., to describe fully the behavior of particular persons.

2. *Simulations illustrating general hypotheses.* In this class of simulations, efforts are made to develop hypotheses about some general class of behavior and to derive some implications of these hypotheses. For example, Cohen, Cyert, March, and Soelberg (1963) attempted to simulate the behavior of a number of different firms in a market system. From sets of assumptions concerning goals related to profits, inventory, production, and sales, Cohen, *et al.* were able to develop a complex and convincing account of the behavior of the market system as well as of the firms imbedded in it.

3. *Simulations for the design of social systems.* Thus far, the simulations we have considered are concerned with simulating events as they actually are, and in this sense simulations such as these are *empirical.* But simulations can be used in a *prescriptive* manner in order to arrive at decisions as to how things should be. It is possible, for example, to simulate social processes like communication networks within complex organizations in order to arrive at the best estimate of the optimal system, taking

into account such constraints as cost, efficiency, and member's morale. Or one might be interested in the same procedures for designing a psychological clinic that would most effectively meet the social, educational, and therapeutic needs of the members, staff, patients, and relatives.

Computer simulation to assist in the design of social organizations may prove of inestimable value. Since trial and error procedures in real life settings may very well prove inefficient, costly, and even dangerous, the advantages of design through simulation procedures should be obvious.

4. *Man-machine simulations for training purposes.* It is possible to create a *feedback system* utilizing the computer to simulate the environment in which human beings are required to behave. In this fashion, the reciprocal effects of the behavior of persons upon their environments and environments upon persons can be studied. By acting, people produce effects upon their environments; the changed environments in turn lead to changes in the behavior of persons imbedded in them. This is what is meant by the term "feedback system." Through use of such a simulated feedback system, the behavior of actual systems can be studied. In addition, persons can be trained to behave effectively in such systems.

The RAND Air Defense simulations are an excellent example. A typical Air Defense Center has a personnel of about 40 people. It maintains continuous radar scrutiny over a given area, identifying aircraft as hostile or friendly and directing, if necessary, interceptor aircraft against suspicious or clearly hostile aircraft. By constructing a close approximation to one such actual center, the physical simulation of the center was developed. Communication networks, radar equipment, central displays, and so forth, were all included in the simulation of the physical environment. Computers employing specially prepared input devices were able to simulate airplane flights over a particular geographical area. Various means of gathering data on the behavior of participants in the simulation (actual Air Force personnel) were employed.

From these simulations, a major conclusion was drawn: operational *flexibility* is a state to be worked towards in the design of a complex system such as this. A completely automated system with rigidly fixed procedures seemed to lack the ability to adapt to unstable situations. In essence, the RAND simulations called attention to the continued importance of well-trained human beings in a flexible organizational environment.

To the four classes of simulations proposed by Cohen and Cyert, we might mention *games* as a fifth approach. In 1944, a monumental work by J. Von Neumann and O. Morgenstern appeared. The book, entitled *Theory of Games and Economic Behavior,* presented a rigorous mathematical approach to the study of certain aspects of behavior. Since that time, well over a thousand articles have appeared in which the competitive or cooperative behavior of interacting human beings has been examined in terms of game theory. Perhaps the best way to capture the meaning of the game approach is to consider an example, the *Prisoner's Dilemma Game.* The ingredients of the game are as follows:

> Two suspects are taken into custody and separated. The District Attorney is certain that they are guilty of a specific crime, but he does not have adequate evidence to convict them at a trial. He points out to each prisoner that he has two alternatives: to confess to the crime the police are sure they have done, or not to confess. If they both do not confess, then the District Attorney states he will book them on some very minor trumped-up charge such as petty larceny and illegal possession of a weapon, and they would both receive minor punishments; if they both confess they will be prosecuted, but he will recommend less than the most severe sentence; but if one confesses and the other does not, then the confessor will receive lenient treatment for turning state's evidence, whereas the latter will get the "book" slapped at him.*

In the game, it is clear that the two persons are not permitted to communicate directly with one another. Hence, each must predict what the other will do, and, more importantly, each must *trust* the other not to selfishly pursue his own interests at the expense of the other. That is, the optimal strategy for both is simply to refuse

---

*From Luce, R. D., and Raiffa, H.: *Games and Decisions: Introduction and Critical Survey.* New York, John Wiley & Sons, 1957, p. 95.

to confess. However, since the opportunity exists for one of the players to exploit the other by confessing and thereby receive a light sentence, a *mixed-motive* situation arises. The term mixed-motive refers to the fact that the subject can adopt a cooperative strategy (one in which he considers his partner's welfare in addition to his own) or a competitive strategy (one in which he pursues his own self-interests at the expense of the welfare of his partner).

The Prisoner's Dilemma Game is an example of a *nonzero-sum* game. In games of this class, the possibility exists that players can make choices that will produce desirable outcomes for both.

In modifications of the original Prisoner's Dilemma Game, the situation is changed to one involving sums of money rather than decisions to confess or not to confess. In this case, a nonzero-sum game is one in which subjects may play in such a manner as to raise pay-off levels for each of the players. The nonzero-sum game is contrasted with the *zero-sum* game in which the possibility of cooperation does not exist. In the zero-sum game, the *sum* of the two pay-offs is zero (what one player wins, the other player loses).

Games such as the Prisoner's Dilemma Game are considered simulations because they attempt to approximate situations that do occur in real life. The mixed-motive situation of the Prisoner's Dilemma Game seems characteristic of numerous life situations in which a person must choose between his own self-interests and those of others.

Formal mathematical models

Certain problems in the study of social behavior are amenable to formal mathematical treatment. Mathematical models, like the simulations we have just considered, are idealized representations of a problem. However, in contrast to simulations, mathematical models are expressed in terms of familiar mathematical symbols and expressions. Certain laws of physics, e.g., $E = mc^2$, are familiar examples of mathematical models. For purposes of clarity, let us consider a simple mathematical model in the study of social behavior.

There is an old saying that "two heads are better than one." This bit of folk wisdom seems to imply that problem-solving by two or more persons will invariably prove superior to that undertaken by the lone individual. Early studies along these lines by Shaw (1932) seemed to support the notion. When individuals and groups were compared based on their abilities to solve certain complicated puzzle problems, groups more often than individuals came up with the solution. Only 14 per cent of the individuals working alone solved the problem, but 60 per cent of the groups came up with successful solutions. Shaw interpreted this difference as being attributable to the effect of *group interaction*.

Lorge and Solomon (1955) questioned Shaw's interpretation of his data. They argued that since the groups added more individuals to the problem-solving situation, it was, in a sense, unfair to compare Shaw's four-person groups to the single individual. In effect, Lorge and Solomon argue that it is unnecessary to postulate some sort of "group interaction" effect to explain the apparent superiority of groups over individuals. Quite simply, with the ability of individuals and group members held constant, the probability of solution is increased as the number of persons is increased. One way of thinking about this is as follows:

1. A group is composed of individuals.
2. It is individuals that solve problems and not groups.
3. The more individuals there are in a group, the more likely it is that one of them will hit upon a correct solution.
4. The apparent superiority of the groups over the individuals is a misleading effect. It really reflects the superiority of comparing the efforts of four individuals to one individual rather than the supposed effects of group *interaction* upon problem-solving.

How might this difference of opinion be resolved? Lorge and Solomon developed a simple mathematical model to argue their case. Let us assume the following:

1. Each individual has a probability (P_I) of solving the problem.
2. In the *absence* of any interaction whatsoever, then, the *group probability of solution* is as follows:

(A) $\text{Probability} \begin{Bmatrix} \text{group of 4 members} \\ \text{solves problem} \end{Bmatrix}$

$= 1 - \text{Probability} \begin{Bmatrix} \text{no member solves} \\ \text{problem} \end{Bmatrix}$

$= 1 - \text{Probability} \begin{Bmatrix} \text{member} \ldots \text{member} \\ 1 \text{ fails} \quad\quad 4 \text{ fails} \end{Bmatrix}$

Expressing these equations in slightly different form yields:

(B) $\begin{Bmatrix} \text{Probability of} \\ \text{group solution} \end{Bmatrix} = \begin{matrix} 1(1 - \text{Probability } I_1)(1 - \text{Probability } I_2) \\ (1 - \text{Probability } I_3)(1 - \text{Probability } I_4) \end{matrix}$

Simplifying (B) leads to the following:

(C) $\begin{Bmatrix} \text{Probability of} \\ \text{group solution} \end{Bmatrix} = 1 - (1 - \text{Probability } I)^4$

Equation (C) above simply indicates that, *in the absence of any group interaction* whatsoever, the probability of a group solution is obtained by the product of the four individual probabilities. Remember that Shaw's data indicated that 14 per cent of the individuals solved the problems while 60 per cent of the groups did so. The best estimate of the individual probabilities (P_I), then, is 0.14. Substituting this value in equation (C) above yields:

$\begin{Bmatrix} \text{Probability of} \\ \text{group solution} \end{Bmatrix} = 1 - (1 - 0.14)^4 = 0.46$

While the model does not perfectly fit the obtained data, it is clear that a very substantial portion of the supposed superiority of the group over the individual (0.60 versus 0.14) can be accounted for by the individual probabilities alone without taking into account hypothetical group interaction effects.

The above example is, of course, a very simple mathematical model. However, it will have served its purpose well if it provides the student with a rudimentary understanding of how formal mathematical models can aid in the understanding of social behavior.

METHODOLOGICAL CONTROVERSY IN PSYCHOLOGY

From time to time, controversies erupt in psychology regarding *the* proper method of inquiry. Proponents of clinical methods have attacked and been attacked by proponents of statistical methods. Experimentalists have engaged both clinicians and statisticians in heated debate. New battles seem to be developing between those committed to mathematical models and those satisfied with experimental methods. From our perspective, such arguments are largely fruitless. There is no such thing as *the* perfect method of inquiry in the study of social behavior. While each method possesses certain advantages not shared by other methods, it also possesses certain disadvantages. Clinical methods, for example, may possess the advantage of permitting intensive studies of the single human being in all of his enormous complexity. But, on the other hand, the clinical method remains essentially subjective. Moreover, it is difficult to see how a science of social behavior can be founded upon data drawn from even the most exhaustive studies of single individuals. It is, after all, impossible to generalize from the particular to the general with any degree of confidence.

Experimental methods may permit rigorous control over variables, but at the same time, one sacrifices the richness of the real life context. Field studies enable one to study the real life context in all its complex manifestations; however, in doing so they frequently require the loss of substantial amounts of control over the situation being studied. Mathematical models may permit extraordinary rigor in the study of social behavior. However, they remain abstract representations of reality. Moreover, only a very narrow range of problems of interest in the study of social behavior are amenable to formal mathematical treatment.

And so it goes. One method enables the psychologist to do this while sacrificing that. Rather than searching for the perfect method of inquiry, it is better to think of existing methods as a substantial body of tools and techniques. The real questions seem to involve *choosing* the appropriate method of inquiry for one's purposes. That is, it is not surprising to discover, after all, that multiple methods of inquiry are necessary if we are to make any sense of the social behavior of human beings. Knowing the advantages and disadvantages of each may permit one to choose intelligently in the search for the appropriate means for answering a given question.

SUMMARY

In this chapter, we have considered the more important methods of inquiry used in the study of social behavior. Our discussion has led us to consideration of the clinical method, correlational methods, experimental methods, quasi-experimental designs, and simulation, gaming, and mathematical models. In each case, we have tried to illustrate the methods of inquiry in the context of actual research in psychology as a social science. Hopefully, the student will have gained a feeling for the substance of psychology as well as for its methods of study from this Chapter.

References

Bain, H. M., and Hecock, D. S.: Ballot Position and Voter's Choice: The Arrangement of Names on the Ballot and Its Effect on the Voter. Detroit, Wayne State University Press, 1957.

Barron, F., and Welsh, G. S.: Artistic perception as a possible factor in personality style: its measurement by a figure preference test. J. Psychol., *33:* 199, 1952.

Cohen, K. J., and Cyert, R. M.: Simulation of organizational behavior. In March, J. G. (ed.): *Handbook of Organizations.* Chicago, Rand McNally & Co., 1965.

Cohen, K. J., Cyert, R. M., March, J. G., and Soelberg, P. In Cyert, R. M., and March, J. G. (eds.): *A Behavioral Theory of the Firm.* Englewood Cliffs, N.J., Prentice-Hall, Inc., 1963.

Cyert, R. M., and March, J. G.: *A Behavioral Theory of the Firm.* Englewood Cliffs, N.J., Prentice-Hall, Inc., 1963.

Hebb, D. O.: *A Textbook of Psychology,* 2nd Ed. Philadelphia, W. B. Saunders, Co., 1966.

Hovland, C. I., and Weiss, W.: The influence of source credibility on communication effectiveness, Public Opinion Quarterly, *15:* 635, 1952.

Jessor, R., Graves, T., Hanson, R., and Jessor, S.: *Society, Personality, and Deviant Behavior: A Study of a Tri-ethnic Community.* New York, Holt, Rinehart and Winston, Inc., 1968.

Laird, C.: *The Miracle of Language.* Greenwich, Conn., Fawcett Publications, Inc., 1967, pp. 15, 25-40.

Lefkowitz, M., Blacke, R. R., and Mouton, J. S.: Status factors in pedestrian violation of traffic signals. J. Abnorm. Soc. Psychol., *51:* 704, 1955.

Lorge, I., and Solomon, H.: Two models of group behavior in the solution of eureka-type problems, Psychometrika, *20:* 139, 1955.

Luce, R. D., and Raiffa, H.: *Games and Decisions: Introduction and Critical Survey.* New York, John Wiley & Sons, Inc., 1957.

Merritt, C. B., and Fowler, R. G.: The pecuniary honesty of the public at large. J. Abnorm. Soc. Psychol., *43:* 90, 1948.

Sawyer, H. G.: The meaning of numbers. Speech before the American Association of Advertising Agencies, 1961.

Sechrest, L. B.: Handwriting on the wall: a view of two cultures. Unpubl. manuscript, N.U., 1965.
Shaw, M. E.: A comparison of individuals and small groups in the rational solution of complex problems. Amer. J. Psychol., *44:* 491, 1932.
Sudnow, D.: *Passing on.* Englewood Cliffs, N.J., Prentice-Hall, Inc., 1967.
Thigpen, C. H., and Cleckley, H. M.: *The Three Faces of Eve.* New York, McGraw-Hill Book Co., 1957.
Von Neumann, J., and Morgenstern, O.: *Theory of Games and Economic Behavior.* Princeton, Princeton University Press, 1944.

CHAPTER

2

Special Problems in Psychological Inquiry

Uncertainty is a fact of life that the student of social behavior must learn to accept. Although many persons may believe that a great deal is known about social behavior, the fact remains that relatively little of the large amount of information in the social and behavioral sciences constitutes *reliable knowledge*. Yesterday's "truths" more often than not turn out to be today's historical curiosities. Today's abundant bright novelties typically seem to tarnish rapidly under tomorrow's more penetrating and critical examination. The student must not suppose that this situation is peculiar to psychology. Uncertainty to some degree characterizes all intellectual efforts of human beings. Consider the following candid remarks by two biologists:

> Despite the logical basis of science, it would be a mistake to give the impression that scientists are never wrong. Nothing could be further from the truth. The astronomer Johannes Kepler once wrote, 'How many detours I had to make, along how many walls I had to grope in the darkness of my ignorance until I found the door which lets in the light of truth.'*

Actually, as Baker and Allen point out, one could write a very large volume indeed on the erroneous experimental findings in physics, chemistry, and biochemistry over the past one hundred years. Lord Rutherford, the celebrated British

---

*From Baker, J. W., and Allen, G. E.: *Hypothesis, Prediction, and Implication in Biology.* Menlo Park, Addison-Wesley Publishing Co., Inc., 1968, p. 34.

physicist, argued that human beings would never tap the energy of the nucleus. The first atomic bomb was dropped a few short years after Rutherford's death. Johannes Müller, the famous German physiologist of the nineteenth century, expressed his belief that the speed of the neural impulse would never be measured. Just six years later, Helmholtz, another great German physiologist, demonstrated that it could indeed be done.

The problem of uncertainty is not peculiar to scientific disciplines; inquiry in the humanities must face the same problem. Henry Steele Commager, the noted American historian, has discussed at length the enormous difficulties confronting the inquiring historian. Although history textbooks frequently give the illusion that past events are known with great certainty, the reconstruction and interpretation of the past is fraught with difficulty. Commager despairs of the seeming paradox of too many and too few facts. On the one hand, the historian is almost overwhelmed by a literal sea of bits and pieces of information of doubtful authenticity and questionable relevance. On the other hand, the truly critical and relevant pieces of data are lacking.

In truth, reliable knowledge in any area is difficult to achieve. But why should this be the case for social behavior? Certainly, there is no lack of data. Each of us is submerged in social behavior for much of our lives, we are involved each day in numerous interpersonal interactions, we find ourselves members of groups of varying sizes and purposes. The mass media provide us with an enormous amount of information concerning events in the society and the world. Moreover, it is apparent that "reasonable explanations" of social behavior are not lacking. Virtually everybody fancies himself a psychologist when asked to explain the behavior of his best friend (or worst enemy), spouse, teacher, or parent.

However, the apparent ease with which observations and explanations of behavior can be made belies the underlying complexity of the problem. Many of our apparently straightforward observations of social behavior do not hold up under careful scrutiny. Human observers are notoriously imperfect. Our beliefs, wishes, emotions, prejudices, values, and so forth, heavily influence what we see and what we do not see. Our seemingly "reasonable" explanations of behavior more often than not turn out to be totally incorrect. In fact, many of our "explanations" are not explanations at all but vague, ambiguous, untestable assertions frequently couched in circular reasoning. For example, consider the concept of instinct. The notion that people behave as they do because of instincts (inborn, unlearned dispositions) captured the imaginations of many persons in the earlier part of this century. But it soon became apparent that the instinct concept, while giving the illusion of explanation, actually explained nothing at all. What do we know when we say that a person fights because of an instinct to hostility, or that a child learns because of an inborn instinct to do so? Can we predict the conditions under which people will fight with one another from the first assertion? And can we predict which children will learn more rapidly than others from the second? Of course not. Upon closer examination, it is apparent that the instinct concept gives the illusion rather than the substance of understanding.

The special problems of psychological inquiry center about two major activities: gathering *observations* of behavior and drawing *inferences* from observations. Neither activity is simple

Figure 4. Two Stonechats attacking a stuffed Cuckoo. In the excitement of discharging a belligerent fixed action pattern, released by the sight of the Cuckoo, the male Stonechat has chewed his protesting mate's foot. In humans, however, the importance of instinctive patterns of behavior remains a matter of debate. (Photo by E. Hosking. *From* Welty, J. C.: *The Life of Birds.* Philadelphia, W. B. Saunders Co., 1962.)

or uncomplex. The skills involved in simply observing and recording behavior accurately are among the most difficult to attain. Moreover, the ability to arrange conditions for gathering observations such that intelligent inferences can be drawn is equally difficult to achieve. The author once taught a course to graduate students in a specialized area of psychology, clinical psychology. The graduate students were asked to go to a nearby psychiatric hospital where they were to make observations on the behavior of particular patients. Upon their return to the classroom, the students were astonished to find that although they had written pages of description, few had actually fulfilled the assignment. Virtually no observations of behavior had been recorded. Instead, the students had faithfully recorded their inferences about patients. They claimed to have seen instances of "unconscious hostility," "classic cases of schizophrenia," "paranoid suspicions," "fragmented egos," and so forth. Unfortunately, few of the students could articulate what it was in the patient's behavior, if anything, that led them to such inferences. Even more interesting was the fact that few of the students recognized that they were *inferring* things about the patients rather than observing behavior! The psychologist (or any human observer) must be alert to the constant danger that he may be observing the activity of his own mind rather than the behavior of the other person. That is, he must be aware that the concepts he uses to make sense of behavior are not a property of the behavior itself.

As we have seen, then, the special problems of psychological inquiry center about observation and inference. Let us examine these problems in greater detail. Why is it difficult to make observations of behavior and why is it difficult to draw inferences from our observations?

Observation, inference, and prediction

Although there are numerous differences among the various methods of inquiry, all appear to share a common intellectual process. Each involves the observation of behavior, the drawing of inferences from such observations, and the effort to predict future behaviors. Let us consider each of these briefly.

Observations may take many different forms. These may range from the direct observation of one human being by another in a real life context to observations obtained by highly sophisticated electronic data gathering equipment in the laboratory. The clinical psychologist listening to his patient's account of an argument with his wife is in the process of gathering observations. The survey research psychologist who measures opinions in a large sample of persons is seeking observations in statistical form. Observations may consist of recordings from an electroencephalograph, a device used for measuring the frequency and amplitude of brain waves. They may consist of performance measures of a group of persons in a social psychological laboratory experiment. The psychological test such as the "intelligence test" or the "personality test" is still another means by which observations may be gathered.

Once observations have been obtained, some sense must be made of them. Few psychologists, if any, are interested in simply developing a large mass of data. The data must be ordered in some meaningful way. In an effort to resolve seeming inconsistencies in his observations, to reduce the complexity of them, and to bring psychological meaning to them, the psychologist attempts to draw inferences. Since he cannot directly observe many processes that are of interest to him, he can only infer them from observations of actual behavior. For example, the psychologist cannot directly observe the social motives of people. The concept of motive lies in the mind of the psychologist and not in the behavior of the person. While motives as such are not directly observable, the behavior of the person is. From numerous observations gathered in different situations, the psychologist may infer that a given social motive exists and importantly influences behavior. However, it is important for the student to realize that the concept of motive may be but one of any number of useful ways to make sense of the behavior of persons, and it is of equal importance for the student to realize that such inferences cannot be drawn in a simple manner. As we shall see, the process of drawing inferences from behavior is a complex one demanding the rigorous application of scientific principles.

Once the psychologist has gathered his observations and drawn his inferences about them, what then? The process cannot stop there. In order to show that his inferences are meaningful, the psychologist must demonstrate that they lead to the *prediction* of future behaviors. If we are to have confidence in the inferences drawn from observations, it must be shown that they are necessary and useful in predicting other behaviors. Once again, it is important to note that we do not lack for what appear to be "reasonable" accounts of social behavior, but simply because an explanation appears "reasonable" is no reason to assume that it is *correct*.

Let us illustrate with an example. David Brown drinks far too much. He is given to driving his car at extremely high speeds on twisting, narrow roads while intoxicated. David has a long record of accidents of numerous kinds. We might infer that David is "driven by either a conscious or unconscious motive to destroy himself." But when we examine this inference more closely, we see that it is a "convenient fiction," that is, we have placed an interpretation upon David's behavior in order to make it more comprehensible to us. While the concept of a "motive to destroy himself" may provide us with the illusion of "understanding" David's behavior, we may, in fact, be very wide of mark. When we ask such embarrassing questions as "Where is this unconscious motive located?", "How much does it weigh?", or "How large is it?", we are made immediately aware of the fact that the concept exists in our minds and not in David's behavior.

How can we be certain that we have indeed discovered why it is that David Brown does what he does? Simply because his behavior appears dangerous and "self-destructive" to us is no reason to assume the existence of a motive toward self-destruction. Without additional information, we would be in great danger of confusing the *attributes* of behavior with *causal* statements about the behavior. For example, we note that children grow tall in the course of their development. However, we cannot on that basis assume that the growth of children is *caused* by a motive to grow tall. The attribute of growth cannot be taken as evidence for a motive for growth. Similarly, the apparent self-destructive nature of David Brown's behavior cannot be taken as the basis for assuming the existence of a self-destructive motive.

Psychological inquiry, when properly conducted, follows sets of rules and conventions for establishing the usefulness of inferences such as this one. In order to establish the necessity for any inference about behavior, we must move beyond the level of mere *description*. For any psychological inference to be useful and necessary, we must show that it has predictive utility. In the hypothetical case of David Brown, if our inference about a motive towards self-destruction predicts nothing at all about David's behavior, we should happily discard it in favor of some other inference. There are, after all, numerous other plausible interpretations of David's behavior we might consider. For example, we might consider the possibility that David cannot control his behavior because he is the victim of the disease of alcoholism. As a consequence, his problematic behavior is directly traceable to a hereditary enzymatic defect that renders his metabolism of alcohol abnormal. Or we might infer that David sincerely believes that "fate has blessed him" for a long and happy life and that nothing really disastrous can come his way. There are probably as many plausible alternative explanations for David's behavior as there are imaginative people to generate them. How are we able to choose among them?

Scientific inquiry as choice among plausible alternative hypotheses

All things are *possible*, but it is the task of scientific inquiry to establish the *probable*. It is, for example, possible that geomagnetic storms on and about the sun are the cause of most human aberrations. It is possible that all human behavior is driven by unconscious motives. Or it is possible that predetermined genetic codes account for all human behavior. However, evidence establishing the probability of each of these statements of possibility does not yet exist.

From this perspective, it is apparent that scientific inquiry proceeds from the possible to the probable. Along the way, the scientist must content himself with successive approximations to something called "reality," and it is the continuing task of the scientific inquirer to design his research so that *alternative explanations* of his data are not possible. In other words, he must design his research in such a manner that his explanation of the data, i.e., the hypothesis which he prefers, cannot be threatened by plausible alternative hypotheses which might be brought to bear upon the same data. Given the many factors which can influence behavior, it is not at all surprising that much of psychological information remains tentative. It is not an easy task to design research so that all known plausible alternative explanations for the data can be ruled out. Moreover, as new information is developed each day and unsuspected discoveries continue to be made, it is not at all difficult to understand why psychological information must be considered tentative. Let us move directly to the heart of the matter: what are the sources of uncertainty in psychological inquiry and what can be done about them?

Sources of uncertainty in psychological inquiry

Perhaps the best way to grasp the meaning of the potential sources of uncertainty in psychological inquiry is to consider them in the concrete setting of an actual experiment. In 1941, Barker, Dembo, and Lewin performed what has come to be regarded as a classic experiment on children. The results of this early experiment are still widely cited in introductory textbooks as evidence for the hypothesis that frustration will lead to regression. Frustration refers to the psychological state that is thought to exist when a person is prevented from attaining some desired goal. Regression is broadly thought of as a return to earlier and more primitive behavior patterns. For example, the ten year old child who once again takes up thumb sucking after having abandoned the habit for a number of years is said to have regressed.

In any case, Barker, Dembo, and Lewin felt that blocking goal attainment would lead to a state of frustration and that this state of frustration would in turn lead to regression. They first had observers rate the "constructiveness of play" of 30 children between the ages of two and five. A set of standardized toys was used, and the children were observed individually. Play that seemed "imaginative" and that involved elaborated and well-structured activities received high ratings of constructiveness. Play that did not seem to the observers to involve those qualities was given lower ratings. After these observations were gathered, a deliberate attempt was made to frustrate the children. Each child was permitted to play with some fascinating new toys for a brief period of time. Then a wire screen was interposed between the child and the toys. He could see the fascinating new toys but could not reach behind the barrier to obtain them. The child was permitted, however, to resume playing with the standardized set of toys used earlier in rating his constructiveness of play. Once again, observers rated the children's constructiveness of play. Hence, two sets of observations of constructiveness of play were available, one prior to "frustration" and one following "frustration." Any decrease in constructiveness of play from the pre-"frustration" state to the post-"frustration" state was taken as evidence for the hypothesis that frustration leads to regression.

Although the hypothesis itself may be intuitively appealing, we must ask whether or not this experiment has demonstrated it. For the moment, let us put aside any feelings we might have that it is true that frustration leads people to behave less maturely and question seriously whether or not this particular experiment provides evidence in support of this common belief.

Incompete experimental design. Our first objection centers around the fact that the experiment is incomplete. The experiment claims to show an effect of frustration. Unfortunately, there is no comparison group against which to demonstrate this effect. That is, would a group of children who were *not* "frustrated" show a similar decrease in their constructiveness of play? Perhaps the results are not attributable to frustration at all but rather to the fact that children tend to get bored rather quickly, especially at these early age levels, and as a consequence of boredom, their play tends to deteriorate across time *whether they are frustrated or not.* Because a *control* group of this nature was not included in the experiment we have no way of knowing whether the observed decreases in constructiveness of play were caused by frustration or a host of other possible factors.

Possible bias in the observers. Since human observers were used to rate decreases in the constructiveness of play, we must ask if every effort was made to prevent the biases of the observers from affecting the results. The observers were aware of the particular hypothesis being investigated, i.e., that frustration leads to regression. They observed the frustration operations introduced into the experiment. Is it possible that they tended to "see" behavior that conformed to their preconceptions of what would happen? Unfortunately, we have no way of knowing whether or not the biases of the observers seriously affected the results that were obtained. We do know, however, that such prejudices even in extremely well-trained observers can lead to serious distortions.

Uncontrolled changes in the subjects. We discussed earlier the possibility that the apparent decreases in constructiveness of play might have been attributable to boredom rather than frustration. Other changes in the subjects across time might have been responsible—for example, fatigue. The children might have grown tired as the experiment progressed. Once again, since the subjects were very young children, this possibility cannot be summarily dismissed. Boredom, fatigue, hunger, and so forth, all may have played a part in decreasing the constructiveness of play. Perhaps it was these changes that were important and not "frustration."

Uncertainty in the choice of the intervening variable. Since the psychologist cannot observe many states or processes directly, he must infer them. In the present experiment it was *assumed* that a state of frustration had been induced. Furthermore, it was *assumed* that this induced state of frustration led to the apparent decreases in constructiveness of play. Frustration is thought of as an *intervening variable.* Intervening variables are hypothetical, that is, they are not directly measureable but are assumed by the psychologist to be necessary in explaining his results. To be sure, Barker, Dembo, and Lewin attempted to define their construct through objective *operations,* e.g., blocking the children from obtaining the fascinating new toys. However, we must still question whether or not these operations led to the assumed state of frustration. Perhaps blocking the children from the desired toys resulted in *anger,* not frustration. Furthermore, perhaps it was anger arousal and not frustration arousal that led to the decrease in constructiveness of play. Or perhaps the blocking of access to the toys aroused *anxiety.* Unfortunately, we have no way of knowing from these data.

From the discussion of this experiment the student should have a clearer understanding of some of the sources of uncertainty in psychological inquiry. Of course, it is possible to eliminate them. For example, it would be easy to simply add a control group of children who are not blocked from playing with the new toys. Observers who are unaware of the purposes and hypotheses of the research could be used. Different observers could be used for the pre-"frustration" and post-"frustration" observations. The addition of each of these changes would increase our confidence in the obtained results if the experiment were to be repeated.

Now that the student has a better understanding of uncertainty, let us consider the special problems of psychological inquiry more systematically and in greater detail. In the following section, we will examine three possible sources of uncertainty, the *subject,* the *inquirer,* and *sampling procedures.*

Sources of uncertainty: the subject

More often than not, the subject in psychological research is an active participant in a social interaction. The seemingly objective term "subject" conjures up visions of a willing, obedient, and essentially passive person devoid of all those complex characteristics that make up human beings. Although many investigators would like to believe that the subject in psychological inquiry plays out a very simple role, nothing could be further from the truth. In actuality, the subject may perceive the research setting quite differently than does the experimenter, who may (and often does) develop hypotheses himself as to what the research is all about. Such hypotheses may strikingly affect results. He may attach undue importance to even the most trivial of experimental behaviors such as a smile, nod of the head, or change in tone of voice. In addition, subjects may be angered by certain research procedures, made anxious by others, or they may be confused by instructions. Most importantly, the experimenter may not even be aware that such *unintended* effects are being produced in his research. Let us consider some of the sources of uncertainty which center around subjects themselves.*

Maturation and fatigue. During the course of a given piece of research, changes may take place in subjects for a variety of reasons. When experimental procedures require intense intellectual or physical effort, subjects may become fatigued. When studies are carried out over an appreciable length of time, the mere fact that subjects are growing older may affect results.

Reactivity of measuring procedures. It is commonly accepted that measurement is not a neutral process. The very act of measuring persons can and does frequently produce unintended reactions. Hence, measurement itself can produce unexpected changes, and this is what is meant by the reactivity of

---

*I am indebted to Professors Donald Campbell, Eugene Webb, Richard Schwartz, and Lee Sechrest, all of Northwestern University, for much of the following discussion.

measuring procedures. For example, a subject in a psychological experiment is well aware of the fact that his behavior is being carefully scrutinized. If people are made to feel that they are "guinea pigs" upon whom research is being conducted, they may respond in a number of different ways, none of which have any bearing on the researcher's initial purpose. They may strive to make a good impression. They may adopt a given *role* which they think the researcher wants them to play. They may distort and misrepresent their opinions, beliefs, and feelings.

It is well recognized that subjects may respond in particular ways to the peculiar social interaction of the "experimenter-subject" relationship. Orne (1962) has discussed the fact that the "experimenter-subject" relationship occurs within a definite *cultural context*, and that the role of subject carries with it well-defined expectations for behavior. Similarly, the role of experimenter also possesses well-defined expectations. Orne believes that it is these mutually held role expectations and not the experimental treatments being studied that determine behavior in many research settings. For example, it was previously thought that subjects could be induced to do socially unacceptable and destructive things under the influence of hypnosis. Early experiments seemed to indicate that hypnotized subjects would go to almost any lengths to satisfy the demands of an experimenter. Unfortunately, these early experiments failed to include comparable groups of persons who had not been hypnotized. Orne discovered that under conditions of the laboratory social setting, *unhypnotized* subjects behaved in much the same manner as did hypnotized subjects. For example, they readily picked up a "poisonous" live snake when requested to do so by the experimenter. When asked by the experimenter to throw "acid" into the face of a laboratory assistant, many did so readily. In an experiment conducted by Milgram (1965), which we will consider in detail later, subjects complied with the experimenter's request to administer what were described as "extremely dangerous" and "lethal" electric shocks to another subject. Of course, unbeknown to the subject, the "acid" was not really acid, the "poisonous" snake was not really poisonous, and the "lethal" electric shocks were not shocks at all. But the point remains that subjects did respond to the demands of an experimenter—demands that they would in all probability view with horror and distain in some other social context.

Response biases. If you watch people walk up stairs in a public building, you will note that most people tend to ascend on the right of the staircase and descend on the left. This illustrates a right-side bias, a tendency to respond in a particular way in this situation. Such tendencies, or sets, to respond in given ways are characteristic of people in a variety of situations. When questionnaires or personality tests are used as the means of gathering observations, response biases can prove very troublesome. For example, subjects will more frequently agree with a statement than disagree with its opposite. This tendency to agree regardless of the actual content of the question is known as the *acquiescence response set.*

Subjects tend to prefer strongly worded statements over moderately or weakly worded statements. When asked to rate a given group of individuals, some subjects may show a consistent preference for the middle range of ratings, some for the upper extreme, and others for the lower extreme.

It is important for the student to note that many of these response biases may operate independently of the actual *content of questions.* As a consequence, the psychologist may attempt to measure some characteristic in his subject, like a tendency toward "authoritarianism," but find that he has, in fact, succeeded in measuring acquiescence response set. As we shall see later, an attempt was once made to establish the existence of a personality type, the "authoritarian personality." It was not until the research had been completed and published that considerable disagreement arose over the basic measuring procedures in the research. Subsequent research has indicated quite clearly that scores on the various measures used to measure "authoritarian personality" were seriously affected by acquiescence response set.

It is quite easy to demonstrate the existence of response biases in a real life setting. The next time an acquaintance stops you on the street and asks, "How are you?" think about all the times in the past that you have answered, "Just fine!"

Sources of uncertainty: the inquirer

In addition to the subject under investigation, all psychological inquiry involves an inquirer. As we shall see, the inquirer himself frequently contributes to the uncertainty by the infor-

SPECIAL PROBLEMS IN PSYCHOLOGICAL INQUIRY 45

mation he generates. At times this may take the form of inappropriate techniques of investigation, or at other times, the logic behind the research may prove questionable. In addition, the behavior of the inquirer vis-à-vis his subjects may introduce unintended consequences. Let us consider these briefly.

Incomplete research designs. As we saw in Barker, Dembo, and Lewin's research on frustration, a critical control group was lacking. Although it might appear that control groups are an obvious requirement in research, in reality precisely what controls are necessary is often unclear. Each experimental situation requires a logic of its own. Moreover, subsequent research may

Figure 5. The study of social thought and behavior is complex and difficult. The student must learn to tolerate uncertainty. (Photo by Cathy L. Jones.)

reveal factors that must be controlled which were not available for consideration at the time a piece of research was completed. However, the failure to provide proper controls, for whatever reason, is common enough in psychological inquiry to require additional stress here.

Experimenter, observer, and interviewer effects. Both the characteristics of the inquirers as well as their behavior in the research setting can influence the nature of the data they obtain. For example, when the inquirer operates in the role of an interviewer in face-to-face contact with his subjects, his race, age, dress, and sex can strongly influence the responses he gets. Most importantly, the *behavior* of the inquirer can have an affect on his results.

In a series of investigations, Rosenthal and his colleagues have demonstrated that the *expectancies* of the inquirer—that is, what he expects will happen in his research—can actually influence results (Rosenthal, 1964). The manner in which such expectancies influence research results is unclear; however, that they can is well documented. Even in the relatively well-controlled laboratory situation involving experiments on rats, such experimenter effects have been noted. Laboratory assistants with one set of expectations for a given experiment rather consistently gathered data in conformance with these expectations. Other assistants with *opposite* expectations for the same experiment collected data in accord with these! Errors, when they occurred in such processes as recording observations or summarizing data, tended to favor the particular research hypotheses under investigation. Precisely how such expectations affect results is still somewhat of a mystery. It is not a matter of deliberate dishonesty on the part of laboratory assistants. On the contrary, it appears that even in the *social interaction* between the human experimenter and the rat subtle influence can take place without the awareness of the inquirer. If such unintended influences can occur in the relatively sterile and objective situation of the animal laboratory, one can imagine their importance in situations involving human subjects. As research has indicated, all sorts of subtle behaviors on the experimenter's part, e.g., smiling, head nodding, manner of questioning, inadvertent vocalizations, tone of voice, and so on, can serve as informative cues to the subject as to how he "should" behave.

Sources of uncertainty: sampling procedures

Psychological inquiry involves a series of important decisions. The inquirer must decide who it is he wishes to study, the situations in which he wishes to study them, and the activities he wishes to study. Since the inquirer cannot usually study all of the persons, situations, and activities in which he might be interested, he is forced to *select* a portion of each from some larger number. The manner in which he makes the selection is extremely important. Obviously, if an inquirer wished to find out what was going on in a given community, he would not stop the first person he met on the street and say, "What's happening?" Similarly, if he wished to understand such a community, he would not confine his observations to a single situation, say, a meeting of the chamber of commerce, nor would he restrict his interests to a single activity. Chances are good that he would *sample* the views of a number of different persons, select a variety of situations in which to make his observations, and concern himself with a variety of social activities within the community.

In essence, the inquirer wishes his sample to be representative of some *larger population to which he wishes to generalize.* The scientific inquirer is rarely interested in making statements about a particular person, a particular situation, or a unique event. Most typically, he is searching for the more general statement that will subsume a host of particulars. For example, he is not interested in Mr. Smith's hostility and its effect upon his son, Charlie. However, he might very well be interested in the more general question of parental hostility and its effect upon the development of children. Similarly, the psychological inquirer would never run experiments if after having done so all he could say was something like, "On Friday, June 13th, 1970, 55 Punxatawney University sophomores behaved in such and such a manner in a particular experiment on nonsense syllable learning involving a 10 word list, five of which began with the letter O and five with the letter P, etc." Quite obviously, no one would really care what 55 Punxatawney University sophomores did on Friday, June 13th, 1970. However, we might very well care if it could be argued that what happened was important for other time periods, for other places and for other persons. However, in order for us to *generalize* with any degree of confidence we must be certain that each of the particulars is representative of the population to which we wish to generalize.

If we wish to make scientific statements about "octogenarians," we would not study nursery school children because obviously the population of "octogenarians" is not represented by nursery school children. Less obviously, if we wish to make statements about the "structure of human intelligence," we would not confine our observations to tests of *mathematical* problem-solving alone. And even less obviously, if we wished to make statements about behavior in groups, we would not restrict our observations to group behavior in a boy scout troop.

One of the most powerful tools available to the psychological inquirer is the *random sample*. When samples of persons, situations, or activities are selected from some larger populations such that each element of the larger populations has an *equally likely* chance of being selected, the samples are said to be randomly selected. It is only in this fashion that the psychological inquirer can assure himself with reasonable probability that his sample is indeed representative of the larger population to which he wishes to generalize. However, it is important that the student realize that the psychologist can only generalize to that population from which he has drawn his random sample. If, for example, he wishes to make statements about undergraduate populations at American universities having an enrollment of over 20,000 students and he draws his samples from this population, he would not be justified in generalizing his findings to small liberal arts colleges, nor, of course, would he be permitted to speak knowledgeably about European universities.

Sampling errors are a common occurrence in psychological inquiry and the student would be wise to remain alert to them. Whenever *volunteers* are used in research, one must be cautious about accepting the findings as general, for it is well recognized that volunteers for research differ from those who do not volunteer in numerous important ways. The mailed questionnaire is notoriously hazardous. Some investigators have foolishly attempted to generalize from questionnaire studies in which less than 20 per cent of the original sample questionnaires were returned. Most importantly, the student should be alert to inappropriate generalizations drawn from exceedingly small samples, from a single experimental study, or from a large number of experimental studies all conducted in the same or highly similar experimental situations. The same experience repeated a thousand times does not equal a thousand *different* experiences! We would have more confidence in consistent results of 20 different experiments involving 20 different sets of randomly selected subjects and 20 different procedures than in consistent results from the identical experiment repeated a thousand times on the same group of subjects.

In any case, the student will encounter reports of many studies in his introduction to psychological inquiry. He should stop and ask himself the following questions:

1. How were the subjects selected?
2. How were the situations selected for study?
3. How were the activities or tasks selected for study?
4. Can we generalize these results to other persons, situations, and activities?
5. What limits on our generalizations are imposed by the sampling procedures employed?

The search for generality in psychological inquiry

In one sense, all statements about human beings are possible. However, it is the task of the research psychologist to establish the *generality* of such assertions, and it may be helpful for the student to bear this in mind in his study of psychology. But what does it mean to speak of the generality of an assertion?

Generality across people. Let us assume that we have conducted exhaustive observations on a single individual, Henry Jones. Further, let us assume that as perceptive and careful inquirers, we have discovered what seems to be a "fact" about Henry's behavior. Are we then justified in assuming that this "fact" will also be true of Henry's neighbor? And without equally careful studies, are we justified in assuming that the "fact" we have discovered by observing Henry Jones is equally true of persons of vastly different social circumstances, ages, cultural surroundings, or occupations? In short, if we pretend to statements about *human behavior* rather than a statement about the unique behavior of a unique person, Henry Jones, we must first establish the generality of our statement across people.

Generality across situations. In addition to generality

across people, it is necessary to establish generality across *situations*. In our example of the hypothetical individual, Henry Jones, it is possible that we may have observed him in *only one* situation. As a consequence, our "fact" about him may be peculiar to that particular situation and not to the numerous other situations in which we might observe him. Would this "fact" about Henry appear in his work situation? Would it be true of him in the marital relationship? Are there social situations in which our supposed "fact" about Henry would not hold at all? It is the task of the psychologist to discover the conditions under which a statement is true and the conditions under which it is not true.

Generality across operations. Generality across *operations* is a third consideration. By operations we mean nothing more than the devices employed to *measure* some aspect of behavior in which we are interested. In psychology, such operations can range from the relatively crude technique of the interview to sophisticated electronic devices for recording the electrical activity of a single cell within the brain. As we have come to appreciate in psychology, measurement is an incredibly complex problem. More frequently than not, two devices that are thought to measure the same thing yield entirely different results. Moreover, it is often the case that we discover, after painstaking research, that a measuring device thought to measure an interesting phenomenon is instead measuring something trivial and unexpected. We may, for example, devise a personality test to measure a person's "hostile-aggressive tendencies." However, if we fail to exercise considerable ingenuity in the development of our measuring device, we may end up measuring nothing more than the tendency of persons to answer all questions in terms of their perceived *social desirability*, that is, the willingness of various persons to answer questions in what they think is a socially acceptable or socially unacceptable manner. As one subject in personality research put it, "That may very well be true of me but I wouldn't admit it to anybody — least of all to myself!"

In our example of the hypothetical individual, Henry Jones, we spoke of conducting "exhaustive observations" of his behavior in order to arrive at a "fact" about him. But our "fact" about Henry's behavior is restricted to the *particular observer* who discovered it. Would a second observer arrive at the same conclusions? Unfortunately, it is frequently the case that two different observers may view the same event and perceive entirely different things.

Temporal generality. Finally, it is important that the *temporal* generality of assertions be established. It is unfortunate that the majority of psychological studies neglect temporal considerations. For the most part, psychologists have studied *short-term influences* over behavior. For example, principles of learning have been established on samples of laboratory behavior which are quite limited in duration. Studies of attitude change have concentrated on momentary shifts in attitudes during brief laboratory manipulations. The majority of studies on memory have been devoted to short-term memory rather than to long-term recall. It is often assumed that the factors that will account for the *acquisition* of behavior will also account for the *maintenance* of behavior over longer temporal periods. Within recent years, evidence has been accumulating that calls this assumption into question. It may, for example, prove necessary to think of short-term memory and long-term memory in terms of entirely different theoretical models, and as the Brelands (1961) point out, it is questionable that the same principles of learning which serve to explain the *acquisition* of responses will also serve to explain their *continued performance* over long periods of time. In their work with animals, the Brelands discovered numerous instances in which learned habits would not continue to be performed even though the *same* conditions of original learning prevailed.

These and numerous other examples indicate clearly that the generality of an assertion across time is an important, although neglected, consideration in psychological research.

Generality and truth

It should now be apparent why the results of any particular piece of psychological research cannot be taken as absolute. One must always bear in mind that the results of any psychological investigation are constrained by the particular sample of subjects employed, the method of inquiry used, the particular situation studied, and the length of time during which the research was conducted. An enormous amount of research effort is necessary before any statement about human beings can be accepted as generally true. Results must be obtained on samples of persons of widely differing characteristics; many different

Figure 6. Psychological inquiry seeks to establish the generality of assertions about human behavior. (Photo by Cathy L. Jones.)

types of measuring procedures must be employed; behavior must be studied under a variety of different conditions; and studies must be extended over lengthy time periods. When all of these conditions have been met, it is only then that the psychologist can begin to speak of general principles of social behavior.

Unfortunately, systematic investigation under all of these varying conditions has not been characteristic of psychological inquiry. Wryly commenting on the extensive use of the white rat and the college sophomore in psychological research, Edward Tolman, the distinguished psychologist, is reputed to have said, "After all, the college sophomore may not be human." Tolman's remark was obviously leveled at the very large numbers of psychologists of his time who apparently believed that a science of human behavior could be constructed upon extensive studies of the rat. But Tolman was also protesting against the striking tendency of academic research psychologists to conduct their studies upon the readily accessible but highly atypical population of college and university undergraduates.

If the psychologist makes pretensions to a science of human behavior, then he has no recourse but to extend his investigations across persons, situations, methods of inquiry, time, methods of measurement, and even across societies and cultures. Then and only then can he legitimately speak of general principles of behavior.

The student must not suppose that this problem of generality is purely academic, irrelevant, or trivial. It is, in fact, one of the most critical problems facing the inquiring psychologist. The history of psychology is filled with discarded or questionable theories all of which failed to take into account the necessary conditions for the development of a general theory of behavior. For example, Sigmund Freud, the famous psychoanalyst, attempted to develop a general theory of *normal* personality development from the study of small samples of *abnormal* persons. He relied almost exclusively upon clinical methods of inquiry. In addition, most of his observations were drawn from the highly atypical and peculiar doctor-patient social situation that characterized psychoanalytic psychotherapy of his time. Of course Freud did not have available to him sophisticated data gathering procedures, complex statistical tools, and other presently available techniques. In this sense, Freud was a victim of history (as we all are!). Consequently, despite Freud's well deserved reputation as a brilliant observer of human beings, the vast majority of his *inferences* about them remain open to question.

Throughout this book, the student will be exposed to reports of research findings and of these findings the student would do well to ask the following questions:

1. Would these results hold for a different sample of subjects?
2. Would these results hold for a variety of different conditions?
3. What might have happened if this investigation were carried out over time?
4. Would these results hold if different measuring instruments had been used?
5. Would a different method of inquiry yield similar results?

The deeper meaning of uncertainty in psychological inquiry

The student should now be in a position to understand the deeper meaning of uncertainty in psychological inquiry. Given the many sources of uncertainty in inquiring into the nature of things, it should now come as no surprise to find that science is more often a way of posing questions and attempting to answer them than it is a stable body of immutable "facts." Considering the increasingly remarkable speed with which such supposed "facts" come and go in all areas of scientific inquiry, it seems reasonable to shift our focus. From our perspective, it is more meaningful to understand the nature of psychological inquiry, its special problems, to grasp the workings of the mind of the psychological inquirer as he puzzles over the meaning of his observations and their limitations, than it is to commit thousands of pieces of information to memory. If, after completing a course in introductory psychology, the student is willing to ask, "How does this psychologist know what he claims to know" and "How do I know what I claim to know about myself and the behavior of others," that is very good. And if he knows how to go about answering these questions, that is very good, indeed. In fact, he will be behaving as a sensitive and perceptive inquirer into the nature of things should behave.

SUMMARY

In this chapter, we have considered the special problems in psychological inquiry. We have examined sources of uncertainty, the nature of knowledge in the study of social behavior, and the nature of inquiry into social behavior. Our examination has indicated that multiple sources of uncertainty exist. Three principal sources of uncertainty are the subject, the inquirer himself, and sampling procedures. Truth in the study of social behavior takes on a rather special meaning. As we have seen, scientific statements about behavior are efforts after generality. At the same time, we recognize that such statements are importantly constrained by a host of considerations.

Throughout this book, the student is encouraged to refer back to this chapter. Although it may seem the least exciting of all, even dull and terribly uninteresting in light of the novelties yet to come, it is perhaps one of the more important chapters for the student to understand. As the student encounters the substance of psychological inquiry, perhaps its importance will become most apparent. Despite the discomfort of recognized uncertainty, we are only truly informed when we know what it is that we do *not* know. And if we know why it is that we think we know something, that is understanding.

References

Baker, J. W., and Allen, G. E.: *Hypothesis, Prediction, and Implication in Biology.* Menlo Park, Addison-Wesley Publishing Co., Inc., 1968.

Barker, R., Dembo, T., and Lewin, K.: Frustration and regression: an experiment with young children. University of Iowa Studies in Child Welfare, *18*: 1, 1941.

Breland, K., and Breland, M.: The misbehavior of organisms. Amer. Psychol., *16*: 681, 1961.

Campbell, D. T., Webb, E. J., Schwartz, R. D., and Sechrest, L.: *Unobtrusive Measures: Nonreactive Research in the Social Sciences.* Chicago, Rand McNally & Co., 1966.

Milgram, S.: Some conditions of obedience and disobedience to authority. *In* Steiner, I. D., and Fishbein, M. (eds.): *Current Studies in Social Psychology.* New York, Holt, Rinehart and Winston, 1965.

Orne, M. T.: On the social psychology of the psychological experiment: with particular reference to demand characteristics and their implications. Amer. Psychol., *17*: 776, 1962.

Rosenthal, R.: Experimenter outcome-orientation and the results of the psychological experiment. Psychol. Bull., *61*: 405, 1964.

CHAPTER

3

Levels of Analysis

Accustomed as we are to thinking of psychology as the study of the individual, we frequently overlook the fact that the *individual level of analysis* is but one of several possible levels at which study can take place. It is certainly true that psychological study must take into account the properties of persons and the processes which take place inside of persons. Hence, the psychologist does concern himself with such factors as the motivations of individuals, personality traits of persons, and the beliefs of persons. However, it is equally true that other factors must be considered as well. With the exception of the occasional recluse, each of us is involved in numerous *interpersonal* interactions: husbands interact with wives, parents with children, students with teachers, and so forth. The vast majority of human beings everywhere find themselves members of *groups* of various kinds. The pursuit of education, health, food, clothing, and shelter requires that each of us participate in *organizations* of varying complexity. Even the recluse can scarcely escape the pervasive and powerful effects of *society* and *culture*.

In short, events of importance to the psychologist can be found at each of these levels of analysis — *individual, interpersonal, group interaction, organizational, societal,* and *cultural*. If we are to make any sense at all of the behavior of human beings, it is important to recognize from the outset of our study that understanding of each of these levels is essential. Variables at all levels of analysis can and do affect our behavior.

Complexity and the study of human behavior

In one sense, we are saying something that any serious observer of human beings has always known. Human behavior is enormously complex, and the factors influencing behavior are multiple. They range from the characteristics of single cells within our brains to culturally transmitted beliefs about the nature of reality. The concept of levels of analysis is one useful way of describing this complexity in an orderly fashion. We find this way of approaching the study of psychology useful for a number of reasons.

First, by keeping these distinctions firmly in mind, we can avoid the *simplistic error* which has colored the thought of laymen for centuries and confused the inquiry of psychologists themselves. The simplistic error arises out of the questionable assumption that events at a single level of analysis are sufficient for the development of an all-encompassing, general theory of human behavior. For example, we are frequently told that nations become embroiled in conflict, people commit suicide, the sexes battle, and so on, because of inborn, unchangeable *instincts* to do so. In this example, virtually all of the behavior of human beings is traced to a single level of analysis, the individual. The concept of "instinct" is thought to explain everything. While it is entirely possible that *some* individual variables may aid us in understanding *some* behavior, it is exceedingly doubtful that a *single* variable at the individual level will explain *everything*. Although they may differ in their surface characteristics, numerous theories concerning human behavior share the questionable assumption that a single level of analysis will prove sufficient in the quest for understanding.

Second, the concept of levels of analysis alerts us to the fact that psychological inquiry can proceed in a number of ways. One can search for relationships *within* each level. For example, it might be argued that personality variables are related to one's political beliefs. Here we are speaking of a possible relationship between two variables both of which lie at the same level of analysis, the individual level.

We might, however, wish to examine relationships *between* levels of analysis. For example, does membership in different organizations give rise to different sets of individual values? Do the professor and the business executive come to hold values characteristic of the organizations in which they pursue their occupational roles? Here one would be concerned with relationships *between* the *organizational* and *individual* levels.

One could also search for relationships which involve several levels of analysis simultaneously, and in this case we speak of relationships *among* levels of analysis. For example, the psychological study of society as a large social system might very well require one to consider many complex interrelationships among a host of variables, many of which lie at different levels.

From our point of view, it is fruitful to think of the proper domain of psychology as ranging across all levels of analysis, and, most importantly, if we are to understand the individual, we shall have to view him from each of these perspectives.

Third, the concept of levels of analysis alerts us to the possibility that many of the events which interest the psychologist are characterized by *reciprocity* between and among different levels of analysis. An individual is not only influenced by his many important interpersonal relationships, but he actively contributes to their nature. For example, a husband's angry remark may call forth a similar remark from the wife. The wife's angry remark may infuriate the husband, and so on. Both are contributing to and being affected by a developing interpersonal conflict. Interpersonal relationships in a work organization not only affect the functioning of that organization, but they are strongly influenced by properties of the organization itself. For example, a worker who feels that he has been treated unfairly may retaliate by destroying company property. The way in which academic organizations limit grades may force students into competitive interpersonal relations. As these examples make clear, reciprocity refers to the fact that people influence and are influenced by events in which they are involved.

Fourth, we are made aware of the fact that psychology is as much a *social science* as it is a biological science. Consideration of the various levels of analysis necessary for the study of human behavior indicates that systematic understanding will continue to elude us if we restrict psychology to the isolated individual separate from his social surrounds. It is often said that the fish will be the last to discover water. In a very real sense, this statement characterizes the study of psychology. Social creatures often seem blind to the fact that they are imbedded in social surroundings and that such surroundings have remarkable and enduring effects upon their behavior.

Fifth and finally, this approach to psychology provides us with a systematic way of organizing our thoughts in the course of this book. Hopefully, in this manner we can avoid the dangers of narrow commitment to this or that doctrine while, at the same time, we can avoid the many useless and pointless arguments that arise from time to time in the study of psychology.

Now let us move more directly to the heart of the matter. In the following, we shall illustrate research bearing on several of these levels of analysis. We shall first examine research *within* the individual, interpersonal, and group interactional levels. In later sections, we will examine relationships *between* and *among* levels of analysis.

WITHIN LEVELS OF ANALYSIS

Individual level: self-esteem and creative performance

Along with attitudes toward others, people, in the course of their development, come to hold attitudes toward themselves. Some persons develop self-regarding attitudes of a very positive nature; they think highly of themselves. We think of these people as possessing *high self-esteem*. Other persons seem to hold very low opinions of themselves, their worth, capabilities, and so forth, and we think of these as possessing *low self-esteem*. Are there consequences of such self-regarding attitudes? Can measures of self-esteem be related to some other aspect of individual functioning?

Coopersmith (1967) decided that the answer to both of these questions is *yes*. In particular, he felt that measures of self-esteem would relate directly to measures of creative performance because creative performances of all types require strength of conviction, ability to tolerate adversity, and a boldness not often found in individuals of low self-esteem. Coopersmith reasoned as follows:

> Since creative products, by definition, represent a departure from the conventional and provide an alternative perspective to that which is popularly accepted, their very expression represents an implicit threat to prevailing standards. Such threats arouse a vigorous response, particularly if they chal-

lenge long-established and culturally valued assumptions. . . . This is as true in the fields of science—the views of Darwin, Freud, and Einstein were initially attacked and rejected—as in the arts and humanities—Picasso, Stravinsky, and Shaw were subjected to harsh critical treatment. But all these men trusted in their judgments, were convinced that their constructions were real and valid, and were willing and able to expose their theories and works to public examination.*

In order to test his hypothesis concerning the relationship between self-esteem and creative performance, Coopersmith needed two independent sets of measurements on a single group of subjects. First, he needed measurements of level of self-esteem. Secondly, he needed measurements of creative performance. For measurement of self-esteem, Coopersmith employed a *self-report* measure (a 50 question inventory answered by each subject) and a *behavioral* measure (ratings by teachers of each subject on sets of behaviors thought to be associated with varying levels of self-esteem).

Three tests of creative performance were employed, the *Unusual Uses Test, Circles,* and the *Draw A Person Test.* The Unusual Uses test provides a measure of the subject's ability to perceive common objects in a unique way. For example, the subject may be asked to think of as many uses as he can for a salt shaker, a book, or a leaf. The number of acceptable alternative functions that a subject can imagine is taken as one index of creative ability. In the Circles test, the subject is given simple, regular forms with which to create an artistic product. The Draw A Person test is accomplished simply by asking the subject to do precisely that. Although the Draw A Person test is sometimes used as a measure of other aspects of personality, in this context it was used as a measure of creative ability in art.

If Coopersmith's hypothesis about self-esteem and creative performance is correct, we would expect that the two sets of measures would show a straightforward mathematical relationship, that is, the greater the self-esteem score, the greater should be the creative performance score.

From data gathered on 1748 children, whose ages ranged from 10 to 12 years, Coopersmith was able to demonstrate the hypothesized relationship. Table 2 shows the average scores for each of the creativity tests for individuals scoring low, medium,

---

*From *The Antecedents of Self-esteem* by Stanley Coopersmith, W. H. Freeman and Company, © 1967.

TABLE 2. Average Scores of Self-Esteem Groups on Three Tests of Creative Performance*

Creativity Tests	Level of Self-Esteem		
	Low	Medium	High
Draw A Person†	1.92	1.66	1.66
Unusual Uses	18.33	30.17	42.33
Circles Test	67.33	77.58	81.58

*Adapted from Coopersmith, S.: *The Antecedents of Self-esteem.* San Francisco, W. H. Freeman and Co., 1967, p. 61.
†Scores on the Draw A Person Test are reversed, i.e., the lower the score, the greater the artistic ability.

and high on both the self-report and the behavioral measures of self-esteem.

As we can see from Table 2, there is a clear-cut tendency for scores on the self-esteem measures to vary with scores on the creative performance tests. The relationship is as Coopersmith predicted: the higher the self-esteem score, the higher the creative performance score.

Recalling our earlier remarks concerning the uncertainty of much psychological information, however, it is important that we view this relationship in light of other aspects of Coopersmith's data. Table 3 shows the relationship between self-esteem scores and mean intelligence test scores.

What is the first thing we notice about these scores in Table 3? They appear to be much like the scores in Table 2 for the various self-esteem groups on the creative performance tests, that is, there appears to be a direct relationship between level of self-esteem and *intelligence* test performance. Unfortunately, we can no longer interpret Coopersmith's data in a

TABLE 3. Mean Intelligence Test Scores for Self-Esteem Groups*

	Level of Self-Esteem		
	Low	Medium	High
IQ	101.53	112.29	121.18

*Adapted from Coopersmith, S.: *The Antecedents of Self-esteem.* San Francisco, W. H. Freeman and Co., 1967, p. 127.

straightforward and uncomplicated fashion. The fact that the various self-esteem groups differed in intelligence test scores suggests that the differences on the creative performance tests may not be attributable to level of self-esteem at all. Rather, the differences on the creative performance tests may be attributable solely to the fact that in Coopersmith's sample of 1748 children, the brightest children tended to score highest on self-esteem, the less bright medium on self-esteem, and the least bright lowest on self-esteem. Since the creative performance tests certainly appear to involve intellectual factors, this alternative explanation for the data seems most reasonable. In other words, Coopersmith's data for the relationship between self-esteem and creative performance *may* be understandable in terms of differences in *intelligence* levels among his various self-esteem groups.

It is, of course, important to note that Coopersmith is not unaware of this difficulty in interpreting his data. The problem is a common one in personality research in which precise experimental control is frequently not possible. Whenever we *select* subjects on differences on one personality variable, we may *unwittingly select them on some other variable as well.* In the present case, Coopersmith selected his subjects on the basis of differences in self-esteem. He then attempted to relate these differences to differences in creative performance. Unfortunately, since self-esteem and intelligence were related in his sample of subjects, and since we have reason to suspect that intelligence is related to the creative performance tests used, we do not really know which of the two variables, self-esteem or intelligence, is affecting the creative performance test scores.

This, then, has been an attempt to illustrate what is meant by psychological inquiry within the individual level of analysis. As we have seen, psychological research at this level of analysis attempts to discover relationships between one set of individual characteristics and another. In Coopersmith's research, an effort was made to relate differences in self-esteem to differences in creative performance. As the student can surmise, research at this level can involve numerous other variables as well. In personality research, the relationships among such variables as psychological needs, drives, traits, skills, attitudes, and beliefs, have been investigated extensively, and we will consider such research in detail in subsequent chapters. However, for the moment, the reader should be content to understand, in broad outline, the nature of research at this level of analysis. Let us now turn to research at the *interpersonal* level of analysis.

Interpersonal level: obedience and disobedience to authority

It is not uncommon in everyday life to find one individual ordering another to inflict painful and even fatal punishments on some person. The soldier commanded by higher authority to kill the enemy, the executioner who, in obedience to the State, shoots, hangs, or electrocutes his helpless victim, and, less dramatically, the unwilling father carrying out mother's orders to spank the erring child all illustrate that obedience to authority in such matters is common.

Milgram, a social psychologist, decided to investigate compliance with authority more thoroughly (Milgram, 1965). In particular, he wished to shed some light on the conditions under which the person would either comply with or defy authority when ordered to administer painful and, in some cases, what were described as "extremely dangerous and severe" electrical shocks to a "victim."

Male subjects ranging in age from 20 to 50 years and drawn from a wide variety of occupations were employed for this study. Upon arrival at the psychology laboratory, subjects were told that they were to participate in an experiment on the effects of punishment on memory and that they would work in pairs, one subject assuming role of "teacher" and the other subject assuming the role of "learner." The "teacher's" task was to teach the "learner" a list of words. Whenever the "learner" made an error, the "teacher" was to punish the learner by administering an electric shock to him. Moreover, the "teacher" was instructed to increase the intensity of shock with each error made by the "learner." In this experiment, the "learner" was not really a subject at all. He was, in fact, an accomplice of the experimenter instructed to behave in certain ways throughout the experiment. The true subject, the "teacher," was unaware of this fact. Moreover, he was unaware that the entire situation was elaborately contrived to make him believe that he was actually delivering real electrical shocks to the other person. Although a shock generator was employed and prominently labeled with statements indicating the intensity of shock from levels of "Slight Shock" to "Danger: Severe Shock," no electric shocks were actually administered.

The following situation was assumed to exist. The naive subject was placed in a social situation in which two demands were made of him. On the one hand, he has been ordered to follow the commands of an authority (the experimenter) to inflict severe harm upon another human being. On the other hand, he is aware of continuing and increasing pressure from the helpless "victim" to stop this cruel and possibly dangerous action.

Milgram first studied two factors, both of which involved physical distance. In the first series of experiments, the distance between the "victim" and the subject was varied. The results of this work showed that obedience to authority *decreased* as the physical distance between the "victim" and the subject *decreased*. In other words, as we would expect, it is difficult to continue to inflict harm upon a person as separation between self and the other person is decreased. In the second series of experiments, the distance between the authority (the experimenter) and the subject was varied. In this case, obedience *decreased* as the distance between subject and authority *increased*. Once again, this is what we would expect because it is easier to disregard pressure from a distant and perhaps absent authority than it is when the authority is looking over one's shoulder to insure that his commands are being carried out.

The unexpected result in Milgram's research, however, was the surprisingly large number of subjects who continued to obey authority despite the cries, protestations, and pleas from the "victim" not to do so. Examination of the tape-recorded comments of one subject are illustrative. The subject had begun in a calm and deliberate manner administering shocks to the "victim." However, when the subject had reached the 150 volt level he became noticeably tense and agitated:

150 volts delivered: You want me to keep going?
165 volts delivered: That guy is hollering in there. There's a lot of them here (remaining memory items). He's liable to have a heart condition. You want me to go on?
180 volts delivered: He can't stand it! I'm not going to kill that man in there! You hear him hollering? He's hollering. He can't stand it. What if something happens to him? . . . I'm not going to get that man sick in there. You know what I mean? I mean I refuse to take responsibility. He's

getting hurt in there. He's in there hollering. Too many left here. Geez, if he gets them wrong. There's too many of them left. I mean who is going to take responsibility if anything happens to that gentleman? [The experimenter accepts responsibility.] All right.

195 volts delivered: You see he's hollering. Hear that. Gee, I don't know. [The experimenter says: 'The experiment requires that you go on.'.] I know it does, sir, but I mean—huh—he don't know what he's in for. He's up to 195 volts.

210 volts delivered.

225 volts delivered.

240 volts delivered: Aw, no. You mean I've got to keep going up with the scale? No sir. I'm not going to kill that man! I'm not going to give him 450 volts!*

Despite his protests that he would "not give him 450 volts" and that he was "not going to kill that man," this subject continued to increase the level of shock beyond 240 volts. In fact, in response to continued pressure from the experimenter, he raised the shock levels to the highest reading on the generator, "Danger: Severe Shock."

What are we to make of this remarkable piece of research? Perhaps it is best to pay heed to the words of Milgram:

> The results as seen and felt in the laboratory, are to this author disturbing. They raise the possibility that human nature, or more specifically the kind of character produced in American democratic society, cannot be counted on to insulate its citizens from brutality and inhumane treatment at the direction of malevolent authority. A substantial proportion of people do what they are told to do, irrespective of the content of the act, and without limitations of conscience, so long as they perceive that the command comes from a legitimate authority. If, in this study, an anonymous experimenter could successfully command adults to subdue a 50 year old man and force on him painful electric shocks against his protests, one can only wonder what government, with its vastly greater authority and prestige can command of its citizenry.†

The research by Milgram illustrates psychological inquiry at the interpersonal level of analysis. As the reader can see, in this type of research individual differences among subjects are not at issue. Rather, the *interactive relationships* that exist between or among persons are taken as the focal point of investigation. In Milgram's research, a particular interactive situation was ex-

---

*From Milgram, S.: Some conditions of obedience and disobedience to authority. *In* Steiner, I. D., and Fishbein, M. (eds.): *Current Studies in Social Psychology.* New York, Holt, Rinehart and Winston, 1965, p. 253-254.

†Ibid., p. 262.

amined, one in which a person by reason of his possession of legitimate authority (the experimenter) successfully manipulates the behavior of another person (the subject) even when the person is reluctant to behave in the manner demanded of him. This example is but one of many that could be used to illustrate the phenomenon known as *social influence*. In subsequent chapters, we will examine social influence in greater detail along with other processes which lie at the interpersonal level of analysis.

Group interactional level: communication structures

A group of persons can be thought of in terms of certain stable and enduring patterns that characterize the interactive behaviors of its members. These are the patterns referred to as the various *structures* of a group. One can speak of the leadership structure, the decision-making structure, the affective or friendship structure, and so on, as a means of referring to particular patterns of behaviors. In this section, we will illustrate psychological inquiry at the group interactional level of analysis by considering one such structure, the *communication structure* of a group.

Bavelas conceived the possibility of systematic investigation of various communication *networks* (Bavelas, 1948). By placing subjects in a situation in which it is possible to control who communicates with whom, one can study the psychological outcomes of various patterns of communication within a group. We can think of such communication networks as ranging from highly *centralized* nets to highly *decentralized* nets. A highly centralized net is one in which all communications flow to a single person in a central position. Group members cannot communicate with each other but must address their messages only to that person in the central position. The central member, however, can address his messages to any group member he wishes. In contrast to the highly centralized network, it is easy to conceive of a highly decentralized net. In this case, everybody can communicate with everybody else and a single central position does not exist. Figure 7 depicts these two extremes.

Although such nets may appear artificial, examples from everyday life can be chosen that seem to fit the diagrams very nicely. For example, the elementary school classroom is quite often structured like the *wheel* in Figure 7. That is, students must address their comments to a single individual, the teacher. Moreover, it is frequently the case that message sending between members of the classroom is discouraged (and often punished). On the other hand, in the informal situation of a party in somebody's living room, the communication net may resemble the *circle* illustrated in Figure 7. That is, persons may communicate with those people near them.

Research with various other types of nets has been accomplished; however, consideration of just these two types will suffice for our purposes. In general, the bulk of research has centered about two consequences of communication structure, *efficiency and morale*. Which network results in the greatest efficiency of the group when performing a task? Which network produces the highest morale among group members?

After nearly 20 years of research on such networks, the results seem to indicate the following (Leavitt, 1951; Shaw, 1964):

1. When the tasks are simple and fairly routine, centralized nets result in greater task efficiency than do decentralized nets.
2. When the tasks are complex, decentralized nets result in more efficient task performance than do centralized nets.
3. Regardless of the complexity of the tasks, decentralized nets result in higher member morale than do centralized nets.

Circle   Wheel

Figure 7. Communication nets: The circle and the wheel.

Although these results seem relatively straightforward, considerable uncertainty is still apparent in the research on communication networks. For one thing, when the groups are studied over longer time periods, the initial advantage of the circle groups on complex problems steadily decreases to a point at which the wheel becomes more efficient (Shaw, 1954; Mulder, 1960).

This finding may reflect the fact that communication structure *per se* might not *directly* influence group efficiency. It is possible that various communication networks produce effects upon the rate at which other structures are developing in the group, and it is these other structures that are important in determining group efficiency. Mulder argues quite reasonably that the rate at which the decision-making structure develops might very well be affected by variations in networks (Mulder, 1960). Communication refers to the flow of information in a group, whereas the decision-making structure determines what decisions are made, how they are made, and who makes them. In the centralized network, for complex problems, it simply takes longer for a centralized decision-making structure to emerge. However, once the centralized decision-making structure develops, centralized communication nets will, according to Mulder, result in superior group efficiency regardless of the complexity of the problems.

Here is an excellent example of the importance of *temporal generality*, which was discussed earlier (see Chapter 2). When the investigation is carried out over time, as was Mulder's study of communication nets, the trend of the data may completely reverse itself, and with such changes in the data, we may derive totally different explanations about what is actually taking place in the research.

In addition to differences in results of investigations which are carried over varying time periods, another source of uncertainty is illustrated in this discussion of communication structure. Much uncertainty in research on group interaction stems from the simple fact that many of the processes we wish to isolate in groups are highly *interdependent*. By varying one structure, we may very well be affecting the development of some other important structure, and it may be the effects upon this other structure that produce our results. As we have seen in the communication network research, variations in networks may affect the rate at which the decision-making structure of the group develops.

Finally, much uncertainty emerges simply because we are a very long way from specifying the dimensions of various *tasks* in psychology with precision. As we have seen, research on communication nets was complicated by task difficulty. One set of results was obtained for "simple" and another set for "complex" tasks. Although we may all think that we are quite sure of what is meant by "simple," and "complex" tasks, in actuality the distinction is not clear at all. Before we can say with any certainty how various tasks affect behavior, much careful analytical and empirical study of the properties of tasks remains to be done.

This example of research at the group interactional level of analysis has provided us with several excellent illustrations of sources of uncertainty in psychological research. Moreover, it should make the discussion on *truth* and *generality* presented earlier (see Chapter 2) more meaningful to the student.

Within levels of analysis: a summing up

We have seen how psychological inquiry proceeds at three levels of analysis: the individual, the interpersonal, and the group interactional. Inquiry at the individual level searches for the ways in which individual characteristics of persons vary with other individual characteristics of other persons. At the interpersonal level the focus of inquiry moves from the individual to *relationships* between individuals. At the group interactional level, inquiry centers around patterns of behavior, which reflect certain social structures and processes, among individuals. In the following pages, we will turn our attention to examples which illustrate inquiry that attempts to establish relationships across *different* levels of analysis. In our first example, we will consider the relationship between *societal* and *individual* behavior.

INTERACTIONS BETWEEN LEVELS OF ANALYSIS

In the past few pages, we have considered research that has attempted to explain events within a given level of analysis. Now we turn to efforts to find relationships between levels of analysis. Is it possible, for example, to explain social conflict within a complex modern *organization* such as the university from an analysis of the many differing *groups* which compose it? Would an analysis of the differing goals of the faculty, the administration, the Students for a Democratic Society, the Black Students Union, and other groups help us to predict the likely course of conflict on American campuses over the coming years?

To take another example: what can we learn about an entire society from sensitive study of the individuals comprising it? Could we predict such things as the rise and fall of great societies from changes in the attitudes, beliefs, and values of their citizens? In the following research we will take up precisely this question. Our example of research illustrating the interactions between levels of analysis addresses itself to the *individual* and *society,* and it poses a profound question: to what extent do the characteristics of a nation's people shape its destiny?

Interaction between the individual and societal levels: need for achievement and economic growth

In recent years virtually everyone has become aware that huge disparities exist in the economic well-being of the peoples of the world. While economic growth continues to soar among northern European and North American nations, vast regions of the earth are populated by destitute, starving, and unbelievably poor people. Robert Heilbroner, the American economist, has indicated that an estimated 10,000 people die each day in underdeveloped areas because of malnutrition. Devastating famines of even greater magnitude than the one which occurred recently in India are routinely predicted by experts in population and food supply. We can gain some understanding of the miserable lives led by many people by considering the average income of residents of Calcutta, India's largest city. Take four million of the poorest people in America, reduce their income to less than 10 per cent of that received by a family on welfare in the state of New York and reduce their food supply to a handful of rice a day. This is the situation faced daily by well over half of Calcutta's seven million people. Perhaps the hideous nature of these realities was best summed up by President Ayub of Pakistan in his recent prediction that "In ten years' time, human beings will eat human beings in Pakistan."

For many Americans, these distant problems are only vaguely perceived and understood. For others, they are considered merely problems of "economic development," problems which will eventually yield to infusions of technological assistance and money. Unfortunately, the situation is not nearly that simple. As more and more thoughtful persons are beginning to understand, the wealth and poverty of nations is far more than an economic matter. The political and social institutions of nations, their internal distributions of power and authority, religious beliefs, relations with other wealthier nations, and even their characteristic psychologies can exert effects upon economic growth.

But what can *individual* psychology contribute to our understanding of world-wide problems of economic growth? One psychologist, David C. McClelland of Harvard University, believes that the psychological study of the individual can contribute a great deal. McClelland rejects the thought that economic

Figure 8. Poverty in Latin America. Can individual psychological variables partially explain differential affluence among the peoples of the world? (From Ray Mitlin, Black Star.)

growth can be explained purely on the basis of economic variables. In fact, he sees psychological and sociological variables as the major factors affecting economic growth. Consider the following quote from his major work on the subject, *The Achieving Society*:

> Interestingly enough, the economic theorists themselves seem to have always felt that sources of change in the economic system lay outside the system itself. Thus it was not really clear to them why technical inventions of practical importance should appear more frequently at one period in history than in another, or why, once having appeared in one country, they should spread more rapidly to country A than country B. Or consider the position of neoclassical economists like Marshall. They placed great emphasis on the importance of saving so that profits could be invested in the expansion of business, but Marshall, at any rate, recognized that thrift is not something which people automatically practice when it is in their interest to do so. Propensities to save and invest and other attitudes necessary for economic growth appear in the end to be not economic but *psychological* variables. As early as 1904, the great German sociologist Max Weber was stressing the fact that such attitudes as economic rationality and the enterprising spirit of modern capitalism were consequences of certain religious world views stressed particularly by Protestant Calvinist sects. He thus laid the groundwork for efforts to understand the social and psychological origins of such key economic forces as rapid technological advances, specialization of labor, population growth, and energetic entrepreneurship.*

In essence, McClelland argues, as did Weber before him, that the rise of modern capitalism cannot be understood on the basis of economic factors alone. Rather, it was changes in the fundamental beliefs of men that gave impetus to economic change. The Protestant Reformation culminated in the production of a new psychological character, one who sought to avoid "damnation" by pursuit of good works and by striving for perfection, for independence and mastery, personal growth and achievement. Moreover, it was these values which eventually led to a striking change in family relationships, which in turn led to child-rearing practices that produced *sons with strong, internalized achievement drives.*

McClelland, then, is asserting that human beings differ from one another in the strength of a particular motive, the *motive to achieve*. Historically, these differences can be traced to the Protestant Reformation, a period which culminated in a major shift in human religious, personal, and social beliefs. It

---

*From *The Achieving Society* by David C. McClelland, © 1961, by Litton Educational Publishing, Inc., by permission of Van Nostrand Reinhold Company.

Figure 9. Motivational theories attempt to explain how behavior is energized and directed. (Photo by Gordon Cole.)

was these changes in beliefs that led to the rise of modern capitalism, which in turn was sustained by altered child-rearing practices that produced sons with high achievement motivation. It is these differences in the strength of motivation to achieve that are important in understanding the differences in the wealth of nations.

Protestantism and level of economic development

The McClelland thesis is indeed an ambitious one. In effect, it purports to explain the decline and fall of entire civilizations on the basis of psychological factors. What evidence does

TABLE 4. Per Capital Consumption of Electric Power for Protestant and Catholic Countries for 1950*

Protestant Countries	Kwh./cap.	Catholic Countries	Kwh./cap.
Norway	5310	Belgium	986
Canada	4120	Austria	900
Sweden	2580	France	790
United States	2560	Czechoslovakia	730
Switzerland	2230	Italy	535
New Zealand	1600	Chile	484
Australia	1160	Poland	375
United Kingdom	1115	Hungary	304
Finland	1000	Ireland	300
Union of South Africa	890	Argentina	255
Holland	725	Spain	225
Denmark	500	Uruguay	165
		Portugal	110
Average	1983	Average	474

*From *The Achieving Society* by David C. McClelland, © 1961, by Litton Educational Publishing, Inc., by permission of Van Nostrand Reinhold Company.

McClelland bring forth in support of his hypothesis? First, he provides data which bear directly on Weber's thesis concerning Protestantism and level of economic development. McClelland gathered data on a number of Protestant and Catholic countries for the year 1950. He reasoned that if Weber's thesis was correct, Protestant nations should show a greater level of development than Catholic nations. The measure of economic level used was kilowatt hours of electricity consumed per capita. McClelland used this measure for two reasons: (1) electricity is the principal form of energy upon which modern industrial society is based and (2) the measure could be established as a unit of international comparability. These data are given in Table 4.

As the data in Table 4 indicate, a marked difference in the level of economic development as of 1950 exists for the samples of Protestant and Catholic nations drawn by McClelland. Even when these data are corrected for such possible effects as differing natural resources, the Protestant-Catholic difference remains.

Achievement-motivated sons and parental expectations

So far, so good. But what of other aspects of the thesis? Is it true that parents can influence the achievement striving of their children? Here McClelland points to an important study on the origins of the achievement motive in early childhood. In 1953, Marian Winterbottom first measured the motive to achieve in a group of 29 boys aged 8 to 10. From stories that the boys made up in response to situations posed by the psychologist, scores thought to reflect differences in achievement motivation were derived. For example, the psychologist might ask the child to tell a story about the situation, "two children playing together." The child might include in his story statements about one child "winning and the other losing," about another child "trying to do his best," and so forth. These would of course be taken as indicative of achievement motivation.

In addition to gathering measures of achievement motivation in the children, Winterbottom also interviewed the mothers of the children. The mothers were asked to say at what age they expected their children to do the following:

1. to know their own way around the city
2. to do well in competition with other children
3. to try out new things for themselves
4. to make their own friends

As the student can see, these questions all have to do with the mother's expectations for the child's independence and mastery of his environment. In accord with McClelland's hypothesis, Winterbottom found that children with high achievement scores were expected to accomplish these goals at a much earlier age than were children with low achievement scores. Moreover, mothers of high achievement-motivated boys tended to reward such early mastery with physical signs of encouragement, e.g., hugs and kisses.

Winterbottom's research, although it certainly does not prove McClelland's assertion about achievement-motivated sons of Protestant families and the rise of capitalism, is at least consistent with the thesis, that is, Winterbottom's study indicates that parental expectations and rewards are associated with level of achievement motivation in sons.

Achievement motivation and economic development

Although the previous studies are consistent with the thesis outlined by McClelland, the most critical data deal directly with the relationship between level of achievement motivation within a given nation and its level of economic development. But how can one measure the level of achievement motivation in an entire nation? McClelland hit upon an ingenious idea: if it can be safely assumed that such things as the myths, folk tales, and educational materials of a nation are representative of its collective concerns, why not employ these as the measure of achievement motivation? McClelland gathered elementary school readers for the years centering around 1925 and 1950. From these samples of educational materials, he derived scores for the amount of achievement motivation reflected in their content. Children's readers from Sweden, Russia, Chile, Japan, Belgium, Germany, Mexico, and a host of other nations were employed.

Armed with achievement motive scores for these two periods, McClelland needed some measure of economic development with which to correlate them. He employed two indices of economic growth. The first measure, discussed earlier, was kilowatt hours of electricity consumed per capita. For the second measure of economic growth, an "international unit" (I.U.), McClelland attempted to measure real national income in different countries. One I.U. is taken as the quantity of goods exchangeable for one dollar in the United States during the period 1925 to 1934.

For each country McClelland used appropriate statistics to compute its *expected* level of economic development from its starting point. This was necessary since gain in development is clearly correlated with initial starting point, that is, the wealthier a nation, the greater is its expected gain over any given period, or, stated more simply, *rate of growth* is correlated with initial position. In effect, the statistics used by McClelland removed this correlation between rate of growth and initial position, thus giving each nation an equal advantage over the period of time studied. Finally, for both measures of expected economic level of development, kilowatt hours and I.U., *actual gain* and *expected* gain were compared. Difference scores that expressed the amount of deviation of actual gain from expected gain were computed.

McClelland now had all the necessary ingredients to test his hypothesis concerning achievement motivation and level of economic development. He possessed achievement motivation scores derived from the content of elementary school readers

TABLE 5. Correlations of Reader n Achievement Scores with Deviations from Expected Economic Gains*

Achievement level by year (readers)	I.U./cap. 1925–1950	Kwh./cap. 1929–1950
1925	0.25	0.53
1950	−0.10	0.03

*From McClelland, D. C.: *The Achieving Society*. Princeton, N.J., D. Van Nostrand Co., Inc., 1961, p. 92.

from the various countries. He possessed two measures of economic development expressed in deviation scores of actual growth from expected growth. All that remained was to compute correlations between the motive scores and the economic development scores. These correlations are presented in Table 5.

What do these correlations in Table 5 tell us? First of all, only one of the correlations is *significant*, i.e., greater than we would expect by chance alone. This is the correlation of 0.53 between achievement motivation for the year 1925 and *subsequent* economic development measured in kilowatt hours of electricity consumed per capita. None of the other correlations is significant, that is, achievement motivation scores for 1925 do not predict level of economic development for real income expressed in I.U. Moreover, achievement motivation scores for 1950 do not correlate with either measure of economic development for the *preceding* years from 1925. For McClelland's argument, the fact that achievement scores seem to predict *subsequent* gain in economic development but do not relate to *previous* gain is all to the good. If the achievement scores for 1950 *did* relate significantly to the measures of economic gain for the *previous* period, then one could argue that it was level of economic development that caused the differences in achievement motivation and not vice versa. Since the achievement scores predicted subsequent gain and were not related to previous gain, McClelland takes this to mean that the *direction* of influence is clear: achievement motivation affects level of economic development.

We can summarize the correlations in Table 5, then, by saying that they indicate mixed support for McClelland's hypothesis. For at least one measure of economic development, kilowatt hours of electricity consumed per capita, achievement scores drawn from elementary readers did predict subsequent differences between actual and expected gain. On the other hand, achievement motive scores did not predict the second measure of economic development, real income expressed in international units (I.U.).

Some puzzles that remain

As we have seen, the research by McClelland was truly an ambitious and imaginative effort. Let us summarize again McClelland's argument. The Protestant Reformation gave rise to a new personality character, one which emphasized the continual striving for perfection, for good works, and for achievement. These changes in religious beliefs, personal values, and orientations toward achievement resulted in a revolution within the Protestant family. Protestant parents behaved toward their children in a manner which produced sons with internalized values characteristic of persons of high achievement motivation. It was these achievement-motivated sons who carried forth the "spirit of capitalism," which gave birth to and sustained the rise of modern capitalism.

Three lines of evidence have been reviewed that bear on these three related but separate parts of McClelland's thesis. We have reviewed data indicating that Protestant nations outdistance Catholic nations in terms of economic development. We have seen in Winterbottom's study that parental behaviors and expectations are indeed related to level of achievement motivation in sons. And finally, we have seen data that directly relates level of achievement motivation in a nation to subsequent gain in level of economic development.

Despite these confirmatory lines of evidence, not all the data bearing on the McClelland thesis is as clear-cut. Some serious puzzles remain.

First, the notion that it is Protestantism *per se* which leads to high achievement motivation is clearly not tenable. In 1960, a study conducted in the United States by Veroff and his colleagues seriously questioned the association of Protestantism with high achievement motivation. In a representative sample of the U.S. population, Veroff *et al.* failed to show a difference in favor of the Protestant parents over the Catholic and Jewish parents with regard to parental expectations for early mastery and independence in children. In fact, Veroff employed the same questions used by Winterbottom in her study of parental expectations and achievement motivation discussed earlier. Moreover, in Veroff's study, Catholic and Jewish boys actually scored *higher* on motive to achieve than did Protestant boys. McClelland's research itself, though it showed a relationship between motivation to achieve and subsequent economic development, did not obtain a clear, significant difference in achievement motivation between Protestants and Catholics.

Second, although it is likely that parental behavior and expectations may affect all sorts of behaviors in their children, the relationship between parental behaviors and achievement striving is not as straightforward as Winterbottom's study would have us believe. It will be recalled that Winterbottom interviewed the mothers of the children in her study. Rosen and D'Andrade (1959) carried out actual observations of *both* mothers and fathers interacting with their children in the home. Although Rosen and D'Andrade's observations of the mother's behavior were in accord with Winterbottom's interview data on the mother's expectations, the findings for the father's behavior were unexpected. Fathers of low-achievement sons appeared domineering and authoritarian in their relationships with their sons. The fathers appeared to react with irritation to their son's mistakes, used specific commands as a means of influencing their son's behaviors, and generally behaved in a domineering fashion. While these results do not directly contradict McClelland's assertion that Protestant families at the time of the Reformation engaged in child-rearing practices that produced sons high in achievement motivation, they do shed some doubt on this proposition. If we are able to believe the data of Winterbottom and Rosen and D'Andrade, then we would insist that the Protestant family at the time of the Reformation *at the very least* would have to have consisted of a warm, encouraging mother who consistently rewarded early independence of her sons and a father who was nondomineering and nonauthoritarian. In the absence of such data for Protestant families at the time of the Reformation, it is impossible to evaluate McClelland's assertion. Whether child-rearing practices in Protestant families at the time of the Reformation were the sociopsychological mechanisms by which achievement-motivated sons were produced or whether some social-psychological mechanism other than the family was responsible is not answerable. Moreover, the fact that more recent studies do not suggest significant differences among Protestant and Catholic families in parental expectations for early mastery and independence in children certainly does not argue in favor of McClelland's hypothesis.

Third, McClelland's thesis is rendered even more problematic by the fact that although achievement motivation derived from elementary readers seems to predict the course of economic development of a nation, *it does not predict the level of achievement motivation in individuals.* The level of achievement motivation in a nation can be measured in two ways. One can attempt to infer it *indirectly* as McClelland did from elementary readers, folk tales, and myths, or one can measure it *directly* in samples of live human beings drawn from the nation. If the indirect method of inferring level of achievement motivation from readers does, in fact, measure achievement motivation and not some other variable, then it clearly ought to correlate positively with direct measures of achievement motivation gathered on live human beings from that nation. Unfortunately, level of achievement motivation inferred from readers does not correlate with direct measurement of individuals. For example, Brazilian readers yield very low achievement motivation scores. However, Brazilian students, when tested directly, score higher on achievement motivation than either German or Indian students, both of whom come from countries whose readers yield much higher achievement motivation scores.

It is unclear why the results of studies of individuals and of readers disagree. Nonetheless, the failure to demonstrate this correlation raises serious questions as to what the scores derived from the readers of various nations actually measure. Do they actually measure "level of achievement motivation within a nation?" Or do the scores derived from the readers measure some other unknown variable which does correlate with economic growth? Unfortunately, we have no way of answering these questions.

Finally, we might well ask why achievement motivation scores derived from readers seem to predict one measure of economic development and not another. It will be recalled that when level of economic development was measured in terms of kilowatt consumption per capita, a significant correlation was found between this measure and achievement motivation scores derived from readers in 1925. However, the motive scores failed to predict gains in real income, the I.U. measure of economic growth. Perhaps one could argue after the fact that the index of real income expressed in international units is not as good a measure as kilowatt consumption per capita. However, that argument appears opportunistic since it will have occurred to us *after* having seen the results. Once again, we have no way of knowing the answer to our question. Why it is that achievement motive scores derived from readers predict one measure of economic growth but not another remains a curious and troublesome puzzle.

Achievement motivation and economic growth: a summing up

Our illustration of psychological inquiry that attempts to establish relationships between two levels of analysis, the individual and the societal levels, has led us to an examination of a complex and ambitious piece of research. As we have seen, McClelland posed a truly profound question concerning the relationship between the destinies of nations and the characteristics of persons who comprise them. Whether or not McClelland succeeded in establishing his hypotheses with complete certainty is not at issue here. Rather, he did demonstrate that it is entirely possible to conduct psychological inquiry such that its results would have meaning for questions at the societal level.

As we have seen, efforts to predict societal variables from individual variables is indeed a complex task, and although we cannot conclude that McClelland has succeeded in proving his point to our satisfaction, we are left to speculate further on the possible relationships between great social, philosophical, and religious movements and their possible effects upon individuals who in turn affect the fate of nations. We can at least see how McClelland was led honestly to his beliefs. The following quote from the Protestant theologican John Calvin makes this quite clear:

> Let us every one proceed according to our small ability, and prosecute the journey we have begun. No man will be so unhappy but that he may every day make some progress, however small. Therefore, let us not cease to strive, that we may be incessantly advancing in the way of the Lord, nor let us despair on account of the smallness of our success; for however our success may not correspond to our wishes, yet our labor is not lost, when this day surpasses the preceding one; provided that with sincere simplicity we keep our end in view, and press forward to the goal, not practicing self-adulation, nor indulging our own evil propensities, but perpetually exerting our endeav-

ors after increasing degrees of amelioration, till we shall have arrived at a perfection of goodness, which indeed, we seek and pursue as long as we live.*

INTERACTIONS AMONG LEVELS OF ANALYSIS

In recent years many persons interested in the study of social behavior have recognized the importance of complex *social systems*. A system is defined generally as a complex of elements related in a causal network in such a way that a change in one element may result in changes in other elements as well as in the system as a whole. The concept of systems is neither new nor foreign to intellectual thought. The human body has been thought of for many years as a complex physiological system. Within biology, the relatively recent science of *ecology* explores the complex interrelationships between living organisms and their living and nonliving environments. As ecological study has indicated, only a tiny amount of knowledge has been established with any certainty about the intricate relationships that characterize the *ecosystems* of man and other creatures. Because of man's ignorance of these patterns of relationships, numerous human interventions into the natural world have resulted in devastating consequences. For example, consider the practice of dumping sewage into offshore coastal waters. Since sea urchins may feed on the sewage, this practice has resulted in rapid buildups in sea urchin populations. Like underwater threshing machines, vast armies of sea urchins decimate offshore kelp forests, and of course the kelp forests and the more heavily oxygenated waters around them are the protective coverings and the homes of a great variety of ocean life. Smaller fish that serve as the staple diets of larger fish are found in great abundance around the kelp forests. As the kelp is progressively demolished by the underwater armies of sea urchins, life disappears from the coastal waters. Here we have an excellent example of an intricate life system, as well as unfortunate testimony to the ignorance of man acting in the natural world of which he is a part.

In addition to the biological ecology of human beings, we can speak of human *social ecologies*. Each of us is imbedded in a

---

*From Calvin, J.: *Institutes of the Christian Religion*, 7th Ed., Vol. 1. (Translated by J. Allen and edited by Benjamin B. Warfield.) Philadelphia. Presbyterian Board of Christian Education, 1936, pp. 775–776.

complex social system. We are likely to be members of various interpersonal pairs, members of a family group, which is in turn imbedded in a social system, and so forth. When the psychologist begins to search for relationships that involve three or more levels of analysis, he has begun the effort toward understanding behavior in a social system.

To illustrate what is meant by this, we will examine behavior in modern organizational settings such as the industrial work situation. In the following discussion, we will see how *organizational* variables can lead to *interpersonal* conflict which then can lead to *individual* psychological stress and discomfort. Our example involves relationships among three levels of analysis: the organizational, the interpersonal, and the individual levels.

Psychological stress, interpersonal conflict, and organizational structure

Conflict seems to be a way of life in modern organizations. Given the different goals, values, and personalities of individuals who make up such organizations, much of this conflict is inevitable. In fact, the appearance of conflict within an organization is often a *healthy* sign of efforts after growth and necessary change. But not all conflict in the modern organization is inevitable or desirable. Conflict that arises out of healthy disagreement and results in constructive change must be distinguished from conflict that arises from improper organizational principles, poor management practices, and faulty administration.

David Hampton, Charles Summer, and Ross Webber have provided us with an excellent account of how the work environment of organizations can produce interpersonal conflict and consequent personal stress (Hampton, *et al.*, 1968). Hampton and his colleagues point out that the manner in which work flow is organized and structured is a potential source of conflict within an organization. The *organizational structure* of a corporation, university, or hospital refers to the formal patterns of communication within such organizations. From knowledge of the structure of an organization, we can gain some understanding of the distribution of authority, patterns of social interaction, and formal channels of communication. These patterns of interaction—who talks to whom, who typically initiates communications, who typically responds to communications, and so on—are important sources of interpersonal conflict. Hampton and colleagues discuss three interaction patterns that can lead to personal stress. These are (1) unidirectional patterns of communication, (2) unpredictable or changing patterns of interaction, and (3) intermittent and inadequate patterns of interaction. Let us consider each of these separately.

Unidirectional patterns of communication

In formal organizations work is often arranged around a strict authoritarian hierarchy. The flow of communications is most typically from the top down; far more communications or commands are initiated from superiors than from subordinates. In some organizations, the distribution of authority is such that virtually no communications can be initiated by persons at the bottom of the authority hierarchy. When this situation exists within an organization, we can speak of a *unidirectional* or one-way flow of communications within that organization. Experience has shown that unidirectional communication systems are not optimal for subordinate morale and happiness. The person who must always *receive* communications and never *initiate* them tends to resent such a system, particularly if the communications he is forced to receive are coupled with criticism. An example from an actual work organization makes this clear. A student who worked as a summer laborer comments:

> On Friday, the general foreman again criticized our foreman (Mike) for his poor work. Mike then began to berate the laborers for their slowness and incompetence.... Under a constant barrage of criticism all day, the workers began to criticize each other's work. The frayed tempers of the laborers caused a further lowering of output.*

This is an excellent illustration of how patterns of interaction can reverberate throughout a social system. The general foreman, obviously worried about how the performance of his group would look "up top," put the pressure on Mike, the foreman on a particular job, who, in turn pressured and berated his men for their poor performance. The men, in re-

---

*From *Organizational Behavior and the Practice of Management* by D. R. Hampton, C. E. Summers, and R. A. Webber. © 1968 by Scott, Foresman and Company. Reprinted by permission.

sponse to Mike, turned their anger upon one another. Finally, this system of one-way criticism so disturbed the relations among the laborers that their output was lowered still further.

Unpredictable and changing patterns of interaction

If given a preference, most of us would probably prefer to work in environments over which we had some control and, moreover, in which we could predict events with some accuracy. Unstable, unpredictable, and erratically changing environments tend to produce stress, anxiety, and extreme personal discomfort. But consider the occupations of many persons in a complex, technological society. Many of us in pursuit of our livelihoods are forced into relationships in which we are dependent upon persons we never meet face-to-face. Often the behavior of these persons can produce effects in a complex system that are totally unexpected and disruptive. Moreover, many of us are forced to work in systems with environments over which we have virtually no control. Consider the following remarks by an airline ticket reservations clerk:

> Suppose that on a busy Sunday in July, I am working in reservations and, inadvertently, I oversell the 8:00 flight by five seats. The effects of such a blunder could easily reverberate throughout the entire system. At 7:30 the ticket counter agent will encounter 76 happy faces and five tigers, holding a total of 81 valid tickets for a plane which seats 76. His job is made that much more difficult, and the ensuing series of unpleasantries delays departure well past 8:00. This puts operations on the spot; a new clearance must now be obtained, necessitating further delay. Finally, the plane is airborne at 8:35.
>
> But this would only be the beginning of events that could be traced to my error. Because of greater traffic than would have been encountered with an on-time 55-minute flight, the trip requires 85 minutes in all, arriving in New York at 10:00 p.m. Over an hour late, fourteen passengers have missed connecting flights, and the ticket counter at Kennedy is inundated with angry fliers....
>
> To complicate matters, there is no way to pass off this feeling of pressure save for kicking the water cooler. We were instructed that a loss of temper in front of a passenger could result in dismissal. Many times I was forced to withstand such searing invective and abuse as would have bowled over a less hearty soul. Little wonder that one of the agents suffered a nervous breakdown while working the ticket counter.*

---

*From *Organizational Behavior and the Practice of Management* by D. R. Hampton, C. E. Summers, and R. A. Webber. © 1968 by Scott, Foresman and Company. Reprinted by permission.

Here we have a terrifying example of how the work environment of a person is characterized by unpredictable events, intricate and complex system effects, and individual stress of probably unbearable proportions.

Intermittent and inadequate interactions

Any cooperative endeavor, whether it be in sports, work, making music or whatever, requires stable patterns of interaction. All too frequently in the modern organizational work situation it is impossible to develop such stable patterns of social interaction because of organizational practices that do not permit long-term and regular interaction. Personnel are assigned and reassigned often and irregularly. Work is often arranged so that persons responsible for that work may have infrequent and sporadic contact with other individuals with whom they are supposed to be cooperating. The effects of intermittent and inadequate patterns of social interaction are again a source of conflict and personal stress. Instead of enjoying stable social relationships, personnel may be confronted with changing faces after short time periods, new groups or coalitions with which they must contend, and fragmented social interactions. As we can readily understand, patterns of social and work interaction such as these can increase the likelihood of personal stress and interpersonal conflict.

Stress waves within an organization

Because the component parts of a complex social system are intricately interrelated, personal stress is rarely an isolated event. Interpersonal conflicts tend to radiate out throughout the organization in complex and unpredictable ways. One can readily appreciate this wavelike action of conflict by making observations within a group such as the family. The mother may be angered by an unfortunate remark made by the father. Rather than confront the father directly with her irritation, she may turn her attentions to the children. Before long a nasty conflict erupts between mother and the children. The father is likely to greet such bickering between the mother and children with further criticism of the mother. Mother may then decide that she is now perfectly justified in an all-out attack on father. In a short time, mother and father are arguing ferociously, the children are fighting with one another, and the baby will likely choose that moment to start screaming.

Stress can, in a similar fashion, radiate outward from a center of interpersonal conflict or personal stress throughout a complex work organization. A further quote from Hampton, Summers, and Webber illustrates that this is the case. A former naval officer discusses the behavior of one of his superiors, the Operations Officer:

> Whenever the Operations Officer became upset, he would soar to a high level of activity. Talking and moving about a great deal, he would go from one compartment to another, giving orders, shuffling papers and griping. Of course, this reaction to stress was detrimental to the efficiency and morale of the department as a whole. Aside from interrupting any work which may have been going on, many of the orders he gave while working off this reaction would be contradictory to those he had given previously.
>
> The results of this could be observed all the way down the line—to the lowest rated man in the department. Because of this pressure from above, a man would react by modifying his usual activity level. Because of the new pattern, interaction with this person would be stressful. This upset person would react with someone else, and so on. As a result, the behavior of a great many men in the department was different than under normal conditions. Indeed, I could tell when the Operations Officer was upset simply by the behavior of my own men.*

As these perceptive observations indicate, events at three levels of analysis must be considered simultaneously if we are to make sense of the behavior. Various features of *organizational structure* lead to given patterns of *social interaction* which in turn can produce important psychological effects upon *individuals.* When considering the behavior of individuals, we must always be on guard against erroneously attributing their behavior to a single level of analysis. For example, a psychologist who attempts to explain all psychological stress as purely a function of things going on *inside the heads* of persons to the neglect of their social and work environments stands in grave danger of creating serious misunderstanding.

In any case, our discussion of organizational structure, interpersonal conflict, and individual stress should illustrate clearly to the student the way in which inquiry involving more than two levels of analysis can proceed. The lesson here is quite simple. Human creatures are members of social systems. We

---

*From *Organizational Behavior and the Practice of Management* by D. R. Hampton, C. E. Summers, and R. A. Webber. © 1968 by Scott, Foresman and Company. Reprinted by permission.

shall have to devote some of our efforts to studying persons as members of these complex social systems if we are to fully understand their behavior.

SUMMARY

In the course of this chapter we have seen how psychological inquiry can proceed at a number of different levels of analysis, and we have considered research both between and among levels of analysis. Our selected examples should make clear to the student that psychological inquiry has a broadly ranging proper domain. The contemporary psychologist is not only concerned with the isolated individual human being but with the important interpersonal, group, organizational, societal, and cultural contexts in which he finds him. Although we may be belaboring the point, the student may not have realized this. Students frequently come to the study of psychology with vague notions drawn from popular culture about what the discipline comprises. While psychology is most certainly the study of the individual, it is at once much more than that. The influences over behavior are multiple and varied. Only *some* of these influences lie within the individual person.

Our discussion of levels of analysis not only gives us a useful way of organizing the vast domain of modern psychology, but it provides us with a useful way to approach our introductory studies. In the following chapters, we will attempt to organize our discussion in terms of the various levels of analysis. In subsequent pages, we will be concerned with the individual, the individual in interaction with others, group interaction, organizational behavior, and the effects of society and culture. Let us begin with the individual human being. How shall we conceptualize the person? How can we study him?

References

Bavelas, A.: A mathematical model for group structures. Appl. Anthrop. 7: 16, 1948.
Calvin, J.: *Institutes of the Christian Religion*, 7th Ed., Vol. 1. (translated by J. Allen.) Philadelphia, Presbyterian Board of Christian Education, 1936.
Coopersmith, S.: *The Antecedents of Self-esteem.* San Francisco, W. H. Freeman and Co., 1967.

Hampton, D. R., Summers, C. E., and Webber, R. A.: *Organizational Behavior and the Practice of Management.* Palo Alto, Scott, Foresman and Co., 1968.

Leavitt, H. J.: Some effects of certain communication patterns on group performance. J. Abnorm. Soc. Psychol., *46*: 38, 1951.

McClelland, D. C.: *The Achieving Society.* Princeton, N. J., D. Van Nostrand Co., Inc., 1961.

Milgram, S.: Some conditions of obedience and disobedience to authority. *In* Steiner, I. D., and Fishbein, M. (eds.): *Current Studies in Social Psychology.* New York, Holt, Rinehart and Winston, 1965.

Mulder, M.: Communication structure, decision structure, and group performance. Sociometry, *23*: 1, 1960.

Rosen, B. C., and D'Andrade, R. G.: The psychosocial origins of achievement motivation. Sociometry, *22*: 185, 1959.

Shaw, M. E.: Some effects of problem complexity upon problem solution efficiency in different communication nets. J. Exp. Psychol., *48*: 211, 1954.

Shaw, M. E.: Communication networks. *In* Berkowitz, L. (ed.): *Advances in Experimental Social Psychology.* Vol. 1. New York, Academic Press, pp. 111-147, 1964.

Veroff, J., Atkinson, J. W., Feld, S., and Gurin, G.: The use of thematic apperception in a nationwide interview study. Psychological Monographs, *94*, No. 12, 1960.

Winterbottom, M. R.: The relation of childhood training in independence to achievement motivation. Unpublished doctoral dissertation. University of Michigan, 1953.

CHAPTER
4

Conceptualizing the Person

For most persons, psychology is the study of the individual. Why does one individual look at the world differently from another? Why do people behave as they do? Why is one person easy to get along with and another difficult? Why do some people develop psychological difficulties, whereas others seem to have more than their fair share of happiness, contentment, and serenity? These and many other questions not mentioned here are certainly the proper domain of psychology. But before we can begin to answer them, we must have some way of conceptualizing these apparent *individual differences* among persons. In fact, we must have some way of conceptualizing the *person*. That is, in order to study persons and their behavior, we must have some units of description and units of analysis with which we can work; and although it might appear a simple enough problem, the truth of the matter is that effective units of analysis in the study of the individual have proved terribly difficult to find. When we view the study of human personality in historical perspective, it is clear that much of the effort of psychologists, as well as of philosophers and other observers of mankind, has been devoted to finding useful ways to conceptualize the person. In this chapter, then, we will consider not only the numerous ways in which persons have been understood, but also the units of analysis that have been considered.

ENERGY THEORIES

Perhaps the theories which most readily come to mind when we consider human personality are those which concern themselves primarily with motivation. Motivation, to a psychologist, means those forces which *energize* and *give direction* to behavior. An unmotivated person is a quiescent one. A motivated person is one who is busily expending energy in seeking to reach a goal, fulfill a need, reduce a pressing drive, and so forth. In this sense, the group of theories that we shall discuss first have been labeled *energy theories*. From this perspective, human beings can be seen as driven by forces, conscious or unconscious, which activate them and give direction to their behavior. The "hot" stuff of passions, urges, impulses, instinctual demands, wishes, and desires are of concern here.

The Instinct Doctrine

Although the concept of instinct had interested social philosophers for some time, intense interest in the notion that inborn and unlearned response tendencies exist and determine behavior grew naturally out of the work of Charles Darwin and other biological thinkers of the late nineteenth century. In *The Descent of Man*, Darwin devoted an entire chapter to showing that no fundamental difference exists between man and the higher mammals in terms of their "mental faculties." He claimed to find "social instincts" in animals; and although he recognized the possibility that many human characteristics could be acquired, Darwin held to the belief that most fundamental instincts of humans were inherited rather than acquired. Bain, the Scottish philosopher, and Spencer, the English philosopher, both wrote extensively on the importance of instinctual tendencies in understanding social behavior. The American psychologist, William James, extended this notion by claiming that for each instinct there was a counterinstinct, experience and reason determining which of the two would prevail. James constructed a list of 49 inborn propensities, including such things as biting, pointing at desired objects, play, curiosity, hunting, and grinding the teeth. Like other instinct theorists, James seemed fond of the practice of making lists of the various instincts thought to exist. However, William McDougall, to whom we now turn, was the champion of all list makers.

McDougall and naive instinct theory

As far as psychology is concerned, naive instinct theory reached its culmination in the writings of William McDougall, the English psychologist. McDougall developed instinct theory in great detail in his *Introduction to Social Psychology,* first published in 1908. Widely reprinted and widely read, this proved to be an influential work. Basically, McDougall asserted what instinct theorists had been arguing for some time: that inborn and unlearned response tendencies exist and determine social behavior. He believed that unless one assumed a fundamental human nature which had basically a "common native foundation," i.e., "instincts," a science of social behavior would prove impossible. McDougall argued that in higher animals basic instincts were capable of modification through blending, organizing, and substitution of an "exciting" object for the original one. However, he insisted that despite such modification, one could still recognize the basic instinctual roots of various actions by the particular emotions that accompany them.

McDougall was fond of lists, as were other instinct theorists. Although he began with a list of just 12 inborn basic propensities, by 1932 his list had expanded to 18 basic propensities, which combined and blended in a host of ways to produce an even greater list of secondary propensities. For example, McDougall was able to give an account of the propensity to "reverence." Reverence, McDougall argued, was a secondary propensity made up of "wonder," "negative self-feeling," and "gratitude," and in the event that someone might ask where does "gratitude" come from, McDougall had a ready answer. Gratitude, it seemed, was also a secondary propensity made up of "tender emotion" and "negative self-feeling!" In any case, this kind of reasoning led to ever increasing lists of instincts upon which nobody could agree. Each theorist had his own list and insisted that his alone was correct and that the others were not. By 1924, at least 849 separate instincts had been proposed to explain human behavior. One theorist even went so far as to suggest that persons are born with a propensity to put their fingers into a hole to see whether or not a squirrel lived there! Perhaps this theorist was not really serious and, like some of the earlier artistic endeavors of Andy Warhol, was poking fun at the senselessness of it all.

It soon became apparent that naive instinct theory as propounded by McDougall and others was a dead end in terms of the expanding lists, arm chair theory, and dreadful circularity of reasoning. As John B. Watson, the early American behaviorist is said to have remarked, "To say that an animal fights because of an instinct to pugnacity or that an animal runs away because of an instinct to fear is not an explanation at all as to why animals fight or run away. It is merely a redundant and circular description of the behavior."

However, the student should not suppose that the instinct doctrine quietly vanished from the scene leaving nary a trace nor ripple. The doctrine was and still continues to be important in modern psychology. As we shall see, a body of theory called *drive theory* was a direct outcome of the instinct doctrine, and we will consider this important body of theory later. For the moment, however, let us continue our discussion of the instinct theorists with a consideration of one of the most influential of all psychological theorists, Sigmund Freud.

Sigmund Freud and sophisticated instinct theory

While we may poke a bit of fun at the naive instinct theorists like McDougall, we cannot dismiss Sigmund Freud's more sophisticated doctrine so readily. Freud, the Viennese neurologist and founder of psychoanalysis, had all the marks of greatness: originality, perseverance, a stubborn belief in the correctness of his convictions, and remarkable productivity. The body of theory and writings that Freud left behind at the time of his death still captivates our imaginations and demands serious scholarly attention.

Freud did not trouble himself with the fashionable practice of list construction nor did he bother with the question of the numbers of instincts necessary to explain behavior. He did, however, feel that it was possible to classify all instincts under two broad categories, the *life* instincts and the *death* instincts. In actuality, the bulk of Freud's work is concerned with the life instincts and, as most people know, with only particular life instincts—those sexual in nature. It is important to note that for Freud the term "sexual" was much broader than one would imagine. Freud conceived of sexual activity in the human as widely diverse and he included in it such primitive forms of behavior as sucking, biting, defecating, and so forth, in addition to actual genital activity. The instincts all derived their energy from a hypothetical pool of energy, *libido*. The total quantity of libido available to a person was thought to be fixed at birth. In order to see the sophistication of Freud's thought, let us examine it in greater detail. In the following paragraphs, we will briefly sketch the relationship between sexual striving and psychological development as it was conceived by Freud.

Freud's account of psychosexual development

It is obvious from the term "psychosexual" that Freud perceived important relationships between the mind and body. In actuality, Freud's account of the development of human personality brilliantly traces the association between psychological development and change in sexual appetites as the infant matures into the young child and finally the adult. In order to develop his thought, Freud needed a number of concepts. One of these, *libido*, we have already mentioned. A second necessary concept was that of *erogenous zones*. Freud conceived of the various parts of the human body as being either sexually sensitive or sexually quiescent. The mouth, the anus, and the genitals were considered to be zones of considerable sexual stimulation and capable of intense sexual sensations during the course of development. Freud also conceived of a process called *fixation*. By this he simply meant that a portion of the total sexual energy available to the individual becomes centered around a particular erogenous zone and remains there, or becomes fixated there. Finally, Freud conceived of the psychic portion of persons largely in terms of something called *defense mechanisms*. Since the open expression of sexual instincts is not socially approved, sexual impulses arising from within the person must be dealt with somehow if the person is to avoid the conscious experience of extreme *anxiety*. These impulses must be *repressed* (automatically shut out of awareness), *projected* (attributed to some other person), or *sublimated* (changed to a socially acceptable means of expression). Now, with these concepts in mind, we are prepared to trace the psychosexual development of the person according to Freud.

The oral stage. In the first year of life, sexual pleasure is largely confined to the mouth and lips. In the early part of this stage, the *oral* stage, sucking and swallowing are characteristic modes of seeking pleasurable stimulation. In a sense, the first task the infant must master is making the distinction between

Figure 10. Sigmund Freud, the founder of psychoanalysis. *From* Jones, E.: *The Life and Work of Sigmund Freud.* New York, Basic Books, 1961.

edible and inedible objects. Swallowing is the first acceptance of something from outside the infant, and spitting out is the first rejection. According to Freud, the primitive forerunner of the psychological mechanism of *identification* with others is derived from the incorporative act of swallowing. Similarily, the psychological mechanism of *projection* (defined above) is derived from the early primitive response of spitting out.

In addition to identification and projection, two other psychological mechanisms were thought to emerge during the oral stage, *fixation* and *regression*. Fixation, which can occur at any stage of development, was thought to occur when a portion of libido would break off and become fixated about the mouth, that is, as the child progressed to another stage of development, some portion of the total amount of sexual energy previously available to him would remain behind in the earlier stage. The potential for *regression* (return to an earlier level of psychosexual development) exists for the individual to the extent that fixation has occurred. Hence, when threatened or stressed, the mature adult with considerable fixation at the oral stage might show regressive behaviors like nail biting, extreme dependency, overindulgence in food or drink, and so forth.

The anal stage. At about the second year of life, libido was thought to become focused primarily about the anus. In the early anal stage, the child derives pleasure from the expulsion of feces. In the late anal stage, the child, discovering that he can drive his parents to extreme discomfort, may use expulsiveness as a means of defying his parents' wishes for him to be clean—or he may defy his parents by refusing to defecate at all. It is small wonder, then, that Freud saw these early happenings in the bathroom as the beginnings of the psychological mechanism of *denial,* i.e., the automatic and unconscious denial of reality. Anybody who has ever spent any time around a two year old can certainly testify that this is a "no-no" period for the child. Negativism, refusal to conform to the wishes of the parent, and so forth, are often considered characteristic of the two year old. Whether such characteristic forms of behavior are attributable to events on the potty is, of course, another matter. However, for Freud, there was a direct and simple connection between the development of denial and the shift of libido from the mouth to the anus.

The phallic stage. At about the end of the third year or the beginning of the fourth year of life, libidinal energy shifts to the genital zone, and, according to Freud, it is here that conflict inevitably lurks within every son destined to play out the famous myth of Oedipus, the king who slayed his father and slept with his mother. Of course, the child does not actually slay his father nor does he accomplish sexual intercourse with his mother, but, again according to Freud, he wants to. Although such sexual hungering after the mother may never be noticeable in the child's overt behavior, it is thought to be revealed in dreams, fantasies, artistic efforts, obsessions, play, and other forms of symbolic enactments.

So at the age of three the child is beginning to experience the dawn of sexual stirrings in the region of his genitals. Mother is a handy sexual object, one who is capable of arousing him, but at the same time the child is aware that he is competing with the father for mother's love and affection. Moreover, he is dimly aware that father is not likely to be nice and understanding about the whole matter. In fact, he suspects that father would very likely castrate him if he were to go through with the act! This fear, *castration anxiety,* as well as the fear of loss of mother's love, results in *repression,* the automatic and unconscious blocking off of sexual feelings toward the mother. Hostility for his competitor, the father, is replaced by identification with him. Sexual strivings toward the mother are converted to tender feelings of love and protectiveness. At this point, the first major conflict of the child has been resolved.

The genital stage. Following a period of what is assumed to be sexual quiescence, the so-called *latency period* (age six to ten), the child enters the genital stage. This is the period of early adolescence which merges finally into adulthood. Shortly before and during puberty the child undergoes a reawakening of interest in older modes of pleasure seeking. The Oedipus conflict may be reactivated. Libidinal activity generally is thought to increase markedly. Aggressive impulses are intensified to the point of unruliness, hunger becomes voracity, and naughtiness may turn toward actual criminal behavior. Most psychoanalytic theorists view this period as a "stormy one" with much turmoil and antisocial behavior in evidence. Whether or not adolescence is indeed inevitably a "stormy" period is open to question, and, more importantly, whether or not particular aspects of adolescent behavior are linked to psychosexual development remains a speculation rather than a firm conclusion. As with much of Freud's thought, as well as with that of those who came after him, we must be careful to distinguish between brilliant and creative myth, which might appear intuitively correct, from established fact.

Adult personality structure and psychosexual development

It is now possible to see the relationship between adult character traits and the course of psychosexual development as Freud conceived it. Depending upon events in the course of psychosexual development, as well as upon the amount of fixation that occurs at each stage, different adult personality structures are thought to exist. The adult who was excessively frustrated during the oral stage is believed to show character traits of dependency, anxiety, and insecurity. On the other hand, the adult who was excessively indulged during the oral period tends to show character traits of optimism and self-assurance, even when such characteristics are unjustified.

The adult with excessive fixation in the anal stage is thought to exhibit pedantry, parsimony, and petulance (jokingly referred to as the three P's). Orderliness and conscientiousness are thought to be characteristic. Obsessive concern with cleanliness, detail, and tightness with money are further thought to be characteristic of the anal adult character.

The phallic character is thought to be exemplified by the professional wrestler, the beach athelete, weight lifter, and motorcyclist. Vanity, exhibitionism, and sensitiveness are linked to early excessive castration anxiety. Phallic characters are said to be narcissistic, unable to form mature relationships with those of the opposite sex, and actually contemptuous of the opposite sex. Sexual conquests are not based upon any real concern for the partner but for vain expressions of masculinity or feminity and even, in some instances, contempt for the sexual partner.

The genital character represents the ideal, although imperfect, culmination of psychosexual development. Capable of genital sexuality, the adult genital character may engage in other forms of sexual expression but finds primary satisfaction in genital contact and activity with the opposite sex. Adequate heterosexual adjustment, sublimation of instinctual drives, and emotional "maturity" are considered characteristics of the genital character.

Summary of Freud's sophisticated instinct theory

It is in fact impossible to present and evaluate a theory as elaborate, provocative, and as subtle as Freud's in this brief space. However, our purpose has not been to present certain aspects of Freud's thought in order to provide an extensive description and appraisal of this important body of theory. Nonetheless, a few words of caution to the student are in order.

In general, the most frequent criticism raised against Freud and psychoanalysis is simply that the theory is not open to confirmation or disconfirmation by scientific methods. There are those, however, who would argue with this common criticism. In many respects, Freud's theory seems more a literary work than a rigorous scientific work and as such it is difficult, if not impossible, to render concepts such as libido amenable to operational definition. Much of what Freud proposed involves totally unobservable events. For example, consider the events thought to comprise the Oedipal complex and its resolution. Libido (an unobservable force) becomes centered about the genitals. Sexual strivings toward the mother (not directly observable) are a consequence. Castration fear (unconscious and not directly observable) leads to repression of sexual strivings toward the mother (repression being automatic and unconscious and thus unobservable). Repression of sexual striving towards the mother permits the identification with the father (this process also being unobservable). In essence, then, Freud begins with an unobservable event and ends with an unobservable one in his account of the Oedipus complex. One might well ask how does he know that this is an accurate account of what takes place. There is, of course, nothing wrong with postulating unobservable events and then attempting through inference to conjecture about their operation. However, one must usually link such unobservable phenomena with observable inputs and measureable outputs. One might, for example, develop interesting hypotheses about what goes on in the heads of people by carefully controlling input and making various predictions about what the output should be if the inner, unobservable phenomenon behaves in the manner in which one thinks it does.

There are, of course, other criticisms of Freud. One suspects that the potential exists for a great deal of confusion between *correlated attributes* of behavior and *causal factors.* For example, if certain changes in behavior do in fact occur as the child moves from the prepubertal phase to puberty, are we justified in inferring that such changes in behavior are attributable to the onset of puberty? Other events are taking place in the lives of children as they age. They move from one school setting to another, the expectations of others toward them change as they age, and so forth.

Finally, one may very well question the methods of inquiry Freud employed to arrive at his conclusions. His methods were most subjective and the possibility of observer bias and observer influence most certainly existed. His sampling of subjects was very limited, consisting, over a lifetime, of a relatively small number of highly selected cases (neurotic patients seeking help through psychotherapy). These shortcomings aside, it is obvious that Freud was a great psychologist, one of unusual brilliance and originality. He worked as a scientist with the methods available to him and, indeed, created new methods. Although we may question many of his *inferences* about behavior, one cannot deny that he was a remarkable *observer* of human beings. Many of his observations still intrigue us, and although his influence has declined in recent years, one must recognize that for nearly half a century, Freud and psychoanalytic thought comprised one of the mainstreams in psychological thought and practice.

The Drive Doctrine

As difficulties became apparent in instinct theory, psychologists turned toward other conceptions. One of these, the drive doctrine, proved to be an influential body of theory. Let us first examine some of the generalities common to most drive theories:

1. People possess a limited number of *primary* drives. These unlearned and inborn physiological drives are thought to be hunger, sex, thirst, and pain.
2. All other drives of the person are *secondary* in nature and are derived from the primary drives.
3. The social drives of persons are learned in accordance with certain laws of learning.
4. People act only to reduce some operative drive. That is, an organism is only moved to action when it is experiencing some deficiency, e.g., hunger, thirst, or sexual arousal.
5. Since people will act only to reduce some drive, all learning depends upon motive arousal and motive reduction.

As already noted, it is clear that the drive doctrine was an improvement over naive instinct theory. First of all, it escaped the problem of arbitrary lists and substituted the notion that a limited number of primary drives exist. Secondly, it focused upon the importance of *learning* in the explanation of human behavior. As a consequence, drive theory did not insist that *all* social behaviors of the person were inborn. Instead, it recognized that *social motives* could be *acquired* by the person in the course of his life. Let us examine this body of theory in greater detail.

Reinforcement theories of learning and the drive doctrine

There were, of course, numerous psychologists associated with the creation and elaboration of drive theory. Perhaps the most notable was Clark Hull, the American psychologist whose efforts after a rigorous scientific behaviorism based upon drive notions were most impressive. According to Hull, learning was a matter of the strengthening of associations between various stimuli and responses. Such associations were formed and strengthened when the activities of the person led to decreases in some operative drive state. All of this sounds terribly complex but is, in actuality, quite simple. Let us consider the work of Dollard and Miller, two drive theorists whose work was of direct relevance to the understanding of human personality. Perhaps, in the context of Dollard and Miller's work, the central ideas of reinforcement theories of learning and the drive doctrine will become clearer.

Drive reduction theory: Dollard and Miller

Dollard and Miller (1950) determined that the learning process consisted of four important ingredients: *drive, cue, response,* and *reinforcement.* Drive was considered to be the *energizer* of behavior, or that which sets the person into action, but drive does not provide direction to behavior. Cues provide the directing function; that is, a hungry person may move about in search of food, but specific cues, such as odors or restaurant signs, will determine where, when, and to what the person will respond. Since learning is defined as the strengthening of an association between a stimulus or cue and a response, the person must be capable of making a reasonable approximation of the response that is to be learned. This may sound somewhat paradoxical to the student. How can the person perform the response which is to be learned? However, one must remember that learning is not defined as the acquisition of a response but as the *strengthening of an association between a stimulus and a response.* In this sense the person already knows the response, i.e., he can perform it, but he must learn to perform the response in the presence of the effective stimulus. Finally in order that the response be learned, reinforcement must occur. Dollard and Miller, and other drive theorists as well, defined reinforcement as the *reduction of a drive.* For example, one reinforces a hungry child by giving him food, or one reinforces a thirsty animal by giving it water. In these two cases, food and water are considered reinforcements because they reduce strong operative drives of hunger and thirst.

Let us briefly summarize what Dollard and Miller have asserted:

1. Learning is the strengthening of associations between a stimulus (cue) and a response.
2. Learning will not take place unless reduction in a drive occurs.
3. Since the person must perform the response in order for the association between it and some stimulus to develop, only motivated persons can learn. That is, since behavior must be energized by some operative drive, an unmotivated person would not perform the response to be learned. Hence learning could not occur.

Significance of the drive reduction theory

At this point in our discussion of drive theory, the student might very well ask, "So what? How does this help me to understand the ordinary behavior of people I'm involved with each day?" An example illustrating how drive theory can be extended is appropriate.

Although it is difficult to define *anxiety* precisely, each of us has an intuitive appreciation of the meaning of the term. We commonly think of anxiety as fear without a recognizable source. Dollard and Miller argued that anxiety can be considered as a strong drive, and in the course of its reduction much learning of significance for the personality of the person takes place. For example, consider the person who engages in a compulsive act like repetitive hand washing. One such person known to the author was compelled to wash his hands over 100 times during the course of a day! If attempts were made to restrain him from engaging in this behavior, he would become visibly upset and disturbed. In this case, the habit of compulsive hand washing was a response that permitted appreciable but temporary reduction in anxiety. Immediately after washing his hands, this person experienced a sudden and welcomed decrease in anxiety. However, this effect was temporary, and anxiety eventually mounted again leading to further hand washing, further anxiety reduction, and so on. In a sense, the person was caught in a vicious cycle of mounting anxiety, compulsive act, and anxiety reduction. It is probable that this troublesome behavior could be traced to early parental training practices in which the child was reinforced for careful washing of his hands and punished severely for dirty hands.

It does not require much imagination to sense the further possible extensions of drive reduction theory. The alcoholic, for example, may be caught in such a vicious cycle. In the beginning, he may drink for a host of reasons, e.g., because alcohol is readily available, because he feels happy or sad, or because he is a success or a failure. In time, however, the alcoholic discovers that alcohol is an effective means of alleviating whatever discomfort is ailing him. Heavy drinking may lead to physical distress as well as psychological and social disruption because of aberrant behavior produced under the influence of alcohol. Hurting desperately both physically and psychologically, the person may very well continue to drink since alcohol, a very effective anaesthesia, is the only thing that affords him immediate comfort. The sense of well-being, euphoria, and lack of anxiety that frequently accompanies the use of drugs, such as marijuana, may also constitute important reinforcements for the person and hence insure the probability that he will continue to use the drug. Users of hard narcotics (morphine, heroin) typically report states under the influence of such drugs which can only be termed totally driveless. Some addicts seem driven only to achieve a state of almost total nothingness: a total lack of drive or anxiety attendant upon entry of the drug into their bodies. Whether or not the same mechanisms can be used to explain psychedelic drug use is of course a different matter. There are enough reasons to suspect that the motivational basis for using drugs like LSD are quite different from those involved in the use of alcohol or marijuana. In fact, there is good reason to believe that persons using psychedelic chemicals are seeking an intensification of experience rather than a reduction in intensity.

Drive reduction theory has been used to explain still other behaviors and attributes. According to Dollard and Miller, many adult characteristics can be traced to early infancy and childhood and to the particular patterns of child-rearing employed. For example, the infant-mother feeding situation may comprise the nuclear basis for such characteristics as sociability or its opposite, social indifference. If the mother permits the hunger drive to mount to reasonable intensity before feeding, sufficient drive level will be accrued to permit appreciable drive reduction when feeding finally takes place. Hence, pleasureable relaxation responses will become associated with the presence of another person (mother). On the other hand, if the child is fed whether he is hungry or not, sufficient drive level will not be obtained, drive reduction of any magnitude will not take place, and pleasurable responses will not become associated with the presence of another person.

Evaluation of the drive doctrine

As appealing as the drive doctrine might seem in explaining certain behaviors, there are now obvious difficulties that restrict its generality. First of all, the assumption that a limited number of primary drives exists from which all other motives are derived has been seriously questioned; much research has been accomplished that does not support this proposition. For example, Harlow, Harlow, and Meyer (1950) discovered that monkeys will learn to solve complicated mechanical problems in the absence of drive reduction. Moreover, monkeys will learn a correct discrimination even if the only reward is gaining access to a novel and stimulating environment (Harlow and McClearn, 1954). Butler and Alexander (1955) demonstrated that monkeys will perform responses only to obtain a view of the world outside a specially designed enclosed cage. In fact, monkeys will learn responses when the only apparent reinforcement is simply gaining a view of another monkey! With regard to the assumed importance of hunger reduction, Harlow (1958) quite clearly demonstrated that *tactile comfort* may be a far more important determinant of the infant monkey's attraction for the mother than reduction of the primary drive of hunger (Fig. 6).

None of these findings, in and of themselves, invalidates the notion that a limited number of primary drives exists. However, one must remember that drive theory was, in part, a reaction to the senseless practice of list-making of the instinct theorists. It would appear that drive theory is heading in the same direction; the list of supposed primary drives is growing. Since many behaviors can be learned in the absence of hunger, thirst, sex, and pain and their reduction, one must conclude that these too are primary. Hence, one must now extend the list of primary drives to include such things as "curiosity," "tactile comfort," "exploration," "problem-solving," "manipulation," and so forth. But what have we actually explained when we say that a monkey learns to open a door because of a "curiosity drive?" Certainly Watson's criticism of naive instinct theory applies here. To say that a monkey explores novel and curious

Figure 11. Harlow's experiments on monkeys raised with wire or cloth surrogate mothers demonstrate the importance of tactile comfort in the development of the young monkey. In this picture, a young monkey, when frightened by a toy bear, chooses the cloth mother to cling to even though food was always available in both the wire and cloth "mothers." (Courtesy of Professor F. Harlow.)

environments because he has a "curiosity drive" seems to amount to a redundant and circular description of the monkey's behavior rather than a serious explanation.

Secondly, the assertion that people will act only to reduce drives is no longer tenable. Experiments indicate that animals will frequently seek more stimulating environments rather than less stimulating environments (Montgomery, 1955; Kish, 1955). Heron (1957) demonstrated that the absence of stimulation can be as aversive as the presence of too much stimulation. Depriving college students of normal sensory input, Heron discovered that *stimulus seeking* behavior on the part of the students became apparent. Most importantly, Heron discovered that normal psychological functioning seemed dependent upon continual and unceasing sensory stimulation.

Finally, the assumption that all learning depends upon drive reduction also no longer appears tenable. We have already considered experiments in which significant learning took place in the apparent absence of drive reduction.

Of course, it is not necessary to discard all of the drive theory. The fact remains that the concepts of drive and drive reduction still provide attractive explanations for many otherwise puzzling forms of behavior. However, it is clear that the *generality* of drive theory is most certainly open to question. Whatever its limits, drive theory clearly cannot explain everything, and indeed no theory can.

Arousal theory: further extensions of drive theory

When it became clear that drive theory was too one-sided, efforts were made to develop a theory that would incorporate the idea that people seem to seek intensification as well as reduction of drive level. As a consequence, the *optimal level of arousal theory* has come into being. According to this theory, neither a high state nor a low state of motivation are desirable. Behavioral efficiency is optimal at a moderate level of arousal. Above this optimal level, performance may be disorganized and inefficient; below this level, performance is also quite inefficient. The theory of an optimal level of arousal permits us to see how emotions or drives can be both organizing and disorganizing. Some persons may work well under moderate pressure and threat, whereas severe pressure might prove disruptive and the absence of pressure might prove unproductive.

In any case, we can now see how energy conceptions have captured the imaginations of psychologists seeking ways to characterize the person. Precisely how useful it is to conceive of a person as a "sea of passions" remains to be demonstrated convincingly, but for the moment, let us consider one further energy conception of persons, that of *need* theory.

Need theories: homeostatic conceptions of human beings

Closely wedded to the concept of drive is the concept of need. In a sense, both characterize the person as striving to maintain a dynamic equilibrium. Both drive theory and need theory were undoubtedly influenced by the ideas of the physiologist Walter B. Cannon. In his major work, *The Wisdom of the Body*, Cannon described the automatic regulatory devices that operate to keep the internal environment of the person in equilibrium. For example, as sugar enters the body and the blood sugar level rises, automatic regulatory processes effect a return of the blood sugar level to its resting state. Cannon referred to these multifarious physiological processes as homeostatic processes. One can think of them as very much like modern feedback control systems such as the thermostat.

If homeostatic principles could accurately describe the physiology of the person, it seemed reasonable by analogy to move to the *psychological* level; that is, since one could consider the person a collection of waxing and waning physiological needs, seeking always to maintain homeostatic balance, one could also assume that persons could be considered as a collection of psychological needs. Psychological needs, then, became the driving force behind human behavior. If one could but discover what a person's needs were, one might be in a position to predict his behavior.

Henry Murray, the distinguished Harvard psychologist, is the man most closely identified with the development of need theory. A prolific writer, a Melville scholar, and a man of great intellectual curiosity, Murray developed a substantial theory of human personality in which the concept of need was afforded a central place. For Murray, needs were hypothetical forces that served to organize perception, intelligence, and action. Persistent and unsatisfied needs would arouse the person to action that would be sustained until satisfaction had been attained. From intensive studies of subjects, Murray (1938) concluded that at least 20 needs could be identified. Some of these are presented in the following table:

Need	Definition
Achievement	To accomplish, to master, to manipulate, etc.
Affiliation	To draw close to others, cooperate, and reciprocate in social interchange.
Autonomy	To be free and independent, to act according to impulse, and to resist authority.
Succorance	To be nursed, protected, loved, assisted, guided, indulged, etc.
Nurturance	To nurture others, protect, guide, assist, etc.
Order	To be orderly, cleanly, precise, etc.

Of course, Murray did not believe that all of these needs were present at full strength in all people. On the contrary, he conceived of persons as differing greatly in the composition of their need structure. One individual might, for example, be high in achievement need and low in the need to nurture others. Another might show the opposite tendency.

Abraham Maslow, the American psychologist, has consistently argued that needs are arranged in a hierarchy. As one general type of need is satisfied, another "higher-order" need will emerge and become operative in the life of the person. At the base of the need hierarchy are the physiological needs such as hunger and thirst. Once these are satisfied, the person seeks to satisfy safety or security needs. Love needs, esteem needs, needs for self-actualization, needs for knowledge, and needs for aesthetic fulfillment complete the hierarchy. In a sense, Maslow is going slightly beyond other need theorists by postulating an order of potency or priority with regard to the structuring of needs within the person.

It is, of course, impossible to say whether or not Maslow's hierarchical conception of needs is factual. No one to this writer's knowledge has demonstrated that this is indeed the case. It is in fact difficult to see how this conception could be demonstrated. Although the term "self-actualization" is an "in" phrase at the moment, it is difficult to find any two persons who mean the same thing when they say it. In sensitivity groups conducted by the author, the phrase has been employed to mean everything from getting rid of one's spouse to creating symphonies with "creative cookery" sandwiched in between. Aside from the semantic nightmare of terms, such as "self-actualization," one has a great deal of difficulty discovering a way to test the proposition that needs are arranged hierarchically. Casual observation suggests that something is not quite right here. The author has known far too many terribly insecure and love-hungry seekers after wisdom to be willing to place "a thirst for knowledge" near the top of a need hierarchy. By all that is reasonable, they should never have passed the second level.

In general, though, we can quickly sense the similarities between the need theorists and the drive theorists. Both postulate hypothetical forces that energize and direct behavior. As in drive theory, the generality of need theory is open to question. In any case, need theory has stimulated some research in psychology, perhaps the most successful and consistent being McClelland's work on need achievement discussed in Chapter 3.

COGNITIVE-INFORMATIONAL THEORIES

As we have seen, energy conceptions of persons as expressed in theories such as instinct theory, drive theory, and need theory quickly captured the imaginations of those interested in human psychology. For many persons, professionals and laymen alike, the answers to the question, "Why do people behave as they do?" seemed to lie entirely in the concept of motivation. For nearly a half a century, the concept of motivation preoccupied those interested in human personality and behavior. In fact, virtually every major classic theory of human personality is in essence a theory of motivation. While theorists disagreed over what the central motivating factors in the lives of persons were, they completely agreed that motivational explanations would eventually suffice for a human psychology.

Psychological theorists seemed incapable of recognizing the fact that numerous determinants of behavior other than motivational ones could exist. In fact, many theorists failed to recognize that while a motive could be *a* determinant of behavior, not *all* determinants were motivational in nature. In effect, such theorists were attempting to explain the behavior of a creature as complex as the human being in terms of a *single variable*. The assumption that all determinants of behavior are motivational in nature leads to serious consequences. If, for example, a person cannot identify the reasons for his behavior, it is often assumed that *unconscious motives* exist and determine his behavior. Persons who are bewildered and confused by their actions, either through professional help or self-analysis, have attempted to root out these supposed underlying unconscious motives that presumably cause them to behave as they do. Little thought is given to the possibility that numerous other factors determine one's behavior.

Within recent years, however, dissatisfaction with motivationally based theories has increased. This is not to say that such efforts after explanation have been abandoned, but many psychologists have turned away from motivational conceptions toward more cognitive theories of behavior. Studies concerned with concept formation, belief systems, cognitive structure, information processing, expectancies, and so forth have recently preoccupied psychologists, and it is to these more recent conceptions that we now turn. In contrast to energy conceptions, the problem of motivation is not central to cognitive-informational theories of behavior.

The psychology of personal constructs: George Kelly

In 1955, George Kelly, then of Ohio State University, published a two-volume work called the *Psychology of Personal Constructs*. Kelly's remarkable effort demonstrated that it was indeed possible to develop a theory of human personality that did not rely upon motivational conceptions. Pondering the entire question of human motivation, Kelly came up with an intriguing question: How might man appear to us if we were to construe him *as if* he were a scientist? That is, instead of thinking of man as driven by forces over which he has no control, in pursuit of homeostatic equilibrium, need satisfaction, and so forth, let us grant to him the same abilities, interests, and characteristics that we psychologists assign to ourselves in our roles as inquirers into human behavior. As Kelly put it:

> Might not the individual man, each in his own personal way, assume more of the stature of a scientist, ever seeking to predict and control the course of events with which he is involved? Would he not have his theories, test his hypotheses, and weigh his experimental evidence?*

Central to Kelly's thought was the notion of *constructive alternativism*. For Kelly, reality certainly exists; however, human beings can never come to know it directly and absolutely. All they can achieve are various *representations* of reality. Upon the turbulent flow of events, human beings attempt to fit "templates," "ideas," "concepts," all structures which in effect bring order to chaos. That is, if there is a fundamental motive behind human affairs, it is necessary to make one's world understandable, coherent, and manageable. According to Kelly, a variety

---

*From Kelly, G. A.: Psychology of Personal Constructs. vol. 1. New York, W. W. Norton and Company, Inc., 1955, p. 5.

of ways exists in which people can structure the events in which they are involved. In fact, people, although they frequently do not realize it, can *choose* among various alternative constructions of events. This is what is meant by the term "constructive alternativism."

For Kelly, the truly interesting properties of people were not their passions, urges, unconscious motives, or anything of the kind. Rather, he was interested in the way they construed their worlds. The basic unit of analysis in the study of the person became the *construct*.

It is easiest to grasp what Kelly meant by constructs by considering how he attempted to measure them. Kelly devised a test called the *Role Construct Repertory Test*. In the first part of the test, the subject was required to list the names of approximately 20 persons who seemed to fit certain descriptions. Some of these descriptions were as follows:

A teacher you liked
Your father
Your worst enemy
Your wife or present girl friend

After the subject had provided names for these descriptions, he was asked to consider sets of three persons at a time and to decide in what way two of them were alike while being essentially different from the third. For example, a subject might say that a teacher he liked and his father were similar in that they were both "understanding" while his worst enemy was "hypercritical." Hence, the dimension "understanding-hypercritical" constituted a construct, one which the subject would employ in making sense of the behavior of other persons toward him. From large numbers of such judgments, Kelly would derive a collection of constructs. In effect, Kelly was searching for a way to see how people's heads were organized with regard to the types of conceptual filters they attempted to fit over the realities of behavior.

The construct systems of people can differ considerably. First, one notices that people appear to differ greatly in the sheer number of constructs available to them. Some persons possess very few interpersonal constructs; others seem to have a rich and varied collection of constructs. Second, the formal attributes of constructs can vary from person to person. For example, one person may possess numerous *permeable* constructs while another may not. A permeable construct is one which is open-ended in the sense that it permits new events to be subsumed under it. One might speculate that "flexible," as opposed to "rigid," persons are those who possess large numbers of permeable constructs.

It is not our intent to present Kelly's theory in all of its full blown complexity and subtlety, but we have mentioned it in enough detail to give the student a feeling for an alternative way to conceptualize the person. We will have more to say about constructs in subsequent pages. For the moment, however, the student should be in a position to see that quite a different psychology of persons emerges when we choose to focus upon the ways in which they structure their worlds rather than upon the forces which drive them.

Cognitive-consistency theories

Within the past several years, a family of theories focusing upon *consistency* have come into being. Although highly similar to each another, the theories are distinctive enough to merit separate discussion. Each grows out of the assumption that human beings strive for consistent, coherent, and harmonious views of the world and the events in which they are involved. Each emphasizes the importance of some cognitively inconsistent event which, in effect, throws the system into a state of imbalance and the subsequent efforts characteristic to return to equilibrium. For example, one may walk outdoors on a perfectly clear, sunny, and cloudless day and encounter rain! The fact that it is raining is inconsistent with all of one's cognitions about bright, sunny, and cloudless days. One might simply accept this discrepancy; or one might look about for a culprit lurking in an upstairs window with a water gun; or one might search the heavens for a stray, unnoticed cloud. In any case, two incompatible cognitions would be the occasion for the arousal of feelings of inconsistency and possible consequent efforts to reduce the inconsistency in some fashion or another.

In a very real sense, consistency theories are extensions of the drive-equilibrium theories discussed earlier, that is, inconsistent events are thought to produce a strain toward inconsistency reduction. Instead of physiological drives being reduced, however, inconsistency theories suggest that the individual is motivated by unbalanced or inconsistent *cognitive* states with pressures toward consistency.

Let us consider these theories in greater detail. There are three major positions: *dissonance, balance,* and *congruity-incongruity theories.*

Cognitive dissonance. Although consistency and inconsistency had captured the imaginations of earlier theorists, it took the inventiveness of Leon Festinger, a social psychologist, to bring the concept to widespread attention within the field of psychology. Working with Carlsmith, Festinger performed what has come to be regarded as the seminal experiment in dissonance theory (Festinger and Carlsmith, 1959). These men created a complicated social situation in which subjects were induced to say something publicly that was in disagreement with their private feelings. They were paid either $1.00 or $20.00 for doing so. Hence, some subjects were offered a small amount of money for lying, whereas others were offered a large amount. Attitude measurements on the issue about which the subjects had lied were gathered after the experiment had been completed. From a common-sense point of view, one would expect that those subjects paid $20.00 would show a greater shift of their opinion away from their private attitude and toward the one they had expressed publicly. After all, $20.00 is a lot of money for a college student (even students at Stanford University, where the experiment was conducted). However, the results were just the opposite. Subjects who were paid only $1.00 showed more positive attitudes toward the position they had taken publicly than did those who were paid $20.00. How can this seemingly baffling result be explained?

Festinger and Carlsmith reasoned as follows: The subject has been induced to say something publicly with which he privately disagrees. As a consequence, he holds two inconsistent cognitions. That is, he says to himself (1) "I feel negative about this thing" and (2) "I'm telling people that it is a pretty cool thing." Presumably the subject is now in an unpleasant state of cognitive dissonance. He must search for ways to reduce the discomfort of this dissonant state. Finally, he hits upon a solution, which is simply to change his private opinion to bring it into line with his public statement. That is, if he can convince himself that he *actually* believes what he has said publicly, then dissonance will be reduced and a state of cognitive equilibrium will be restored.

The difference between the subjects who were given $20.00 and those given $1.00 is explained by the variable of *amount of justification*. Subjects offered $20.00 could explain their public lying simply on this basis. They could say, "Well, I know I don't feel this way, but $20.00 is a lot of money." In other words, they were given sufficient justification for lying. Hence, little dissonance should be aroused and dissonance reduction would not need to occur, i.e., the subject felt no need to change his private opinion.

The subject paid only $1.00, however, is in quite a different psychological position. He has presented publicly a position with which he privately disagrees. Moreover, he has done this for only a paltry dollar! Under these circumstances sufficient justification has not been provided, a state of dissonance exists, and the subject attempts to reduce it by changing his private opinion.

Since this early experiment by Festinger and Carlsmith, an enormous number of studies on dissonance arousal and reduction have been made. Dissonance theory has generated much heat and controversy, more than any other cognitive-consistency theory. Among psychologists, one can identify a variety of positions. There are those who have always maintained that the existence of something called dissonance and its effects have never been adequately demonstrated in any respectable scientific sense (Chapanis and Chapanis, 1964). There are those who feel that dissonance may exist but that it is not terribly important in explaining behavior (Freedman, 1968). Finally, there are those who remain vigorous supporters of the theory, although they recognize both its methodological and conceptual problems (Aronson, 1968). We will have occasion to discuss extensions of dissonance theory in later sections. For the moment, the student should be content to understanding the concept of dissonance as well as the manner in which it is thought to operate in human affairs.

Balance theory. In the Festinger and Carlsmith experiment, inconsistency between private belief and public behavior was examined. It is possible for other types of inconsistency to exist. In 1958, Heider wrote extensively about the importance of inconsistency between *cognition* and *feeling*. Heider was concerned mainly with interpersonal relationships. It is perhaps easiest to understand his concept of *balance* by considering several states which could characterize a unit of three persons. Consider the hypothetical persons, Harry, Joe, and Bill, all of whom are known to each other, and the following situation:

>State 1. Harry likes (+) Joe; Harry likes (+) Bill; and Joe likes (+) Bill. State 1 is a balanced state since the relationships among the three persons are positive. But suppose the following situation existed:
>
>State 2. Harry likes (+) Joe; Harry likes (+) Bill; but Harry has discovered that Joe *dislikes* (−) *Bill.*

According to Heider, State 2 reflects an unbalanced triad and consequently pressure towards change exists in State 2. It is possible, for example, that Harry might change to a negative attitude toward Bill.

Extensions of Heider's notions concerning discrepancies between knowing and feeling have been carried out by Rosenberg (1960, 1968). Rosenberg reasoned that an attitude may have several components. Our *beliefs* about an object are a part of our attitudes, but we also have *feelings* toward objects. For example, a person may believe that wars are necessary, but his feelings about persons killing one another are quite negative. In this case, an unbalanced state would exist since that belief and affect are quite inconsistent with one another.

With these thoughts in mind, Rosenberg gathered measurements of persons' beliefs and feelings about important social issues. For example, subjects were asked to state their beliefs as well as their emotional reactions to issues such as "Negroes moving into all-white neighborhoods." Once the person's beliefs and reactions were known, he was hypnotized and his feelings were deliberately distorted. If a person felt quite negatively about blacks moving into white neighborhoods, it was suggested to him, under hypnosis, that "The thought of Negroes moving into all-white neighborhoods will make you happy."

It is important to note that while under hypnosis, the subject was not given any suggestions about his *beliefs.* If, for example, he felt that blacks moving into an all-white neighborhood would result in a fall in property values, no effort was made to change this belief. Only the feeling state was altered under hypnosis. Following the hypnosis session, the person's feelings and beliefs were again assessed. Rosenberg discovered that along with a change in feeling, the person's beliefs showed changes as well. A person who previously believed that blacks moving into an all-white neighborhood would result in a fall of property values showed evidence of believing, after a change in his *feelings* had been effected, that this would not happen.

Rosenberg used the balance principle to explain this change in belief. He reasoned as follows: If the feeling component of an attitude can be altered, a state of imbalance involving affect and cognition will occur. As a consequence, pressure toward bringing affect and belief into balance or consistency will be generated by the person by altering his beliefs to bring them into line with his feelings.

Congruity-incongruity theory. Congruity-incongruity theory grew out of the work of Charles Osgood working on the problem of *meaning* (Osgood, 1952). Osgood recognized that more than one type of meaning exists. One can speak of *denotative* as opposed to *connotative* meaning. Denotative meaning deals with *signs*; when a specific sign signifies a specific action, we are dealing with an instance of denotative meaning. For example, a dot on a page of music signifies that the performer is to strike a given note and to hold it for a given duration. Similarly a *Stop* sign denotes a specific action to be taken by a motorist.

Connotative meaning concerns *symbols* rather than signs. In connotative meaning we are not concerned with a one-to-one relationship between a sign and what it signifies. Rather, we are concerned with symbols that suggest something because of association, convention, or relationships. For example, to some persons a marijuana cigarette may connote "evil," "degradation," "crime," and "violence." To others it may connote "pleasure," "relaxation," "warmth," and "fun." The lion can symbolize "courage;" the fox, "craftiness." Many of the difficulties in human communication arise simply because words connote different underlying meanings to different persons. Few arguments arise over the meanings of signs but words and what they symbolize can generate much heat.

Osgood devised an ingenious way to measure the connotative meanings of concepts. The *Semantic Differential* is a test consisting of a number of scales that permit one to assess a number of connotative meaning dimensions suggested by given concepts. Perhaps the most important dimension of meaning that enters into our concepts is the *evaluative dimension*, i.e., things are most frequently judged either "good" or "bad." For example, if we ask persons to comment upon almost anything, one of the first questions they address themselves to is an evaluative one, e.g., is it "good" or "bad," do I "like it" or "dislike it," and so forth.

Osgood speculated about what might happen if inconsistencies occurred among the connotative meanings that people attached to various concepts (Osgood and Tannenbaum, 1955). Suppose, for example, that we administered the Semantic Differential to a group of subjects and discovered that they felt (1) quite positively about Richard Nixon and (2) equally positively about America's role in Viet Nam. Let us further suppose that Nixon made an address in which he made strikingly negative statements about American involvement in Viet Nam. According to Osgood, a state of cognitive incongruity would exist. Two previously positive concepts (Nixon and America's role in the Viet Nam war) have become associated by means of a negative assertion (Nixon's negative pronouncements on American's involvement in the war). According to congruity-incongruity theory, change must occur somewhere. Either the person's attitude toward Richard Nixon would change, by becoming more negative, or his attitude toward the Viet Nam war would change, also by becoming more negative. Congruity-incongruity theory would predict that *when inconsistency among the connotative meanings of concepts occurs, changes toward consistency must take place.* As the popular song says, "something's gotta give."

Summary of consistency theories. Once again, in the short space provided it is difficult to give an adequate account of a complex and varied body of theory and research such as that which has grown up around the principle of cognitive consistency. These theories, particularly dissonance theory, have stimulated an enormous amount of research. Interesting and fruitful elaborations and extensions of consistency theory have recently appeared in the work of Newcomb on balance (1968), of Rosenberg on cognitive-affect inconsistency (1968), and in the work of McGuire on the structure of human thought (1968).

However, the point has been made: human beings appear to strive for consistent and coherent views of their worlds and of the events in which they are involved. Exactly what the conditions are under which such striving will take place and exactly what the consequences of such striving will be remain to be clarified by systematic research. Much like drive-equilibrium theories, theories of cognitive consistency focus upon equilibrium as a desired state of human beings. In fact, it is not difficult to see the intellectual heritage of theories such as dissonance theory. The concept of drive reduction is obviously closely allied to that of dissonance reduction. When one remembers that persons seem to also seek intensification of stimulation under certain conditions, it would not prove at all surprising to discover that a similar situation exists for dissonance arousal and reduction. It is entirely possible that conditions exist under which persons deliberately seek out inconsistency rather than consistency in their perceptions of events in which they are involved. If one is to trust the anecdotal evidence, at least part of the fascination with the use of psychedelic chemicals seems to be the fact that novel, contradictory, ambiguous, and inconsistent glimpses of reality are provided by such experiences.

In any case, it would appear that persons do strive for consistency under certain conditions: consistency between belief and behavior, belief and affect, and consistency among evaluative meanings of various concepts. The importance of such striving for consistency, the extent to which it can be applied to human affairs, and the conditions under which it will occur remain to be clarified.

Theories emphasizing choice

Within recent years, the search for a satisfactory unit of analysis in the study of the person has led to increased interest in the more "rational" aspects of human beings. Rather than conceiving of persons as blindly driven about by such things as needs, drives, instincts, and so forth, it is possible to think of them as possessing some ability to control their actions and their possible futures. In short, persons can exercise *choice*. Given several possible alternative courses of action, persons can state *preferences* for given actions as well as for the expected outcomes of such actions. Preference-expectation theories, which view human beings as conscious and deliberate choosers, decision-makers, and problem-solvers, have recently attracted much attention in psychology.

The study of individual and collective choice has, of course, interested others as well as psychologists. Mathematicians, economists, political scientists, and administrative scientists have all concerned themselves with the complex problems involved in choice behavior. Early theories of individual choice were provided by the philosophers John Stuart Mill and Jeremy Bentham. Mill and Bentham proposed that the principal goal of human behavior is to seek pleasure and avoid pain. From this perspective, the value of an action is conceived of as a ratio of its pleasure-giving aspects to its pain giving aspects. Accordingly, the human being *ought* to act so as to *maximize* his pleasure. Whether or not human beings *do* act in this manner is of course a debatable matter. In point of fact, the vast majority of psychological disorders, problems, and disabilities seem to indicate that persons frequently do not act in their best interests. The so-called "neurotic paradox" is concerned precisely with this apparent perversity of human beings. That is, if people do act in order to maximize pleasure, then why is it that so many persons persist in making the *same* disastrous mistakes over and over again? One would have to hypothesize that some persons enjoy being miserable!

Leaving the "neurotic paradox" aside for the moment, one can see classic theories of choice seem to share the following assumptions:

1. A set of alternatives exists from which choices can be made.
2. A set of preferences exists according to which the chooser ranks the alternatives.
3. The chooser attempts to select that one alternative which is preferred to all others in the set.
4. A uniformly preferred alternative exists when the chooser's rankings have the property of transitivity. (If alternative A is preferred to alternative B, and alternative B is preferred to alternative C, then alternative A is preferred to alternative C. A transitive-preference ordering of this nature is called an ordinal-utility ranking.)
5. The chooser will prefer that alternative with the highest ordinal-utility ranking, i.e., he will *maximize his utility*.

But, as we shall see, it is not an easy or a straightforward matter to apply this economic theory of choice to the individual choices made by individual persons. First of all, we must recognize that the preference for any given outcome is importantly influenced by its *probability of occurrence*. Not all outcomes are equally likely. The *value* of any outcome is, in part, determined by its probability of occurrence. One would very likely value a highly desired but highly improbable outcome less than a moderately desired but likely outcome.

Taking into account the probabilities of events as well as the values assigned to them, it is possible to compute something called the *expected value* of an action. The expected value of an action is obtained by first stating all the possible outcomes of an action, assigning a value and a probability to each and then averaging. It is perhaps easier to see this in a formula:

Assume a set of outcomes, $i = 1, 2, 3.....n$,
a set of values, one for each outcome,
$v(1), v(2), v(3).....v(n)$, and
a set of probabilities, one for each outcome,
$p(1), p(2), p(3).....p(n)$.
Expected value $= v(1)p(1) + v(2)p(2) + v(3)p(3) +.....+ v(n)p(n)$.

In this sense, then, human beings can be construed as attempting to maximize their expected outcomes. Of course, the objection may be raised that people rarely go about calculating the objective probabilities of events in a world in which all the outcomes of their actions are known. In this case, it is possible to substitute *subjective* probabilities for the objective probabilities in the above equation and then derive what are called subjective expected values. Even with the use of subjective expected values, however, it is not clear that persons will behave in the neat, rational fashion predicted by classic economic models of choice. Quite frequently persons appear to adopt less than optimal strategies. During the Second World War, for example, fighter pilots in the Pacific encountered situations in which incendiary shells would be appropriate one-third of the time and armor piercing shells two-thirds of the time. When left to their own choice, pilots would arm themselves with incendiary and armor piercing shells in a ratio of one incendiary shell for every two armor piercing shells. On the surface, this would appear an optimal choice. But let's see:

Calculating the odds of having the appropriate shells in a given situation yields $⅓ × ⅓ + ⅔ × ⅔ = ⁵⁄₉$. Hence, the pilots' strategy leads to a probability of $⁵⁄₉$ that the appropriate shells will be available in a given situation. But suppose that the pilots had simply armed themselves with armor piercing shells on every occasion; what would the probability of being correctly armed be then? In actuality, they would have been correctly armed two-thirds of the time: $⅓ × 0 + ⅔ × 1 = ⅔$.*

From this example, we can readily appreciate the fact that human beings do not appear to behave completely rationally in

---

*The author is indebted to J. L. Bower (1968) for this example.

accordance with the economic theory of choice. In the preceding example, it was clear that the pilots simply engaged in *event matching,* i.e., they chose shells in accordance with the proportion of times that each type would be appropriate. Quite typically, in the psychology laboratory subjects confronted with similar types of choice problems resort to event matching rather than to utility-maximization as predicted by economic theory.

It will be helpful at this point to draw a distinction between *normative* theories and *empirical* theories. Normative theories are prescriptive in the sense that they have something to say about how people *ought* to behave. Empirical theories are concerned with how they *actually do* behave. Classic economic theories of choice are normative theories because they are concerned with the optimal way a choice can be made. The psychologist, on the other hand, is interested in how people actually go about making choices.

Herbert Simon, working with his colleagues at the Carnegie Institute of Technology, has made precisely this distinction between classic economic theory as a normative theory and empirically based choice theories. Simon, concerning himself less with how decisions ought to be made, favored studying how decisions actually are made in the real life context that daily confronts the chooser. According to Simon, it is not possible for any isolated single decision-maker to achieve a high degree of rationality. Actually the decision-maker rarely, if ever, knows all of the possible consequences of his actions. Moreover, what knowledge he does have is fragmentary and uncertain. In the real life context the numbers of alternatives are so great and the information necessary to evaluate each so complex and costly to obtain that persons resort to great simplification. In order to function at all, the person must restructure the situation in which he finds himself, and it is in this restructured situation that choices are actually made rather than in the complicated "objective" situation of reality.

Simon views human beings as possessing *bounded rationality,* rather than as the supremely rational maximizer of utility that emerges from classical economic theories of choice; moreover, he sees them as engaged in a process of *satisficing** rather than

---

*A satisficing process is one in which a chooser examines alternatives one by one until he discovers an alternative that is satisfactory to him. It is contrasted with a maximizing process in which a chooser examines *all* alternatives and selects that one which is not only satisfactory but optimal in the sense that it is the best of all possible choices that could be made.

maximizing (Simon, 1957). The concepts of bounded rationality and satisficing are really quite simple to grasp. According to Simon, the chooser cannot attend to all of the information bearing upon a given choice nor can he appreciate all of the alternatives and the consequences of each alternative. The chooser attempts to deal with a highly simplified version of the objective choice situation. He attends to only a few alternatives at a time and ignores the larger potential pool to which he might attend. He focuses upon information that is relevant to the few alternatives he considers and ignores the greater pool of information which is available. In this sense, the chooser can be said to possess limited rationality or, as Simon puts it, bounded rationality.

Instead of obtaining all of the possible outcomes and choosing that one which maximizes his utility, the chooser examines alternatives one at a time until he finds one that is satisfactory. That is, the chooser conducts a search among alternatives and continues the search until a satisfactory alternative is discovered. For example, consider a person buying a new car. A utility maximization theory would require that all available models be ranked by the chooser and that a clear preference hierarchy be established. A satisficing theory would simply have the chooser conducting a limited search among a smaller set of the available models. When the chooser discovered a car that met his requirements as well as the constraints under which he was operating (price), he would most likely choose that one.

Simon makes use of still another concept, that of *level of aspiration*. In a crude sense, level of aspiration is a fluctuating acceptance level or level of satisfaction for the person. One can think of it as a value that changes across time as a function of experience. If the person is successful at a task, he is likely to raise his aspiration level slightly. If unsuccessful, he is likely to lower his aspiration level. In the choice situation, the chooser examines alternatives until he finds one that satisfices his level of aspiration. If an alternative cannot be found, the person tends to lower his level of aspiration, accepting the first alternative that satisfices this new level of aspiration.

Simon, then, has drawn a clear distinction between two quite different processes. Utility maximization is designed to lead to the "best" or "optimal" choice, whereas satisficing leads to a choice that is "satisfactory" but not necessarily the best that could be made.

Whether or not a utility maximization theory or a satisficing theory best describes what persons actually do in choice situations remains to be answered. One carefully conducted study (Solberg, 1966) suggests that choosers in real life situations do not conform to either theory. Solberg conducted interviews with graduate students who were in the process of making job decisions. Eighty-seven per cent of the graduate students studied terminated their search for alternatives ten days or more before the date on which they reported making a final decision. Seventy-four per cent of the students had one or more acceptable alternatives available to them two weeks or more *before they terminated the search for alternatives.* According to Simon's theory, this should not have occurred. Search for new alternatives should have been discontinued when a satisfactory alternative was discovered.

In any case, the choice situation is a rich and complicated one, one that will require considerable research effort before a clear picture of how human beings go about making choices becomes available. We have examined only a tiny portion of the available literature on choice. The student should be aware that a large and complex body of literature in economics, mathematical psychology, and political science bears upon this topic. However, our point has been made. It is possible and indeed fruitful to view the person as capable of least bounded rationality. As the student is now in a position to appreciate, quite a different psychology of persons emerges when we concentrate upon the person as a conscious and deliberate chooser of alternative futures rather than a passive victim of forces over which he has no control.

The self concept

For many persons, psychology is the study of the elusive "me." Each of us is aware that we exist in a world of many other physical and social objects. Boundaries between ourselves and that "which is out there" certainly do exist. Allport (1955) has presented us with some curious examples. Suppose that you have pricked your finger. You would not think anything at all about placing the finger in your mouth and gently sucking blood from the puncture. But imagine that your blood has been placed in a glass. Would you even consider drinking a quantity of it? Or for that matter, although each of us constantly swallows our own saliva, who among us could possibly expectorate into a glass and then drink its contents? As Allport points out, when these fluids are within the boundaries of the "perceived self," they do not appear alien, strange, or unusual to us. However, when they are placed outside the boundaries of the perceived self into the external world, our attitudes toward them undergo change.

This sense of self as distinct from one's surroundings as well as our fascination with ourselves as "experiencers" continue to intrigue us. The study of self cognitions has attracted a host of persons, both within and without psychology. The "ego," "self-concept," "body image," 'self-image," "phenomenal self," "proprium," "ideal self," "actual self," and the "actualized self" are but a few of the terms employed by various theorists to describe this elusive sense of personhood which underlies experiencing. Wiley (1968) has recently summarized these self referent constructs as follows:*

1. A person as an entity separated from others is experienced.
2. A sense of being the same person continues over time.
3. Physical characteristics as experienced are included in the concept.
4. One's behaviors as experienced and remembered are included, especially if associated with feelings of intent or being under the control of the experiencing person.
5. A degree of organization or unity among items included in the self concept is experienced. On the other hand, some theorists postulate semiautonomous subdivisions which can be logically incompatible with one another. There is no statement as to how to reconcile these two views on the internal organization of the self-concept.
6. Self percepts and self concepts are not distinguished by the theorists.
7. The self-concept includes a person's evaluations as well as his cognitions.
8. The self concept is described as involving degrees of conscious or unconsciousness.

An enormous amount of both theory and research has been devoted to the self concept. Carl Rogers, the American psychologist, is probably the most celebrated self theorist. According to Rogers, a common and universal tendency exists in

---

*From R. C. Wylie, The present status of self theory, in Borgatta and Lambert (eds.), *Handbook of Personality Theory and Research*, © 1968 by Rand McNally & Company, Chicago, p. 740.

all persons, the tendency toward actualization of self. By self-actualization Rogers means the tendency for the person to actualize his inherent potentials in a manner consistent with his conscious view of himself and in a manner which will maintain and enhance life. The person, according to Rogers, possesses needs for *positive regard from others* as well as *positive self-regard*. The person thrives on positive regard and acceptance from others and experiences disappointment and frustration when met with disapproval. Not only is the person affected by the attitudes of others toward him, but he also comes to hold self-regarding attitudes of approval or disapproval as well. Because the person has need of positive regard from others, he will seek to gain their approval. It is in this process of approval seeking that the self concept develops. In time, the person will come to hold cognitions of himself that have grown out of his experiences of approving or disapproving significant other persons.

When only *some* of the person's actions, thoughts, and feelings are supported by significant other persons, the person falls victim to approval seeking rather than self-actualization. His concept of self will be importantly influenced and limited by what others think of him and by their selective approval and disapproval. When such *conditions of worth* exist, the person cannot seek to fulfill his potentialities but instead must limit himself to those actions, thoughts, and feelings that will lead to positive regard from others. According to Rogers, self actualization is fostered by social situations characterized by *unconditional positive regard*. By this he means simply that the person is loved, supported, and accepted regardless of his actions, thoughts, and feelings. There are no conditions of worth. Under conditions of unconditional positive regard, the person is not forced to shape and limit his behavior in order to gain the approval of others. Quite simply, he can be "himself," whatever that might be.

As Rogers points out, there are serious consequences of inordinate approval seeking. Not only is the person prevented from pursuing self-actualization but excessive dependency on others and on their opinions can result in considerable defensiveness. Studies by Crowne and Marlowe (1964) lend support to this contention. Crowne and Marlowe first devised a test that measured the extent to which subjects relied upon others for approval. They then administered the test to subjects in a variety of contexts. Some of their results were as follows:

1. Approval-dependent patients in psychotherapy tend to terminate prematurely and without improvement. Since the psychotherapy situation is one which requires the patient to be open, honest, and trusting, approval-dependent persons find the situation filled with conflict. On the one hand, they are asked by their therapist to honestly explore with him their thoughts, feelings, and experiences. But on the other hand, if one actually does so, one might reveal things that might shock and disgust the other person and thus lead to disapproval. Under these conditions of conflict, the approval-dependent person chooses to leave the field of conflict.

2. In anticipation of rejection and threat to self-esteem, approval-dependent persons resort to the self-protective behavior of conformity.

3. The fantasy life of approval-dependent persons seems characterized by strong wishes for affiliation with others but at the same time by fear of rejection by others. In actuality, approval-dependent persons are less well liked by their peers. They are, in fact, perceived by their peers as highly defensive.

It is, of course, impossible to discuss all of the studies bearing upon self concept in this brief space. However, examination of a few areas of research are most interesting. In a host of studies reviewed by Wiley (1968), it is clear that sex differences in self concept do exist. Different stereotypes for the female and male roles exist and self concepts do seem to conform to these stereotypes. College women do tend to perceive self in accordance with the "female stereotype," and this stereotype of "women in general" is less favorable than that of "men in general."

Experimental studies of induced success and failure have been conducted extensively. In general, subjects are not likely to lower their self-evaluations following a single experimentally induced failure. They are more likely to raise their self-evaluations following success, however. Experimentally induced failure can lead to various defensive behaviors such as failing to recall failure information accurately, discrediting the source of failure information, and blaming others for one's failures.

Finally, extensive investigations of the relationship between self-insight and adjustment have been conducted. Unfortunately, as Wiley points out, the vast majority of these studies are inadequate methodologically, and few, if any, conclusions can be drawn from them. In only one of three adequately conducted studies was there a suggestion of a relationship between insight and degree of personal adjustment. This question must remain unanswered until adequately designed research covering a wide variety of behaviors is conducted.

Despite the attractiveness of the self concept, it has not proved a particularly easy phenomenon to investigate empirically, but much the same thing could be said of virtually every other concept that psychologists have entertained. Nobody ever guaranteed that the study of human thought and behavior would be easy and uncomplex!

In any event, one cannot afford to ignore the importance of various beliefs, attitudes, and feelings about the self. Whether or not concepts like self-actualization will prove useful in a scientific sense remains to be demonstrated. However, it seems quite clear that the self will remain a feasible unit of analysis in modern psychology for some time to come. As long as persons permit themselves to remain dependent upon other persons, places, or things for self-images of worth and importance, self theorists will have a great deal to say about human misery. Moreover, while concepts such as self-actualization may very well prove to be semantic nightmares, it seems intuitively plausible that we have barely scratched the surface with regard to the limits of the potentialities of human beings. Much of what we consider as our realistic limitations often seems to be little more than social definition of what is correct, possible, and feasible. Unfortunately, each of us tends to internalize the thoughts of others and to accept external definition of what is possible rather than our own inner convictions. In many respects, the constraints are really in our *heads* rather than in the nature of things. The trick is knowing which is which.

SOCIAL ROLE CONCEPTIONS

The theories that we have discussed up to this point vary in the extent to which they consider the person as a social creature. Instinct theory, for example, treated the person as though he existed in a social vacuum. The self theorists did recognize the importance of the social surroundings of the individual. Roger's emphasis upon positive regard from significant persons renders his theory, in part, a theory of social behavior. When dealing with *role conceptions* of persons, however, we arrive at the other end of the spectrum. No other concept of the person is as explicitly social in nature as is role theory. From this perspective the person is seen as an integral part of a social system. Let us examine this way of conceptualizing persons in greater detail.

As Thomas has recently pointed out, there is no single agreed upon definition of role (Thomas, 1968). However, if there is a thread of commonality that runs through the many definitions that have been offered, it is as follows: A social role is the set of expectations that defines what the behavior of a person occupying a given position in a social system should be. Quite simply, each actor in a social system can be construed as occupying a given position. For example, in a work situation there may be such positions as "laborer," "foreman," "middle manager," "general manager." Associated with these various positions are *expectations* for particular behaviors. One does not expect a general manager to sweep the floors of the machine shop, nor does one expect to find the laborer in an industrial concern making important decisions concerning what products will be produced and marketed. These particular behaviors fall outside the set of role expectations that are associated with the positions of "general manager" and "laborer."

From the perspective of the role theorist, much of the behavior of persons is predictable from little more than knowledge of the positions they occupy in given social situations. Consider the ordinary classroom situation. The vast majority of both the teacher's behavior and the behavior of the students is situationally controlled; that is, there are characteristic sets of behavior associated with the positions "teacher" and "student." We expect students to behave in a given way and we expect teachers to behave in other ways. For the most part, both teachers and students conform to these expectations. Actually, many persons are made very uncomfortable when actors do not behave in accordance with the expectations associated with the positions they occupy. The author has noted, for example, that even though students say they dislike authoritarian, directive teacher behavior in the classroom, many show extreme discomfort and anxiety when the professor abandons this type of instructional style in favor of more democratic and nondirective methods. Part of these feelings are undoubtedly explained by the fact that many persons may dislike a given social interactive situation but will resist changing it simply because they have grown *competent* in manipulating the situation to their own ends. A changed situation brings with it a certain amount of uncertainty and demands for new skills and competencies, some of which the person may not possess. The author was intrigued by the remark of a very unhappy person: "I don't like the way I am at all—but at least I know how to get what I want the way I am. I'm afraid of change because I don't know how I'll do if I were to change. I guess I'm not a very happy person but at least I know what I'm doing!" From the perspective of this young man, it is not surprising then that he resisted personal change. To him, a sense of *competence* was far more important than a sense of well being, which may or may not be present if he were to change.

But aside from the challenge of change in terms of the necessity for new skills and competencies, it is probably true that disconfirmation of expectations can be, under certain conditions, in and of itself an unpleasant experience. Of course this statement demands qualification. Slight to moderate deviations from expectation can actually be perceived as delightful, amusing, and pleasant. For example, a novel harmonic progression in a piece of music can excite and stimulate us if it does not deviate too much from what we had expected. On the other hand, if one were forced to listen to music that continually and markedly departed from one's expectations, it would very likely be regarded as "noise."

The concept of expectations, then, is of central importance in role theoretical conceptions of human beings. The behaviors of actors in given social situations are importantly influenced and constrained by the expectations that others hold toward them as well as by the expectations they hold toward themselves. These expectations are derived from the positions that actors occupy. Let us examine role factors in greater detail.

Role conflict. A person is said to experience role conflict when the role expectations placed upon him by others are incompatible, thus rendering it impossible for him to conform to both sets of expectations at the same time. As anyone who has been caught in such a situation can testify, role conflict is a most unpleasant experience. When one must attempt to meet two sets of expectations which contradict each other, personal and interpersonal disruption is a common outcome. Unfortunately, role conflict is more prevalent than most people realize. Kahn, Wolfe, Quinn and Snoek (1964), in a representative sample of the labor force of the United States, discovered that 48 per cent of those studied reported being caught at various times between two sets of people who each expected different things of them. Some positions are more likely to involve role conflict than others. The position of "foreman" is an example of a high role-conflict position. Mediating between the expectations of subordinates and the expectations of superiors can prove to be a difficult if not hazardous way of making a living.

Role ambiguity. When the expectations for a given position are incomplete and ambiguous, a condition of role ambiguity is said to exist. Students who have been given little notion about what to expect in the form and substance of given evaluations frequently show excessive anxiety and personal discomfort. In the study by Kahn and his associates mentioned earlier, it was discovered that role ambiguity was related to emotional reactions of tension and futility, low job satisfaction, and low self-confidence.

Role overload. When role expectations exceed the person's capacities to meet them, a condition of role overload exists. The housewife in American society is frequently depicted as caught in a situation of role overload. She is expected to be sexy, a good mother to the children, an efficient manager of a small business enterprise, an understanding and sympathetic "buddy" for the husband, a chauffeur for the kids, and so on. It is little wonder that numerous women show signs of personal emotional distress in the face of such excessive demands for a variety of role performances.

Role discontinuity. During the course of his life, a person may find himself in a variety of positions, e.g., he may move from the position of "student" to that of "head of household" to "retired." When there is little transferability of skills from one position to another, a condition of role discontinuity exists. To the extent that there is little continuity in the transition from one position to another, the possibility of personal discomfort and stress is increased. A college graduate recently turned "young mother" commented woefully to the author: "I spent the last four years painting pictures, talking philosophy and political ideas until the wee hours of the morning, reading, going to plays, concerts, dancing, and now all I do is sit around a house in the suburbs waiting for *him* to get home, changing diapers, and staring at the walls or that idiotic boob tube. What the hell kind of life is this?" It is obvious from this example that nothing in the position "college student" was even remotely related to the position "housewife-mother." Unfortunately, until society takes seriously the necessity of providing intelligent transitions from one position to another in the lives of its citizens, enormous costs measured in human misery, confusion, and unhappiness will continue to exist. There is little doubt that role discontinuity is both a societal and a personal problem; it is one of great importance but one about which little, if anything is done.

Role taking skills and aptitudes. In order for a person to perform a given role, it is clear that he must possess the necessary role-relevant skills. Obviously one cannot occupy the position "brain surgeon" without possessing certain necessary role-relevant skills. Less obviously, things like "dependency," "hostility," and "aggression" can be viewed as skills which the individual can choose to either perform or not perform. The author has discussed at length the possibility of viewing many personality characteristics of persons as *skills* rather than motives (Wallace, 1966 and 1967). Not all persons are capable of assuming an "aggressive" role, for example, in interaction with others. I have suggested that it might be very fruitful to consider a person as possessing a repertory of interpersonal skills and roles and that selection from this repertory will determine what behaviors the person will display.

Whether or not a general *aptitude* for role taking exists still remains to be demonstrated. Sarbin (1964) has demonstrated relationships between a measure of aptitude for role taking and specific role enactments. However, such relationships must be demonstrated across a wide variety of behaviors before one can speak confidently of a general aptitude for role taking.

In this portion of the chapter, we have examined briefly role theoretical approaches to the person. As we have seen, much of the behavior of persons is related to the positions they occupy in given social systems. Role theoretical conceptions forcefully remind us that we cannot ignore the social context in which behavior occurs. Any adequate conceptualization of the person must treat him as a social creature rather than as a being behaving in a social vacuum. We will have occasion to refer to role conceptions in subsequent pages. For the moment, let us turn our attentions to other conceptualizations of the person.

CONDITIONED RESPONSE THEORY

It would be impossible to discuss conceptualizations of the person without mentioning conditioned response theory. In actuality, we have already discussed one form of conditioning in our presentation of drive reduction theory; namely, that of instrumental learning. However, in this section we will present the more general case of instrumental learning and contrast it with classical conditioning.

Classical conditioning

The discovery of the conditioned reflex is attributed to the brilliant Russian physiologist, Ivan Petrovich Pavlov. In his investigation of the digestive glands which was conducted around the turn of the century, Pavlov noticed peculiarities in the behavior of his experimental animals that less curious men might very well have missed. Dogs, for example, would begin to secrete digestive juices upon seeing the person who typically was responsible for feeding them. Pavlov became fascinated by these "psychic secretions" and arranged to study them experimentally. He reasoned that when food was placed directly in the mouth of the animal, an inborn and unlearned salivary response occurred. However, salivation at the mere sight of food or of objects associated with food was a *learned* response, not an inborn response. Pavlov soon discovered that nearly any stimulus that was associated with food could become an effective stimulus for eliciting salivation. For instance, arbitrary stimuli, such as bells or lights, could be made to evoke the conditioned salivary response.

Pavlov's method was quite simple. A light or a bell (the stimulus to be conditioned) was repeatedly presented immediately before food (the unconditioned stimulus) was placed in the mouth of the experimental animal. This process was repeated until the bell or light eventually produced the salivation response. In a sense, Pavlov succeeded in capturing in this simple experiment a convincing experimental demonstration of a principle upon which philosophers had speculated in numerous weighty tomes: the *principle of association*. It is not surprising that Pavlov's apparently simple discovery attracted both widespread interest and widespread hostility. Scientific workers recognized the importance of Pavlov's work, whereas humanists attacked it bitterly. Pavlov was considered, as was Freud, a threat to *reason*, an important element in nineteenth century thinking. It appeared that influenced by Freud and Pavlov, reason would rapidly give way to the irrational processes of conditioned reflexes and unconscious instincts.

The reactions of the humanists of Pavlov's time did little to stem the growing tide of interest in Pavlov's discovery of the conditioned reflex. Since Pavlov's early experiments, an enormous amount of research on the nature of conditioned responses and the variables affecting them has been conducted. There have been attempts to explain nearly every important class of human behavior, from neurotic behavior to language learning, in terms of conditioning. Quite recently psychotherapies based upon conditioned response theory have appeared and have shown considerable promise. Systematic desensitization therapy, introduced by Joseph Wolpe in 1958, is based on the assumption that conditioned anxiety responses lie at the heart of most psychological difficulties. Wolpe has argued that if such conditioned responses can be "deconditioned," troublesome behaviors such as phobias, sexual impotence, and psychosomatic complaints can be removed. Dekker and Groen (1958) provided a convincing account of the occurrence of asthmatic attacks based upon conditioning. They discovered that if an asthma attack could be made to occur to known allergenic substances in the laboratory, through association previously neutral stimuli could gain the power to elicit asthma attacks. For example, after patients inhaled allergenic substances that promptly produced an asthma attack in the laboratory, the mere sight of the inhalator was sufficient to evoke asthmatic responses on subsequent occasions.

Remembering that *awareness* of the process is not necessary for conditioning to occur, one may reasonably suppose that many seemingly irrational fears of persons may very well be the outcome of automatic conditioning processes. When such conditioning occurs in early childhood, it is even more difficult to establish the origin of certain adult fears, anxieties, and compulsions.

As we can readily appreciate from the examples given, Pavlov's seemingly disarmingly simple discovery of "psychic secretions" has had enormous influence in modern psychology. Perhaps the greatest extensions of conditioning theory have been carried out by Russian psychologists. Recent reports from

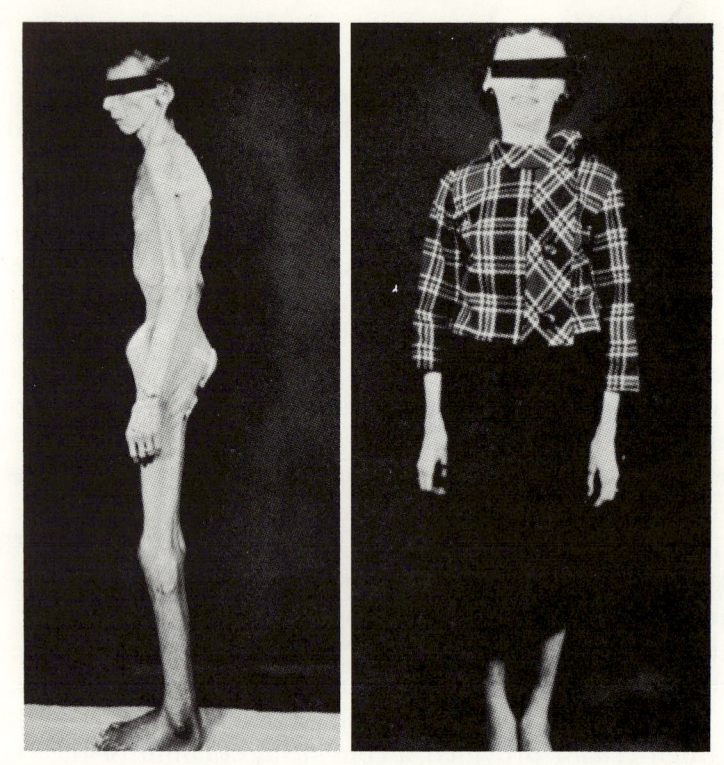

Figure 12. A case of anorexia nervosa, a psychological disorder in which the person is unable to eat. This case illustrates one of many important applications of operant conditioning procedures. The photo on the left was taken prior to the introduction of conditioning procedures to restore a normal pattern of eating. The photo on the right was taken after operant conditioning procedures had been applied. *From* Bachrach, A. J., Erwin, W. J., and Mohr, J. P.: The control of eating behavior in an anorexic by operant conditioning techniques. *In* Ullmann, L. P., and Krasner, L. (eds.): *Case Studies in Behavior Modification.* New York, Holt, Rinehart and Winston, Inc., 1965. p. 153.

Russia (e.g., Razan, 1961) indicate that remarkable progress in the study of conditioned responses has been made. The types and varieties of conditioned responses that have been brought under experimental control in Russian laboratories are truly fascinating.

Instrumental learning

In addition to classic conditioning, psychologists have extensively studied another form of learning, namely instrumental learning or operant conditioning. Central to instrumental learning is the notion that behavior is controlled by its consequences. Responses that lead to reinforcement will continue to be performed, whereas performance of responses that do not lead to reinforcement will cease.

The work of the Harvard psychologist B. F. Skinner immediately comes to mind when reinforcement theories of learning are considered. Skinner thought of responses as belonging to one of two classes, *elicited* responses or *emitted* responses. Elicited responses are those for which a known stimulus exists. For example, in the classic conditioning situations of Pavlov, salivation was a response to a known stimulus (food powder in the mouth). Typically, elicited responses are nonvoluntary responses involving the autonomic nervous system.

On the other hand, emitted responses are those for which a known stimulus does not exist. The responses are simply emitted, they are not elicited by an experimentally controlled stimulus. Responses involving the skeletal musculature are considered to be emitted responses. Behaviors such as riding a bicycle, playing the piano, and throwing a ball are also considered to be emitted responses. Elicited responses can be studied through classical conditioning procedures, whereas emitted responses cannot. In order to study emitted responses, Skinner devised a particular type of instrumental conditioning procedure referred to as operant conditioning. In the operant conditioning procedure, a hungry animal is permitted to explore an experimental environment. Through a series of trial and error responses, the animal finally discovers a response that leads to reinforcement. For example, a hungry pigeon may find that pecking at a circle results in a grain of food while pecking at a square does not. The circle is referred to as the *discriminative stimulus* and the grain of food as the *reinforcement*. In time the pigeon will learn to discriminate between the circle and the square and will confine its pecking to the circle until a sufficient number of nonreinforced trials occurs. When reinforcement does not occur, the response is said to undergo *extinction*.

One cannot dismiss this deceptively simple experimental situation as trivial. Instrumental learning studies have been conducted on a host of creatures and a wide variety of behaviors. There seems to be little question that this general proposition—that behavior is controlled by its consequences—contains a strong element of truth. While the effects of punishment are quite complex and, in many respects, still not completely understood, numerous behaviors in both humans and lower organisms have been brought under control by means of positive reinforcement. Reinforcement theories of learning have been extended and elaborated to include such diverse things as programmed learning, control of deliquent behavior, and treatment of severely disturbed children.

Despite the proved effectiveness of positive reinforcement under certain conditions, one must be cautious about generalizing the principle that behavior is controlled by its consequences. As we have seen, single variable explanations of human behavior, although attractive in their simplicity, are not sufficient to account for something as complex as human behavior. One must frequently know a great deal more than the consequences of a given act to understand why it is performed or why it is not reliably performed.

SUMMARY

Throughout this chapter we have been concerned with the more important units of analysis and description that have been used in the study of the person. We have examined energy conceptions of persons, cognitive-informational conceptions, role theoretical formulations, and conditioned response conceptions. In the space of a single chapter we have not been able to consider all possible units of analysis and our discussion has therefore been selective.

The student should now be in a position to realize that alternative conceptions of the person do exist and do have important consequences for the study of social thought and behavior. Obviously the need theorist focuses upon quite different things than does the theorist who is interested in choice. The psychologist who concerns himself with the way persons structure their worlds in terms of personal constructs will approach the study of behavior quite differently than one who is enamored of the concept of unconscious motivation. The conception of persons as operating in social vacuums rather than as integral parts of dynamic social situations has obvious implications.

If we have done nothing more than stimulate the student to think about the "lenses" through which he views his own behavior and that of others, then we have accomplished a great deal. As we will see, the ways in which we choose to think about persons are important determinants of what we "think" we know about them. More often than not we tend to "see" our theories of behavior and our concepts of persons rather than the reality of behaviors and individual lives.

References

Allport, G. W.: *Becoming: Basic Considerations for a Psychology of Personality*. New Haven, Yale University Press, 1955.

Aronson, E.: Dissonance theory: progress and problems. *In* Abelson, R. P., et al. (eds.): *Theories of Consistency*. Chicago, Rand McNally and Co., 1968.

Bachrach, A. J., Erwin, W. J., and Mohr, J. P.: The control of eating behavior in an anorexic by operant conditioning techniques. *In* Ullmann, L. P., and Krasner, L. (eds.): *Research in Behavior Modification*. New York, Holt, Rinehart and Winston, 1965.

Bower, J. L.: Descriptive decision theory from the administrative viewpoint. *In* Bauer, R. A., and Gergen, K. J. (eds.): *The Study of Policy Formation*. New York, The Free Press, 1968.

Butler, R. A., and Alexander, H. M.: Daily patterns of visual exploratory behavior in the monkey. J. Comp. Physiol. Psychol., *48*: 247, 1955.

Cannon, Walter B.: *The Wisdom of the Body*. New York, W. W. Norton and Company, Inc., 1939.

Chapanis, N. P., and Chapanis, A.: Cognitive dissonance: five years later. Psychol. Bull., *61*:1, 1964.

Crowne, D. P., and Marlowe, D.: *The Approval Motive*. New York, John Wiley & Sons, Inc., 1964.

Dekker, E., and Groen, J.: Reproducible psychogenic attacks of asthma. *In*: Reed, C., et al. (eds.): *Psychopathology: A Source Book*. Cambridge, Harvard University Press, 1958.

Dollard, J., and Miller, N.: *Personality and Psychotherapy*. New York, McGraw-Hill Book Co., 1950.

Festinger, L. and Carlsmith, J. M.: Cognitive consequences of forced compliance. J. Abnorm. Soc. Psychol., *58*: 203, 1959.

Freedman, J. L.: How important is cognitive consistency? *In* Abelson, R. P., et al. (eds.): *Theories of Cognitive Consistency*. Chicago, Rand McNally & Co., 1968.

Harlow, H. F.: On the meaning of love. Amer. Psychol. *13*: 673, 1958.

Harlow, H. F., Harlow, M. K., and Meyer, D. R.: Learning motivated by a manipulation drive. J. Exp. Psychol., *40*:228, 1950.

Harlow, H. F., and McClearn, G. E.: Object discriminations learned by monkeys on the basis of manipulation motives. J. Comp. Physiol. Psychol., *47*: 73, 1954.

Heider, F.: *The Psychology of Interpersonal Relations*. New York, John Wiley & Sons, Inc., 1958.

Heron, W.: The pathology of boredom. Scientific American, *199*:52, 1957.

Kahn, R. L., Wolfe, D. M., Quinn, R. P., and Snoek, D. J.: *Organizational Stress: Studies in Role Conflict and Ambiguity*. New York, John Wiley & Son, Inc., 1964.

Kelly, G. A.: *The Psychology of Personal Constructs*, Vol. 1. New York, W. W. Norton and Company, Inc., 1955.

Kish, G. B.: Learning when the onset of illumination is used as a reinforcing stimulus. J. Comp. Physiol. Psychol., *48*: 261, 1955.

Maslow, A. H.: A theory of human motivation. Psychol. Rev., *50*: 270, 1943.
McDougall, W.: *Introduction to Social Psychology*, London, Methuen and Co., 1908.
McGuire, W. J.: Theory and structure of human thought. *In* Abelson, R. P., *et al.* (eds.): *Theories of Consistency*. Chicago, Rand McNally & Co., 1968.
Montgomery, K. C.: The relation between fear induced by novel stimulation and exploratory behavior. J. Comp. Physiol. Psychol., *48*: 254, 1955.
Murray, H. A.: *Explorations in Personality*. New York, Oxford University Press, 1938.
Newcomb, T. M.: Interpersonal balance. *In* Abelson, R. P., *et al.* (eds.): *Theories of Consistency*. Chicago, Rand McNally & Co., 1968.
Osgood, C. E.: The nature and measurement of meaning. Psychol. Bull., *49*: 197, 1952.
Osgood, C. E., and Tannenbaum, P. H.: The principle of congruity in the prediction of attitude change. Psychol. Rev., *62*: 42, 1955.
Razan, G.: The observable unconscious and the inferable conscious in current Soviet psychophysiology: Interoceptive conditioning, semantic conditioning, and the orienting reflex. Psychol. Rev., *68*: 81, 1961.
Rogers, C. R.: *Client-centered Therapy: Its Current Practice, Implications, and Theory*. Boston, Houghton, Mifflin Company, 1951.
Rosenberg, M. J.: Cognitive reorganization in response to the hypnotic reversal of affect. J. Pers., *68*: 39, 1960.
Rosenberg, M. J.: Hedonism, inauthenticity, and other goads toward expansion of a consistency theory. *In* Abelson, R. P., *et al.* (eds.): *Theories of Consistency*. Chicago, Rand McNally & Co., 1968.
Sarbin, T. R.: Role theoretical interpretation of psychological change. *In* Worchel, P., and Byrne, D. (eds.): *Personality Change*. New York, John Wiley & Sons, Inc., 1964.
Simon, H.: *Administrative Behavior*. New York, The Macmillan Company, 1957.
Skinner, B. F.: *The Behavior of Organisms*. New York, Appleton-Century-Crofts, 1938.
Solberg, P.: Unprogrammed decision. *In Papers and Proceedings, 26th Annual Meeting, Academy of Management*, pp. 3–16, 1966.
Thomas, E. J.: Role theory, personality, and the individual. *In* Borgatta, E. F., and Lambert, W. W. (eds.): *Handbook of Personality Theory and Research*. Chicago, Rand McNally & Co., 1968.
Wallace, J.: An abilities conception of personality: some implications for personality measurement. Amer. Psychol., *21*: 132, 1966.
Wallace, J.: What units shall we employ? Allport's question revisited. J. Cons. Psychol., *31*:56, 1967
Wiley, R.: The present status of self theory. *In* Borgatta, E. F., and Lambert, W. W. (eds.): *Handbook of Personality Theory and Research*. Chicago, Rand McNally & Co., 1968.
Wolpe, J.: *Psychotherapy by Reciprocal Inhibition*. Stanford, Stanford University Press, 1958.

CHAPTER

5

The Psychological Study of the Person

In the previous chapter we examined the many ways in which psychologists have attempted to conceptualize the person. Our attention now turns to the numerous substantive findings that have flowed from these conceptions. As we have stressed previously, a psychological concept is an *invention*. It is a novel product of the mind of the psychologist and not an *inherent* property of the behavior to which it may refer. For the psychologist, any given conceptualization of the person may seem intriguing, exciting, and intuitively plausible. He recognizes, however, that a concept is not an end in and of itself in the study of social thought and behavior. It is an important beginning. Once a way of construing the person has been invented, the important questions become pragmatic ones. "Is it *useful* to think of social thought and behavior in this manner?" "Does the concept help me to explain, understand, and predict behaviors in ways that I could not if I did not have it?" "Does the concept involve vague, imprecise, and ambiguous terms, ones that seem to convey meaning but in reality do not?" "Does the concept have meaningful implications for the actual behavior of persons, or is it 'full of sound and fury, signifying nothing'?"

Although the psychologist may be terribly fond of his inventions and even, in many cases, emotionally involved with them (after all, psychologists are human too), he must still test them against reality. As we noted in Chapters 1 and 2, the *evaluation* of the thought of the inventive psychologist is not a simple and uncomplicated process. There are far more blind alleys in the search for knowledge than one might suppose. It is only in retrospect that we perceive the simple fact that the path was truly narrow and that many more incorrect choices were available to us than correct ones. Psychological conceptualizations of the person have led to an enormous number of choices, some correct and some incorrect. The ticklish problem is simply knowing at any point in time which is which. When we examine the many findings in the study of the individual, we are confronted by an enormous body of information; some fraction of this information is reasonably reliable and certain, some less than certain, and some is highly uncertain. In approaching the following body of substantive findings in the study of the person, it is important for the student to bear in mind that the well-trained psychologist himself regards much of the information available to him as *tentative* rather than absolute. An examination of the history of any science, especially one in its formative stages, has a way of instilling humility in the person who feels that he is in possession of the truth.

But enough of this. Let us turn to what it is we psychologists think we know about the person.

SOCIAL MOTIVES AND THEIR MEASUREMENT

What is it that drives people, that arouses them to action and gives direction to their behavior? How can we understand such a thing? We really cannot simply ask people to tell us about their motives, since most people would not be able to articulate what it is that directs their behavior and determines what goals they strive for. In many instances, people will offer what appear to be *justifications* for their behavior rather than descriptions of their motivations; that is, they often seem to invent accounts of their own behavior so as to make it appear purposeful and reasonable to themselves and to others. In order to appreciate the difficulties involved, one might try finding a solution oneself. How would you go about measuring a motive that you are convinced exists and is important in determining social behavior? If you take such an exercise seriously, you will surely find that it is not an easy matter to invent a means of measuring social motives.

Let us consider how psychologists have approached the problem. In the following discussion, we will concern ourselves with perhaps the most exhaustively researched social motive of all, namely, the achievement motive.

Achievement Motivation

Need for achievement

We have already considered the achievement motivation in the discussion of McClelland's attempts to explain differential economic development among nations of the world (see Chapter 3). Let us examine this important social motive more closely.

Approaching the problem of measures of motivation in general, McClelland (1958a) set down four necessary criteria. These were as follows:

1. *Any measure of motivation should reflect the presence or absence as well as the variation in strength of the motive.* This requirement is quite simple and straightforward. If we have devised a measure of motivation to achieve, for example, our measure ought to at least tell us whether or not the motive is present in any given individual. Beyond telling us something about mere

Figure 13. Human motivations are complex and not readily apparent in the actions of persons. (Photo by Gordon Cole.)

presence, the measure ought to tell us something about the relative strength of the motive in the person; that is, does the person seem to possess a great deal, a moderate amount, or very low motivation to achieve?

2. *Any measure of a given motivation should reflect the presence of only that motive and not of other motives as well.* This requirement states that our measure should be "pure"; that is, if we set out to measure achievement motivation in a person, we hope to be certain that our measurements reflect only achievement motivation and not "approval motivation," "affiliation motivation," or any one of a host of other possible social motives. Although this criterion is a logical necessity, and as such may seem terribly obvious, it is in fact difficult to achieve measurements in psychology that are "pure" in the sense that they measure *one and only one thing*. More often than not our measures reflect many things other than the single item we are interested in measuring, and often we are unaware that this is the case.

3. *Any measure of a given motivation should be reliable.* The term "reliability" refers to the *accuracy* of measurement. A reliable measuring device is one which yields consistent scores for the person across time. Suppose a certain thermometer gave readings of 98, 76, 84, and 104 degrees for the same person within a half-hour period. We would discard it as a totally unreliable instrument. Psychological measurements must meet the same criteria of stability and consistency if they are to be useful.

4. *Any measure of motivation should provide "relational fertility."* Quite simply, our measurements should relate to something other than themselves if they are to be useful and interesting. In the case of measurements of a social motive, we might, for example, want to know if they predict such things as the person's willingness to take risks, occupational choices, job satisfaction, and so forth.

When we examine the great amount of research generated by McClelland's approach to the achievement motive, we are impressed with the extent to which efforts have been made to meet these four criteria. We will see how successful these attempts have been, but let us first examine McClelland's approach to measurement.

The thematic apperception test and achievement motivation

Seeking a way to measure achievement motivation, McClelland was intrigued by the fact that our fantasies often reveal the motivational bases for our actions. Each of us who has taken the trouble to be analytical about our daydreams is aware that these are often filled with themes of power, recognition by others, magnificent achievements, sexual strivings, and so forth. McClelland decided to capitalize upon these intriguing attributes of fantasy by measuring achievement motivation in the *creative* productions of people. The Thematic Apperception Test is one way of doing this. If we present people with pictures of other persons under moderately ambiguous and unstructured circumstances and ask them to "tell a story" about what is happening in the picture, in doing so they may often reveal a great deal about themselves. Since the picture is "unstructured," the person must find some way of imposing "structure" upon it. It is in this process of structuring the reality of the picture that the person *may* tell us something about himself, his typical concerns, and his strivings.

Imagine a picture of a girl staring out of a window into the fog. A story that might reflect considerable achievement motivation would be as follows:

> She is sitting there dreaming about her future. Perhaps she will grow up to be a great concert pianist—or maybe a brilliant doctor, one who attends to the needs of poor people in far-off Africa. She wants so much to know where the fog comes from and where it goes—where life comes from and where it goes. Perhaps one day, if she studies long and hard enough, she will know.

McClelland and his associates have developed a complex scoring system by which the strength of achievement motivation present in stories such as this one can be measured.

Now that we have some understanding of how McClelland measures achievement motivation, let us see if subsequent research indicates that the criteria for measurement mentioned earlier have been met.

Does McClelland's method actually measure achievement motivation? When we consider what a measure of achievement motivation should relate to, the subject of actual achievement in school immediately comes to mind. Surely a measure of achievement motivation should predict actual school achievement. When we remember that actual school achievement is affected by many variables other than motivation to achieve, however, the situation becomes more complex than we had imagined. Efforts to relate need achievement scores to actual school achievement have yielded inconsistent results. In some studies involving high school students, low but positive relationships to school grades have been found (Birney, 1968). However, the results for college students are not at all clear cut; some studies reported no relationship and others even reported *inverse* relationships. Cole, Jacobs, and Zubok (1962) found in one study that when scholastic aptitude was held constant, students enrolled in the honors program had *lower* need achievement scores than did students who exhibited merely average performance. In a second study, these investigators found that the students *lowest* in need achievement at the start of their freshman year actually performed the *highest* by the close of the semester. Similar findings by Broverman, Jordan, and Phillips (1960), from studies in a different context, led these investigators to conclude that rather than showing a direct relationship to overt behavior, fantasy measures are *compensatory*. That is, high need achievement scores are obtained by persons who are *unable* to express their need for achievement in a real life context.

In an attempt to account for the fact that need achievement scores do not consistently predict actual achievement in school, McClelland argues that academic settings are not conducive to the kinds of achievement striving shown by high need achievement people. According to McClelland, people with a high need for achievement prefer to solve problems set by *themselves* rather than by *others*. Actual achievement in academic settings reflects such things as being able to follow instructions, examination taking skills, and a willingness to solve problems posed by others. Many of these skills are not prized by the high need achievement person. Hence, we should not expect to find relationships between need achievement scores and actual achievement.

If McClelland's line of reasoning is correct, we should expect to find consistent *inverse* relationships between need achievement scores and performance in academic settings. That is, if it is true that high need achievement is incompatible with the academic setting as McClelland claims, then one should find high scorers performing poorly and low scorers performing well. While there is actually evidence in the study by Cole, Jacobs, and Zubok mentioned earlier that this is the case, the *positive* relationships reported between need achievement and grades for high school students confuse the issue. For McClelland's argument to hold, we would have to assume that the high school situation and the college situation are radically different in that the high school situation encourages independent problem setting and solution, indifference to following instructions, and so forth, and that the college situation encourages the opposite. This does not seem plausible.

There are similar difficulties involved with the other argument, that states that one cannot expect to find consistent relationships between a measure of achievement motivation and school grades simply because school grades reflect things other than motivation to achieve. If we were to take this argument seriously, then no single variable ought to relate to school achievement; but this is not the case. Consider measures of intelligence as an example. Even though we grant that grades are determined by many things, measures of intelligence consistently relate positively to school achievement.

What we know about motivation tells us that a highly motivated person will, other things being equal, perform better than a poorly motivated person (assuming that motivation is not at such a high level that it actually interferes with performance). We really cannot vindicate McClelland quite so easily because the very *meaning* of the concept of need achievement is at issue here. In fact, the absence of a consistent pattern of relationships between need achievement and actual achievement leaves us in a quandary as to what McClelland's method of measurement *actually measures*. Does it measure need achievement or some other unknown variable? What is the relationship of fantasy to overt behavior in the measurement of achievement motivation? Does high achievement in fantasy reflect a compensatory mechanism in persons whose achievement drives are frustrated? Unfortunately, we really do not know the answers to these questions with any certainty.

As we promised the student at the beginning of this chapter, it is not an easy matter to establish the usefulness of the inventions of a psychologist. It would be nice to leave the student with a comfortable feeling of certainty—he would be happier even though ignorant—but the reality of psychological research does not permit the luxury of certainties. Once again, the serious student of social thought and behavior must learn to tolerate uncertainty. But let us continue our discussion of need for achievement. Perhaps the puzzle posed by research on the relationship between need achievement and actual achievement will become clearer.

Is McClelland's measure of need achievement a reliable one? As we mentioned earlier, reliability refers to the accuracy and consistency of measurement. A persistent difficulty in the case of need achievement measurement is that the stability of the measure across time is quite low (Birney, 1968). When subjects are tested with the same form of the test on two separate occasions or when the second testing is accomplished by means of a different but highly similar test (a parallel form), correlations ranging from 0.20 to approximately 0.59 have been obtained. By most psychological testing standards these correlations are quite low as far as the reliability of a measuring device is concerned. Quite simply a low correlation, of 0.20 for example, means that if a person's achievement motivation was measured on one day and again on another day, the person might seem to possess *high* achievement motivation on the first testing and *low* achievement motivation on the second day!

Of course one might argue that motivational states like need achievement are subject to temporary *arousal* by fluctuating environmental conditions; that is, a person is not *chronically* high need achievement-oriented. Achievement, like other needs or motives, waxes and wanes as situations arouse them and activity quiets them. Hence, one cannot really expect a motivational state to be consistent from one day to the next, and one therefore cannot expect measurement of such states to be highly stable.

Does the need achievement measure show relational facility? Although it is still difficult to see how any measuring device that yields unreliable scores can be used to establish relationships with other variables, the history of research on need achievement provides us with ample evidence that this can and does occur. Need achievement has been related to a host of other variables ranging from preference for aesthetic designs to memory for tasks completed to tasks not completed. It has been used to predict risk-taking behavior, persistence on difficult tasks, and even, as we noted in Chapter 3, the economic behavior of entire nations. Precisely how a measure of such low reliability could enjoy such predictive success is, of course, one of those curious puzzles with which we will have to live. However, it is clear that the achievement motivation measure has produced many relationships with other variables. Before leaving our discussion of need achievement, let us see how achievement motivation has been combined with other variables to afford interesting predictions.

Motive, expectancy, and incentive: need achievement and risk-taking

In a truly imaginative approach to risk-taking, Atkinson (1958) demonstrated the advantage of considering motivation in combination with other variables in order to predict behavior. Atkinson's account of risk-taking involves three variables, namely, *motive, expectancy,* and *incentive.* Suppose that a person is confronted with performing a given task. Not only may he be motivated to succeed, he may also be motivated to avoid failure. We would, of course, expect different results if his motive to succeed were equal to his motive to avoid failure, if his motive to succeed were greater than his motive to avoid failure, or if his motive to succeed were far less than his motive to avoid failure. In the first instance, when both motives are equal, we would find the individual in much conflict. In the second instance, the motive to succeed predominates, and in the final instance, the motive to avoid failure is dominant.

In addition to considering the relative strengths of these two motives, we must also consider the person's *expectancy* of succeeding (his *subjective probabilities* of success). For example, the person may be motivated to succeed but he may perceive the task as so difficult that his subjective probabilities of success are quite low. Obviously this person would differ from one whose motive to succeed was equally high but whose subjective probabilities of success were also high.

But knowledge of the relative strengths of motive to succeed and motive to fail in conjunction with subjective probabilities is still not sufficient to predict the person's behavior. We must also have some appreciation of the *incentive* value of success for the person. Does he value success highly or does he place a low value on succeeding at this task? But what determines the incentive value of success? Let us assume that incentive value is a *positive linear function* of the difficulty of the task; that is, as the difficulty of a task increases, the incentive value of success also increases. In other words, succeeding on a very difficult task is far more rewarding to the person than succeeding on a very easy task. Given this assumption and representing task difficulty as subjective probability of success, we can write incentive values as follows:

Incentive value of success $= 1 -$ Probability of success
(1) $I_s = 1 - P_s$

Conversely, the negative incentive value of failure (how much it embarrasses us to fail) is as follows:

$$\text{Negative incentive value of failure} = \text{Negative probability of success}$$
$$(2) \ I_f = -P_s$$

From equation (1), when the probability of success is very high, say 0.90, the incentive value of success is quite low $(1 - 0.90 = 0.10)$. However, when the probability of success is very low, say 0.10, then the incentive value of success is quite high $(1 - 0.10 = 0.90)$.

From equation (2), when the probability of success is very high, say 0.90, the negative incentive value of failure is also quite high (-0.90). In other words, it embarrasses us greatly to fail on easy tasks. Similarly, when the probability of success is quite low, say 0.10, then the negative incentive value of failure is also quite low (-0.10). We do not mind so much when we fail at tasks that are extraordinarily difficult.

In other words, Atkinson is postulating that overall motivation to achieve is a joint function of motivation to succeed times probability of success times incentive value of success. Conversely, the overall motivation to avoid failure is a product of motivation to avoid failure times probability of failure times negative incentive value of failure. We can represent these by the following equations:

$$\text{Motivation to achieve} = M_s \times P_s \times I_s, \text{ and}$$
$$\text{Motivation to avoid failure} = M_f \times P_f \times I_f$$

From these equations, Atkinson concludes that differences will be apparent in individuals who differ in the relative strengths of motive to achieve success and of motive to avoid failure when they are asked to choose and perform one of several tasks in which the probabilities of success vary as well. The person high in success motivation but low in motivation to avoid failure will tend to select tasks of *moderate* probability of success. The person high in motivation to avoid failure will tend to select tasks which are extremely high in probability of success (easy tasks) or extremely low in probability of success (very difficult tasks). Why should this be? It is easy to see why the failure avoidant motivated individual will select easy tasks. He is willing to minimize the amount of incentive success value he receives in order to insure avoiding failure. But he may also accomplish his purposes by seeking to minimize the *negative incentive value of failure* by deliberately selecting extraordinarily difficult tasks—"Nobody can blame me if I fail on such a difficult task."

For the person high in motivation to succeed, the overall motivation to achieve is highest when the probability of success and the incentive value of success are moderate. Given a choice among tasks of varying levels of difficulty, the person with a high motivation to succeed will voluntarily choose to perform those tasks of moderate probability of success and of moderate incentive success value.

Atkinson's analysis is entirely consistent with an experiment on risk-taking behavior conducted by McClelland (1958 *b*). In this experiment McClelland had kindergarten students perform a simple ringtoss game in which each child was asked to throw a ring over a peg placed on the floor. The child could stand as close to the peg as he wished. Consistent with Atkinson's analysis, high achievement-motivated five year olds tended to choose to throw at a moderate distance from the peg (moderate risk-taking), and low achievement-motivated children chose to stand very near the peg (low risk-taking) or very far from the peg (high risk-taking).

Even though other researchers have suggested weaknesses in Atkinson's model and modifications as well (Birney, 1968), it is nevertheless an ingenious and important contribution to the understanding of the manner in which motivation, expectancy, and incentive combine to affect the degree of risk that persons are willing to assume.

Summary of achievement motivation

Although need achievement has stimulated an enormous body of research, of which we have only scratched the surface in this chapter, some curious puzzles and difficulties remain. First, the fact that the need achievement measure does not relate consistently to overt achievement in the academic setting has been glossed over too quickly. While the arguments explaining the lack of relationship are plausible, one finds oneself pondering precisely what it is that the achievement motivation measures if it does not predict behavior in actual achievement settings. Second, the poor reliability of the measure is a further difficulty that has never been dealt with adequately. It is curious that this measure has resulted in so many significant relationships with other variables and that other more reliable and stable instruments have not. Why this should be is not altogether clear.

Nevertheless, one cannot help being impressed with the sheer amount of research that the achievement motivation measure has generated as well as the relational fertility it has demonstrated. Even though one might hold serious doubts about what it is that the measure actually measures as well as the accuracy with which it measures it, there cannot be any question that its use has illuminated a number of intriguing relationships. Most certainly, Atkinson's efforts to combine motivation, expectancy, and incentive are a most significant contribution to our understanding of risk-taking behavior.

Power, Manipulation, and Machiavellianism

Psychologists are, of course, interested in social motives other than achievement. In Chapter 4, for example, we considered research directed toward understanding the *approval motive*. In Chapter 7, which deals with interpersonal interaction, we will deal with the *affiliation* motive and other motives that are aroused when one person interacts with another. Still other motives of interest to the psychologist concern the disposition of one person to exert control over another, to manipulate the other person, to exercise social power over another, and so forth. What of power and manipulation motives? Can the psychologist tell us something about these?

In American society circa 1970, it is not at all unusual to find psychologists interested in the motivation for social power. Within recent years the many struggles for power taking place in a variety of arenas, e.g., the traditional political party, the radical political party, the high school, university, and ghetto, tempt one to conclude that power games have become a national indoor and outdoor sport. But that analogy is, of course, far too frivolous for the seriousness of the crises that confront American society, crises regarding questions of the distribution of social, economic, and political power.

It is not difficult to understand why persons in a societal context such as modern America seek to develop and extend their own bases of power and influence. A careful examination of a day in the life of almost any corporate executive ought to convince even the most ingenuous of recent business administration graduates that he should learn something about the art and mastery of manipulation—if only to know when he is being manipulated and to be able to mount effective countermanipulation tactics of his own. But one does not have to turn to the "dog eat dog" world of corporate management for instances of Machiavellianism (the subtle art of manipulating others; named after the Italian theorist of such matters, Machiavelli). One can very likely find evidence of its practice in the local PTA, garden club, in small town politics, and even in the relationship between two lovers. It would seem that whenever two or more persons interact with one another, the probability that attempts at interpersonal influence of some kind will occur are quite high. As one student of Machiavellianism, Richard Christie, has remarked:

> As an undergraduate these [Machiavelli's ideas] had impressed me as thoroughly detestable. After some years of experience with department chairmen, deans, college presidents, governmental officials, and foundation executives, my reaction was different. Some of them had apparently taken Machiavelli to heart or had independently discovered similar techniques of manipulating others.*

As many humanistically oriented student radicals are now painfully aware, radical politics is not immune to power struggles and attempted manipulation. The divisive and almost bizarre struggles for control in evidence at the recent SDS (Students for a Democratic Society) National Convention in Southside, Chicago, should convince even the most idealistic person that radical politics are really *politics* after all. The various tactics employed by factions such as the Revolutionary Youth Movements and the Progressive Labor Party-Worker-Student Alliance to gain control of the national leadership of SDS were clearly blatant, although amateurish, efforts after manipulation.

To take another perspective, we can readily appreciate why minority groups in America have recently increased their efforts to gain social, economic, and political power. The slogans "Black Power" and "Power to the People" are fully understandable when one considers the manner in which minorities such

---

*From Christie, R., and Geis, F.: Some consequences of taking Machiavelli seriously. *In* Borgatta, E. F., and Lambert, W. W. (eds.): *Handbook of Personality Theory and Research.* Chicago, Rand McNally & Co., Inc., 1968, p. 261.

as the black American and the Mexican-American have been excluded systematically from full participation in American society.

In one sense, then, it is not difficult to see why many persons in American society develop manipulative styles of social interaction. In truth, much of social reality consists of interpersonal, group, and organizational contexts in which the arts of influence and manipulation have been developed to a high degree. Like sex, however, power is a dirty word in American society. Although we are taught the skills of manipulation and the virtues of possessing power by our parents and others in the course of our development, paradoxically we are simultaneously taught to *deny* that we have even the slightest interest in such matters. It is socially unacceptable in American society to admit to wanting to control others. Witness the reaction of white America to the realistic demands of black Americans for "Black Power." From the horrified reactions of many white Americans one would have thought that the society functioned entirely upon love, charity, fair play, and good will rather than on the seeking and exercise of power by individuals, special interest groups, political parties, foundations, large corporations, and so forth. One would have thought that the black American was asking for something strange, evil, and alien rather than merely a voice in such matters as economic self-determination, education of his children, and control over his own community—things which white Americans regard as commonplace and take for granted.

Why does one individual differ from another in the *degree* to which he wishes to control the behavior of others? Why must one individual always have things go his way in a group while another is content to sit back and let others make important decisions for him? Why does one individual rely almost exclusively upon manipulative styles of interaction while another prefers other ways of interacting? Why do some individuals deliberately choose contexts of interaction in which manipulation and influence are practiced to a high degree? There are, of course, no certain answers to these complex questions but efforts to explain them have been attempted.

Personality and politics

Harold Lasswell, a political scientist with a long-standing interest in the relationship between psychology and political science, has attempted to apply the principles of psychoanalytic psychology to the concept of power motivation. From his considerable knowledge of both psychoanalytic theory and political figures of the past and present, Lasswell has developed an interesting hypothesis concerning the power seeker. According to Lasswell, the power seeker pursues power as a means of compensation for "deprivation." He attempts to overcome "low estimates of self" by changing the environment in which he operates (Lasswell, 1948).

But deprivations must not be too severe if the complete collapse of the personality of the individual is to be avoided. The power seeker must also have been exposed to extreme indulgence as well. It is from this situation of extreme deprivation and extreme indulgence that the *tensions* necessary for power craving arise in the person. Perhaps this is most readily illustrated in the life of Genghis Khan, the legendary Mongolian seeker after power. Born into a Mongol family that had once known greatness but that later was confronted with great poverty and adversity, Genghis Khan's early life experiences were characterized by great physical and social deprivation. Counterbalancing these extreme deprivations, however, was a mother who indulged her sons greatly with both love and affection and stories extolling the heroic virtues of the Mongol past. Moreover, Khan was taught that it was not himself or the Mongols who were to blame for their adverse position but *forces outside of himself and his people*. Considering the tensions that arose out of extreme deprivation on the one hand and extreme indulgences on the other hand, Lasswell does not find it surprising that Genghis Khan came to believe that "a man's highest job in life is to break his enemies, to drive them before him, to take from them all the things that have been theirs, to hear the weeping of those who cherished them, to take their horses between his knees, and to press in his arms the most desirable of their women" (Lasswell, 1948, p. 92).

The pursuit of power as a means of overcoming low self-esteem growing out of deprivation is seen in other instances. Upward mobility by seeking after power is fostered in a home in which one of the parents, usually the mother, experiences a blighted career. The father may feel that he failed to achieve the position suitable to him in life. The mother may feel that she had "married beneath her station." In both cases the child is expected to carry through with the frustrated ambitions of his parents. The parents of course derive *vicarious* satisfactions from the achievements of the child.

If the person himself experiences deprivation when his own career aspirations are frustrated, intense power cravings may arise. This is especially true when the responsibility for failure can be projected outward onto the society at large and away from self. Lasswell feels that the great philosopher and economist Karl Marx was launched into his career as a sharp social critic when the Prussian establishment of his day refused him a position as a professor in a Prussian university.

Physical deformities can also serve to set up the necessary tensions for compensatory power seeking. Lasswell points to the withered arm of William II of Germany, the short stature of Napolean, Queen Elizabeth's doubts about her physical beauty, Mirabeau's disfiguration by smallpox, and Franklin D. Roosevelt's struggle with the aftereffects of infantile paralysis.

According to Lasswell, then, the power seeker is one who yearns for power over others in order to quiet the pain of low self-esteem. The tensions arising out of extreme deprivation and extreme indulgence are necessary before power striving will appear. While Lasswell's hypothesis is intuitively appealing, there are certain problems associated with it. Even though one may certainly find examples in history of persons who fit the hypothesis, one can also discover those who do not. As William Domhoff has amply pointed out in his recent book *Who Rules America,* inherited advantage rather than early deprivation is the most certain path to a seat of power, at least in American society. From a variety of sources Domhoff makes it clear that America is currently producing more leaders who have enjoyed inherited advantage than at any other time in history. The Kennedys, the Rockefellers, Adlai Stevenson, Robert Fiske Bradford (former governor of Massachusetts), Henry Cabot Lodge, Dean Acheson, Christian Herter, and many others have all enjoyed the benefits of enormous wealth rather than early deprivation.

In his book Domhoff considers those who were involved in one of the most significant and potentially dangerous crises that confronted American society within recent years, namely, the Cuban missile crisis. In attendance at *the* top-level meeting in which decisions were made concerning what to do about the presence of Russian missiles in Cuba in 1962 were the following:

John F. Kennedy, President of the United States
Lyndon B. Johnson, Vice-President
Robert F. Kennedy, Attorney General
Dean Rusk, Secretary of State
Robert McNamara, Secretary of Defense
C. Douglas Dillon, Secretary of the Treasury
Boswell Gilpatrick, Deputy Secretary of Defense
McGeorge Bundy, presidential adviser
Adlai Stevenson, U. S. Ambassador to the United Nations
John McCone, Director of the Central Intelligence Agency
Dean Acheson, former Secretary of State
Robert Lovett, former Secretary of Defense
General Maxwell Taylor, presidential military adviser
Major General Marshall S. Carter, Deputy Director of the CIA
George Ball, Undersecretary of State
Edwin W. Martin, Assistant Secretary for Latin American Affairs
Theodore C. Sorensen, presidential speechwriter and adviser

If we view power as the potential to exercise influence over the lives of others, then we must regard those present at this particular top-level policy making meeting as possessing enormous power. When we examine the family histories of those present at this historic meeting, we note that at least nine of them can be characterized as having risen from initial positions of enormous affluence rather than early deprivation and that none of those remaining could be said to have experienced extreme deprivation. Assuming then that occupying a seat of power is related to motivation to achieve power (a perfectly reasonable assumption), one would say from these observations that Lasswell's hypothesis does not appear tenable.

Of course Lasswell might argue that deprivation might take many forms and meanings other than those embodied in money, material goods, and affluence; and if we looked closely at the lives of the rich, we would find various psychological and other kinds of deprivations, such as insufficient love, affection, and recognition. Although this may very well be true, it is difficult to test. The meaning of deprivation becomes so broad then that one could find "evidence" of deprivation in the lives of virtually everyone. A *selective* reading of any man's history would permit us to validate the hypothesis.

In actuality, as Domhoff carefully documents, a disproportionate representation of the affluent is found in all arenas of the American power structure—political, corporate ownership, governmental, and so forth. Such observations led Domhoff to conclude that America is ruled by a *power elite* whose membership is heavily tipped to the side of those with inherited advantage. The sociologist C. Wright Mills arrived at a similar conclusion concerning the existence of an American "power elite."

Even though Lasswell's hypothesis concerning deprivation and indulgence may explain power motivation in certain cases, it is clearly insufficient to explain it in all cases. One must search for additional variables which determine differential power seeking.

Machiavellianism

A different approach to the problem of individual differences in manipulative tendencies has been provided by the work of psychologist Richard Christie (Christie and Geis, 1968). Through extremely careful procedures and with much testing and refinement of questions, Christie and his colleague were able to develop a test that measures the extent to which persons agree with or disagree with machiavellian tactics in their interactions with others. From their work with the measurement of preference for machiavellian tactics, Christie and Geis concluded the following:

1. Preference for machiavellian tactics does *not* appear to be related to measures of psychological abnormality, social class, intelligence or ability, and political ideology.

2. In general, males tend to score higher than females on preference for machiavellian tactics.

3. Endorsement of machiavellian tactics seems to be clearly associated with the extent to which a person is involved in a set of complex formalized role relationships with other people. The more involved a person is under such circumstances, the more likely he is to endorse machiavellian tactics. For example, a study of medical school students revealed that those specializing in psychiatry (high formal role involvement with others) scored highest in their endorsement of machiavellian principles and those specializing in surgery (low formal role involvement with others) scored lowest. Interestingly enough, social psychology graduate students scored the highest in machiavellian tendencies of any group tested. This is not surprising considering the recent emphasis in experimental social psychology on experiments involving manipulation as well as deception of persons.

4. Those who agree with machiavellian principles appear to have greater success in coping with the demands of American society than those who do not. For example, those who endorse manipulative tactics get better grades in college than those who do not endorse such tactics. (Remember that preference for machiavellianism is *not* correlated with intelligence or ability measures.)

From Christie's data, we can conclude that the preference for manipulative styles of interaction is a social-psychological phenomenon rather than a purely individual one. The fact that machiavellian preferences seem to correlate to the extent to which people are involved in complex formalized role relationships with others is most intriguing. One might very well conclude that people differ in tendency toward manipulative styles of interaction largely because they have been *socialized* that way in the occupational roles they have chosen. Certainly, as in the case of the social psychology graduate student, there is much evidence to support this hypothesis. Within recent years a number of critics of the deception experiment in social psychology (one in which subjects are deliberately deceived as to the real purposes of the experiment and the nature of procedures employed) have expressed alarm over the consequences for the subject. One might very well extend this argument and ask what are the consequences for the experimenter or for those being trained to assume the role of "social psychologist"? Is it possible that cynical, manipulative, and antihumanistic attitudes are imparted to graduate students in psychology departments where the deception experiment is not only publicly practiced but privately encouraged? Of course we do not know the answer to this question. However, the possibility of such an outcome should not be overlooked by those responsible for the training of graduate students in psychology. Naturally there are good reasons why subjects should remain unaware of the true purposes behind many experimental situations; the subject's awareness might distort the data or make precise control over conditions impossible. Even granting this line of argument, one might still question the manner and the social context in which such deception is conducted. Moreover, it seems reasonable to suppose that ingenious experimenters could devise ways to test hypotheses other than by the elaborate deceptions that characterize much contemporary experimental social psychology.

The fact that those who endorse machiavellian tactics show evidence of greater success in coping with the demands of American society is a further observation of considerable interest. It may very well be that individual differences in manipulative preferences reflect individual skills in such tactics in social contexts in which such tactics lead to reward. That is, if one possesses a certain skill or set of skills that lead to reward in a given social context, he will very likely utilize them, and if "conning" the professor is one way to get a good grade (with intelligence and ability held constant), it is not surprising to find students who have this skill using it to this end. In other words, preference for manipulation may arise (1) because the person is skilled in such tactics and (2) because various social contexts reward the exercise of such skills. The problem then becomes one of determining what life experiences foster the growth of manipulative skills and what life experiences do not. Quite simply, people tend to use the skills that they perceive in themselves, especially if the exercise of such skills leads to rewards. Hence, people who are competent in manipulative games will very likely choose to utilize such skills in interaction with others. There are, however, individuals who do possess such skills but choose *not* to perform them even if performing them would lead to reward. About such exemplary persons we know very little indeed.

Hostility and Aggression

Perhaps no other topic of conversation has more engaged people's emotions in contemporary America than that of violence. The events of the Democratic Convention, televised from Chicago, prior to the presidential elections of 1968 brought into sharp focus the fact that violence in America is not restricted to criminal elements. That there has been an increase in the use of violent tactics to gain specific ends in American society cannot be denied; nor can it be argued that the use of violent tactics is one-sided in the current struggles on America's campuses and in its cities. The Chicago Democratic Convention demonstrated the existence of police violence in the service of "law and order" as well as the use of violence in the service of social justice. One is quick to add, however, that neither police nor protestors can be characterized as people who rely exclusively upon violent tactics. Such a portrayal of either would grossly distort both groups and create stereotypes that neither conform to the facts nor provide a basis for intelligent and rational solution of the difficulties that confront us. It cannot be denied that some demonstrators at the Chicago Democratic Convention came fully prepared to engage in violent acts, which they did carry out. However, it is equally true that a variety of conditions, including preparations of the police for the convention, set up expectations that violent action might very well prove necessary. That both sets of expectations erupted in violent actions on both parts is now obvious. A care-

Figure 14. America, 1970. The distribution of power in American society is questioned. (Photo by Gordon Cole.)

ful reading of the Official Report to the National Commission on the Causes and Prevention of Violence (Walker, 1968) will convince even the most skeptical reader that police violence as well as demonstrator violence must be contended with if mass violence, such as that which occurred in Chicago, is to be avoided in the future.

Police violence was a fact of the convention week. Were the policemen who committed it a minority? It appears certain that they were—but one which has imposed some of the consequences of its actions on the majority, and certainly on their commanders.... That some policemen lost control of themselves under exceedingly provocative circumstances can perhaps be understood; but not condoned. If no action is taken against them, the effect can only be to discourage the majority of policemen who acted responsibly, and further weaken the bond between police and community. Although the crowds were finally dispelled on the nights of violence in Chicago, the problems they represent have not been. Surely this is not the last time that a

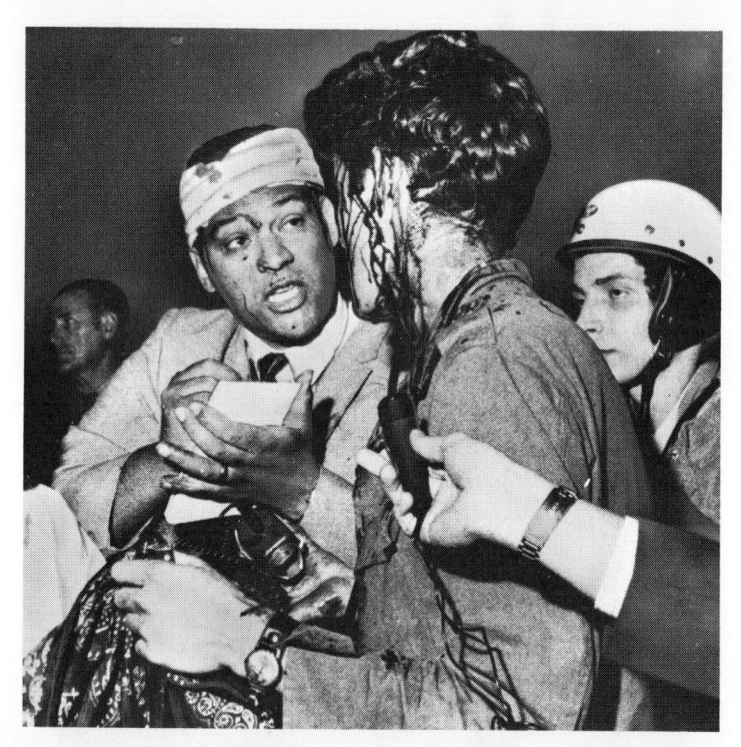

Figure 15. Police violence was a fact of the Chicago Democratic Convention of 1968. In this picture, NBC newsman John Evans (with bandaged head) interviews photographer Dan Morrill; both men were victims of attacks by police officers. (Courtesy of Wide World Photos.)

violent dissenting group will clash head-on with those whose duty it is to enforce the law. And the next time the whole world will still be watching.*

A federal official describes the way the action on Michigan Avenue began:

> I heard a 10-1 call (policeman in trouble) on either my radio or one of the other hand sets carried by men with me and then heard 'Car 100—sweep.' With a roar of motors, squads, vans and three-wheelers came from east, west, and north into the block north of Jackson. The crowd scattered. A big group ran west on Jackson, with a group of blue shirted policemen in pursuit, beating at them with clubs. Some of the crowd would jump into doorways and the police would rout them out. The action was very tough. In my judgment, unnecessarily so. The police were hitting with a vengeance and quite obviously with relish.... †

An exhaustive study of the violence that erupted at the Democratic Convention in Chicago would be of considerable interest. However, we do not have space here to conduct such a study. Let us now turn to several of the more important ways in which psychologists have attempted to understand hostility and aggression.

Perhaps the most longstanding and popular conception of hostility stems from the belief in *catharsis*. One can trace this idea back to Aristotle's theory of the function of tragedy in theater. According to Aristotle, audience reactions at the theater serve to "drain off" emotions which might otherwise overwhelm the individual in real life. This cathartic effect of emotional expression has been elaborated by Freud and other psychoanalytic theorists, and quite recently it has found expression in the writings of the European ethologist Konrad Lorenz (1963). Basing his conclusions on observations of lower organisms, Lorenz advocates that aggression is an inborn instinct. From this, he is led to the familiar arguments that "dammed-up aggressive drives" must be redirected, sublimated, and so forth, through such activities as sports, "mountain climbing, diving, offshore and ocean sailing, but also [through] other dangerous undertakings, like polar expeditions and, above all, the exploration of space," all of which "give scope for militant enthusiasm, allowing nations to fight each other in hard and dangerous competition without engendering national or political hatred" (Lorenz, 1963, p. 282).

---

*From Walker, D.: Rights in Conflict: *Official Report to the National Commission on the Causes and Prevention of Violence.* New York. Signet Books, 1968, Foreword.
†Ibid.

Not all psychologists accept Lorenz's account of aggression and the ways in which it can be handled. Bandura and Walters (1963), for example, cite a host of studies in which children observing another person engage in aggressive activities show an *increase* in aggression rather than a decrease. This is, of course, in direct opposition to Aristotle's view of the value of catharsis. In one study, Kenny (1962) first measured children's tendencies toward aggression. He then permitted one group of children to engage in highly aggressive physical and verbal play while another group was encouraged to engage in nonaggressive play for an equivalent time. If the catharsis hypothesis as advocated by Lorenz were correct, we would expect those given the chance to "drain off" their aggressions through the "sublimated" aggressive doll-play situation to show less aggression than the group who did not have this opportunity. In contradiction to the catharsis hypothesis, however, the children who had engaged in *nonaggressive* play showed a greater decrease in aggression than those who had engaged in aggressive play.

More recently, Berkowitz (1968) has demonstrated that witnessed violence serves to increase aggression rather than decrease it. In one series of studies, Berkowitz and his colleagues first angered students through the use of ridicule and electric shock. The ridicule and shock was administered to the students by "partners." At the conclusion of the experiment, the student who had been shocked was given a chance to change roles with his "partner." However, before the reversal of roles was accomplished, the ridiculed and shocked students were shown movies. One film showed a nonviolent scene involving a race between the first two men to run the four-minute mile. The second film, however, was a most violent one displaying the brutal beating of one boxer by another from the Kirk Douglas movie *Champion*. Some of the students were shown the nonviolent movie and others the violent movie. For those who were shown the violent movie, a further experimental treatment was added. Half were led to believe that the brutal beating of Kirk Douglas in the film was *justified,* i. e., that he had it coming; the other half were led to believe that the severity of the beating was not justified, i. e., that he got more than he deserved.

The results of this experiment are quite interesting. The filmed violence had no cathartic effect whatsoever. In fact, for the students who were led to believe that it was justified, the filmed violence seemed to release their own aggression toward their "partners" rather than purge it. These results were confirmed in five independent experiments conducted in laboratories other than Berkowitz's.

In further research, Berkowitz demonstrated the importance of the presence of stimuli associated with hostility, namely, shotguns and revolvers. Using the same situation in which the subject was first shocked by his partner and was then permitted to reverse roles and shock his partner, Berkowitz demonstrated that the mere presence of weapons in the vicinity of the subject at the time he shocked his partner resulted in an increase in aggression. This occurred whether or not the subjects reported awareness of the weapons. Apparently one need not be angry in order to have the mere presence of weapons increase aggressive responding. In one study, nonangered children permitted to play with toy guns showed greater subsequent aggression than children who were not permitted to play with guns.

Further evidence that is contradictory to the catharsis hypothesis stems from Berkowitz's demonstration of a "snowballing effect." When the person is permitted to express aggression by attacking another any number of times, the intensity of the aggression appears to *mount* rather than decrease as the number of aggressive acts increases. As Berkowitz puts it, people seemed to "feed" on their own aggressive responses, with aggression producing further aggression.

There are numerous implications of considerable social relevance that one can draw from these findings. Certainly, the fact that witnessed aggression gives rise to further aggression says something about the nature of television programming and movies. Aside from the fact that a person may learn the actual *techniques* of violence from these media, e.g., how to throttle a hapless victim, make a bomb out of odds and ends from the garage, and so forth, witnessed violence appears to lower the inhibitions of persons to commit aggressive acts themselves. Moreover, the fact that the mere presence of the instruments of violence such as revolvers and shotguns can serve to increase the likelihood of general aggressive behavior is most certainly relevant to the current debate over control of firearms in the United States. As Berkowitz points out, we frequently fail to appreciate the fact that many violent acts are *impulsive* in nature. For many persons who have committed violent acts it is almost certainly true that in a moment of rage, justified or unjustified, a weapon was available. They simply picked it up and "pulled the trigger." The mere sight of a weapon is frequently sufficient to lower inhibitions to its use.

An early theory of aggression held that frustration was a necessary condition for aggressive responses to occur. This theory also maintained that the frustrated person would frequently *displace* his aggression away from the object of his aggressions to other targets. Displacement is especially likely against those who are not in a position to retaliate. For example, the angry and frustrated man might not express his aggression against his boss but would take it out on his children or perhaps the family dog. Although it is certainly true that frustration may be *one* of the factors leading to aggression, it is now quite clear that it is not the only factor. Aggressive responses can occur without frustration. Moreover, it is equally clear that frustration can lead to responses *other* than aggression. One person may typically respond to frustration with aggression; another may withdraw. Another may act "childishly," and still others may find effective ways of coping with frustration either by altering their approach to a frustrating problem or by altering their goals in order to achieve an equally attractive but more easily attainable goal. At this time psychologists are not able to predict which of these responses to frustration will occur in any given individual without first extensively studying the individual and his various life circumstances. It is probably true that each of us possesses more than one and perhaps several possible responses to frustration.

Much the same can be said with regard to the hypothesis that people may displace aggressive responses. While displaced aggression may be *one* of the responses to frustration, it is clearly not the only one. Moreover, the conditions under which displaced aggressive responses will occur require considerably more research before accurate predictions can be made. The ability of the target to retaliate is obviously one important factor. We are more likely to select a victim for our displaced aggressive responses who is not in a position to strike back. The similarity of the target of the displaced aggressive response to the original object is a further consideration. Hence, the husband may displace aggression more rightfully directed at his mother onto his wife. However, the manner in which similarity operates in displaced aggressive responses is not clearly understood.

SOCIAL MOTIVES AND THEIR MEASUREMENT 165

Quite recently the phenomenon of *rising expectations* has been postulated as a factor in the occurrence of violence and aggression. The argument states that it is only when a downtrodden people like the American blacks experience a period of rising expectations coupled with eventual frustration that appreciable amounts of aggression appear. Davies (1969) has traced the history of revolutions in terms of periods characterized by a prolonged interval of rising expectations and gratifications followed by a short period of reversal in which the gap between expectation and actual gratification received widens until it becomes intolerable. According to Davies, the unbearable tensions and hostility generated by the gap between what people want and what they can get culminates in violent rebellion or revolt. In the American Revolution, the American Civil War, the French Revolution, the Nazi revolution, and, more contemporaneously, the rebellion of the black man in America, Davies claims that a prolonged period of rising expectations and gratifications followed by a sudden reversal can be noted. This relationship between rising expectations and sudden economic reversal is illustrated for the Nazi revolution in Germany in Figure 16.

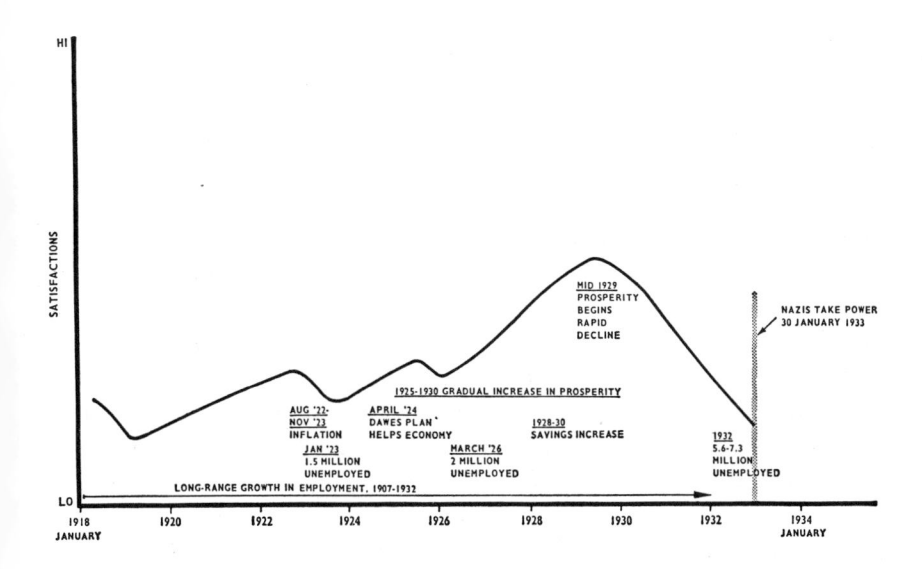

Figure 16. Economic satisfactions and the Nazi Revolution. *From* Davies, J. C.: The J-curve of rising and declining satisfactions as a cause of some great revolutions and a contained rebellion. In: Graham, H. D., and Gurr, T. R.: *Violence in America: Official Report to the National Commission on the Causes and Prevention of Violence.* New York, The New American Library, 1969.

Although we can use historical examples to buttress any hypothesis we wish and cannot therefore be certain that Davies is not reading his history *selectively*, we are intrigued by the hypothesis. For example, it may be true that during periods of rising expectations rigid controls over people are progressively relaxed, the stirrings of protest tolerated, and the *inhibitions* of downtrodden people to violent protest are progressively lowered. This could be especially true when, as in the case of the American black, a substantial portion of the majority expresses support in the legitimacy of its cause. When public opinion no longer permits the brutal repression of a minority, it is not surprising that a downtrodden group, sensing the increased liberalization and permissiveness, will show increases in aggressive demands for their rights and even violent reactions when efforts are made to reinstitute repressive controls by a frightened government.

In other words, it may very well be that the *inhibition* to aggression and violence is lowered among persons anxious to better their position. This may come about since it is precisely during periods of rising expectations attendant upon equally rising general prosperity that governments may relax repressive measures against some of its citizens as well as make at least minimal efforts to satisfy them. However, a sudden economic reversal may bring with it an effort to reinstate previous repressive controls. But the situation has changed; the government is no longer dealing with a group of persons whose threshold for aggression is quite low. Having witnessed the positive effects of aggression during the permissive periods of rising expectations, a downtrodden people might well react with further aggression to attempts of the government to reestablish repressive controls. The government in turn might react with further repressive controls and thus lead to further protest. Once this occurs, the familiar pattern of escalation of conflict takes place and culminates in either massive government violence or revolution.

We have concentrated on the lowering of the threshold for aggression during periods of rising expectations, whereas Davies has concentrated upon the sudden gap that occurs between such expectations and gratifications as the critical factor. We do not view our analysis as opposed to Davies' hypothesis. It may very well be true that both the frustration of expectancies and the lowering of inhibitions to the use of aggressive tactics, as well as other factors, will prove necessary to explain the occurrence of revolutionary violence.

Summary of Social Motives and Their Measurement

In this portion of the chapter we have examined several important social motives: the achievement motive, the power and manipulation motive, and hostility and aggression. There are, of course, other motives that we could examine. However, it is not our purpose to provide the student with a handy summary of the findings of psychological research concerning all of the social motives of human beings. From a more searching discussion of a limited set of motives we hope that we have introduced the student to many of the puzzles and complexities that confront the psychologist or any other inquirer into human behavior who searches to understand the motivations of human beings.

ANXIETY, CONFLICT, AND DEFENSE

In addition to the study of social motives, psychologists interested in the individual have devoted an enormous amount of effort to the study of anxiety, conflict, and defense. Let us consider each of these briefly.

Anxiety

Personality and anxiety

It has long been commonly observed that individuals differ in anxiety-proneness. Some individuals seem almost perpetually "up tight," frightened by this, upset about that, tense in many social situations, "nervous," and so on. Other individuals appear to go about their affairs in a state of almost perfect serenity hardly troubled by even the most stressful of circumstances. Are there consequences of such wide individual differences in anxiety-proneness? Psychological research indicates that there are.

Self-esteem and anxiety. One would suspect that a relationship between self-doubting and anxiety exists; that is, a person very unsure of himself is one who is easily threatened in interpersonal situations. Unsure of his own capabilities and excessively afraid of failure, both socially and intellectually, it is not surprising to find that these persons of low self-esteem are characterized by excessive anxiety. Suinn and Hill (1964) and Rosenberg (1962) have reported substantial relationships between measures of self-esteem and measures of anxiety. Those who tend to evaluate themselves quite lowly also show signs of greater anxiety when compared with other persons on typical measures of anxiety. More recently Coopersmith (1967) has reported a very substantial correlation between measures of anxiety and measures of self-esteem. Once again, in Coopersmith's research the direct relationship between anxiety and self-esteem is clearly shown.

Guilt-proneness and anxiety

Anxiety-prone subjects are also guilt-prone according to the research of Lowe (1964). Taking great care to separate his measures of anxiety and guilt so that distinctly different concepts were measured, Lowe found a substantial relationship between anxiety-proneness and guilt-proneness. Of course many theorists, e.g., Freud and Horney, have argued that guilt is merely a type of anxiety—moral anxiety. However, Lowe's careful research suggests that a distinction between the two can be achieved and that there is some advantage in considering the anxiety-prone person as one who is likely to show evidence of guilt-proneness as well.

Creativity and anxiety

Wallach and Kogan (1965) studied an entire population of fifth grade students in a suburban middle-class school. Although the investigators were interested in a number of personality variables, their results for anxiety and creativity are of interest here. By measuring both intelligence and creativity Wallach and Kogan were able to divide their sample in terms of high intelligence-low creativity, high intelligence-high creativity, low intelligence-high creativity, and low intelligence-low creativity. The lowest anxiety scores were reported for the group of boys who possessed high intelligence but low creativity. The highest anxiety levels were found in boys with both low intelligence and low creativity. Intermediate levels of anxiety were found in the two highly creative groups.

From one perspective it is easy to see why boys of high intelligence but low creativity were low in anxiety. In the typical public school classroom they are in complete command of their environments. They possess sufficient intelligence to cope adequately with the demands of their teachers. More importantly, their low creativity is not an undesirable attribute in the typical elementary school classroom where *conformance* of thought rather than modification of thought is usually rewarded. Also it is not difficult to see why boys of low intelligence and low creativity score high on anxiety. Since one of the tests used by Wallach and Kogan was a measure of *test* anxiety and considering the histories of failure on the part of low intelligence-low creativity boys, their high scores on the anxiety measure are not surprising.

It is difficult, however, to explain the intermediate levels of anxiety reported for the two highly creative groups. Behavioral observations of the high intelligence-high creativity group suggested that they showed the least doubt about their work and about themselves and were reported to have the highest self-confidence. Hence, we would expect this group to be quite low in anxiety. Boys low in intelligence but high in creativity were reported to be the least sure of themselves, cautious, and the most deprecatory toward themselves and their work of all the children studied. Clearly this group should have scored highest on anxiety.

It is possible that the high intelligence-high creativity boys scored higher on anxiety than their equally intelligent but less creative classmates precisely because they tend to perceive things in unique and different ways. The possibility that teachers alternately reward and punish deviant (nonconforming) thought may create an uncertain situation for the highly intelligent, highly creative child in the elementary school classroom. He never knows how the teacher might respond to his productions. As a consequence he may experience more anxiety than his high intelligence-low creativity classmates whose "perfect" (conforming) responses are nearly always "correct" and nearly always likely to bring forth praise and reward from the teachers.

Of course we cannot generalize the same line of argument to explain the differences between the two low intelligence groups. Why boys of high creativity but low intelligence score lower on anxiety than boys of low creativity and low intelligence is not altogether clear. Perhaps creative responses from low intelligence boys affect the teacher differently than creative responses from high intelligence boys. Perhaps the teacher more *consistently* rewards "creativity" in low intelligence-high creativity boys (since she cannot reward their intellectual products, the teacher rewards evidence of creative abilities). As a consequence of possessing at least one "marketable" skill in the elementary school classroom, the low intelligence-high creativity boy has at least one means of obtaining some relief from persistent failure, something which his less creative classmate of equally low intelligence does not possess. Consequently, the low intelligence-high creativity child may be partially protected from the experience of anxiety in the classroom (he can at least do something which brings forth teacher praise), whereas the low intelligence-low creativity child is not protected because he has no skills to compensate for low intelligence). But, of course, we are speculating here far beyond Wallach and Kogan's data.

School achievement and anxiety

Anxiety has been shown rather consistently to relate negatively to school achievement and test performance, i.e., the higher the anxiety, the lower the achievement level. In one recent study, Hill and Sarason (1966) clearly demonstrated the effects of anxiety upon school performance. With what is called a *longitudinal study* they studied *test-taking anxiety* in children over a five-year period by measuring their progress from the first to the sixth grades. Children who gained in measured *test-taking anxiety* showed the lowest gains in standardized achievement test scores as they progressed through school.

Curiosity, sensation-seeking, and anxiety

In still other studies anxiety-proneness has been shown to be negatively related to "curiosity" and "sensation-seeking." As we would expect, fearful and anxious people are not among those who seek the uncertainty of novel environments or ideas, nor are they likely to seek out situations that are characterized by high levels of sensory stimulation. Perhaps anxiety-prone persons already experience such a high level of arousal that further stimulation from curious or sensual environments is simply unbearable. The lesson here might be "Don't take a high anxious friend to a light show; she might 'freak out'!"

Learning and anxiety

Janet Taylor Spence (1963) has provided us with an interesting account of the manner in which anxiety enters into learning. Working within the framework of drive theory, Spence reasoned that anxiety is a drive. She further reasoned that in a simple and uncomplicated learning situation, increases in anxiety ought to *facilitate* learning. However, in complicated learning situations anxiety would interfere with learning. Spence's hypotheses about anxiety were based upon Hull's learning theory, in which drive was thought to energize habits. If we think of the person as possessing a number of *response hierarchies*, each consisting of a number of responses arranged in order of their relative strengths, it is possible to see how anxiety will aid a simple learning situation and hinder a complex learning situation. Consider a response hierarchy corresponding to the term "great men." A person might have this class arranged in his head as follows (in decreasing order of response strength):

Great Men

A. Presidents of the United States
1. Lincoln
2. Roosevelt
3. Kennedy
4. Truman

B. Famous Writers
1. Hermann Hesse
2. Ouspensky
3. John Barth
4. Terry Southern
5. Blake

C. Famous Composers
1. Stravinsky
2. Bartok
3. John Cage
4. John Lennon

Suppose we asked this person to play a variety of Twenty Questions, a game called "Guess the Great Man I'm Thinking of." Since presidents of the United States are at the top of his hierarchy and since Lincoln is at the top of this category, we would expect our subject to respond with "Lincoln." This response is the most *dominant* or probable response in the person's response hierarchy corresponding to the stimulus "great men." The least dominant response, and hence the least probable response, is "John Lennon" under the heading famous composers.

Anxiety as a drive facilitates the performance of highly dominant responses. When the "correct" response is high in the hierarchy (as, for example, it would be with "Lincoln"), anxiety will actually lead to better performance. However, when the "correct" response is low in the hierarchy (as it would be with "John Lennon"), anxiety will interfere with performance. This follows from the fact that anxiety as a drive is a *multiplier* of the strength of habits; that is, an increment of anxiety will result in proportionately greater increases in the strength of dominant habits over weaker habits. Stated quite simply, under conditions of strong anxiety, highly dominant responses are energized more than responses that are low in the hierarchy. A highly anxious person asked to play our guessing game might very well continue to search for the solution among highly dominant responses long after the less anxious person had abandoned dominant responses in favor of searching for responses low in the hierarchy.

In the context of the simple learning situation in which the simple reflex of the "blink" is conditioned to a stimulus accompanying a puff of air, highly anxious subjects condition more rapidly than do less anxious subjects. However, in a situation where subjects must learn fairly complex verbal material, the situation is reversed with highly anxious subjects showing less efficient learning than subjects who are low in anxiety.

In addition to the fact that highly anxious subjects condition more rapidly than do less anxious subjects, highly anxious subjects also show more *generalization* of conditioned responses. If we were to condition a highly anxious person to respond emotionally to the stimulus of a musical tone of 440 cycles per second, he would very likely show some emotional response to tones of 438, 436, 434, and 432 cycles per second as well. The less anxious person, on the other hand, might show some response to 438 cps, hardly any response to 436 cps, and no emotional response to 434 and 432 cps. The gradient of generalization for the highly anxious person is *much* broader than that of the less anxious person; that is, he responds to many more stimuli that bear some similarity to the original stimulus to which he was conditioned than does the less anxious person.

The fact that more rapid conditioning and greater generalization are characteristic of the highly anxious person is more significant than meets the eye. Consider the highly anxious child who happens to be bitten by a dog. He may quickly develop a phobia about dogs, and, most importantly, this phobia may involve dogs in general as well as other furry, four-legged animals, e.g., cats, mice, monkeys, and so forth. The less anxious child might respond fearfully to the dog that bit him as well as to other dogs that are highly similar to that dog. However, he might very well be able to tolerate other types of dogs and other furry, four-legged creatures. As the author has pointed out elsewhere (Sechrest and Wallace, 1967), the more rapid conditioning and broader generalization characteristic of highly anxious persons may serve to explain some aspects of neurotic behavior. The neurotic person may be one who, for whatever reasons, possesses a high chronic anxiety level. Through unfortunate life experiences he develops a conditioned anxiety response, and this response generalizes broadly, giving rise to further emotional responses and further anxiety which, in turn, results in further conditioning. As more and more stimuli in the neurotic person's environment become capable of eliciting conditioned anxiety, the person becomes progressively more debilitated. When we remember that conditioned responses can occur *without awareness,* the situation becomes even more complicated. A person may enter adult life fearing such seemingly innocuous things as elevators and not have the slightest idea why. When we review the many and diverse things of which people report fears, automatic conditioning becomes a plausible explanation.

Many years ago G. Stanley Hall once obtained a sample of fears from over 1700 persons. People, it seems, fear an incredible array of things. Thunder, reptiles, strange persons, and darkness were among the most common. But people also reported fears of high winds, water, high places, meteors, mice, bats, comets, eclipses, cloud forms, people with prominent teeth, the Northern Lights, and even, in one case, the "man in the moon." When we further realize that one need not have direct experience with a feared object but can learn through vicarious conditioning procedures (see Chapter 7), explanations of fear by conditioning become more plausible and especially so in the highly anxious person.

Conflict

A person is said to be in conflict when two mutually exclusive and incompatible response tendencies exist simultaneously. He may, for example, wish to *approach* some goal and at the same time wish to *avoid* it. The person who wishes to enter college but at the same time fears that he will fail is caught in an *approach-avoidance* conflict, as is the man who is both attracted by but fearful of an attractive, intelligent, and highly aggressive female.

There are other types of conflict. A person may wish to approach two equally desirable goals but the attainment of one means that he must forgo the other. This occurs, for example, when a man must choose between two equally attractive job offers. When a person is forced to choose between two equally attractive goals, he is caught in an *approach-approach* conflict. Similar to the approach-approach conflict is the *avoidance-avoidance* conflict: the person must choose between two equally unattractive goals—as when mother offers Johnnie his "choice" between spinach and turnips, both of which he equally detests.

The person trapped in the *double approach-avoidance* conflict is faced with two goals, each of which contains both positive and negative features. The girl with two men on the string for marriage may find herself totaling up both the positive and negative features of each only to find that such attributes are evenly balanced. "On the one hand, Jack has a superb sense of humor but he snores. Bill doesn't snore but he whistles those aimless tunes through his teeth incessantly. But then, Bill has a lot of money—but so does Jack," and so on and so forth.

Perhaps the most extensively studied form of conflict is the approach-avoidance variety. Miller and his colleagues (1959) presented a schematic drawing of the approach-avoidance conflict in terms of intersecting gradients. These are depicted in Figure 17.

In Miller's analysis it is assumed that the gradient of avoidance is far steeper than the gradient of approach. Hence, as one approaches a simultaneously feared and desired goal, the tendency to avoid will become proportionately stronger than the tendency to approach. Clear-cut tendencies to approach will be obtained only at some distance from the goal. From this analysis we can conclude certain things. Perhaps, most importantly, it would be foolish to attempt to resolve a conflict by forcing oneself to directly approach a feared goal. This would only tend to elevate conflict to unbearable levels since avoidance tendencies are highest in this region. Therefore it makes no sense to force a child who is both attracted to and frightened to death of wild animals at the zoo to stand within five feet of the lion's cage. Such a practice would merely intensify his conflict and cause him to run in a panic if not otherwise restrained. One might, however, attempt to deal with a conflict by reducing the avoidance gradient. For the child in the previous example this might be accomplished by reading stories about wild animals to him while he is quite relaxed and happy, having him draw pictures of lions and tigers quite secure in their cages, and so forth. This might be coupled with visits to other animal housing centers, e.g., animal hospitals, farms, and the local pound. By exposing the child gradually to the elements that make up the complex situation of the zoo and by doing so

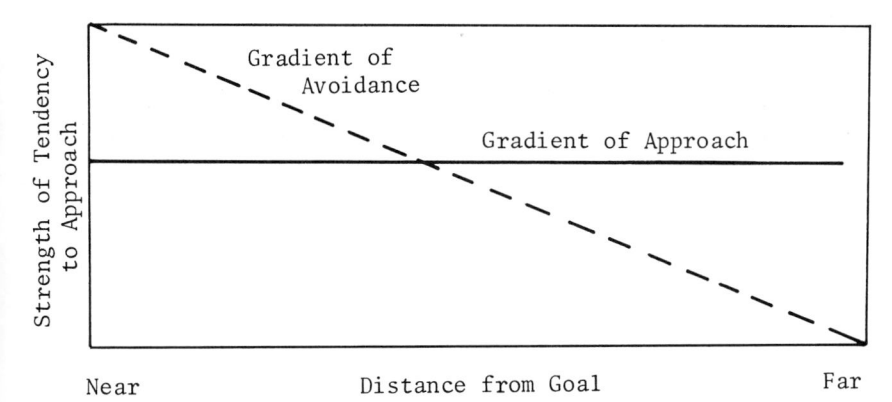

Figure 17. Simple graphic representation of an approach-avoidance conflict. The tendency to approach is the stronger of the two tendencies far from the goal, whereas the tendency to avoid is the stronger of the two near to the goal. Therefore, when far from the goal, the subject should tend to approach part way and then stop. In short, he should tend to remain in the region where the two gradients intersect. (*From* Miller, 1959; *after* Miller, N. E.: Experimental studies of conflict. *In* Hunt, J. (ed.): *Personality and the Behavior Disorders.* New York, The Ronald Press Company, 1944.)

under relaxed and nonanxiety-provoking circumstances, it might prove possible to decrease some of his fears associated with zoos. Through this procedure of progressive desensitization to the cues which evoke anxiety in the child, it might prove possible to eventually get the child to approach the feared object (the zoo) once his avoidance gradient has been lowered.

The author once used precisely this technique in his clinical practice with children. A child who was caught in a terrible conflict about school attendance—attracted on the one hand and repelled on the other—responded very well to systematic attempts to lower her avoidance gradient by progressively desensitizing her to anxiety-provoking cues associated with school attendance.

Although Miller's analysis of conflict in terms of intersecting gradients of approach and avoidance is intuitively appealing, not all psychologists are in agreement with the model. Quite recently Mahrer (1966) has questioned both the assumptions about the relative slopes of the approach and avoidance gradients as well as the deductions from these assumptions. Briefly Maher finds that actual gradients do not conform to Miller's assumptions about them. Moreover, it is often the case that when animals (rats) are deliberately dropped into what should be an avoidance area, they tend to run *toward* the goal rather than away from it as Miller's model requires. Also, when conflicts are viewed in a *temporal* sense rather than in a spatial one (e.g., time elapsing before a feared and desired event occurs rather than physical distance from a goal), the findings do not conform to the conflict model at all. Once again we see the necessity for establishing the *generality* of a psychological finding. While Miller's model may be useful for some purposes, Maher's criticisms make it clear that it cannot be generalized to other forms of conflict nor can it account for all of the findings within its own frame of reference.

Defense

The psychological study of defensive behaviors owes its intellectual heritage to Sigmund Freud. Defense mechanisms such as repression, projection, rationalization (see Chapter 4), and so forth, are thought to protect the individual from the conscious and disruptive effects of anxiety. All individuals are thought to possess and utilize such patterns of anxiety avoidance. For the most part, such defenses are considered to be automatic and unconscious parts of the personality, occurring without the awareness of the person.

Repression, the automatic shutting out of awareness of disturbing impulses or thoughts, is by far the most heavily researched defensive response to anxiety. The data are by no means clear. However, results consistent with the hypothesis that forgetting, similar to the process of repression, can occur have been reported. Levinger and Clark (1961), for example, took physiological measures of "emotionality" while subjects responded to a word association task. The experimenter might say the word "green" and the subject might respond with the word "grass." While this was taking place, physiological measures of his "emotional responses" were also gathered. The experimenters were able in this fashion to gather the differential emotional responses that subjects might make to various stimuli. After the subject had completed the list of word associations, he was asked to try to remember his original responses as the list was repeated. Interestingly enough, the subject showed inferior ability to recall those words on which he displayed increased "emotionality." This finding, although it does not prove the existence of repression, is at least consistent with it.

The study of *perceptual defense* has a long and checkered history. The term grew out of the observation that recognition thresholds for anxiety-provoking words seemed higher (it took longer to recognize them) than for neutral words. Thus, for example, if a subject were to look into a tachistoscope (an instrument by which the duration of exposure of a stimulus can be precisely controlled) and see the word "house," he might very likely require less exposure time to recognize the word than if it were a "taboo" word such as bitch, belly, or Kotex. Even though psychologists agreed that recognition times varied for so-called taboo words and neutral words and that recognition of taboo words apparently took longer, they were not in agreement as to how this finding might be explained. There were those of course who argued that the higher thresholds for recognition of taboo words was evidence of a "defensive perceptual process." Other psychologists pointed out that more simple explanations might be offered. One obvious alternative explanation was simply that subjects recognized the taboo words but were reluctant to say them out loud in the formal context of a psychological experiment. Another argument focused on the differential *familiarity* of taboo words versus neutral words. Since taboo words might very well be less familiar to subjects than neutral words, this fact alone would explain why it took longer for subjects to recognize them, and in that case one need not postulate a process of perceptual defense to explain the finding.

It is now clear, however, that even when these two alternative explanations for the data are controlled for, a process of *perceptual vigilance* exists in addition to the process of perceptual defense (Ericksen and Pierce, 1968). Although some subjects seem to take longer than others to recognize emotionally reactive stimuli, others seem to require even *less* time when comparisons with neutral stimuli are made. Perceptual vigilance is the term used to describe the case in which recognition time is even shorter than one would expect it to be for neutral stimuli. The existence of both of these processes was hypothesized by Postman, Bruner, and McGinnies in 1948 when they first undertook studies of this nature.

Quite recently, however, personality psychologists have postulated the existence of two different types of persons; namely, *repressors* and *sensitizers.* Repressors, as the name implies, are those who use avoidance defenses when confronted with emotionally reactive stimuli. They tend to rely upon repression as a major defense against anxiety. Sensitizers are thought to be the opposite. They are likely to be quite alert to emotionally reactive words and not rely at all upon repression. In perceptual recognition situations repressors take longer to recognize an emotionally reactive stimulus; sensitizers take less time to recognize such a stimulus. In real life contexts repressors are those who are likely to minimize threat and unpleasant life experiences in line with their preference for avoidance and repressive defenses. Sensitizers are likely to augment threat rather than reduce it; they are constantly on the alert for signs of threat and rejection in their interpersonal relationships. Repressors are likely to say only socially desirable things about themselves, to have favorable self-concepts, and generally avoid thinking unpleasant thoughts. Sensitizers are more willing to admit socially undesirable things about themselves, to admit to unfavorable self-concepts, and seem more willing to dwell on the unpleasant aspects of life. Sensitizers show greater appreciation of sexual and aggressive humor, things that are apparently not very pleasing to repressors. Repressors are less likely to remember tasks in which they have failed.

In general, then, we can conclude that the twin processes of perceptual defense and perceptual vigilance do exist and do influence behavior. However, the *conceptual similarity* of these processes to Freud's concept of repression is not altogether clear. Remember that Freud conceived of repression as the automatic and unconscious forgetting of anxiety-provoking impulses or content. The relationship between this type of process and elevated recognition is not clear. Obviously, subjects, even repressors, *will eventually report recognition of a stimulus* if exposure times are sufficiently lengthened. In fact, there is but a fraction of a second difference between defensive perception and normal perception. This hardly seems an experimental analogy to Freud's view of the severity and pervasiveness of forgetting as delineated in his concept of repression.

When subjects recall fewer of the words that are associated with "emotionality" in a word association test, it is equally uncertain what relationship this observation might have to Freud's concept of repression. If the experiment were carried out for several additional trials and the subjects then attempted to remember the forgotten words, they might quickly recover them.

It is difficult to draw firm conclusions with regard to defenses other than repression. Although clinical observations verifying the importance of such things as rationalization, projection, and denial continue to be readily available, controlled experimental demonstrations of such processes have not been achieved. Quite recently a process similar to "denial" has been reported by Lazarus (1964). Lazarus had male college students view a film on puberty rites among a primitive people. The rites involved a painful scene in which public circumcision was performed on a group of boys. Two different soundtracks accompanied the film. One soundtrack augmented the repugnant aspects of the situation by commenting on the severe pain sustained by the boys, the unsanitary conditions under which the operation was performed, and so forth. Another soundtrack was employed that extolled the virtues of the rites and minimized the repugnant features by claiming that it was a "joyous" occasion for the boys because it marked their transition to manhood. In a sense, the augmenting sound track facilitated sensitizing defenses and the minimizing soundtrack facilitated the defensive process of "denial." That is, the emotionally traumatic aspects of the film could be denied more readily by the observers who heard the minimizing soundtrack. Lazarus gathered both verbal and physiological measures of the reactions of his subjects to the film and the two different soundtracks. As was expected, viewers exposed to the soundtrack which facilitated "denial" of the painful aspects of the circumcision rites showed lower anxiety in both their verbal reports and physiological responses.

Once again, however, one is not certain as to how these results relate to Freud's concept of the defense of denial. One could argue that rather than demonstrating the existence of denial, the experiment simply demonstrated that the one stimulus (the film plus the minimizing sound track) was simply less emotionally traumatic than the other stimulus (the film plus the augmenting sound track). In other words, one could achieve the same effect by showing one group a film depicting the horrors of a concentration camp and another group a film about the joys of butterfly hunting. The differences in emotional reaction likely to occur would be entirely a function of the fact that two different stimuli, one emotionally provocative and the other emotionally neutral, had been shown. In other words, differences in emotionality would be attributable to differences in the stimuli and not in a "denial" process taking place inside the viewer.

We may conclude, then, that processes *consistent* with such concepts as repression and denial have been suggested by psychological research. Moreover, it appears likely that a personality dimension of repression-sensitization may also exist. The precise relationship of these processes to the concept of defense mechanisms as advanced by Freud remains uncertain and in need of further research.

Tactics versus defenses. Quite recently, Sechrest and Wallace (1967) have provided an extended discussion of an alternative to the classic concept of defense. These authors view many interpersonal behaviors as *learned tactics* in the service of overall strategies in interpersonal interaction. In Chapter 7, in which interpersonal interaction is considered, we will consider the concept of tactics further.

THE SELF CONCEPT

As we pointed out in Chapter 4, psychologists have long been interested in such things as the attitudes of a person towards himself, self-perceptions, beliefs concerning the self, and expectations about self. In this section, we will briefly consider efforts to translate such interests into research.

The perceived self and the ideal self

Much of the research on the self concept has centered on the fact that people seem to possess a view of the self as it is at the moment as well as a sense of what they would like it to be. We can speak of the *perceived self*, or actual self, and the *ideal self*. A considerable amount of research has gone into determining the effects of discrepancies between the perceptions of the self as it is and as the person would like it to be. Byrne (1966) has recently summarized much of this research. It would appear that in some studies the extent of this self-ideal discrepancy is related to measures of maladjustment in a straightforward, linear fashion, i.e., the greater the discrepancy, the greater the maladjustment of the person. However, Byrne questions whether or not this simple linear relationship is the correct one. He reasons that self-appraisals can be subject to deliberate lying and misrepresentation, unconscious distortion, inaccurate perception of reality, and so forth. On this basis, he concludes that one must consider *unrealistically low* self-ideal discrepancies as well as extremely high self-ideal discrepancies in maladjusted persons. In other words, Byrne is arguing that either a very low discrepancy or a very high discrepancy is indicative of maladjustment. Byrne is convinced that the relationship between self-ideal discrepancy and maladjustment is not linear but actually *curvilinear*. He further argues that persons high in repressive defenses are likely to show low self-ideal discrepancies, whereas those high in sensitizing defenses are likely to show very high self-ideal discrepancies. As a consequence, we can expect extreme repressors to be maladjusted while reporting low self-ideal discrepancies and extreme sensitizers to be maladjusted as well while reporting high self-ideal discrepancies. Indeed, as Byrne points out, research seems to support this hypothesis in which the self-ideal discrepancy is viewed from the perspective of the typical defensive style used by the person.

Parental behaviors and attitudes and self-esteem.

In an extensive study of the factors giving rise to self-esteem, Coopersmith (1967) has provided us with several fascinating findings. It is clear from Coopersmith's research that in children widely accepted public notions of the effects of success, status, and physical appearance upon self-esteem do *not* bear up under careful scrutiny. Self-esteem did *not* relate significantly to height and physical attractiveness. Moreover, it appeared to be only weakly related to social status and academic performance.

The most significant findings in Coopersmith's research concern significant persons, parents or peers, in the lives of children. Favorable treatment by such significant persons is likely to enhance feelings of self-worth and self-esteem. Interestingly enough, Coopersmith shows that the setting of definite *limits* on their children's behavior by parents is one factor associated with high self-esteem. Contrary to much of the lore on *total permissiveness* as a parental strategy, Coopersmith found that excessive permissiveness did not result in elevated levels of self-esteem. The highest levels of self-esteem were found in the children of parents who set quite explicit limits on what the child could and could not do but who still provided the child with ample freedom for self-expression and self-determination. In other words, high self-esteem was associated with families in which parents maintained a clear expression of "parental authority." Coopersmith concludes that a child in such families "concludes that he is indeed significant to his parents, which is evidenced as much by their restrictions as by their attention and concern" (Coopersmith, 1967, p. 244).

In a direct study of the person's perceptions of the attitudes of his parents toward him and his own self-concept, Jourard and Remy (1955) found that self-regarding attitudes correlated quite highly with perceptions of the parents' attitudes toward the self. The more a person tended to perceive his parents' attitudes toward himself as favorable, the more positive was his self-concept.

In an interesting study Suinn (1961) demonstrated that the extent to which one accepted one's parents correlated to the extent to which one accepted oneself. By having his subject report on his own self-ideal discrepancy as well as on his father's, Suinn was able to make comparisons among the discrepancies between the actual self and the ideal self and discrepancies between the subject's perceptions of the father's actual self and ideal self. A subject with a low self-ideal discrepancy was defined as one who accepted himself. A subject who perceived his father as having a low self-ideal discrepancy was defined as one who accepted his father. Subjects who had low self-ideal discrepancies were found to be more likely to attribute low self-ideal discrepancies to the father as well.

Accuracy of self-perception and perceptual defense

From research it would appear that persons who possess an accurate self-concept are less likely to be defensive than those who do not. Chodorkoff (1954) had subjects give self-descriptions and then had expert judges give descriptions of the subject. Of course, the judges did not use the subject's self-descriptions as a basis for judgment but made their judgments independently. The accuracy of self-perception was measured by the size of the discrepancy between the person's self-perceptions and the judges' perceptions of him. The lower the discrepancy, the greater the accuracy of self-perception.

Chodorkoff then had his subjects perform in a typical perceptual defense task. He discovered that accuracy of the self-concept was related to low measures of defensiveness. The greater the accuracy score, the more rapidly the subject recognized "threatening" stimuli. It would appear, then, that accuracy of the self-concept is associated with a nondefensive style at least in the typical perceptual defense experiment.

Mood fluctuation and self-acceptance

From our own life experiences we are given to expect that our moods will be much more positive when we are in a period of self-acceptance; conversely, we are likely to be in the "dumps" when we find it difficult to accept ourselves. Of course this is a bit like the chicken and the egg problem. Which comes first, a wave of depression followed by a drop in self-acceptance or a drop in self-acceptance followed by a wave of depression? It is often difficult to tell. However, from research on mood fluctuations conducted by Wesman and Ricks (1966) it is clear, at least for Radcliffe and Harvard students, that depression is associated with significant drops in self-esteem, the appearance of self-derogatory attitudes, and marked obsession and preoccupation with self.

Another intriguing finding of the work by Wesman and Ricks on mood variability concerns the fact that people could be categorized as either *very stable* or *highly variable* in mood fluctuation. That is, some persons seemed to vary very little in the day to day fluctuations of their moods. Others seemed to ride wild roller coasters of elation and despair, plunging from the heights to the depths within the course of a single day and over several days. Do stable and variable persons show differences in self-concept? Wesman and Ricks' findings indicate that they do.

When considering the ways in which their actual selves differed from their ideal selves, stable men felt that they were much too "cautious, too isolated, and insufficiently warm, friendly, free, and spontaneous." On the other hand, variable men felt that they "spread themselves too thin, could not fulfill their ambitions, and were lacking in composure and the ability to absorb frustrations." As Wesman and Ricks put it, "The self-ideal descriptions suggested that stable men had subjected inner pressures to the demand of steadiness in confronting the environment, and had been rewarded with emotional stability and 'character.' The variable men were more subject to inner turmoil, and were more vulnerable, but were rewarded with a more intense inner life and greater responsiveness and originality" (Wesman and Ricks, 1966, pp. 249-250). Once again, we are reminded that life may be little more than a series of trade-offs in which it is quite difficult to maximize everything. If we are to believe Wesman and Ricks' findings concerning stable and variable men, one can achieve the steadiness of "character" at the expense of a rich inner life. But originality and a rich inner life come at the expense of greater inner turmoil, as shown by the moody men studied. Of course, there is no reason to believe that this is necessarily the case. The careful study of the lives of many great men, particularly those who undergo spiritual transformation in the quest for mystical and religious experience, suggests that inner richness can occur without paying the high price of inner turmoil and careening moods. The trick, of course, is in knowing how to reach such an enviable state of complex and creative serenity. About that psychologists know very little, but the ancient mystics apparently knew a great deal. Perhaps as psychologists turn their attentions to such things as meditation, fasting, and various systems of mystical beliefs, more will be revealed.

SUMMARY

In this chapter, we have attempted to introduce the student to some of the enormous body of work that has been accomplished in the study of the individual. Obviously we could not hope to cover it all. There is much that we have not considered, e.g., intelligence and its measurement, development of the person, the study of formal cognitive structures and processes, perception, sensation, and so forth. We have, however, treated topics such as social motives and their measurement, anxiety, conflict, and defense, and the self-concept. Our discussion has led us to consider the achievement motivation, power, manipulation and machiavellian motives, hostility and aggression, the personality correlates of anxiety-proneness, the nature of intrapersonal conflict, research on defense mechanisms, repression and sensitization as a personality dimension, and a host of studies concerned with self-esteem and self-acceptance.

Our approach has been clearly selective. The topics chosen seem particularly relevant both to the student and to the problems of social thought and behavior characteristic of contemporary American society. By treating some of these topics in greater depth and forgoing any attempt at extensive but necessarily superficial coverage, we hope to have presented with greater clarity the nature of research at the individual level of analysis. Hopefully the student is aware of the many complexities that lurk here as well as the ways in which the inquisitive psychologist goes about his business.

Our attentions now turn from the individual level of analysis. In the next two chapters we will concern ourselves with psychological inquiry at the interpersonal level of analysis. Our first problem concerns interpersonal knowing. What does it mean to "know" something about another? What is it that affects what we come to "know" about other persons? As we shall see, these are fascinating questions.

References

Atkinson, J. W.: Motivational determinants of risk-taking behavior. *In* Atkinson, J. W. (ed.): *Motives in Fantasy, Action and Society*, New York, D. Van Nostrand Co., Inc., 1958.

Bandura, A., and Walters, R. H.: *Social Learning and Personality Development*. New York, Holt, Rinehart and Winston, 1963.

Berkowitz, L.: *Roots of Aggression: A Reexamination of the Frustration-Aggression Hypothesis*. Menlo Park, Atherton, 1968.

Birney, R. C.: Research on the achievement motive. *In* Borgatta, E. F., and Lambert, W. W. (eds.): *Handbook of Personality Theory and Research*. Chicago, Rand McNally & Co., 1968.

Broverman, D. M., Jordan, E. J., and Phillips, L.: Achievement motivation in fantasy and behavior. J. Abnorm. Soc. Psychol., *60*: 374, 1960.

Byrne, D.: *An Introduction to Personality*. Englewood Cliffs, Prentice-Hall, Inc., 1966.

Chodorkoff, B.: Self-perception, perceptual defense, and adjustment. J. Abnorm. Soc. Psychol., *49*: 508, 1954.

Christie, R., and Geis, F.: Some consequences of taking Machiavelli seriously. *In* Borgatta, E. F., and Lambert, W. W. (eds.): *Handbook of Personality Theory and Research*. Chicago, Rand McNally & Co., 1968.

Cole, D., Jacobs, S., and Zubok, B.: The relation of achievement imagery scores to academic performance. J. Abnorm. Soc. Psychol. *65*: 208, 1962.

Coopersmith, S.: *The Antecedents of Self-Esteem*. San Francisco, W. H. Freeman and Co., 1967.

Davies, J. C.: The J-curve of rising and declining satisfactions as a cause of some great revolutions and a contained rebellion. *In: Violence in America: Official Report to the National Commission on the Causes and Prevention of Violence*. New York, Signet Books, 1969.

Domhoff, G. W.: *Who Rules America?* Englewood Cliffs, Prentice-Hall, Inc., 1967.

Ericksen, C., and Pierce, J.: Defense mechanisms. *In* Borgatta, E. F., and Lambert, W. W. (eds.): *Handbook of Personality Theory and Research*. Chicago, Rand McNally & Co., 1968.

Hill, K. T., and Sarason, S. B.: The relation of test anxiety and defensiveness to test and school performance over the elementary school years: a further longitudinal study. Monogr. Soc. Res. Child Develop.; *31*: 1, (Serial No. 104), 1966.

Jourard, S. M., and Remy, R. M.: Perceived parental attitudes, the self, and security. J. Consult. Psychol., *19*: 364, 1955.

Kenny, D. T.: An experimental test of the catharsis theory of aggression. Unpublished doctoral dissertation. University of Washington, 1962.

Lasswell, H.: *Power and Personality*, New York, W. W. Norton and Company, Inc., 1948.

Lazarus, R. S.: A laboratory approach to the dynamics of psychological stress. *In* Grosser, G. H., et al. (eds.): *The Threat of Impending Disaster*. Cambridge, The M.I.T. Press, 1964.

Levinger, G., and Clark, J.: Emotional factors in the forgetting of work associations. J. Abnorm. Soc. Psychol., *62*: 99, 1961.

Lorenz, K.: *On Aggression*. New York, Harcourt, Brace and World, 1963.

Lowe, M. C.: The equivalence of guilt and anxiety as psychological constructs. J. Consult. Psychol., *28*: 553, 1964.

Mahrer, B.: *Principles of Psychopathology*. New York, McGraw-Hill Book Co., 1966.

McClelland, D. C.: Methods of measuring motivation. *In* Atkinson, J. W. (ed.): *Motives in Fantasy, Action, and Society*. New York, D. Van Nostrand Co., Inc., 1958a.

McClelland, D. C.: Risk-taking in children with high and low need for achievement. *In* Atkinson, J. W. (ed.): *Motives in Fantasy, Action and Society*. New York, D. Van Nostrand Co., Inc., 1958b.

Miller, N. E.: Liberalization of basic S-R concepts: extensions to conflict behavior, motivation, and social learning. *In* Koch, S. (ed.): *Psychology: A Study of a Science*. New York, McGraw-Hill Book Co., 1959.

Postman, L., Bruner, J., and McGinnies, E.: Personal values as selective factors in perception. J. Abnorm. Soc. Psychol., *43*: 142, 1948.

Rosenberg, M.: The association between self-esteem and anxiety. J. Psychiat. Res., *66*: 91, 1962.
Sechrest, L. B., and Wallace, J.: *Psychology and Human Problems.* Columbus, Charles Merrill, 1967.
Spence, J. T.: Learning theory and personality. *In* Wepman, J., and Heine, R. W. (eds.): *Concepts of Personality.* Chicago, Aldine, 1963.
Suinn, R. M.: The relationship between self-acceptance and acceptance of others: a learning theory analysis. J. Abnorm. Soc. Psychol., *63*:37, 1961.
Suinn, R. M., and Hill, H.: Influence of anxiety on the relationship between self-acceptance and acceptance of others. J. Consult. Psychol., *28*: 116, 1964.
Walker, D.: *Rights in Conflict: Official Report to the National Commission on the Causes and Prevention of Violence.* New York, Signet Books, 1968.
Wallach, M. A., and Kogan, N.: *Modes of Thinking in Young Children.* New York, Holt, Rinehart and Winston, 1965.
Wesman, A. E., and Ricks, D. F.: *Mood and Personality.* New York, Holt, Rinehart and Winston, 1966.

CHAPTER 6

Interpersonal Knowing

As we go about our affairs, each of us, whether he likes it or not, must interact with many different persons. In the course of these interactions we come to "know" things about the other persons with whom we interact. We may, for example, decide that this person is to be trusted but that one is not. We seem attracted to some persons and repelled by others. A host of impressions vie for our attentions. The other persons we meet seem industrious, shy, ambitious, friendly, sneaky, hostile, cheerful, suspicious, angry, fearful, creative, nasty, pedantic, and so forth.

At times we seem intensely interested in anticipating the future behaviors of other persons. The husband, for example, is frequently more than mildly interested in his spouse's probable reaction to his decision to do this or that. Certain students are reputed to be masters of the game of predicting what particular professors will ask on examinations. Boy-girl relationships, at least in American society, seem fraught with dangerous uncertainties, and efforts to predict the future take the form of questions such as, "I wonder what he will do if I do that" or, "How might she react if I suggest that?"

These and many other possible examples suggest that the process of coming to know others is one of central importance for understanding interpersonal interaction. These judgments of others, the impressions we form of them, the ways in which we categorize them, and our efforts to predict their likely behaviors have important implications for our behavior toward them. Obviously our behavior toward a disliked person is likely to be quite different from our behavior toward a person to whom we are attracted; and if we construe another person as a "hostile" person, we are very likely to behave differently in his presence than in the presence of a person construed as "friendly." Our expectations about the future behaviors of others with whom we interact can and do exert powerful influences over our own behavior.

In short, though many of us are hard pressed to give a reasonable account of how it is we have come to "know" something about others, the fact remains that we do arrive at such conclusions. Moreover, these conclusions about others importantly affect our behavior toward them.

The assumed incompatibility of analytical and subjective skills

From the outset of our discussion it is important to note that resistances to analytical understanding of interpersonal knowing do exist. For many persons interpersonal knowing is the outcome of more subjective skills frequently labeled "intuitive" skills. Many of these persons are unwilling or reluctant to examine analytically the bases for their conclusions about others. For some, the use of analytical skills in interpersonal interaction is regarded as objectionable or even, perhaps, dangerous. For others, careful analysis appears incompatible with warm, spontaneous, and exciting interpersonal interaction. Impressed by the compelling immediacy of their perceptions of others, many persons refuse to entertain the possibility that their perceptions might, in some instances, be highly idiosyncratic or even downright incorrect. It is intriguing to note that the belief that each of us is blessed with marvelous powers of "intuition" persists despite the fact that it has proved terribly difficult to define "intuition," that our "intuitive" perceptions are frequently shown to be wrong, and that research has amply demonstrated that much more than "intuition" is involved in coming to know others.

Despite these commonly held assumptions that analytic skills are inappropriate for understanding interpersonal knowledge, it would appear that the facts are to the contrary. From our perspective, knowledge about the process of coming to know others cannot but help one to become a more sensitive, aware, perceptive, and sophisticated person in his interaction with others. Considering the complexities of the process as well as the many pitfalls which await the unwary traveler who must pass through this difficult terrain each day of his life, it would appear that one needs all of his wits about him all the time.

The assumption that certain intellectual skills are somehow incompatible with the most desirable qualities of spontaneity, warmth, and sensitivity in interactions with others certainly requires careful reexamination. Obviously, one can imagine situations in which careful intellectual analysis would be highly inappropriate, e.g., the passion of the lovers' embrace. On the other hand, one can easily imagine situations in which such analysis is indispensable, e.g., decision-making situations in which large expenditures of human and material resources are at stake. But for the most part, the vast majority of human interpersonal settings call for both analytical and subjective skills. The poet e. e. cummings had a point when he wrote:

> Since feeling is first,
> whoever pays attention to
> the syntax of things will
> never wholly kiss you. . . .

However, it seems a bit ironic that Cummings chose to develop his convictions about the primacy of feeling in one of the most intellectually demanding of all literary forms, the short poem.

From our perspective, it is more fruitful to think of intellect and emotion as complementary and capable of integration in the life of the person rather than as incompatible and even antagonistic forces. It is probably true that intellect and emotion are incompatible only to the extent that we *choose* to think of them as such.

Interaction with others, then, involves much more than feeling. There is much that we can come to know that will help in our quest for understanding of why it is that we arrive at certain conclusions about other persons. In this chapter we will examine the nature of interpersonal knowing. We will consider the many factors that affect the impressions we form of other persons and the judgments we make of them, the ways in which we categorize others, and the bases for our predictions of their behavior. As we shall see, interpersonal knowing is a subject of vital interest to the student of social thought and behavior.

The human being as a complex information processing system

It is possible to view a creature as complex as the human being from many different perspectives, and although each of these perspectives may advance our understanding to some degree or another, it is clear that none of them are totally adequate for comprehensive understanding of human behavior. Obviously human beings are at once much more than a bundle of "habits," a collection of "traits," a hodgepodge of "needs," or, as we suggest here, "complex information processing systems." Nonetheless, analogies such as these are useful for certain purposes. Conceiving of human beings as complex information processing systems seems particularly useful for understanding interpersonal behavior. But what does it mean to conceptualize the human being in this manner?

At each moment of his life, the human being is literally bombarded with large amounts of information. Information from the *external* environment in the form of visual, auditory, tactile, olfactory, and gustatory physical energies is unceasing. Stimulation from *within* our bodies contributes as well. Sensations arising from receptors in our muscles, tendons, and joints provide us with information necessary for proper locomotion. From receptors in the inner ear we are provided with information for establishing spatial orientation, body tilt, and body movement. Our thoughts, fantasies, and dreams further expand the pool of information to which we are exposed. Clearly we cannot attend to all of this information at once. As intricate as the human information processing system is, it seems to possess limits on the amount of information with which it can deal at any given moment in time. As a consequence, human consciousness can include only a minute portion of the vast amount of potentially available information on any given occasion. In this sense, human beings are highly *selective* information systems; that is, from the vast amount of potential information to which we could attend, we attend to only a tiny fraction. We are selective in terms of the information that is actually *registered* as well as in terms of the particular information we *seek*.

Information overload, cognitive strain, and interpersonal knowing

As we shall see, the limitations on the human information processing system in the face of almost overwhelming complexity have important implications for interpersonal knowing. As the amount of information to which we attend increases, cognitive strain also increases. At some point the effort and personal discomfort involved in further increases in information result in increased *selectivity* and even *active avoidance* of further information. The strain on cognitive processes such as judgment, memory, logical reasoning, categorizing, and so forth, becomes too burdensome for the individual to bear as conditions of *information overload* are approached. Perhaps it is this process that underlies the humorous remark, "Don't confuse me with further facts; my mind is already made up!"

But what has all of this to do with interpersonal knowing? As in the comprehension of physical objects and phenomena, cognitive processes such as judgment, categorization, memory, and so forth, are involved in the comprehension of *social* objects. Each individual that we meet is truly an enormously complex creature. Rather than deal with the many complexities of each individual human that we encounter, we tend toward selectivity; that is, we attend to some information about the person and ignore other information. We seek out certain information about the other person while not troubling ourselves with other information.

Consider the familiar social phenomenon known as *stereotyping*. On the basis of some distinguishable attribute such as skin color, hair length, ethnic background, or religious preference, individual human beings are lumped together indiscriminately and treated as if they possessed other attributes common to that class. Hence, blacks are often regarded by racially prejudiced persons as lazy, dishonest, hypersexual, and born with a natural sense of rhythm. "Hippies," a truly fictional social category, are invariably described by many persons as dirty, lazy, addicted to dope, and morally depraved. Jews are still thought by many as "crafty" and not to be trusted in business matters. One must not suppose, however, that stereotyping is restricted to racially, ethnically, or religiously prejudiced people. Numerous other distinctions serve as the bases for stereotyping. Body build, occupation, hair color ("blondes have more fun"), style of dress, and so forth, can be employed for the creation of misleading and irrational categorizations of human beings.

It is probably true that stereotypical thinking is characteristic of virtually all of us. Since it is a socially encouraged and even directly taught process, even the most aware person can scarcely escape its temptations in the face of information complexity. However, we must not suppose that the use of stereotypes is totally valueless. An *accurate* stereotype can actually aid one in the difficult task of judging others. Because large numbers of persons within a given society share common values, beliefs, and patterns of behavior, it is possible to construct a reasonably correct view of the *generalized other*. That is, what is true of one member of a given society or a segment within that society may *probably* be true of another as well.

Our problems in the use of stereotypes arise when we rely upon inaccurate stereotypes and when we fail to consider possible differences as well as similarities among persons. For example, in the current debate over campus turmoil in this nation and others, one searches in vain for a carefully differentiated portrait of the various participants. Unfortunately, many observers prefer to deal with such complexities in terms of familiar stereotypes of "students," "faculty," and "administrators." There seems to be little recognition of the fact that students differ greatly in terms of their goals, values, beliefs, and typical patterns of behavior. Such differences are characteristic of faculty and administrators as well. When each participant in a social conflict situation persists in construing the other in terms of stereotypes, solutions do not appear and conflict tends toward further escalation.

Stereotyping is but one of a number of ways in which human beings attempt to deal with information complexity, and in subsequent pages we will examine other strategies for dealing with such complexity. For the moment, however, the student should have a rudimentary understanding of the significance of apparent limitation in the information processing capacities of human beings. Information complexity and overload give rise to cognitive strain, which in turn produces pressures toward selectivity. Often our "knowledge" about others reflects the information to which we have chosen to attend rather than information we might consider.

The active nature of social inference

The study of human perception in its most general sense is one of the most intriguing areas of inquiry in psychology. When we stop and consider the matter closely, it becomes apparent that our senses and brains do not act faithfully to record that which is "out there." In point of fact, the study of perception has been stimulated largely by the many seeming paradoxes of human perception. We are struck by the many *noncor-*

respondences between the physical world and the world of our senses and perception. For example, consider the *perceived size* of objects. It is clear that the perceived size of an object does not depend solely upon the size of the image falling upon the retina of the eye. Or to take another example, the phenomenon of *apparent movement* indicates that we may perceive movement when none has, in fact, occurred. Various *constancy* phenomena are further examples of noncorrespondence between the physical world and the world of perception. Objects will display a constancy of shape even though our viewing angle may change radically.

For centuries poets have made extensive use of noncorrespondence by attributing properties to objects that they obviously do not possess. Terms such as "angry" oceans, "noble" mountains, and so forth, evidence the tendency of human beings to elaborate the physical world in terms of properties that it does not possess.

It is clear from these and many other possible examples

Figure 18. A sophisticated social perceiver is one who is aware of the process by which he arrives at conclusions about others. (Photo by Cathy L. Jones.)

that human perception is an active rather than a passive process. Human beings are constantly *interpreting* information from their senses. Although we do not realize that such is the case, our "knowledge" about the physical and social worlds surrounding us is a collection of inferences about the nature of physical and social reality. In many cases, we leap far beyond the available information to arrive at conclusions. Often our inferences about ourselves, others, and events in which we are involved are based upon scanty, fragmentary, and even contradictory information.

In approaching the study of interpersonal knowledge, it is important to remember the distinction between *observation* and *inference,* as drawn in Chapter 2. Many of our difficulties in interpersonal interaction stem from the fact that two observers may view the same event but draw completely different inferences from their observations. Each, however, will insist vigorously that he has recorded faithfully the truth of the matter. Unfortunately, each may have failed to learn an important lesson in the conduct of human affairs. There is no such thing as a completely passive observer. Any account of the nature of things represents an active elaboration on the part of the observer; and it is here that psychological analysis begins. What is it that influences the inferences we draw about the nature of ourselves, others, and events in which we are involved? Let us begin to answer this question.

PROPERTIES OF THE OBSERVER

Only by the wildest stretch of the imagination can we conceive of the person as an "empty" organism reacting indiscriminately to and controlled totally by external stimulation. The person does not "check his complexity at the door" when he enters into interaction with others. He brings into such interactions the experiences of his past and his hopes for the future. His beliefs, values, emotions, preferences, attitudes, and expectations combine in intricate and often poorly understood ways to influence the way he thinks about a given interaction as well as the ways in which he is likely to behave. His purposes for entering the interaction, his goals for the interaction, and what he expects to achieve by interacting are further important determinants of what he is likely to perceive. The language that he possesses for describing other persons may act as a very effective filter for what is registered in his consciousness.

In short, the properties of the observer himself are critical determinants of the inferences he draws in interaction with others. Let us first consider these numerous properties of observers and the ways in which they influence the conclusions drawn about others.

Inferential sets and interpersonal knowledge

If we can identify the goals toward which an observer is striving in any given interaction, it becomes possible to make some statements about the information to which he will likely attend and about the inferences he will draw from such information. Two social psychologists, Jones and Thibaut (1958), have given us a convincing account of the importance of what they term "inferential sets." The term "set" is generally defined as a tendency or predisposition to respond in a given way. An inferential set is a tendency toward certain inferences in interaction with others. The goals of the person in any given interaction give rise to particular inferential sets. Let us consider briefly three inferential sets discussed by Jones and Thibaut.

Value-maintenance set. When the person in interaction with others is seeking *confirmation* of or *social support* for his beliefs, values, or emotional feelings, a value-maintenance set arises. For example, an executive who is uncertain about several decisions he has made might call a meeting with his subordinates for the ostensible purpose of discussing his decisions with them. In actuality, however, the executive might use the interaction to solicit support for and approval of these decisions. Uncertain about the correctness of his actions and seeking social support for them, the executive might very well focus upon information from the group of subordinates that confirms his prior actions and beliefs. Moreover, it is likely that he would tend to ascribe positive attributes to those whose opinions agreed with his own. The important point is that the value-maintenance set can act as a selective filtering device in interpersonal interaction. When we are seeking social support for our beliefs, values, and actions, it is likely that we will be more sensitive to information relevant to this purpose than to information that is not.

Situation-matching set. Individuals may approach interactions with the sole purpose of judging the actions of other persons and administering rewards or punishments to them. Examples of this inferential set, the situation-matching set, are not difficult to find. Many mothers, seemingly obsessed with bringing their children up "correctly," appear incapable of viewing their children's behavior in alternative ways. The important question for such a mother is simply, "Is he being good or bad?"

In this example there are serious consequences of excessive situation-matching, both for the development of the child and for the interaction between the child and its parent. Perfectly innocent behaviors, which might go unremarked in another household, are construed as "bad," and punishments are administered accordingly. Even positive characteristics, e.g., curiosity and high energy levels, may be labeled "bad" under mother's scrutiny, and through punishment the child may be trained away from desirable traits. Moreover, the parent who consistently approaches her child's behavior in terms of a situation-matching set will find that many more occasions for discipline are likely to arise than if alternative inferential sets were employed. As a consequence, the quality of the parent-child relationship is likely to take on certain undesirable features.

Finally, concern with situation-matching may prevent one from ever coming to understand the other person with whom he interacts. When the issue becomes one of deciding when to reward and when to punish, one is involved in the exercise of *power*, not the search for understanding. The mother who persists in construing the behavior of her child as deserving of either reward or punishment only may never come to understand her own children. The teacher who waves the grading curve over his students like a club may have conforming and obedient students in his classroom but he will not succeed in educating them, nor will he ever know what his students really think of his ideas.

Causal-genetic set. When our primary reason for interacting with another person is to discover why he behaves as he does, we are operating under a causal-genetic set. It seems reasonable to suppose that a person will attend to a broader base of information when he attempts to discover the reasons for the behavior of the other person rather than when he attempts to decide upon the social acceptability of the behavior. The professional psychologist typically operates under the causal-genetic set. He does not enter interaction with his client in order that he might make moral pronouncements about the unacceptability of his client's behavior, nor does he attempt to gain support from his client for particular values, beliefs, or attitudes that he, the psychologist, might hold. Although the psychologist might unwittingly pursue such goals on occasion with his clients, his interests, for the most part, are directed toward discovering why it is that his client behaves as he does. The psychologist may conduct a thorough search of the client's past as well as a careful analysis of his current life situation in search of clues for the client's behavior. As one can readily appreciate, a search of these proportions can lead one to consider an enormous amount of information about the other person that would not be considered under some other interactional set.

Summary of inferential sets. As we have seen, the goals and purposes of the observer in any given interaction can importantly influence what information he seeks and what information he finds. Jones and Thibaut's account of inferential sets is an intuitively appealing explanation of how the goals of the observer enter into the perception of the other person. At least one study (Jones and deCharms, 1958) has provided some empirical support for their hypotheses. When different inferential sets were deliberately aroused in groups of observers attending to the same situation (a fictional "tape-recorded interview" with two American soldiers who had signed propaganda statements against the United States while prisoners of war in Korea), different perceptions in the groups were obtained. Persons who listened to the tape recording with one inferential set had different perceptions of the two soldiers than those who listened under another inferential set.

Language and interpersonal knowing

There is an old truism that goes something like this: What happens to us in life is not nearly so important as what we *choose to tell ourselves* about what has happened. There is more than a grain of truth in this simple but profound statement. Caught in the rush of events, we often overlook the simple fact that we could choose to tell ourselves many different things about events in which we are involved. Although reality may exist in some objective and abstract sense, all that we can come to know of it consists of various representations. Upon the raw stuff of experience we impose symbolic representations—efforts to make our worlds comprehensible and predictable to us. The manner in which we choose to construe events in which we are involved is hardly trivial. For example, many of us know of persons with seemingly identical life experiences. However, their attitudes toward such experiences seem radically different. One man may choose to look upon adversity as an opportunity for significant learning. Another, facing the same adverse conditions, may come to the pessimistic conclusion that fate has willed to him an unhappy and unfortunate existence. Considering these widely differing representations of experience, it is not surprising to find that characteristic patterns of behavior vary. The person who construes adversity as the occasion for significant learning may very well learn from it, alter his methods or goals, and continue striving. The person who sees adversity as a sign of fate's control of his life might very well lapse into apathy and inactivity.

In short, it is our representations of reality that are important for psychological understanding. For most persons language is the means through which such representations are accomplished, and it is for this reason that language becomes important for interpersonal knowing. In a very real sense, language is the filter through which the raw stuff of experience is channeled. By the use of verbal labels and categories, it becomes possible for us to achieve some *differentiation* among the many objects, both physical and social, that make up the buzzing confusion of our everyday environments. In a very real sense, language determines what we see and what we do not see. Each of us has had the experience of being told the name of a particular flower and then suddenly finding it everywhere we look. In this sense, verbal labels make certain events more *salient* than others. The well-trained botanist very likely sees radically different things when looking at a field of wild flowers than does the layman. Similarly, the well-trained psychologist observing behavior is likely to see things that an untrained person would not notice. The fact that the botanist and the psychologist possess languages that are very different from that used by the layman helps, in part, to explain the fact that they may perceive things that others would not notice.

Styles of interpersonal description

Interpersonal languages differ rather strikingly from person to person. When we ask a group of subjects to write a description of their "best friend," individual differences in style of description emerge. Consider the following descriptions obtained from two different subjects when they were asked to describe one of their classmates:

Subject 1. Bob is tall and good looking. He has blue eyes and blonde hair. When he smiles, he is really handsome. Some of the other fellows here at school are good looking too, but not like Bob. He's the very best. I like him because he's always cheerful and friendly and he never gets mad at anybody.
Subject 2. Bob is a complicated guy. On the surface, he seems a model of self-confidence. But I know better. He's just as mixed-up as the rest of us, afraid of the draft, afraid he won't make it into college. I think he goes around smiling all the time 'cause he wants everybody to like him. But Bob's a good leader. He can get things done. He keeps himself under control real well but there are times when he can flare up and let you have it if he wants to. He pretends grades don't mean anything to him but they do. How would I describe him?—anxious to please, wants to make class president, insecure, kind.

As we can see from these examples, interesting differences are apparent in the styles of interpersonal description. Subject 1 describes her classmate Bob almost entirely in terms of *physical* rather than psychological attributes. This subject speaks almost as though Bob's most interesting characteristics were his apparent "good looks." The description is meager in terms of psychological characteristics. In addition, Bob is described in terms of consistently socially desirable characteristics—he is friendly, cheerful, and he never gets mad. In this sense, the description is one which focuses upon *congruence* among socially positive characteristics. Nothing negatively valued is mentioned. There is no incongruity at all.

Subject 2, on the other hand, presents a much more complex description of Bob. He concentrates almost entirely upon his estimate of Bob's *psychological* characteristics. Moreover, Bob is described in terms of socially acceptable as well as socially unacceptable terms. Some *incongruity* among Bob's characteristics is present in Subject 2's description. In this sense, we feel that Subject 2 has given us a far more differentiated picture of Bob than did Subject 1.

From this example, we can see that interpersonal descriptions vary along a number of important dimensions. First of all, descriptions can emphasize either *physical* or *psychological* characteristics. They can consist of *congruent*, socially acceptable characteristics with evidence of pressure toward consistency or *mixtures* of congruent and incongruent traits. Interpersonal descriptive styles which tend toward congruent characteristics may achieve a consistent picture of the other person at the expense of accuracy. That is, pressures toward consistency in description may result in a distorted picture of the other person. After all, it is possible for a person to be both "meticulous" and "spontaneous" even though we may *assume* that it is not.

Language and trait inference

As we have seen, we often "read" the activity of our own minds rather than the actual behavior of the other person. It is for this reason that language is of central concern in understanding interpersonal knowing. Much of what we think we know about others stems directly from the ways in which we represent their behavior. Each of us possesses an interpersonal "dictionary," sets of terms, concepts, and so forth, which we use in making sense of the behavior of other persons. Our interpersonal "dictionaries" frequently limit what we see and what we do not see in interaction with others. A person with a rich network of interpersonal concepts is likely to see quite different things in the behavior of other persons than one who does not possess such a store of concepts.

Most importantly, fairly stable relationships exist among the various terms that make up our interpersonal dictionaries; that is, we tend toward a consistent structure in our linguistic representations of behavior. Some concepts are strongly associated with each other and weakly associated with others. For example, "warm" people are also thought to be "spontaneous," while "cold" people are not. Although it may be true that "warm" people are more likely to be "spontaneous" than "cold" people, the fact remains that such *prior* associations do exist and do bias our perceptions of others. As a consequence of such preexisting linguistic relationships, we are in constant danger of *assuming* certain qualities in others when they may not, in fact, exist. A classic experiment by Asch (1946) illustrates this point quite nicely.

Asch gave two groups of college students lists of characteristics describing a hypothetical person. The lists were identical with the exception of a single word. One group received the following list: intelligent, skillful, industrious, *warm*, determined, practical, and cautious. The other group received the following list: intelligent, skillful, industrious, *cold*, determined, practical, and cautious. As we can see, the lists were identical except for the presence of the adjective warm in one and the adjective cold in the other. The students were asked to write an impression of the hypothetical person after they had seen the lists of characteristics.

Asch's findings indicated several striking differences between the two groups of students. When the hypothetical person was described as warm, 91 per cent of the students also thought him "generous," 65 per cent thought him "wise," 90 per cent thought him "happy" and 51 per cent thought him "imaginative." In contrast, when the hypothetical person was described as cold, only 8 per cent considered him "generous," 25 per cent "wise," 34 per cent "happy," and 19 per cent "imaginative."

Asch's study indicated, then, that subjects would assume quite different things about a person having been given information about a central characteristic, in this study warmth or coolness. But one might well ask if these differences are really important. Would such different assumptions actually affect the behavior of the person in interaction with others? Happily, a further study by Kelley (1950) provides us with the necessary information. In effect, Kelley repeated Asch's experiment but used a real rather than a hypothetical person. Prior to the appearance of a "guest lecturer" in their classroom, two different groups of students received descriptions. As with the Asch experiment, the descriptions were identical with the exception of the terms "very warm person" in one and "rather cold person" in the other. Once again, impressions of the guest lecturer showed important differences in the two groups. However, the important finding in Kelley's study was that effects upon the students' behavior were noted. Kelley had observers record the numbers of students participating in discussion with the lecturer. A larger number of students chose to interact with the guest lecturer when he had been described as very warm than when he was described as rather cold.

Naive personality theories

Each of us strives for a consistent and coherent view of the behavior of ourselves and others. Although we may not be formal personality theorists, each of us seems to possess what might very well be called a naive theory of personality. We have our hypotheses about the behavior of others, our hunches about what makes our friends behave as they do, our beliefs about the best way to raise children, and so forth. These naive theories of personality may very well be important determinants of our perceptions of others. If, for example, one firmly believes in the concept of the "unconscious mind," one is likely to think about the behavior of others in quite different terms than one who does not hold to such a concept. Or, to take another example, if one believes that most of the important determinants of his present behavior were formed many years before in events that happened during early childhood, he is likely to think about behavior quite differently than the person who views his behavior as more currently determined. These and many other "exotic" beliefs are very likely quite important in the perception of one's own behavior as well as in that of others.

An interesting experiment by Matkom (1963) indicates the importance of naive personality theory. Matkom reasoned that judgments about others often involve two components, what a person "appears to be" and what a person "really is underneath it all." Some persons are content to use surface behavior or the "apparent personality" to arrive at conclusions concerning others. Other persons are rarely content with surface behavior and seem convinced that the "truth" lies much deeper in the "real personality." In other words, some persons seem disposed to see both "apparent" and "real" levels of personality as consistent with one another. Others tend to see large discrepancies between the apparent and real levels of personality. Matkom was interested in discovering whether or not there were important consequences of such beliefs.

Using psychological tests as well as the judgments of psychologists, Matkom first categorized his subjects as either "well-adjusted" or "poorly adjusted." The subjects were then shown a movie in which an interview was being conducted. The subjects were asked to write their impressions of the person being interviewed in the film, first with regard to "what he appears to be like" and secondly, what "he really is like." Matkom found that the degree of discrepancy between judgments of real and apparent personality varied with degree of adjustment. That is, the more maladjusted a subject was, the more he tended to see large discrepancies between surface behavior and the "real" person. Moreover, in addition to larger discrepancies between the apparent and real personalities, maladjusted subjects tended to describe the real personality as considerably more *unfavorable*.

In any case, not only is our language important in influencing what we think we know about others, but our unexamined beliefs and hypotheses also influence our perceptions of other persons. Moreover, Matkom's research indicates, these may have important relationships to our own psychological functioning. There is an important lesson to be learned here. In interacting with others, one must take every precaution that one is not viewing his own naive personality theory rather than the actual behavior of the other person.

Cognitive complexity-simplicity

Human beings differ in terms of the number of interpersonal concepts they possess. One person may view virtually all of the behavior of others through the lenses of a mere handful of concepts. Another person may possess a rich and sizeable repertory of concepts that he uses to make sense of the behavior of others. The psychologist George Kelly devised an ingenious test for measuring the number of constructs a person typically employs in construing others. This test, the *Role Construct Repertory Test*, asks the subject to consider three people at a time and to decide in what ways two of them are alike while being essentially different from the third. For example, the subject might be asked to consider his "best friend," his "father," and his "favorite teacher." He might indicate that his "best friend" and his "favorite teacher" are alike in that they are *understanding* but that his father is *insensitive*. In this case, the construct dimension *understanding-insensitive* would be an important dimension along which judgments of others are made. From a sizeable number of three-person judgments such as those mentioned, it is possible to gain some information about the number of constructs the subject possesses as well as the nature of them.

Persons who possess relatively few interpersonal constructs are said to be *cognitively simple;* persons with numerous constructs are thought to be *cognitively complex.* Whether one is cognitively complex or simple seems to have important implications for interpersonal knowing. Cognitively simple persons seem to assume great similarity between themselves and others. When asked to make judgments about themselves and others, cognitively simple persons seem more sensitive to similarities between themselves and others. Cognitively complex persons, on the other hand, seem more sensitive to differences between themselves and others. Several studies (e.g., Bieri, 1955; Leventhal, 1957) are in agreement that when asked to judge others, cognitively simple persons are more capable of predicting similarities between their own behavior and that of others, whereas cognitively complex persons are more capable of predicting differences.

In one study conducted by the author, cognitive complexity-simplicity was related to the typical method of behavior control used by teachers. Cognitively simple teachers were found to employ punishment extensively, whereas cognitively complex teachers seemed to rely more upon reward as a means of influencing and controlling the behavior of their students. A teacher with very few interpersonal constructs (especially "evaluative" ones such as "good-bad") is likely to regard a wide range of student behaviors as deserving of punishment. However, as the number of constructs is increased, it is likely that the range of student behaviors relevant to the decision "punish-not punish" decreases. For example, the teacher who possesses and uses constructs such as "curious," "emotionally troubled," and "high need for activity" might prove more capable of tolerating and understanding many behaviors in the classroom than a teacher who does not possess such constructs.

Generality of cognitive complexity-simplicity

Thus far we have spoken of cognitive complexity-simplicity as though it were a generalized trait of persons. Unfortunately, the evidence for generality is not straightforward. Allard and Carlson (1963) found some evidence for generality across several measures. However, the methods of measurement used by Allard and Carlson all seemed quite similar. When a large number of *different* measures of cognitive complexity-simplicity were used, generality was not obtained (Vannoy, 1965). In other words, we may expect that a person will appear cognitively simple on one set of measures and cognitively complex on another set of measures. That this should be the case is not at all surprising. The author has been acquainted personally with numerous individuals who displayed such a striking inconsistency. A brilliant engineer who could reason remarkably well about complex *physical* systems seemed almost childlike in his approach to complex *social* systems and problems. Although he could handle multivariate problems in an engineering context, he seemed incapable of appreciating the fact that social problems would not yield to single variable explanations! It seems highly probable that the evidence for generality of cognitive complexity-simplicity will continue to be mixed, with some persons appearing quite complex in some areas of functioning and simple in others.

Temporal focusing and interpersonal knowing

Human beings dwell in three time fields simultaneously: the past, the present, and the future. However, it is interesting to note that individual orientations toward time seem to vary considerably. Some individuals seem to be focused primarily on the past. Others seem obsessed with the future. Still others seem to live in a continuous present. Many elderly people, for example, appear to have difficulty discussing future events or, for that matter, concentrating upon their present interactions. Highly ambitious persons seem totally obsessed with future events. In interactions with such persons one often gets the impression that very little of themselves is brought into present interaction. They seem to be "somewhere else" — and indeed they often are. Their consciousness seems flooded with anticipations, plans, schemes, wishes, and aspirations, all of which lie in the psychological future.

But what does temporal focusing have to do with interpersonal knowing? The answer is reasonably straightforward. A person's temporal orientation or focus is an important determinant of his state of consciousness. It is important, at this point, to recall our earlier discussion of *selectivity*. Since human consciousness seems quite limited in that it can focus upon only a small number of events at any moment in time, information selectivity occurs. One important determinant of what is registered in our awareness is our temporal orientation.

First of all, our focus upon events that *have already* happened or upon events that *may* happen distracts us from perceiving present events. If we are caught in obsessive thought about the past or about the future, we may literally fail to perceive much that is happening at the moment. Secondly, concern with the future or the past may channel our perceptions in given ways. For example, the person who strongly desires some possible future state may seek out and perceive only that information in interaction with others that is relevant to the desired future state. Hence, his knowledge of others with whom he interacts may be limited only to that which is relevant to some possible future; other aspects of persons may very well go unrecognized. Similarly, the person who focuses primarily upon the past may have a tendency to "read" present interactions through the lenses of past experience. In either case, it seems reasonable to suppose that *present* experience is almost certain to be perceived differently.

The author has noted with curiosity that students rarely seemed to remember information given in the last few minutes of class. Questioning of the students revealed that their awareness was flooded with images of their "rising from their seats," "walking to the door of the classroom," "meeting a friend after class," and "hurrying to another class." In short, images of themselves in the immediate future seemed to compete with careful attention to present events. In still another classroom exercise, the author, while lecturing, casually took out a cigarette, traced eight or nine circles with it in the air, moved it horizontally several times, then placed it in his mouth and lit it. Some time after this striking behavior, the author asked if any student could recall what he did with the cigarette. Quite remarkably only a few, if any, students perceived this extraordinary way of lighting a cigarette. Most students, when asked to demonstrate what the author did, acted out a conventional sequence of events in lighting a cigarette. In essence, the students were perceiving their *expectations* for the chain of events which normally follows after a person reaches for a cigarette.

Of course there are numerous alternative explanations in these uncontrolled classroom demonstrations. In the example in which students showed surprisingly poor recall of events that occurred near the close of class, competition from images concerning their immediate futures is only one possible explanation. It may simply be that students were tired as the lecture neared completion or that attention could not be sustained for a complete hour. In the example of the cigarette lighting, it might actually be that in concentrating upon what was being said, the students simply failed to note that the instructor was lighting a cigarette. When asked to recall the manner in which it was done, they simply produced a conventional account of this behavior. In any case, the hypotheses derived from these simple classroom demonstrations require controlled testing in other contexts.

Expectations, derived either from past experience or in anticipation of future events, seem to be a potent influence over what is perceived in interaction with others. Human beings seem to have a propensity for busily engaging in the making of plans for the future. Unfortunately, we also seem to have a propensity for living in our plans rather than in the actuality of the moment when they finally materialize. Once again, we seem to be in danger of reading the activities of our own minds rather than the reality of other persons and their behavior; that is, we often "see" what we expect to see rather than what is actually taking place.

Strategies in coming to know others

As we have noted earlier, it is obviously impossible to seek out and evaluate all potential information about the other persons with whom we come in contact. In face-to-face interactions we are literally bombarded with more information than we could possibly handle. As a consequence, most persons seem to develop what might best be termed as *information reduction strategies*. Persons seem to develop one or more methods by which the total amount of information to which they might attend is reduced to a smaller and more manageable pool. Of course, there are problems in calling such simplifying methods "strategies." In point of fact, it is probably true that most persons are unaware that they are attending to only a minute portion of the total amount of information about others to be had. Moreover, the simplifying methods used by most persons are not deliberate as the term "strategies" implies. However, it is equally true that persons can be made aware rather easily of various methods they do employ and could employ in coming to know others. Once aware of these methods, they could exercise choice among a set of possible methods. For these reasons, the term "strategies" seems a reasonable one to employ in the following discussion.

Categorization and information reduction. Human beings do not deal with their worlds in bits and pieces. Categorization of some kind or another seems to be the rule. Information reduction through categorization is taught with the very beginnings of language learning. One can scarcely escape the all-pervasive effects of social influence that go on unceasingly from early childhood into the adult years in the form of direct linguistic instruction about the nature of the world and persons in it. It is not at all surprising that much of our thought about ourselves and others is stereotypical in nature. Stereotypy is a natural consequence of ordinary language training in American culture as well as in most, if not all, others. As we shall see, information reduction strategies used in coming to know others are directly based upon categorization.

Assumed similarity. A commonly used strategy in coming to know others is *assumed similarity*. When one is confronted with the task of understanding another person, he can proceed by assuming that other persons are very much like *himself* and base his conclusions on this assumption. As a strategy, assumed similarity has its strengths and weaknesses. If one happens to live in a culture in which individuality is discouraged and conformity to group norms is characteristic, then assumed similarity is an ideal strategy. Chances are good that everyone in such a culture is, in fact, very much like oneself, and if one has the good fortune to know himself rather well, then the task of coming to know others can be quite simple. Moreover, one is likely to be extremely accurate in his perceptions of others.

On the other hand, if one happens to live in a culture in which individuality is prized, rewarded, and expected, then assumed similarity can be a dangerous strategy indeed. Obviously, when the probability of meeting someone with similar beliefs, values, and motivations is quite low, it is hazardous to use oneself as a means of gauging the possible reactions of other persons. When one is traveling in foreign countries, the limitations of assumed similarity are often painfully apparent.

Generalizing attributes of behavior to assumed stable traits of the actor. When we note a person behaving "irresponsibly," we are often tempted to conclude that we are dealing with an "irresponsible" person. Oftentimes we do so without ever taking into account such things as the frequency of the behavior, the context in which the behavior occurred, the state of the actor at the time, and so on. This confusion of aspects of behavior with assumed stable traits of the actor is common enough to deserve mention here. Perhaps the greatest danger associated with this strategy is the clear possibility of confusing *attributes* of behavior with *causal* statements about behavior. For example, once we have decided that a person is "irresponsible," we are likely to explain all of his behavior on this basis. If we are asked, "Why did John do such an irresponsible thing?" we are likely to answer, "Well, it's because he's an irresponsible person." The circularity in this example is readily apparent. One can readily appreciate the fact that explaining an irresponsible act by saying that it was committed by an irresponsible person is really a pseudo-explanation, i.e., it is not an explanation at all but a redundant statement. Less obviously, to say that persons who have hallucinations are schizophrenic and that they hallucinate *because* they are schizophrenics amounts to the same type of pseudo-explanation. Although people under the influence of certain drugs may seem quiet and withdrawn, we have no reason to assume that persons take drugs in order to "escape from reality." Most certainly, knowing that a given person uses drugs is hardly sufficient information for concluding that that person is an "escapist" or "immature." Such cliché-ridden explanations for behavior may be quite common and they may give one a comfortable sense of knowing something about other people, but in actuality they tend to obfuscate issues rather than clarify them.

In short, one must be extremely careful in moving from categories of acts to categories of people. Even the most celebrated psychological theorists of the past have fallen victim to this most common information reduction strategy.

Assumed characteristics and role perception. Each of us occupies some position in the social systems in which we function. Associated with such positions are fairly clear-cut prescriptions for behavior, and we can speak of these sets of prescriptions for behavior as *social roles*. It is interesting to note how much we tend to assume about a person knowing little else than his formal social role. In many instances elaborate fantasies have been constructed around given occupations. Airline stewardesses, for example, are thought to be sexually uninhibited, cheerful, courteous "swingers." In ultraright-wing political circles, knowing that a man is a university professor (especially in California) is sufficient evidence for inferring that he is a political radical, a communist sympathizer, and dedicated to warping tender young minds with radical thought. In radical left wing circles, policemen are sadistic, brutal, and hostile to nonconformists. Although it may be true that there are radical university professors and that some policemen abuse their authority, it is quite another matter to stereotype all persons who happen to have chosen these occupational roles.

A fascinating study by Mason Haire (1955) illustrates quite nicely the manner in which role perception can influence inferences about others. Haire chose to work in the area of labor-management relationships. He first selected a group of managers and a group of labor representatives. To these subjects he presented pictures and descriptions of two hypothetical persons. The pictures and descriptions were identical except that some subjects were told that the person was a member of management and other subjects were told that the person was a member of the labor force. Hence, while all other aspects of the hypothetical persons were held constant, their occupational roles were systematically varied. As Haire expected, the perceptions of the hypothetical persons varied considerably when they were described as either members of management or labor. For example, when one of the hypothetical persons was presented to managerial subjects as a member of management, 74 per cent of these subjects thought the hypothetical person to be honest and 71 per cent thought him to be mature. In contrast, when the same hypothetical person was presented to managerial subjects as a *labor* representative, only 50 per cent saw him as honest and only 34 per cent as mature! Similar differences were obtained when representatives of labor were asked to judge "management" and "union" hypothetical persons. Considering these striking differences in perception between management and labor, it is not surprising that union-management negotiations frequently become quite troublesome. In any case, Haire's study provides us with convincing evidence as to the importance of role perception in coming to know others.

As a strategy, role associated inference has obvious limitations and serious hazards. Although one may be able to predict some characteristics of persons simply from social role, it is clear that this strategy leads quite readily to the construction of distorted pictures of many persons.

Sterotyping as a strategy. As we mentioned previously, stereotyping is difficult to avoid even for the most cautious of social observers. It requires considerable effort to continue to attempt to view others in carefully differentiated and individual ways. The temptation to yield to stereotypical perception of others in the face of complexity is always present. However, as difficult as it may be, one must continually strive to come to know the reality of other persons and their behavior rather than the illusions of stereotypes. The consequences of irrational social stereotypes are readily evident in American society. The black man has suffered gravely from the insane stereotypical beliefs of the white man in America. The tragic consequences of such insanity are everywhere apparent, e.g., the devastating human tragedy of ghetto life, poverty, misery, racial strife, and so forth. That skin color alone can serve as the basis for inferring such characteristics as intelligence, morality, motivation, and values continues to be one of the most fantastic forms of insanity ever visited upon human beings.

The process of stereotypical perception expresses itself in numerous ways. Hair seems to make a lot of people very "up tight." Why this should be the case is not altogether clear, but the fact that it does is quite evident. The author once had the enormous displeasure of watching an entire "respectable" and "normal" American community, Laguna Beach, California, whip itself into a terrible frenzy of self-righteousness and downright hatred bordering on violence over the influx of long-haired, different looking youths into the community during the summer. The police chief of the community was soundly booed and harrassed by a group who called themselves the "Concerned Parents Association" when he firmly refused to take extralegal action against the transient young people. Talk of forming "vigilante" groups to go around placing youths under citizens' arrests for all sorts of minor violations of city ordinances was rampant. Letters to the editor of the local newspapers overflowed with hate-filled comments concerning the "hippies" and their supporters. The city manager of Laguna Beach took space in the local newspaper to expound his own political and social philosophy concerning such matters as child-rearing, drug use, and so forth, finishing with a series of four articles and a detailed account of how citizens' arrests of "hippies" could be made.

The fact that such incredible social ignorance and hatred, which grew out of stereotypical thinking on the part of the citizens of Laguna Beach, did not explode in outright violence remains a stroke of good fortune, of which they are very likely

VOTE FOR
☆ GOLDBERG
☆ OSTRANDER
☆ LORR

The Only Local Businessmen Running for Council

TO RESTORE OUR GOOD IMAGE AND SAVE LAGUNA BEACH FROM THE FURTHER FISCAL WASTE AND IRRESPONSIBILITY — ALSO FROM **THE BLIGHT OF THE HORRIBLE HIPPIE HORDES.**

PAID FOR BY CITIZENS' COMMITTEE FOR COMPETENT GOVERNMENT
CHAIRMAN, BART McHUGH, 650 MYSTIC VIEW, LAGUNA BEACH

Figure 19. Stereotyping is frequently a factor in the political process. This advertisement, which concerns a city council election, dramatically illustrates the extent to which social stereotypes can culminate in intense emotional reactions. (From the *Laguna News-Post*, April 8, 1970.)

unaware. Of course, throughout this entire period of mass "psychosis," constructive and workable solutions to the problems that were posed by large number of transient youths did not appear. The reliance upon stereotypical thinking prevented the occurrence of rational planning and intelligent management of social conflict.

Even though obvious examples of stereotypical thinking are not difficult to see clearly, one must not be deluded into thinking that since he is not racially or ethnically prejudiced, he is free of stereotypical thought. It is, for example, as ridiculous for "liberal" whites to imbue blacks with all sorts of positive characteristics as it is for prejudiced whites to associate negative characteristics with blackness. Unfortunately, we shall continue to pay extraordinary costs in terms of human suffering until we learn that there simply is no substitute for accurate perception of *individuals*. As difficult as such perception may be to achieve, its rewards in terms of interpersonal and societal functioning can be truly enormous.

Deliberate misperception. A possible but rarely used strategy in coming to know others is something I choose to call *deliberate misperception*. Since our expectations for the behavior of others and our prior conceptions about them heavily color our perceptions of them, we must constantly check our present perceptions. One way in which such testing can be accomplished is to entertain alternative hypotheses about the other person and then observe his behavior quite carefully while holding the alternative hypothesis in mind. When one entertains a hypothesis which is directly opposed to that which one normally holds concerning another person, then one is using the strategy of deliberate misperception. For example, if another person is typically construed as "hostile," one might try to construe him as "friendly." Bearing this alternative construct in mind, does the behavior of the other person now appear differently to us? Does one now notice things in the behavior of the other person that previously went unnoticed?

As a strategy, deliberate misperception has interesting possibilities. Since it creates a "bias" in the opposite direction from one's previous conceptions of others, it permits one to break up old expectations for behavior and often creates a fresh context in which observations can take place. Moreover, since one's *own behavior* toward another person may change as one's constructs about the person changes, deliberate misperception permits one to assess whether or not the perception of the other person is a function of the interaction between self and other. That is, if another person may appear to us as "hostile," our behavior toward the other person may in turn suggest "hostility" on our part, thus leading to outright "hostility" on his part, which confirms our original perception, leading to further "hostility" on our part, and so on and so forth. Whether or not our perceptions of the other person are the outcome of *reciprocal interaction* rather than careful observation of the *properties* of the other person is a question that rarely occurs to us.

Deliberate variation in the contexts of observation. Oftentimes our knowledge about others is based upon observation in a small number of situations or contexts. In many cases, we may even base our conclusions upon observations in only a *single* context. However, we must be aware that situations exert powerful influences over behavior. When we fail to vary our observations across a wide variety of situations, we often erroneously conclude that a given characteristic is a *property of the person* rather than *a sample of behavior in a given situation*. For example, if we observe a particular child in a particular classroom with a particular teacher, our conclusions might be quite different than if we had observed the same child in a different classroom with a different teacher. The student will recall our earlier discussion of psychological inquiry, sampling, and the problem of generality of knowledge. The present problem is, in essence, no different. Whether one is trying to understand behavior in the laboratory or in the everyday world, the problem of generality across situations is still present. Deliberate variation in the contexts of observation is an important strategy in coming to know others. Unfortunately, it is rarely practiced. As a consequence, we frequently attribute properties to persons when we should be considering persons in given situations.

Behavioral tests for one's hypotheses. Surprisingly few of us stop to check our hypotheses, first impressions, vague intuitions, and so forth, against the actual behavior of others. Quite often we seem unable to even verbalize the bases for our knowledge about particular others. If we think we know something about others, then we ought to be able to verbalize what it is we know, explain the basis for it, and predict something about the future behaviors of the persons from it. In this sense, the strategy suggested here is an evaluative one. By carefully observing behavior in given situations appropriate to our hypotheses, it is possible to check upon the adequacy of our thinking about particular persons with whom we interact. As an exercise, the student might try writing a nontrivial description of several of his best friends. And he might try attempting to predict the behavior of these friends in situations in which he has not observed them previously. Although often difficult, this exercise usually illuminates quite clearly the terribly imprecise way most of us attempt to conceptualize other persons. Moreover, failures to predict the behavior of persons who are "well known to us" are often more revealing and intriguing than if we had correctly predicted it. In any case, testing one's hypotheses about others against actual samples of behavior is one means of assessing what it is we think we know about others.

Summary of strategies. We have attempted to illustrate the methods that are used or could be used in coming to know others. The list we have presented is certainly not exhaustive; the student can very likely think of others, and this is, of course, to be encouraged. In the often difficult task of arriving at correct understanding of other persons, one needs as many methods of proceeding as one can devise. The important point to note, however, is that simplifying methods of some kind or another are characteristic of social perception. The vast amount of interpersonal information to which we are exposed each day of our lives must be handled in some way. The limitations on human information processing and increased cognitive strain resulting from information overload render information handling strategies a necessity. The important questions involve *choice* among possible strategies under varying conditions and for varying purposes. One must always be aware of the advantages and limitations of selectivity. Hopefully, such awareness will help to make each of us more intelligent, perceptive, sympathetic, and wise observers of the human scene.

Affective states, attention, and social perception.

In addition to the goals, language, constructs, beliefs, attitudes, and strategies of the observer, various emotional states can also affect what the observer sees and does not see. It is a well-known fact that under conditions of great emotional arousal, decreased accuracy of perception is encountered. Under stress, individuals show marked inability to concentrate, attention span becomes quite short, and perceptual errors are common. In problem-solving, for example, emotional arousal tends to narrow attention to cues that are situated in the center of the visual field, with peripheral information going unnoticed (Easterbrook, 1959). In a dramatic demonstration of the effects of arousal, Hernandez-Peon, Scherrer, and Jouvet (1956) showed that an arousing *visual* stimulus could actually interfere at the neurological level with the transmission of a simultaneous *auditory* stimulus to the brain. Using a cat as a subject, these investigators were able to record the response of the cochlear nucleus (the first relay station from the ear to the brain) to a continuous auditory stimulus. When a rat in a bottle was suddenly placed before the cat, the response of the cochlear nucleus to the auditory stimulus was greatly reduced. In effect, the cat had been deafened by an intense *visual* experience.

In addition to the fact that emotional arousal can directly affect the ability of the person to process information efficiently, other disruptive effects upon cognitive processes are apparent. Once again, it is a commonplace observation that, under stress, individuals do not think clearly. In studies of people caught up in natural disasters (Tyhurst, 1951), it was discovered that a very large number of people showed complete breakdowns in adaptive and rational behavior. When informed that they were threatened by fire or flood, many showed virtual paralysis, some became hysterical, and others refused to leave the seeming security of their beds.

It is not surprising, then, that under conditions of strong emotional arousal our perceptions of other persons can be distorted greatly.

Individual differences in ability to judge others

Although it seems intuitively correct to assume that persons differ greatly in general ability to judge others, it has not proved easy to establish the correctness of this assumption. Despite several decades of research, the existence of a general ability to judge others continues to resist clarification. Early studies that were thought to show the existence of such a general ability have been extensively criticized on methodological grounds (Cronbach, 1955). More recent studies in which appropriate controls have been used have yielded mixed results. Hatch

(1962) in an elaborately controlled study was able to demonstrate some generality and above chance prediction for good judges. However, much of Hatch's results was attributable to chance alone with little accuracy demonstrated even among those considered to be "good judges."

In a series of studies Cline and his colleagues (1964) have demonstrated that the ability to judge others may possess some generality but that it is quite complex and consists of more than one component. Using a mathematical technique called factor analysis, Cline's group analyzed the results of a number of judging tests. They concluded that while it was possible to speak of a general ability to judge others, this ability, like "intelligence," consisted of at least two factors and probably more. The two factors identified were *stereotype accuracy* and *differential accuracy*. Quite simply, this means that one might be an accurate judge over several judging tests because one has an accurate stereotype of others or because one is able to predict differences between individuals. This result seems in keeping with the findings for cognitive complexity-simplicity discussed earlier.

In any case, even though there is a widespread assumption that people differ in a general ability to judge others, it has proven terribly difficult to establish this common-sense notion in terms of research and objective data. Although some evidence for generality exists, it is not impressive.

PROPERTIES OF THE OBSERVED

Up to this point in our discussion we have concentrated upon the observer. Obviously, however, those persons whom we observe and their attributes do influence our knowledge about them. Let us now consider some of the important cues to which meanings are attached that are transmitted by others.

Physical characteristics

Perhaps the most primitive form of information about others concerns physical appearance. Secord, Dukes, and Bevan (1954) showed that certain physical characteristics are often associated with specific psychological characteristics. Dark complexioned men with heavy eyebrows, coarse hair, a straight mouth, and an oily skin are frequently perceived as hostile. Fat persons are often thought of as jolly, whereas the absence of excess flesh is taken to signify "shrewdness" or "calculation." One remembers the famous line from Shakespeare, "Yon Cassius has a lean and hungry look."

An amusing study by McKeachie (1952) revealed that the wearing of lipstick produced reliable differences in judgments of college women by college men. Girls who wore lipstick were judged more frivolous, more anxious, less conscientious, and more interested in the opposite sex than those who did not.

As we have already mentioned, skin color can and does serve as a cue for inferences of all sorts concerning other people. Hair length, style of clothing, presence or absence of eye glasses, and so forth, all serve as cues for judgments of the other person. Thinking about such characteristics one is reminded of the numerous school boards throughout the nation who permitted themselves to be drawn into public controversy over such idiotic matters as style of dress and hair length of their students. Often members of such boards would make explicit their beliefs that the behavior of students could be controlled by controlling their appearances. Mustaches, side burns, and length of miniskirt were measured meticulously, and the student showing a bit too much hair or leg was sent home for barbering or tailoring! One would be hard pressed to justify such incredible demands for mindless conformity on any grounds—legal, moral, ethical, or scientific. It is hard to believe that one could change the behavior of a motorcycle gang by dressing them in white dinner jackets. In any case, as the kids frequently put it, "You ought to be concerned with what is *in* our heads rather than *on* them." But we can readily see, in this example, the very great importance placed upon surface, physical characteristics in our judgments about others.

Eye contact

Whether or not a person with whom we are communicating maintains or avoids eye contact is a most significant bit of information. Expressions such as "He wouldn't look me in the eye when he said it" are, of course, quite common and reveal the naive importance attached to eye contact. We are likely to regard a female who maintains very close eye contact with a nonintimate person as quite "bold" and even perhaps "seductive." It is an amusing exercise to attempt to maintain eye contact with strangers that one encounters while travelling. One soon discovers that it is almost impossible. If a male tries to catch and hold the eye of an attractive female, she will almost invariably break it off after a very brief glance. If a male tries to maintain eye contact with another male, it is even worse! When I try to recall long hours of waiting in airline terminals, I remember little beyond large numbers of very bored people trying desperately to pass the time without looking at one another.

The anthropologist Hall (1963) discussed eye contact at length. He concluded that the amount of eye contact displayed by the communicator was indicative of his attitude toward the person he was addressing. Mehrabian (1969) has reviewed a host of studies of eye contact and has concluded that attitudes are indeed communicated by degree of eye contact. In general, positive attitudes between communicators is associated with greater eye contact. In addition, degree of contact varies with status relationships. It would appear that eye contact is greatest when one is addressing a moderately high-status person and lowest when one is addressing a very low-status person. Punishments, such as unfavorable comments upon the performance of another person, can lead to a decrease in amount of eye contact.

Distance

When we stop and think about it, it comes as no surprise to find that we tend to maintain fairly stable distances between ourselves and others. We permit and encourage intrusions into our "personal spaces" by those of whom we are fond and resent such intrusions by disliked people. In a broader cultural perspective, it is clear that definite boundaries exist for various types of relationships. Hall (1964) has claimed that in the United States measurable distances for given types of interaction exist. Intimate interpersonal interactions are typically conducted with a distance between participants of 6 to 18 inches. Casual interpersonal interchanges take place across a distance of 30 to 48 inches, and public interaction situations take place at 30 or more feet.

Against this cultural backdrop of what is and what is not a correct distance in a given context, deviations in either direction are the occasion for interpretation. If a communicator strays outside the permissible limit or draws too close, the other party in the interaction may infer a negative attitude on the part of the communicator. Important relations exist between status and space. The amount of space allotted to a person for his own use is often taken as an indicator of his status and importance.

Once again, the travelling situation is an instructive (and oftentimes amusing) one in which to demonstrate these relationships for oneself. The next time you board a nearly empty bus, avoid all of the unoccupied double seats and deliberately sit next to a person. On occasion the author has had lone females rise and move to another unoccupied seat. Males tend to stare straight ahead rather stonily. It is obvious from these simple examples that people are prone to question one's intentions when one deliberately intrudes into their spaces when the intrusion could have been avoided.

The author once had a friend who had been born and raised in France. Her conception of a casual conversation with someone was to draw herself up directly under his nose, stare intently into his face, and talk a mile a minute. Whether this is a characteristic of French women generally is not known to the author. However, on several occasions it was quite amusing to watch disconcerted males and females alike being "driven" across the room during a conversation with her at a cocktail party. As each participant tried to maintain a preferred distance, one moving closer and the other away, the interchange looked more like a dance than a conversation.

From these examples, then, we can see that distance is an important cue in interpersonal knowing. Inferences about attitudes, feelings, status, and intentions are readily drawn from the distance the other person maintains in interaction with oneself.

Postural cues

Persons may derive information from cues concerning posture alone. Sarbin and Hardyck (1955) presented subjects with "stick figure" drawings in various poses and asked for judgments of such poses as "sleepy," "thoughtful," "sexy," "relaxed," and so forth. Interestingly enough, subjects readily took on the task of attributing characteristics to the stick figures even though the only cue present for judgment was posture. More recently, Mehrabian and Friar (1969) have investigated postural arrangements indicative of relaxation-tension. They have concluded that a curvilinear relationship exists between the attitude of a communicator toward the person he is addressing and the degree of relaxation; that is, relaxation is either very high or very low for a disliked person while it is moderate for a liked person. Similarly, one is more likely to assume a position with arms akimbo while communicating with disliked persons than with liked persons. Body orientation (facing toward or away from a person) is also an important cue in inferring attitude.

From these and numerous other studies not mentioned here, we see that posture can be used as information to arrive at knowledge about others.

Verbalizations and vocalizations

Of course, much of what we come to know about others stems directly from what they say about themselves, their feelings, beliefs, values, and aspirations. George Kelley, an imaginative psychologist himself but one who apparently tired of the seemingly inexhaustible ingenuity of psychologists in coming up with intricate and indirect methods of "measuring personality," is purported to have said, "If you want to find out something about someone, you might try asking him—chances are good that he might just tell you!"

Albert Mehrabian, another imaginative psychologist in his own right, might agree with Kelley but for entirely different reasons. Mehrabian (1968) has put forth the intriguing claim that verbal information is far less important than either vocal information or facial information. In fact, Mehrabian claims that the total impact of a message from a communicator is as follows:

$$\text{Total Impact} = 0.07 \text{ verbal} + 0.38 \text{ vocal} + 0.55 \text{ facial}$$

Mehrabian might agree then that it is a good idea to ask for information but he is likely to ignore the actual content of the answer in favor of carefully noting the tone of the voice and the facial characteristics that accompany the verbal utterances. Of course, the fact that vocalization and facial expressions are important in understanding what is being communicated has been known to those in theater for centuries. In the practice of clinical psychology, numerous theorists have discussed the importance of such information. Harry Stack Sullivan, the famous psychotherapist and personality theorist, would not sit directly across from his patient. He preferred to sit at an angle to his patient so that the visual display would not distract him from sensitively listening to the changes in pitch, shifts in amplitude, and so forth.

By varying the tone of one's voice, it is possible to say "I hate you" and have somebody know you love him. Or one can say "I love you" and leave the distinct impression with the other person that he is thoroughly disliked. For that matter, completely unintelligible speech can be interpreted by different persons with considerable agreement as to the tone of feeling of the speaker, his attitudes in a situation, and so forth. By passing spoken language through electronic filtering devices, it is possible to remove its content while leaving changes in pitch, amplitude, and so forth, unchanged. Subjects asked to infer characteristics of the speaker from samples of electronically expurgated talk readily, and with considerable agreement, make such judgments.

PROPERTIES OF THE CONTEXT

In addition to the observer and the observed, we must consider the context in which observation takes place if we are to fully understand how knowledge about others is developed. Behavior does not take place in a social vacuum. Obviously our knowledge about others grows from observing them in given social situations. Often we erroneously conclude that the person is the *cause* of his own behavior when we should conclude that *external* forces acting upon the person are the important determinants. Think about your own behavior. A moment's reflection reveals that you are very likely a "different" person in the many different situations in which you find yourself. A person's behavior in the classroom may differ dramatically from his behavior in a favorite bistro. Or one may behave quite differently in the presence of this friend rather than that one. One may behave differently in a face-to-face interaction with just one other person rather than in a small group of persons. Clearly, situations can and do exert very powerful influences over our behavior. Let us briefly consider the context in which behavior occurs and the manner in which it may affect what we think we know about others.

Locus of causality

Human beings tend to look upon social events as having causes. In some cases, the person himself is seen as being the cause of some social event or act. In other cases, external forces are seen as the cause of his behavior. Locus of social causality concerns the question "Where are the determinants of behavior, inside or outside the person?" Suppose that, for example, upon visiting a friend's home, you observed his younger brother playing the violin. You might conclude, "He really doesn't like to practice but his mother makes him" (external determinant). Or you might conclude, "He wants to play the violin because of his great love of music" (internal determinant).

What is it that determines where we place the locus of social causality? Perhaps the most important factor is the *saliency* of the external forces acting upon the person in the context in which we observe his behavior. When the external forces are very apparent, we are likely to perceive these as the cause of the person's behavior. However, when external forces are not readily apparent, we tend to jump to the conclusion that the person himself is the cause of his own behavior. In our example of the young violinist, if we had observed his mother threatening to withhold his allowance if he did not practice, we would have been drawn to an explanation quite different from that of internal motivation.

Locus of causality is not a trivial question in understanding social behavior. Consider the arguments that rage over the deviant person in our society. Law enforcement officials generally perceive cause as residing in the person. Social scientists, on the other hand, are generally more receptive to external factors, e.g., social environments, early childhood experience, and so forth. Our perceptions of locus of causality influence what we do with deviant persons. When we perceive the person as the cause of his behavior, we tend toward punishment as a means of changing it. On the other hand, if we perceive the deviant member of society as having been influenced greatly by forces outside of himself, we tend toward rehabilitation and environmental alteration as a means of changing his behavior.

The belief that forces deep within the person are the cause of his behaviors has colored the practice of psychotherapy for many decades. Quite recently these longstanding assumptions about deep underlying unconscious forces have been questioned, in the practice of psychotherapy. Interesting new lines of psychotherapy based upon changes in the patient's reactions to external stimuli have suggested much promise.

One can readily appreciate, then, that perceived locus of causality is not a trivial issue. The management of criminal behavior and psychological therapy have both been importantly influenced by assumptions concerning the perceived locus of cause of behavior. In many instances, failure to comprehend the fact that behavior takes place in social contexts has led both psychological theorists and criminologists to erroneous theories concerning the origin of certain behaviors, the factors which maintain them, and the means by which these behaviors could be changed.

Intentionality and social contexts

Social acts can be perceived as "accidental" in nature or deliberately intended. It is clear that we are constantly drawing inferences about whether or not a given form of behavior was deliberately caused or occurred accidentally. Consider the following situation: Johnnie (age 7), while rushing about excitedly, bumps into little Willy (age 6). Poor little Willy jumps up, brushes himself off, and goes back to his play without a whimper. Willy's mother says to Johnnie's mother, "Oh, never mind, it was an accident." But suppose,

poor little Willy in his bright new sashes,
was knocked into the fire where he was burned to ashes.

What then, Mom? Willy's mother is likely to regard the whole event as deliberately caused by that brat, Johnnie. In short, the *severity of the consequences* of our actions greatly influences other persons' tendencies to perceive our acts as intentional and to hold us responsible for them.

An ingenious experiment by Walster (1966) illustrates this point quite nicely. Walster was interested in the fact that many unfortunate events transpire that are largely unavoidable. Nonetheless, we are often held responsible for them. What determines whether or not one is to be held responsible for one's actions? Walster reasoned that the severity of the consequences of our actions would prove an important factor. She arranged a situation in which persons listened to various tape recordings in which a hypothetical motorist, Lennie, was described. In one condition, Lennie received a minor dent in his fender. In another condition, Lennie's car was completely demolished. In a third condition, it was mentioned that Lennie's car *might* have rolled down a hill and struck some people. In a fourth condition, it was mentioned that Lennie's car *did* roll down a hill and *did* strike some people. Walster's results clearly indicated that as the severity of the consequences of Lennie's accident increased, the more subjects held him directly responsible for his actions.

As with locus of causality neither is perceived intentionality a trivial matter. Suppose that a man in a moment of anger takes out a gun and shoots at his wife. Suppose that he misses. Legally, he can be charged with something like assault with a deadly weapon. But suppose his aim is as deadly as his intentions and he hits her squarely between the eyes, rendering her one dead wife. Now, what are the charges against him — murder! As anyone can appreciate, assault with a deadly weapon, while certainly not trivial, is hardly as serious as murder.

Perceived justifiability

To the extent that we perceive another person's actions as justified, we are likely to regard them quite differently than when they are perceived as unjustified. Once again, the context in which behavior occurs importantly influences our perceptions of justifiability. Pastore (1952) conducted an interesting study in which this was demonstrated. He constructed two forms of a questionnaire. In one form, a set of highly frustrating circumstances was illustrated and no adequate explanation was provided for them. In the other form, the same set of circumstances were depicted but a nonarbitrary reason for them was offered. For example, one of the items on the questionnaire was as follows: "Your date phones at the last minute and breaks the appointment without an adequate explanation" (inadequate explanation). "Your date phones at the last minute and breaks the appointment because she had become suddenly ill" (nonarbitrary explanation). Subjects were asked to identify with the situations and to respond as they would. Subjects given the arbitrary and inadequate explanations responded with considerably more hostility to frustration. From Pastore's study we conclude that the perception of justifiability for given acts can determine the magnitude of our responses to frustration.

Relative freedom versus inhibition in given contexts

Social contexts differ greatly in terms of the degree of social *control* present. Some situations permit considerable freedom of responding while others are very "uptight" indeed. Our knowledge of other persons under these varying conditions of social control can vary as well. Under condition of great social control, we may come to know only a fraction of the true feelings, beliefs, and values of other persons. When punishments are employed, persons may shape their behavior accordingly, but their underlying beliefs, attitudes, values, and feelings may remain unchanged.

Reciprocity and interpersonal knowing

It is important to bear in mind that the observer himself and his behavior more often than not make up part of the social environment of the observed. One must constantly be alert to the fact that one's own behavior can importantly influence the behavior of the other person. That is, each of us contributes to and is affected by our interpersonal interactions. Much of the behavior that we observe in interaction with others is linked directly to our own. This is what is meant by the term "*reciprocity.*" Once again, we must not suppose that the behavior of the other person is occurring in a social vacuum. Much of what we see in the behavior of other persons may be there simply because we have behaved in a manner to insure its occurrence. The husband, for example, who thinks his wife is angry with him may respond angrily to her. She, in turn, observing real hostility in her husband, may reciprocate with genuine hostility, thus providing "confirmation" for the husband's earlier perception.

As observers of others, we would like to believe that our perceptions are objective and free of distortion. However, we frequently forget that self has a great deal to do with the behavior of the other person with whom we are interacting. Often we erroneously conclude that given behaviors indicate stable properties of the other person when we should conclude that we have had a great deal to do with shaping the behavior. One is reminded of George Bernard Shaw's famous play *Pygmalion*, in which Professor Higgins teaches a London flower girl how to be a lady. After her transformation, the flower girl has quite a different view of matters than her mentor, Professor Higgins. She insightfully remarks:

> You see, really and truly, apart from the things anyone can pick up (proper dressing, proper speaking, etc.), the difference between a lady and a flower girl is not how she behaves, but how she's treated. I shall always be a flower girl to Professor Higgins, because he always treats me as a flower girl, and always will; but I know I can be a lady to you, because you always treat me as a lady, and always will.

SUMMARY

In this chapter we have examined the important problem of coming to know others. As we have seen, the properties of the observer, of the observed, and of the context of observation all affect what it is we think we know about other persons. We have considered the goals, language, naive personality theories, strategies, constructs, beliefs, and emotions of observers and related these to interpersonal knowing. In addition, we considered the nature of interpersonal information transmitted by the observed. Finally, we briefly discussed the context of observation and how this affects interpersonal knowing.

Our discussion of interpersonal knowing has focused upon the necessity for information reduction methods in a world abundantly rich in information. As we have seen, the limitations upon human information processing abilities give rise to cognitive strain, which in turn leads to efforts to reduce the amount of information to which one is exposed. Although there is nothing inherently objectionable in information selectivity, a sophisticated observer of others is one who is aware that such selectivity takes place. Moreover, a sensitive, perceptive, and aware person in interaction with others is one who can choose his methods of arriving at understandings of the behavior of other persons. Knowledge of the process through which interpersonal knowing is accomplished cannot help but make one a more intelligent consumer of interpersonal information. At the very least, it can aid one in avoiding the dreadful stereotypy that characterizes much social thought. Perhaps it might even permit one to come to know individuals rather than the "social fictions" of one's own imaginings.

References

Allard, M., and Carlson, E. R.: The generality of cognitive complexity. J. Soc. Psychol., 59: 73, 1963.
Asch, S. E.: Forming impressions of personality. J. Abnorm. Soc. Psychol., 41:258, 1946.
Bieri, J.: Cognitive complexity-simplicity and predictive behavior. J. Abnorm. Soc. Psychol., 51: 263, 1955.
Cline, V. B.: Interpersonal perception. In Maher, B. (ed.): Progress in Experimental Personality Research. Vol. 1, pp. 221–281. New York, Academic Press, Inc., 1964.
Cronbach, L. J.: Processes affecting scores on "understanding others" and "assumed similarity." Psychol. Bull., 52: 177, 1955.
Easterbrook, J. A.: The effect of emotion on cue utilization and the organization of behavior. Psychol. Rev., 66: 183, 1959.
Haire, M.: Role-perceptions in labor-management relations: An experimental approach. Industrial and Labor Relations Review, 8: 2, 1955.
Hall, E. T.: A system for the notation of proxemic behavior. Amer. Anthropol., 65: 1003, 1963.
Hall, E. T.: Silent assumptions in social communication. Disorders of Communication, 42: 41, 1964.
Hatch, R. S.: An Evaluation of a Forced Choice Differential Accuracy to the Measurement of Supervisory Empathy. Englewood Cliffs, Prentice-Hall, Inc., 1962.
Hernandez-Peon, R., Scherrer, H., and Jouvet, M.: Modification of electrical activity in cochlear nucleus during "attention" in unanesthetized cats. Science, 123: 331, 1956.
Jones, E. E., and deCharms, R.: The organizing function of interaction roles in person perception. J. Abnorm. Soc. Psychol., 57: 155, 1958.
Jones, E. E., and Thibaut, J. W.: Interaction goals as bases of inference in interpersonal perception. In Tagiuri, R., and Petrullo, L. (eds.): Person Perception and Interpersonal Behavior. Stanford, Stanford University Press, 1958.
Kelley, H. H.: The warm-cold variable in first impressions of persons. J. Personality, 18: 431, 1950.
Leventhal, M.: Cognitive processes and interpersonal prediction. J. Abnorm. Soc. Psychol., 55: 176, 1957.
Matkom, A.: Impression formation as a function of adjustment. Psychological Monographs, 77, whole no. 564, 1963.
McKeachie, W. J.: Lipstick as a determiner of first impressions of personality. J. Soc. Psychol., 36: 241, 1952.
Mehrabian, A.: Communication without words. Psychology Today, Sept., 1968.
Mehrabian, A.: Significance of posture and position in the communication of attitude and status relationships. Psychol. Bull., 71: 359, 1969.
Mehrabian, A., and Friar, J. T.: Encoding of attitude by a seated communicator via posture and position cues. Cons. Clin. Psychol. 33, in press, 1969.
Pastore, N.: The role of arbitrariness in the frustration-aggression hypothesis, J. Abnorm. Soc. Psychol., 47: 728, 1952.
Sarbin, T. R., and Hardyck, C. D.: Conformance in role perception as a personality variable. J. Cons. Psychol., 19: 109, 1955.
Secord, P. F., Dukes, W. F., and Bevan, W.: Personalities in faces: I, an experiment in social perceiving. Genet. Psychol. Monogr., 49: 231, 1954.
Tyhurst, J. S.: Individual reactions to community disaster: the natural history of psychiatric phenomena. Amer. J. Psychiat., 107: 764, 1951.
Vannoy, J. S.: Generality of cognitive complexity-simplicity as a personality construct. J. Pers. Soc. Psychol., 2: 385, 1965.
Walster, E.: Assignment of responsibility for an accident. J. Pers. Soc. Psychol., 3: 73, 1966.

CHAPTER

7

Interpersonal Interaction

When we view psychology in historical perspective, it is quite apparent that the vast majority of theories and studies have been concerned with the isolated individual. Classic theorists of personality, for example, seemed so enamored with hypothetical processes thought to be taking place within persons that they scarcely seemed aware of the fact that persons have *environments.* Experimental psychologists, on the other hand, while recognizing the importance of events external to the individual, conducted extensive investigations on the effects of *physical* stimuli. However, *social* stimuli were, for the most part, neglected. It was not until very recently that the experimental laboratory situation (even that one involving the human experimenter and rat subject) was widely recognized as a social interactive situation.

When we examine the realities of the everyday lives of persons, it is difficult to see why so much of psychology has been devoted to the study of the isolated individual. In actuality, for most human beings a solitary state seems more the exception rather than the rule. Aside from the hours spent sleeping, human beings spend very little time alone; typically our time is spent in the presence of one or more persons. As one young and rather disillusioned university professor bitterly complained, "Life, it seems, is nothing more than a series of committee meetings!" Although we are quick to sympathize with the young professor's complaint, life is certainly much more than committee meetings. It is also a never-ending series of two-person interactions. At the close of a day, it is instructive to reflect upon what has happened. When we take the time to do so, we find that our day has consisted of a host of encounters with other persons. Two-person interactions of all kinds will have absorbed much of our energies and attentions. We will have very likely assumed a variety of roles in a variety of interactional contexts. In the course of a day, we may have found ourselves in a student-teacher relationship, a doctor-patient relationship, a parent-child relationship, an intense love relationship, a casual interaction with a stranger, a police officer-citizen relationship, a seller-buyer relationship, and so forth. It is equally instructive to note that our behavior has very likely changed as we moved from one context of interaction to another and as we shifted from role to role.

Surely all these comings and goings and happenings among people have a great deal to do with how they think and how they behave. But like the proverbial fish that is the last to discover water, human beings seem woefully ignorant of the fact that they have social surroundings and that such surroundings can and do exert powerful influences over the ways in which they think and behave. Other people are a lot of fun! True enough. But they are a mess of other things as well. They try to persuade us, influence us, control us, love us, hate us, change our opinions, shape our behavior to conform with their wishes, get us to buy things we do not need, seduce us, get us to marry them, help us, educate us, and even, at times, try to destroy us. While all of this is going on, we really do not sit back passively and watch the show. In fact, we are very likely trying to do the same things to others. It would be surprising indeed if these often intense and frequently passionate encounters between humans had very little to do with their thought and behavior!

In this chapter, then, we will take up the matter of interpersonal interaction. For the most part, we shall concentrate upon two-person interactions. In subsequent chapters, our attention will shift to multiperson interactional contexts.

THE PURPOSEFUL NATURE OF HUMAN INTERACTION

Even though it is undoubtedly true that numerous human associations do not involve intent or purpose, true social interaction does. People choose to interact with another person because they expect the interaction to serve some end. In this sense, social interaction is purposeful and guided by the interests of the participants. In the course of human social interaction, needs are fulfilled, beliefs about the nature of reality are supported and validated, opinions are confirmed, skills are acquired, emotions aroused and quieted, ideas about self are either confirmed or disconfirmed, commodities exchanged, and so forth. Unlike the celebrated hairy-chested everybody's Marlboro man who climbed the mountain "because it was there," people do not choose to interact with other people simply because "they are there." People who interact usually have some purpose. Of course, a person may choose to interact with a *particular* other person because of that person's proximity and availability. Studies of the development of friendship patterns, for example, clearly indicate that sheer propinquity is an important determinant of relationship. Festinger, Schachter, and Back (1950) found clear effects of spatial location upon friendship patterns in a housing development. Newcomb (1961) and Priest and Sawyer (1965), while studying friendship choices among college students, discovered that friends tended to come from the same areas of their dormitories. Although propinquity is clearly a variable of some importance in predicting *who* will associate with *whom*, the question of why people choose to interact in the first place is an altogether different question. In this portion of the chapter, we will consider several of the more important reasons for human interaction.

Social comparisons and information seeking

Although we rarely stop to consider it, we are frequently dependent upon others for certain types of *information*. Lacking clear objective data for many of our beliefs, values, and emotional reactions, we seek *confirmation* from others. Each of us, in effect, attempts to build a reality of self and a social reality; but it is difficult to establish such realities in the absence of information from others. How can one, for example, decide what is the "correct" or "proper" opinion to hold on a given political or moral issue? Should one engage in premarital sexual relations? Is it proper to smoke pot? How should one feel about radical political movements? How should one react to a shattered love relationship? How should one respond to a clearly unjustified attack upon self by another person? These and many similar questions constitute terribly important questions for all of us at various points in our lives. Unfortunately, the reserve book room of the library does not contain a book that details the "correct" answers. Unlike physical reality, social realities are not constructed upon hard, objective data.

If we cannot find the answers to these important questions indexed in a weighty tome entitled "What You Should Believe and Why," where do we turn for the necessary information? The answer is really quite simple—to other people. The attitudes, beliefs, emotional reactions, and behaviors of others are readily available to us. In the course of our lives we are immersed in a vast sea of social behavior. By interacting with others, we find the necessary information for constructing a social reality. Through interaction, our values, beliefs, opinions, and feelings are either confirmed or disconfirmed.

Festinger (1954) has written extensively on the need for *social comparisons* in the construction of a self and social reality. A belief, value, or opinion is "proper" to the extent that it can be located in some reference group; that is, we look to others who hold beliefs and attitudes similar to our own for the validation of further beliefs and attitudes. The radical student may very well seek out other radical students for confirmation of his feelings about the latest pronouncement from the chancellor's office. Youthful pot smokers are not likely to engage their local "narc" in a conversation about the winning qualities of grass as opposed to bourbon. The superpatriot, incensed over real or imagined insults to the flag, is likely to validate his feelings by interacting with other incensed superpatriots.

In the absence of hard and objective data, people turn to other people for information about how they should feel and what they should believe. The necessity for confirming information in the construction of a social reality is a major reason why human beings choose to interact with one another. In the course of such interactions, social comparisons yield useful information.

Uncertainty, social comparisons, and affiliation

When a person feels completely certain as to the validity of his beliefs, the need for social comparison information from others is quite low. As a consequence, pressure toward affiliating with others is low. On the other hand, when a person is terribly uncertain about himself, his beliefs, and so forth, the need for social comparison information can be quite pressing. Under such circumstances it is not surprising that the tendency to affiliate with others will be strong. A series of ingenious experiments by the social psychologist Stanley Schachter (1959) attempted to establish the effects of uncertainty upon affiliation. In actuality, Schachter investigated the effects of fear arousal as well as of uncertainty upon the tendency to affiliate. Let us examine what he did.

Schachter led groups of college girls to believe that they would receive electric shocks in the course of a psychological experiment. In one condition, *strong* fear was aroused by describing the forthcoming shocks as "intense" and "painful." In a second condition, *low* fear was aroused by describing the shocks as "very mild" and capable of causing a sensation resembling "tickling" or "tingling" rather than pain. After Schachter had prepared the girls for the experimental situation, he gave them the choice of either *waiting together* (affiliation choice) or *waiting alone* (nonaffiliation choice) for a period of time before the experiment would begin. Under these conditions, Schachter discovered that 63 per cent of the girls in the high-fear arousal group chose to wait together (affiliate) while only 33 per cent of the low-fear arousal group chose to wait together. In a further experiment, Schachter demonstrated that when given the opportunity to choose between waiting with girls about to undergo the same experience or with girls not scheduled for the experiment, girls chose to wait with other girls about to undergo the same experience. Realization that the other person shares one's fate, then, is a further important determinant of affiliative choice.

Although Schachter's findings are consistent with the notion that subjects chose to affiliate because of uncertainty associated with high-fear arousal, it is not possible to rule out other plausible alternative interpretations from these findings alone. Perhaps it was true that the girls in the high-fear arousal condition were uncertain about the appropriateness of their emotional reactions and were seeking social comparison information from other girls about to undergo the same experience. On the other hand, one might argue that uncertainty was present in both the high- and low-fear conditions, but that the difference in affiliative tendencies between the two groups was attributable to the fact that greater concern over the consequences of the experience led the high-fear girls to affiliate. Still another hypothesis could involve drive reduction (see Chapter 4). From past learning experiences (e.g., a mother quieting and comforting a frightened child), persons may associate other persons with fear reduction. Even the laboratory rat will show a more rapid extinction of experimentally induced fear when it is provided with a mate with which to face the threatened situation.

A clever experiment on fear arousal, uncertainty, and affiliation conducted by Gerard and Rabbie (1961) attempted to shed light on some of these alternative explanations for Schachter's data. Gerard and Rabbie arranged a situation similar to Schachter's. However, by means of a bogus simulated electronic "feedback" device, subjects were given "information" about their own fear level as well as about that of others. Actually, Gerard and Rabbie discovered a total of six conditions. These are depicted below:*

Level of Fear	No Information	Information About Self Only	Information about Self and Others
High	1	2	3
Low	4	5	6

Gerard and Rabbie reasoned as follows: If persons choose to affiliate because of uncertainty, then the tendency to affiliate should be *lower* among those given information about themselves and about others and highest among those given information only about themselves or no information at all. In order to follow this line of reasoning, the student has only to refer back to our previous remarks about uncertainty and certainty and information seeking. If the person already is certain about his own reaction and where he stands in comparison with others, then his need for social comparison information, and hence his affiliative tendencies, should be less than for the person who is uncertain.

As in many social psychological experiments, the data from Gerard and Rabbie's experiment provides both confirmation and disconfirmation for their hypothesis. On the one hand, there is clear evidence for uncertainty reduction since fewer of

---

*From Gerard, H., and Rabbie, J. M.: Fear and social comparison. J. Abnorm. Soc. Psychol., 62:586, 1961.

the subjects who had been given information about their *own and others'* emotional reactions chose to affiliate than did subjects given information only about their *own* reactions. Unfortunately, the findings for the no-information condition create problems. If the uncertainty hypothesis is correct, we would expect those subjects given no information at all to experience the greatest amount of uncertainty and, hence, to show the greatest amount of affiliative behavior. Unfortunately, this did not take place. Although the subjects with *no information* chose to wait with others more often than did the subjects who had *information about self and information about others,* the *no-information* subjects showed less affiliative tendency than did the *information-about-self-only subjects.*

How can we explain this unexpected finding? It is possible that giving a person information about his own reactions while denying him information about others' reactions results in *sharpened sensitivity* to uncertainty. That is, the person who has been given information about himself but who is not able to anchor it in comparison with others may experience even greater uncertainty than the person who has been given no information about self. But we must be careful with such after-the-fact explanations. Even though plausible, our suggested explanation amounts to a statement of faith in the correctness of the original hypothesis in the face of seemingly disconfirming information.

One other comment about Gerard and Rabbie's experiment is in order. Because all the high-fear conditions showed greater affiliative tendencies than did the low-fear conditions regardless of the information received by the subjects, we must conclude that although uncertainty reduction may be operating in the experiment, other factors associated with *fear* are operating as well. In other words, while uncertainty reduction may be *a* determinant of affiliation, it is not the only determinant. Even in this well-controlled laboratory experiment by Gerard and Rabbie, other factors contributed to affiliation.

Of course, the study of uncertainty, social comparison, and affiliation includes more experiments than those mentioned here; we cannot review all of these in this brief space. It should be sufficient to note, however, that the majority of these are at least consistent with the notion that *one* of the important determinants of affiliation is the need for social comparison information necessary to reduce uncertainty.

Expected gain and social interaction

The construction and maintenance of a personal and social reality is but one of the reasons persons seek out others. Social interaction is related to a host of purposes, and in this sense it is multiply determined. In the course of social interaction, multiple wants are satisfied, advice and assistance are solicited and given, status and ego needs are fulfilled, affectional and sexual strivings are met, work is accomplished, and money is made. In each of these examples, we sense the purposeful nature of human interaction. Each of the participants in an interaction brings with him goals, aspirations, wishes, desires, and wants. He or she enters the interaction with the expectation that the other partner can be counted upon, either willingly or reluctantly as the case may be, to provide satisfaction. To the extent that each partner in the interaction is capable of fulfilling the expectations of the other, a satisfactory interaction ensues. Unfulfilled expectations, on the other hand, lead to the unfortunate consequences associated with difficult and unhappy relationships, e.g., marital strife, divorce, interpersonal hostility, mutual attempts at psychological destruction, and even physical violence. One partner in an interaction may prove so interpersonally incompetent that he or she is quite incapable of meeting even the most modest of demands from the other person. Another person may place such totally unreasonable and unrealistic demands upon the partner that no one could possibly expect to meet them. Unfortunately, no one yet has worked out a calculus that tells one precisely how much one should give and how much one should get in an interpersonal interaction. The questions of "what is a fair price?" and "what is a fair share?" are ones that cannot be answered in any absolute and abstract sense. What is a "fair price" in one relationship may be far in excess of what one must pay in another relationship. Clearly there are relationships in which one is wisest to expect nothing much less anything resembling the "fair share" of other relationships.

Actually, the answers to these important questions involving expected and actual gains in interaction lie in the interactions themselves. Through processes very similar to bargaining and negotiating and through the use of various tactics and countertactics, persons seem to arrive at interpersonal accommodations. Offers are made ("If you promise to love me, I promise to buy you a new refrigerator"), threats are bandied about ("If you don't stop drinking, I'm going to go home to mother"), compromises are effected ("You can go fishing on our vacation, but I'm going to San Francisco"), and so forth. While there are undoubtedly those who would object strongly to conceiving of the stuff of human interaction in these terms, one can only reply that there is nothing inherently disgusting about the notion that people expect different things from one another and there is nothing inherently disgusting about the use of such processes as bargaining and negotiating to obtain them. Such relatively peaceful processes are surely preferable to the all-out war that characterizes many stressful and unfortunate human encounters. Moreover, as we have seen, the important questions concerning "price" and "fair share" are not resolvable in any absolute and final sense. It is in the course of the real life struggles between human beings that compromises are effected and interpersonal accommodations reached. Finally, the test of any analogy is in its usefulness and not in how it strikes our ethical or aesthetic sensibilities. Not that these sensibilities are unimportant. Given the choice between two equally useful analogies, this author would clearly choose that one most in line with his value system as well as that one which most elegantly tickled his aesthetic sensibilities. But let us move directly to the issue at hand. How does it aid our understanding to construe human interaction in terms of the expected gain and the tactics through which such gain is pursued?

INTERPERSONAL TACTICS

The notion that interpersonal relationships can be viewed as "games" recently achieved widespread popular appeal in the writings of Eric Berne. His book *Games People Play* consists largely of clever accounts of interpersonal behaviors in a variety of interactional contexts. Typical of Berne's compendium of people-games is the game of "See what you made me do." This game deals largely with the assignment of blame. The object of the player is to end up always in the happy position of being blameless while others about him are cast in the light of incompetent bunglers. For example, the person in the process of performing a delicate, skilled operation of some kind is interrupted by another person. He makes a dreadful error, like dropping the entire can of nutmeg into the Christmas wassail bowl or he gets heavy handed with the vermouth so that his martinis are 18 to 1 rather than a chic 36 to 1. He turns to the intruder in a rage and says, "See what *you* made me do!" According to Berne, the game of "See what you made me do" can be extended to one's work situation in which, for example, the superior can "democratically" ask the subordinate for suggestions only to be in the happy position of having someone to blame if things do not go properly. In his analysis of this game, Berne states that the principal aim of the game is vindication. He feels that it may be related to premature ejaculation in its mildest forms or, in its strongest forms, to rage based upon castration anxiety.

It is difficult to evaluate Berne's approach to interpersonal interaction through his concept of "games." On the one hand, the writing is undeniably clever and appealingly witty. On the other hand, one wonders if Berne has done anything more than relabel phenomena that have been well-recognized for many years. For example, the game of "See what you made me do" seems to involve little more than *blame assignment.* The fact that people will assign blame to others for their own actions under certain conditions has been more than amply appreciated for many years. What we need to know and what Berne does not tell us are *the conditions under which blame assignment will occur* and the conditions under which it will not. Unfortunately, Berne's analysis does not extend itself to these more pertinent scientific questions. Finally, one may well ask how Berne seems to know things that are not strikingly obvious at first glance. Why is the game of "See what you made me do" related to premature ejaculation in its milder forms and rage borne of castration anxiety in its stronger forms? How does Berne know this? Is it because sufficient cases of premature ejaculation and rage based on castration anxiety have been documented through controlled observation of players of the game to support the hypothesis? Unfortunately, we have no way of knowing. Despite its cleverness and obvious charm, the book seems more a prescientific collection of anecdotal and stereotypical accounts of hypothetical interactions. In some instances, the accounts can be dangerously misleading. From personal and intimate knowledge of the lives of well over a thousand alcoholics, this author finds Berne's account of the so-called "alcoholic" game superficial, incredibly speculative, and more than a shade abusive to millions of persons caught in the miseries of a disease that may very likely prove to be biochemical in origin rather than psychological. In any case, the remarkable stereotypy that characterizes Berne's account of a disease that manifests itself in a myriad of ways is deplorable.

Ingratiation tactics

A more convincing account of the usefulness of "game analyses" of interactions is provided by the careful work of the social psychologist Edward Jones (1964). By "ingratiation" Jones means the tactics one person employs to make himself more attractive to another. Jones has distinguished three classes of ingratiation tactics. First, one can attempt to ingratiate himself with another by *flattery*. There are obvious dangers associated with such a tactic in that inordinate flattery can lead to suspicion and rejection on the part of the other person. Second, one can ingratiate himself with another by *opinion conformity*. Since it appears to be true that most people are attracted to others who hold similar opinions, the ingratiator can capitalize upon this fact. Finally, the ingratiator can concentrate upon his own manner of *self-presentation*. By subtly selecting only those aspects of himself for presentation to another that are undeniably positive and exemplary, he can carefully manage the impression that the other forms of him.

According to Jones, ingratiation in an unequal power relationship—in an interaction between a subordinate and a superior—is one means by which the person of lesser power can augment his influence over the person of greater power. If the subordinate can succeed in making himself more attractive to the superior, he will also very likely have increased the amount of influence he has over the superior. How does this come about? A superior will be less happy about disapproving of the work of a subordinate that he finds attractive than of one he finds unattractive. Also, since it gives us pleasure to compliment and reward those we like, it seems reasonable to suppose that an attractive subordinate will receive a greater share of rewards than will an unattractive subordinate. In this sense, ingratiation tactics give the subordinate a degree of influence over a more powerful person that he might not otherwise have. In a series of experiments, Jones and his colleagues demonstrated that ingratiation tactics could be reliably produced in subjects in interpersonal interactions in which one person possessed greater social power than the other.

As Jones pointed out, ingratiation tactics differ in one crucial respect from mere conformity to the opinions of a more powerful person. The ingratiator must cleverly conceal his true motives for compliance. Whereas the conformist does little beyond bringing his beliefs and opinions in line with those of the other person, the ingratiator must make the fact of his conformity seem *spontaneous* and *uncalculated*. For example, a subordinate who adopts his superior's beliefs about some particular issue might act, if he chose to use ingratiation tactics, as though he were thoroughly impressed with his superior's "brilliant" analysis of the issue. He would certainly not convey to the superior that he is conforming to his opinion simply because he (the superior) is the "boss."

Marital tactics

Perhaps one of the most interesting applications of game analogies has been provided by Bernard (1964) in her analysis of marital interactions. Bernard conceives of marriage as a "mixed-motive" game (see Chapter 1). From this perspective the marital situation is one in which continuous bargaining and negotiating takes place. Typically, the partner with the least interest in maintaining the marriage is the one with the stronger position. This, by the way, is true of other interpersonal relationships as well. The person most committed to the continuance of a given relationship over time is the one in the most vulnerable position. The employer who has a sizeable and readily available labor pool may be far less committed to a relationship with any given employee than one who does not have such a pool of talent available. Similarly, the female with five men on the string is in a better bargaining position with regard to any one of them than the "going steady" type with her "one and only."

Returning to Bernard's analysis of marital interactions, let us consider the variety of moves available to each partner in the marriage game.

Refusal to communicate. One of the marriage partners may simply use the tactic of refusing to communicate at all on issues of importance to the marriage. In effect, by refusing to discuss problems at all, one partner may quite effectively limit the options available to the other partner. While such a tactic can have disturbing consequences for the other partner who wishes to communicate and the marriage, it may be of considerable use in marriages where one of the partners is verbally and intellectually inferior to the other. The less intelligent partner may handle the situation by simply refusing to discuss matters at all.

Fait accompli. One partner can make a "first move" response that leaves the other no alternatives whatsoever. For example, the husband may arrive home in an expensive new Jaguar and cheerfully announce, "Hey, honey, look what I picked up on the way home from the office." Or, to take another example, the wife may greet her husband at the door and say something like, "I know you are tired, dear, but I promised the Henrys that we would love to drop in for their son's graduation party tonight." There is absolutely no defense against extreme first moves such as these. One can only shrug one's shoulders and hope for a more manageable first move on the partner's behalf the next time around. It is frequently the case that the continued use of *fait accompli* by one partner will result in angry retaliation by the other. When both partners to the interaction choose first moves so as to leave the other with no alternatives, it will not be long before open warfare occurs.

Strategic threat. One partner who threatens objectionable behavior if the other does not "shape up" creates an instance of strategic threat. The husband who threatens to have an affair if his wife does not start looking and acting "sexier" is using the strategic threat. The wife who threatens to open charge accounts at all the local department stores if the husband does not increase her portion of his pay check has also resorted to the strategic threat. In order to be effective, strategic threats must be *credible*. One does not, for example, say to the partner, "If you wear that old blue suit again, I'm going home to mother." A threat of this magnitude is simply not credible. But if the wife were to say, "If you wear that old blue suit again, I'm not going to the party," the husband might very well think twice about his attire, especially if the occasion is a dinner party at the boss's home.

Strategic promise. In contrast to the strategic threat, the strategic promise occurs when one partner promises something quite desirable if the other will act in a given way. For example, "If you paint the garage door, dear, I'll fix you your favorite dinner tonight."

These are several of the tactics that Bernard proposes for understanding marital interaction. Of course, in actual practice strategic threats and promises may occur much more subtly than depicted in our examples. In fact, a clever bargainer in the marital interaction would very likely imply what the bargaining conditions were rather than state them as boldly as in these examples. However, it is clear from Bernard's analyses that much of what takes place under the euphemism "marital bliss" can be construed profitably from the perspective of various interpersonal bargaining and negotiating tactics. We do not mean to imply that marriage is nothing but a game of bargaining and negotiating; nor do we mean to imply that all the interaction between a husband and wife can be construed in this manner. Even though there is ample evidence to suspect that things such as strategic promise, strategic threat, and fait accompli take place within even the most stable of marriages, other means of maximizing expected gain in the marital relationship are available.

One reasonably attractive alternative could be labeled "Do your own thing, but love me and be available when I really need you." Although such a marriage sounds more like a non-marriage, it has the attractive features of discouraging wretchedly excessive dependency while increasing the likelihood that each partner could better approach self-fulfillment. Many marriages degenerate into the weary business of bargaining simply because partners have not learned to *release* their mates with love. It is unfortunate (and perhaps even tragic) that many a good man and woman have had to forgo exploring their potentialities because they have had to move "lock-step" through life with unimaginative, restrictive, and excessively dependent partners.

INTERPERSONAL INFLUENCE

Social scientists have long been concerned with the apparent ability of one person to exert influence upon another. People do succeed in altering each other's beliefs, values, and even, in some cases, entire life styles. The influencing process has been approached from many different perspectives, e.g., the analysis of social power, attitude change, persuasion, communication, social learning, and social reinforcement. In this section, we will concern ourselves with the nature of interpersonal influence.

Bases of power

An interesting approach to social influence has been provided by two social psychologists, French and Raven (1959). French and Raven distinguish five separate *bases of power*. In effect, the term "bases of power" refers to the *means* by which influence can be accomplished. Let us examine these in greater detail.

Reward power. If a person believes that another person has control over desired resources, then the other person possesses reward power in that situation. Quite simply, we will tend to attribute power to those individuals who can control and dispense highly valued commodities. By "commodities" we do not mean simply material things. Any highly desired resource, e.g., love, affection, sex, money, goods, services, and so on, can enter into the determination of reward power.

There is little question that enormous control over the behavior of another person can be accomplished through the careful administration of *social reinforcements*. A large body of evidence from research indicates that a host of interpersonal behaviors can serve to increase the likelihood of and maintain responses to which they are applied. Head nods, smiles, expressions of agreement, vocalizations such as "mm-hmm," verbalizations such as "good," "fine," "right," "yes," and so forth, have been demonstrated under certain conditions to be effective reinforcers. For example, Greenspoon (1955) instructed subjects to emit words at random for a period of time. Whenever a subject emitted a plural word, Greenspoon responded with a simple "mm-hmm" (positive reinforcement), but he would respond with "huh-uh" (punishment) when the subject emitted a singular word. Under these social reinforcement conditions, the number of plurals emitted increased significantly while the number of singulars decreased. Although Greenspoon, in this early work, claimed that few subjects were aware of the contingency between their behavior and the experimenter's reinforcements, subsequent work has seriously questioned the proposition that behavior in such situations can be controlled effectively without the awareness of the subject (Spielberger, 1962). Aside from this rather complicated question of the state of the subject's awareness of what is happening to him, a host of further studies clearly indicate that behavior can be brought under experimental control by the use of social reinforcers.

The student must not be put off by the apparent simplicity of social reinforcement. That the behavior of others can be controlled effectively through use of social reinforcement is a powerful principle, one of which each of us should be well aware. If essentially trivial behaviors like head nodding and saying "mm-hmm" can affect our behavior, think of what more potent social reinforcements, such as the giving and withholding of love and affection or the dispensing of disapproval, can do to us. Since our behavior is so susceptible to manipulation, we would do well to have all our wits about us in interaction with others. We might, for example, find ourselves agreeing with fascist principles under the guise of democratic ones simply because others smile when we endorse them. That this is not such a far fetched idea is illustrated by an experiment by Singer (1961). Singer administered a personality test thought to measure tendencies toward fascism, the so-called *F Scale*. Some representative items from the test which indicate fascist tendencies are as follows: (1) "Sex crimes, such as rape and attacks on children, deserve more than mere imprisonment—such criminals should be publicly whipped or worse." (2) "People don't place enough emphasis on respect for authority." When subjects endorsed an antiauthoritarian item or disagreed with an authoritarian one, Singer would simply say "good" or "right." Under these conditions of social reinforcement, prodemocratic, antiauthoritarian responses increased steadily. One has only to use one's imagination to predict what might have happened if Singer had reinforced fascistic attitudes.

In the hands of a manipulator, social reinforcement techniques could well be put to improper use. In the hands of well meaning persons, however, such procedures have been used effectively and beneficently. For example, Lovaas, a clinical psychologist, has made what only can be described as remarkable strides in the treatment of severely disturbed children, so-called autistic children. Working with mute autistic children, Lovaas succeeded in developing language through use of social reinforcement procedures where others have failed consistently with other conventional therapies (Lovaas, *et al.*, 1966).

It is important that one be cognizant of the potent effects of social reinforcement for still another reason. Often in our roles as influencers of others we *unwittingly reinforce the very behaviors we are trying to modify*. The mother who gives in to a child's tantrums, whining, or crying is reinforcing the very pattern of behavior she would like to see changed. A particularly interesting example of unwitting social reinforcement comes from the author's clinical practice with children. One of the children seen in psychotherapy by the author had the habit of rubbing his eye severely when anxious or threatened. This symptom had reached disturbing proportions since the child could no longer attend to school work, and moreover he had begun rubbing the eye so incessantly that serious irritation of the entire area was produced. The mother had tried allergenic desensitization therapy for a lengthy period on the premise that the problem was allergenic in nature, but this accomplished nothing. Then, starting from the premise that the problem was psychological in nature, psychotherapy was begun. After six months the child showed remarkable improvement. He was reading in school, and the eye and the area surrounding it was clear and rubbing had ceased. Suddenly a dramatic reversal of all of these gains occurred. Questioning of the mother revealed that she had become uncomfortable about having discontinued the child's allergy shots and had rescheduled the child with his allergist. On the day prior to the return of the symptoms, she had removed the child from school and taken him for his shots where he was rewarded profusely with social reinforcements ("You are a big, brave boy") as well as with candy. Following his injections, the boy was taken by the mother to an ice cream shop situated directly across from the child's school (where he would have been if mother had not removed him) and treated to an ice cream sundae. Under these conditions of social reinforcement, it is not at all surprising that the eye rubbing reappeared the next day. It was necessary to convince the mother that her unwitting reinforcement of the symptom had to cease before progress could again be made.

In any event, it is important that we carefully scrutinize our own behavior in interaction with others. When we do so, we may find that much of the behavior of intimates that we regard as objectionable is paradoxically being maintained by our own unwitting social reinforcing behavior.

Coercive power. Analogous to reward power, coercive power is concerned with punishment. If a person believes that another person possesses the ability to mediate punishments, then the other person is seen as possessing coercive power. Although the use of punishment as a means of influencing and controlling the behavior of another person may lead to rapid compliance with the wishes of the punisher, obvious difficulties accompany its use. Aside from our humanistic and moral objections to its use, punishment is simply not an effective or desired means of influencing another. Its effects are often unpredictable and frequently characterized by undesired side effects. Although there are conditions under which punishment can lead to a long-term behavioral change, it more typically leads to a *temporary suppression* of the behavior to which it is applied. In the course of clinical practice with children, the author never ceased to be surprised at the apparent resistance of highly punitive mothers to seeing that frequent and often brutal punishment of the child did not result in permanent modification of undesirable behaviors. Punishment does not tell a person what he *ought* to do, it simply tells him what he must *not* do. In this sense, punishment possesses very low information content. Since the child is left to figure out what it is he must do in order to satisfy the parent who relies upon punishment, it is not at all surprising that he may discover new patterns of behavior equally objectionable to the parent or, in confusion, return to previously punished patterns of behavior.

In addition to the fact that punishment is an inefficient means of controlling behavior, it has the added disadvantage of producing avoidance responses in the punished person. Hence, it becomes increasingly difficult to exercise any influence whatsoever upon the punished child who will run away from or avoid in other ways a punishing agent. The child who is punished in school for misbehaving may, for example, suddenly develop morning nausea, abdominal pains, headaches, and so forth, all of which are designed to convince his mother that he is too ill to go to school. School avoidance patterns (appropriately termed "school phobia") can prove extremely resistant to treatment.

Finally, the parent who relies exclusively upon punishment must realize that by doing so, she is *directly teaching* the child that punishment is the means by which behavior can be controlled. Consequently, it is not unusual to discover that the children of highly punitive parents are often, in turn, highly aggressive, hostile, and punitive in their own relationships with other children.

Referent power. People tend to identify with one another. This fact gives rise to the possibility of referent power. If two persons are attempting to influence our behavior, it is highly likely that we will be more open to influence from the one with whom we identify rather than from the one with whom we do not identify (other things being equal, of course). The author has witnessed dramatic instances in a variety of group psychotherapeutic settings in which persons who, for many years, having resisted changing extremely self-destructive patterns of behavior, discovered a person in the group who had "lived their life" or, as the saying goes, "told their story." Influenced by such strong conditions of identification with this person who had undergone their life experiences, these people showed an abrupt change of attitude and became open to influence from the person with whom they had identified and eventually from other persons in the group. Such increased susceptibility to social influence growing out of identification is commonly observed in self-help groups such as Alcoholics Anonymous, Neurotics Anonymous, and Weight Watchers Anonymous. It is almost uncanny to observe a sick alcoholic, who has continued to lose the battle with the bottle for over twenty years and appears to have no chance whatever to control and eliminate his obsession with alcohol, discover a recovered alcoholic with whom he can identify and change his behavior as a consequence. Although such dramatic reversals of maladaptive patterns of behavior are rightfully regarded with caution, they occur with such regularity and frequency in groups such as Alcoholics Anonymous and Synanon (a self-help group for drug addicts) that psychologists would do well to study them intensively. Of course, in groups such as these many things are taking place besides identification of the one person with another person or with the group as a whole. Social reinforcements are dispensed for appropriate behavior, views of personal and social realities are shared, advice is given, love and affection are openly shared, and belief systems are transmitted. Nonetheless, it is often clear in many cases that nothing seems to work until identification occurs. The fact that we are more open to influence from those "who have been there themselves" is not surprising. Such people appear to us as highly *credible* resource persons — they "know what is happening."

Identification with another, of course, may have many bases. One of the most poignant and chilling accounts of identification is Bettleheim's description of *identification with the aggressor,* which occurred among concentration camp victims in Germany during the Second World War (Bettleheim, 1943). A prisoner himself, Bettleheim gathered careful observations of behavior in the camp in which he was interred. Bettleheim's training as a psychiatrist was of obvious value in his role as participant-observer. It is most astonishing to read Bettleheim's account of the manner in which inmates identified with their cruel and sadistic captors. Prisoners would go to almost any length to find scraps and pieces of old German uniforms which they could make into garments that resembled those of their guards. When it became necessary to punish one of their own kind who had violated the prisoner's own rules of conduct, they frequently used the same brutal and inhuman methods of torture as did their Nazi captors.

Of course, the fact that people will identify with those who hold social power in a situation is, in some respects, not surprising. We do not find it at all unusual that a child will imitate his father or some other powerful and significant male figure. For the concentration camp victims, the fact that their captors possessed absolute *fate control* over their lives was surely a factor leading to imitation. In the face of death, it is not difficult to understand that persons would magically come to believe that their own base of power would be augmented by assuming the attributes of those holding power. Moreover, it is possible that the inmates believed that by increasing the similarity between themselves and their captors they might thereby decrease the possibility that they would be perceived as alien, strange, and different. It is easier to murder a man who is thought to be foreign to one's own self. Witness American propaganda about the differences between the South East Asian and the middle-class American. "They" are not supposed to value life as much as we. "They" are sneaky, crafty, and not to be trusted. "They" have selfish motives. "They" are different from us in a host of ways. If you want to practice violence upon some other person, you must first dehumanize him. And if you wish to dehumanize a person, you must first create differences between yourself and him. After all, *you* are human, *he* is not. It is then that you can kill him with a clear conscience.

Legitimate power. Situations exist under which we accept the fact that another person has the "right" to influence us. By reason of office, role, or position in a recognized and accepted authority hierarchy, we grant the other person *legitimate* power. The military, for example, is a system of levels of legitimate power. The Catholic Church with the Pope at the pinnacle of power is another example. We must not suppose, however, that legitimate power, once granted, is something that endures forever. The present struggles across the "generation gap" suggest that legitimacy is being challenged at all levels of society and with regard to a variety of issues. In fact, authority hierarchies of all kinds are being put to severe tests. It is almost as though the glue of assumptions that holds social organizations together were rapidly coming apart under intense reexamination and questioning. Those who hold power are inclined to believe that it is legitimate (simply because it has always been), whereas those who do not hold power do not share such convictions. As a consequence, *some* senior professors and administrators in the modern university resent the fact that many students no longer regard their positions of power as legitimate. Many students no longer feel that a professor or administrator has the right to exercise fate control over their perceptions of reality, values, political convictions, and styles of life. In the students' eyes legitimacy is "up for grabs." Considering such differing perceptions of legitimacy, it is not at all surprising that power struggles are taking place on university campuses (not only in America but throughout the world).

The current struggles for power serve to remind us that much of social reality is assumed rather than fixed in absolutes once and forever. Moreover, it is apparent that we know very little about the ways in which consensus about legitimacy is reached. Some research by Raven and French (1958) is revealing. These men reasoned that there are a variety of ways in which a person can come to hold a given position in an organization; election and appointment are the two most obvious. They conducted an experiment in which two identical work situations were created with the exception that in one the supervisor was elected by the participants and in the other he was appointed. Comparing the two supervisors on their ability to influence, Raven and French discovered that the elected supervisor had a more effective influence on his subordinates than did the appointed supervisor. In general, it would appear that persons are more willing to accept an authority structure as legitimate when they themselves have had a hand in creating it than when they have not. In our discussion of organizations and society, we will examine this important question of participation and perceived legitimacy in greater detail. For the moment, however, we will content ourselves with the observation that legitimacy can serve as a basis for social power.

Expert power. Persons perceived as possessing expert knowledge of some issue or topic are generally more successful influencers than those considered nonexpert. Obviously, if we want to know whether fluoridation of public waters constitutes a severe threat to our health, we might be more persuaded by the opinions of a man who has studied the matter for a number of years rather than one who has not. On the surface, it appears perfectly reasonable to conclude that experts on given topics will be listened to carefully and will possess enormous potential for influence. In actuality, however, not much is known about the conditions under which expert testimony will influence and when it will not. Anti-intellectualism has raised its ugly head frequently enough in American society to cause this author to conclude that expertise is often ignored or even ridiculed, particularly in political and social matters. Although it would appear that Americans are enormously impressed with technological expertise, social competence and expertise are downgraded in favor of polemic "know nothingness," ignorance bordering on superstition, and political chicanery. If we were particularly susceptible to influence by expert opinion in social matters, we would not find ourselves in the current ecological, racial, and militaristic crises. Ecologists, for example, have expressed repeated warnings, to no avail, over the years concerning the extremely hazardous profit-oriented exploitation and abuse of our ecological surroundings. The brilliant but ethically sensitive physicist J. Robert Openheimer was publicly humiliated and harassed (and later decorated) for his prophetic statements about the role of the scientist in human affairs and the ultimate dangers of uncontrolled nuclear development. Social scientists have been crying in the wilderness for years about the explosive nature of racial ignorance, prejudice, and exploitation. However, it has taken Watts and a host of other devastated American cities in addition to a crisis in black and white of incalculable seriousness to awaken white America to the plight of the black man and the frightening consequences that it portends for all of us.

But of course, in the larger social context of society, many other forces are at work to mitigate the role of the intellectual and expert opinion. Political offices must be won even if it means catering to social stupidity. Profits must be made even if in the making of them human environments are rendered unfit for human beings. Aside from these larger issues, though, in the context of two-person interaction, it is reasonable to suspect that expertise can serve as a basis for power and influence over others. A study by French and Snyder (1959) is illustrative. When the ability to influence of air force noncommissioned officers was examined, it was discovered that those noncoms rated more intelligent by their subordinates were more influential in affecting judgments made by their men than were those considered less intelligent.

French and Raven's analysis of the bases of power provides one with a useful conceptualization of the means by which influence can be accomplished. Let us now turn to the topic of *social learning*.

Social learning

In Chapter 4 we briefly examined two forms of learning, namely, instrumental learning and classic conditioning. As we have seen, both forms of learning deal with the individual learning in an isolated and nonsocial context. In the present discussion our attention has shifted to the person learning in interaction with others. The fact that both instrumental learning and classic conditioning can take place *vicariously* (i.e., through observation of others) greatly extends our understanding of how various beliefs, values, and behaviors can be acquired in social creatures such as human beings.

Novel response learning in social contexts. In an amusing discussion of the inadequacies of traditional theories of learning, Bandura (1966) poses the intriguing question, "How would you teach a child to say *supercalifragilisticexpialidocious?*" You might, Bandura suggests, adopt a teaching strategy based upon "random trial and error with reinforcement for the correct response." But how long would you have to wait for the child to say anything even remotely resembling *supercalifragilisticexpialidocious* so that you could reinforce him? Since the probability of a response as novel as this defies calculation, you would very probably have to wait forever! The student will recall from Chapter 4 that instrumental learning theories require that the learner perform the response so that reinforcement can be administered.

As Bandura points out, traditional theories of learning cannot readily account for the learning of totally novel responses. But of course theorists like B. F. Skinner, whom we discussed in Chapter 4, would argue that there is no such thing as a totally novel response. Behavior, his argument would go, is built up from molecular units to larger units. Moreover, Skinner would argue that since "I can take a pigeon and by carefully reinforcing tiny bits of behavior and shaping and molding these tiny behavioral fragments into progressively larger patterned units of behavior, I can teach what amounts to *rare* patterns of behavior in the pigeon. For example, I can get pigeons to play ping-pong, rats to drive little rat-mobiles, pigs to play the piano, and so forth. And if it isn't novel for pigeons to play ping-pong, for rats to drive little rat-mobiles, and pigs to play the piano, then God really doesn't make little green apples." While it is doubtful that Professor Skinner would address himself to Dr. Bandura in these terms, the message is clear. One can produce very novel responses through operant conditioning procedures by carefully constructing larger units from smaller units.

Even so, one wonders if *most* human learning, especially language learning, does, in fact, take place as Skinner describes it. Moreover, with regard to the *efficiency of learning strategies*, it is obvious that for more complicated human learning, operant procedures leave much to be desired. We must be careful to distinguish several things here. Because we can demonstrate that learning can take place through operant conditioning procedures, we cannot conclude therefore that learning cannot take place in *other* ways; nor can we conclude that operant conditioning is the most *efficient* or the *optimal* way in which learning can occur. Of course, Professor Skinner would never argue that his experiments preclude other ways of learning, nor would he argue that operant procedures are the most efficient.

According to Bandura, the learning of complex and novel responses can be accomplished quite readily and simply through the use of *behavioral models*. If we wish to get a child to learn to say *supercalifragilisticexpialidocious*, we might try putting him in the presence of a verbally competent adult, have the child direct his attention to the adult, and have the adult repeat the word until the child shows evidence of having learned it. In short, Bandura argues that much learning of significance for human beings takes place in human social situations through the observation of others. Once again, it is important to remember that the behavior of others is readily accessible to us. We frequently do not have to ask them to tell us what they are trying to do. Their actions show us. The means by which they approach problems, solve important life dilemmas, and achieve their most brilliant successes and their most dismal failures are readily available to us. Mothers, for example, transmit patterns of child-rearing directly to their children in their roles as social models. Many a distressed young mother has stumbled upon an important truth, and despite the fact that she can hardly forgive her own mother for treating her the way she did, the young mother discovers, much to her horror and amazement, that she is inflicting the same damaging practices upon her own children.

A wide variety of behaviors can be transmitted by way of live social models. Delinquent patterns of behavior, values, beliefs, behavior control strategies, attitudes toward persons of minority groups, and neurotic patterns of behavior can be learned through social learning processes. The parental admonition "Don't do what I do, do what I say" seems to be based upon the fact that parents are well aware that children will very likely respond to the former and ignore the latter. Nonetheless, many parents find it difficult to see the relationship between their own behavior and their children's behavior, particularly when negatively valued behaviors are at issue. The father, for example, who has handled the majority of life's problems by first soaking them thoroughly in the genuine drug, ethyl alcohol, is horrified that his son is smoking "pot." Alcohol, it seems, is not a genuine drug but marijuana is—at least to the father. The fact that America has been, for some time, a drug-oriented society is apparent in such things as excessive alcohol consumption, inordinate barbiturate, tranquilizer, and amphetamine consumption, as well as almost magical beliefs that pills of all kinds and descriptions are good for whatever ails you. At one level, there seems to be little difference between adult audiences getting a kick out of Dean Martin's legendary capacity for booze and the delight of youthful audiences at the so-called "hippie-tribal-love-rock" musical *Hair*, in which the virtues of smoking pot are extolled. The fact that youth and their elders are bitterly divided over the *choice* of chemicals to influence their states of consciousness hardly seems to separate them that widely. Considering their social surroundings, it is not surprising that youth are experimenting with a variety of chemicals. From one perspective, taking drugs is as American as apple pie.

An experiment by Ross (1962) is representative of an enormous number of studies that have been conducted recently on social learning. Ross wondered if exposure to a deviant model would result in decreased resistance to deviation in the observer. She arranged a clever experiment in which children observed a child model either conforming to a rule ("You are permitted to take only one toy") or violating the rule. When the observing children were given free access to the toys, those who had observed the deviant model who had broken the rule showed greater rule violations than those who had observed the conforming model. Bandura and his associates (1961) have demonstrated that very novel aggressive responses can be learned by way of observational learning. Moral opinions, ability to delay gratification, and altruistic responses have all been shown to be influenced by social learning processes.

Conditioned emotional responses. Berger (1962) has more than amply demonstrated that emotions can be conditioned through vicarious classic conditioning procedures. Observers watched as a person received what were described as painful electric shocks. Immediately prior to the onset of the shock, a buzzer was sounded. By attaching an apparatus to the observers which recorded autonomic nervous system activity, Berger was able to study the build up of a conditioned emotional response in his observers. In time, the observers developed a conditioned emotional reaction to the buzzer which preceded the onset of shock to the person they were observing. In other words, though shock had never been administered, the observers showed a conditioned emotional response. Mere observation of the conditioning of another person was sufficient to elicit the response.

Once again the student is cautioned not to regard Berger's work as trivial. The fact that conditioned emotional responses can occur merely as a function of observation has immensely important implications. Many of the seemingly inexplicable fears of persons may be explained on this basis. For example, a child who has never had an unfortunate experience with animals herself may show an inordinate and inappropriate fear of dogs. The origin of the fear response may stem from the fact that she once observed another child being bitten. Bandura (1966) gives a particularly chilling account of vicarious emotional conditioning in a Ku Klux Klan meeting in the deep South.

256 INTERPERSONAL INTERACTION

Children ranging in ages from babies to teenagers watched as their parents ranted, raged, and expressed horror that the black man was out to kill them, rape their women, and commit all sorts of other unimaginable atrocities. One does not need much imagination to see quite clearly how intense emotional responses in the children could become conditioned to the pejorative term "nigger" or to the sight of blacks. The effects of such early emotional conditioning are pervasive and remarkably resistant to extinction. The author once knew a distinguished professor of psychology who had been born and raised in the South. Although he was scrupulously correct and just in his dealings with black colleagues, he admitted privately that his innermost emotional reactions to blacks were uncontrollably negative. Although he had managed to overcome the intellectual basis of his early training about blacks and certainly could not

Figure 20. Humans learn by observing the behavior of others. (Photo by Gordon Cole.)

be called prejudiced, he could not alter his emotions, even though he was ashamed and embarrassed by them.

Factors affecting social learning. In the course of a day we are exposed to many different potential behavior models. What determines which of these will influence our behavior? First of all, the *consequences* of the behavior of the model are important. In general, persons tend to imitate patterns of behavior that lead to positive consequences and not to imitate patterns of behavior that lead to negative consequences for the model. The characteristics of models are also important in determining who will be an effective model and who will not. Models that have control over desired resources are more likely to be imitated than models who do not. This, of course, is quite similar to French and Raven's account of reward power discussed earlier. High-status models are more likely to be imitated than are low-status models. Prestigeful models possess greater influence potential than do those not exhibiting this attribute. Finally, it is probably true that we are more likely to imitate those with whom we identify than those with whom we do not. Again, this seems quite similar to French and Raven's concept of referent power.

COMMUNICATION AND INTERPERSONAL INTERACTION

For many students of social behavior the process of communication lies at the heart of social interaction. According to George Herbert Mead (1947), the most fundamental acquisition of human beings is the capacity to use significant symbols. Consider two persons interacting. One of the persons makes a gesture which the other perceives. The gesture, according to Mead, is a significant symbol if it calls forth the same response in the receiver as it does in the sender. In a sense, if the receiver shares the sender's cognition or has the capacity to "assume the role of the other" with respect to the gesture, a significant symbol has been communicated. Communication between persons involves far more, then, than the mere exchange of information. Intertwined with communication are such things as empathy, the ability to assume the role of the other person, shared meanings, and tendencies to act in similar ways. In order to see this more clearly, let us first consider the development of communication skills.

Development of communication skills

The name Jean Piaget is virtually synonymous with the study of cognitive development in children. Working in relative obscurity on problems of cognition in children at a time when stimulus-response psychology was all the vogue, Piaget amassed a number of intriguing observations of the course of cognitive development in children. Quite typically, his experiments involved intensive studies of small numbers of children at varying age levels. By posing conceptual problems to two, three, and four year olds, Piaget was able to offer intriguing hypotheses about the structure of intellect in the child as development unfolded. He claimed to have found various *stages* of development with each stage characterized by the appearance of particular cognitive skills. For example, consider the differences between the *preoperational*-stage child (ages two to seven) and the *concrete operational*-stage child. Suppose that we take two identical glasses and fill each with water to exactly the same level. Both the preoperational and the concrete operational child will agree that the glasses hold the same amount of water. Suppose, however, that in full view of the children the water from *one* of the glasses is poured into another much narrower and taller glass. Now when the children are asked to say which glass holds more, the original glass (still in full view of the children) or the taller and narrower glass, the preoperational child will claim that the taller and narrower glass holds *more* water, whereas the concrete operational child will correctly state that both glasses still hold the same amount of water. Of course, the preoperational child is led to his error because he makes his judgment upon the basis of the water *level* in the two glasses. Since the water level is *higher* in the taller and narrower glass, there must be more water in it. According to Piaget, the concrete operational child has learned the principle of *conservation,* i.e., that amounts do not change simply because they are transformed in various ways. The preoperational child, on the other hand, is victimized by his immediate perceptions. He cannot move beyond immediate perception to more abstract levels of thought. As a consequence, he reacts to transformations even though such transformations leave basic qualities such as amount unchanged (Piaget and Inhelder, 1962).

Piaget has made much of the *egocentrism* of the young child. According to Piaget, egocentrism is a pervasive characteristic of the thought of the young child that consists of a very general lack of recognition of "points of view." Consequently, the young child does not appreciate the fact that his views may differ from those of others and typically is unable to take the role of another, see things as the other sees them, empathize, and so forth. In effect, the young child has no basis upon which to build communication with others. He does not possess the ability, as does the adult, to seek and locate in the minds of others bases upon which true interactive communication can be built.

Flavell (1963), a careful Piaget scholar, perceives social interaction as the means through which the child is finally "liberated" from egocentric thought and communication. In the course of his interactions with peers, particularly through disagreements and arguments, the young child is forced to recognize that other points of view exist and that his own perceptions must be reexamined in light of those of others. In Flavell's conception we clearly see the intertwining of communication and social interaction. The development of communication skills takes place in the stuff of interpersonal interaction.

Piaget (1926) conducted several interesting studies on the importance of egocentrism in the young child. For example, he recorded the spontaneous utterances of children, aged 4 to 7, and analyzed them carefully. First, he established that a very high percentage of the utterances could be classified as egocentric. Second, he found that the majority of children's conversations at these age levels could be considered *collective monologues* because the children seemed to speak *at* rather than *to* one another, neither paying much attention to the other's messages nor appreciating the impact of their own messages upon the other.

In a further study, Piaget first told a child a story. The child was then instructed to relate it to another child who in turn was to relate it back to Piaget. Because they fail to take the other's point of view, children in younger age groups do not communicate effectively, and as listeners, they often fail to grasp the information communicated even though they may think they have.

A more recent study by Krauss and Glucksberg (1965) lends support to Piaget's observations. Pairs of children were separated by a screen. One child was to describe a particular design to the other in such a way that the listener could correctly select it from a set of designs in front of him. Three year olds simply could not understand the general requirements of the task. Four year olds understood but could not perform adequately. In general, the younger children tended to give highly idiosyncratic descriptions, such as, "It looks like Mommy's hat." Of course, the listener, never having seen "Mommy's hat," was in no position to use such information for a correct identification. Here is an excellent illustration of the speaker's failure to appreciate the position of the listener.

Recent work by Flavell and his colleagues (1968) throws considerable light upon the nature of communication and role-taking skills. From a series of studies, Flavell concludes that before one can achieve effective communication with others, the following must be known:

Existence. One must first appreciate that there is such a thing as "perspective." That is, he must first realize that his perceptions, thoughts, and beliefs about a given situation need not coincide with what others perceive, think, and believe.

Need. One must perceive a need for analyzing the other person's point of view. In short, one must feel that such an analysis will prove useful in achieving one's ends in the particular interaction.

Prediction. One must know how to carry out his analysis. He must be in possession of the necessary skills to discriminate the other person's relevant role attributes in the situation.

Maintenance. One must learn how to maintain the results of this analysis of the other in one's own awareness. Considering the fact that one's own egocentric perceptions will continue to compete for one's attention in interaction with others, it is difficult to maintain a clear and undistorted view of the other and of the nature of his messages.

Application. One must possess the ability to apply the results of the analysis of the other. How does one convert that which one has learned about other into an effective verbal message?

Considering this collection of complex and difficult skills necessary for effective communication and sensitive appreciation of the position of the other person with whom one is attempting to communicate and interact, it is little wonder that communication between persons is often an "Alice in Wonderland" experience. It is curious that despite extensive language learning in the schools, children are rarely, if ever, taught the subtleties of effective and sensitive interpersonal communication. It is small wonder that many persons who lack instruction fail to develop the important skills that Flavell has outlined above. While we are horrified at the thought of permitting mathematical skills to develop in a random and haphazard way, we seem woefully ignorant of the fact that the extremely important skills of interpersonal communication and role-taking are sadly neglected in the formal social developmental training of children. Given these unfortunate circumstances, who would be surprised that each of us finds it extraordinarily difficult to communicate those seemingly elusive but very important inner thoughts and feelings to others and equally difficult to grasp them when another haltingly tries to communicate them to us?

Communication of expectancies

That expectations can be communicated to others and can importantly influence their behavior is one of the more exciting hypotheses to emerge from relatively recent social psychological theorizing. The term *self-fulfilling prophecy* refers to the general case in which a *prediction* about behavior can shade over into *control* over the behavior. One expects that one will fail and one does. Or one expects that some other person will fail and he does. The intriguing question here is simply are we good predictors of events or have our predictions *insured their occurrence*? It is clear that our predictions about events in the *physical* world can rarely, if ever, influence them. The meteorologist's predictions about the weather, for example, can in no way affect whether or not it rains. However, when we concern ourselves with *social* events, it is quite clear that our predictions can have important effects upon the occurrence of these events. The public opinion poller, for example, who advertises his predictions about the outcomes of a political race may help to convince undecided voters whom they should vote for. The parent who expects her daughter to smoke "pot" and be promiscuous may communicate such expectancies in the form of subtle, indirect, and unfair accusations ("The next thing I know you'll be running around with that crowd at the beach, smoking marijuana and getting into trouble"). After sufficient unfair accusations, the daughter may say something like, "What the hell, I might as well do it since I'm being accused of it all the time anyway."

The Harvard psychologist Robert Rosenthal, whose work we mentioned in Chapter 2, has extensively investigated the effects of self-fulfilling prophecies. In his most recent work, *Pygmalion in the Classroom* (Rosenthal and Jacobson, 1968), the history of interest in the problem of self-fulfilling expectations is explored and new light is shed on the matter. Psychologists and sociologists have long been struck by the fact that behavior seems to be importantly influenced by interpersonal and self-expectations. Racial relationships seem complicated by the fact that whites expect blacks to fail while blacks themselves expect to fail. An experiment by Bavelas reported to Rosenthal in a personal communication (see Rosenthal and Jacobson, 1968, p. 6) is of definite interest here. Supervisors in an industrial setting were given *false* performance scores from tests of intelligence and aptitude for a number of female applicants. The supervisors were told that one group of women had very high scores and that another group had very low scores. At a later time, performance evaluations were gathered on the women's subsequent work. Supervisors tended to evaluate more favorably those women who had been described as superior. The important finding, however, was that the actual production records of the supposedly "superior" group were *actually superior*! One appealing interpretation of Bavelas's findings (but certainly not the only one) is that supervisors' expectations for superior performance were communicated to the supposedly "superior" group, and it was these expectations that resulted in actual superior performance. Of course, we can only conjecture from these data. In the absence of information about the condition in which no information at all about test scores was given, we do not know if the difference between the "superior" and "inferior" groups reflects the fact that the false test scores raised performance in the superior group or lowered performance in the inferior group as compared with a no-information group.

A more convincing demonstration of interpersonal self-fulfilling prophecies is provided by Rosenthal and Jacobson's work (1968). Working in an elementary school that possessed an "ability-tracking" system (children worked in a fast, slow, or medium track depending upon evaluations of their ability), Rosenthal used a procedure similar to Bavelas's. The children were first tested on standard tests of intelligence. Following the testing, the teachers were told at the beginning of the year that they could expect certain of the children to be intellectual "bloomers" during the course of the year. About 20 per cent of the children were so described to the teachers. Since the children designated as those likely to undergo intellectual "blooming" in the course of the year were selected by means of a table of random numbers and not by actual test scores (the teachers, of course, did not know this), the expectations for sudden spurts in intellectual growth during the year were *in the teachers' heads* and not in the nature of things.

The results of Rosenthal's work were quite clear. In comparison with a control group about whom no expectations had been communicated, Rosenthal found that far more of the supposed intellectual "bloomers" showed dramatic increases in *measured intelligence* (IQ) by the close of the school year than did control group subjects. Whereas 19 per cent of the control group subjects showed increases in IQ of over 20 points, fully 47 per cent of the intellectual "bloomers" showed IQ gains of over 20 points!

Curiously enough, these results were particularly pronounced in minority group children, i.e., Mexican-American children. Even more striking was the fact that within the Mexican-American group, the advantage of teacher expectations was positively correlated with the degree of "Mexican-ness" of the children's faces. That is, the more typically Mexican the child appeared, the more he benefited from positive expectation on the part of the teacher. Given the fact that expectations for such children among many caucasian middle-class teachers is ordinarily the opposite of those artificially created in this experiment, one can only wonder about the causes of minority group educational failure in predominantly caucasian middle-class schools. As the student can readily appreciate, the work of Rosenthal and Jacobson has enormous implications for education generally and for minority group education in particular.

COMMUNICATION AND INTERPERSONAL INFLUENCE

Our discussion of Rosenthal and Jacobson's work on interpersonal self-fulfilling prophecies has led us quite naturally to a consideration of communication and interpersonal influence. In the course of interpersonal interaction, communication is the means by which influence is accomplished. Through the exge of information we persuade others to adopt our beliefs opinions as reasonable, and they in turn succeed in altering ... In this section, we will briefly consider the factors associated with information exchange between persons and social influence. The communication setting consists of three major ingredients, namely, the message being communicated, the sender of the message, and the receiver of the message. Let us first consider properties of the message.

Properties of the message

There are a host of ways in which messages differ from one another. In some, the persuasive appeal can be "one-sided" in the sense that only a single position is presented and advocated. Other messages may be "two-sided" in the sense that both pro and con positions are presented even though only one is advocated. Messages can be deliberate and consciously aimed at an audience or "unintended" or incidental. As we noted in Chapter 6, interpersonal information can be verbal or nonverbal. Let us begin with an examination of incidental communication.

The incidental communication. In a clever experiment Allyn and Festinger (1961) demonstrated that incidental information can be more effective in changing opinions than information that is at the focus of attention. Allyn and Festinger exposed groups of high school students to a highly polemical speech *against* teenage drivers. Of course, such a speech would not be particularly popular with this audience. Under one condition, the students were told to concentrate upon what the speaker was saying so they could answer questions later about the arguments presented (focal information condition). In the other condition, the students were asked to focus on the speaker's *personality* rather than on what he actually said (incidental information condition). When opinions were measured after the speech, subjects who had been told to concentrate upon the speaker's personality showed greater changes in the direction of the speaker's position than did those who were told to concentrate upon his speech. What can be made of this peculiar finding? When we concentrate upon a speaker's personality rather than what he is saying, he seems to possess more of an ability to persuade us!

In order to understand this curious finding, we must take the position of the listener. When he is presented with a persuasive attempt to take up a position he does not agree with, the listener is not passively inactive. The chances are good that he is actively refuting the speaker in his own mind, thinking up counterarguments, seeking out weaknesses in the speaker's line of reasoning, and so on. Consequently, he is actually engaged in a process of reconvincing himself of the correctness of his own position while attending to the opposite position of the speaker. Now what might happen if we shifted the listener's attention away from his own position in relation to the speaker's position by asking him to concentrate upon the speaker's personality? In effect, we may have effectively interfered with this inner process of argument in the listener. As a consequence, he becomes more susceptible to influence.

A further experiment by Festinger and Maccoby (1964) supports this hypothesis. Fraternity boys were required to listen to a sound track which advocated the end of the fraternity system. Under one condition, the sound track was accompanied by a film of an actual speaker giving the address. In another condition, the sound track was accompanied by a totally irrelevant film involving the peculiar antics of a modern painter. If the incidental communication is more effective than the direct and focalized communication, we would expect the sound track accompanied by the irrelevant film to be more effective in changing opinion than the sound track accompanied by the relevant film. This is what in fact occurred. That incidental communications are generally more effective than deliberate and focalized ones is not known. However, the next time one happens to *overhear* a particular political opinion being discussed, one might be well advised to take it under advisement carefully!

The double-bind communication. One must not suppose that a message is a single, unitary thing. Interpersonal messages can be taken at a variety of levels. There is an *intellectual* content to a message in the sense that it says something at an overt level. But messages also often involve an *emotional* content as well. Mehrabian's work discussed in Chapter 6 pointed to the fact that a message has a verbal and nonverbal content. One can communicate one message verbally while simultaneously communicating its opposite by another means. Hence, one can say "I love you" at the verbal level but communicate "I hate you" at the nonverbal level. Such contradictory messages have been called double-bind messages (Jackson, 1960).

A double-bind message is one that involves two incompatible and contradictory messages. For example, the female who keeps sending "come hither" messages verbally and simultaneously *behaves* as though she wished you were in Afghanistan has developed the art of double-bind communicating to its highest degree. She may tell you that you are without question her "one and only love" only to break off dates at the last minute with a never-ending series of weak excuses. Anybody who has ever been involved in a serious and important relationship with a person who persists in sending double-bind messages can readily testify that an experience of this nature can be disturbing indeed. In fact, it can be "mind-blowing." Whether or not one can use the double-bind hypothesis to account for the development of a severe mental disorder (e.g., schizophrenia) as some investigators have done (Jackson, 1960) is, of course, another matter.

Jackson proposes that schizophrenics are those who have been caught up in intense relationships with a double-binding communicator (most typically, the mother-child relationship) and cannot escape. Under these circumstances, the child learns that his only defense is to become a double-binding communicator himself. He takes recourse in the disorder of schizophrenia, one characterized by incredible cognitive, linguistic, and communication peculiarities. Jackson's hypothesis is undoubtedly ingenious, imaginative, and creative. It is, in fact, deserving of far more extensive research investigation than it has received. Whether or not it can be used as a basis for explaining a disorder like schizophrenia (which in actuality may ultimately be shown to be biochemical in nature) of course remains to be seen. But within the "normal" range of variation in interpersonal relationships, the hypothesis that disturbed interpersonal relationships can be produced by discrepant and contradictory patterns of communications remains most intriguing.

Formal properties of communication. There is a host of formal properties of communications that have been shown to be important. For example, if you are attempting to persuade someone else, is it better to state your conclusion *explicitly* or to *imply* it? The results of a series of experiments seem to indicate that the answer has to do with the complexity and familiarity of arguments as well as with the intelligence of one's audience. If one is presenting complex and unfamiliar arguments to persons of lesser intelligence, then it is more effective to present one's conclusion explicitly (Cohen, 1964). Much the same can be said for presenting a "one-sided" or a "two-sided" persuasive appeal. With more intelligent persons a "two-sided" appeal, one in which both pro and con positions are given, is more effective than a "one-sided" appeal. With less intelligent and less well-educated persons, a "one-sided" appeal is more effective. In addition to intelligence level of the audience, the effects of a "two-sided" appeal also involve an *order* effect. If one decides to use a "two-sided" appeal, which should one present first, the pro argument or the con argument? In social psychology, this issue has been labeled the *primacy-recency* issue. In effect, the issue is concerned with the relative strengths of the first (primary) position heard or the last (recency) position heard. Unfortunately, there is no general statement that can be made—neither primacy nor recency has the advantage under all conditions. One factor concerns *public commitment*. If a listener is required to publicly state his position after hearing the first side of an argument and before hearing the second side, a rather clear primacy effect is obtained. If public commitment is not made following the first side of the argument, there seems to be no clear advantage to the first issue presented.

The type of appeal, whether it is fear arousing or emotionally neutral, is a further consideration. The evidence regarding this issue is clearly mixed; some investigators claim that fear arousing communications are effective in influencing persons, whereas others claim just the opposite. Unfortunately, we do not have the space here to delve into this interesting but complex question.

Attributes of communicators

The nature of the communicator himself can enter into the determination of the effectiveness of a persuasive communication. In Chapter 1, we reviewed a classic study by Hovland and Weiss concerning the *credibility* of the communicator. In general, the results of many experiments clearly indicate that variations in the credibility of communicators does result in variations in the amount of attitude change achieved. The more trustworthy, expert, and credible a communicator is perceived, the more he is able to exert influence over his listeners. One is reminded here, of course, of French and Raven's *expert power* concept discussed earlier in this chapter.

Aronson, Turner, and Carlsmith (1963) have conducted research work concerned with the credibility of the communicator in relationship to the amount of opinion change he advocates. That is, if you were asked to address a group of highly prejudiced persons and you really wished to change their opinions about something like the supposed "biological inferiority" of the black man, how far from their original opinions should you try to move them? The answer depends upon how credible you are in their eyes. If you are perceived as a highly credible person by such groups, you can advocate far more opinion change than if you are perceived as having moderate or low credibility.

Recalling our discussion of interpersonal knowing presented in Chapter 6, one can readily imagine other attributes of communicators that can affect the degree of influence they possess. Considering the tendency toward stereotypy that exists in most persons, one can readily appreciate the possibility that communicator attributes such as skin color, hair length, hair color, and manner of dress can all enter into communicator effectiveness. Obviously, if one wishes to influence one's local John Birch Society, one does not appear before them bearded, beaded, and carrying a well-worn copy of *Confessions of a Lady of Pleasure*. On the other hand, if one wants to influence long-haired, transient youth populations, a double-breasted blue suit, crewcut, pocket handkerchief, black socks, bow tie, and a "Support Your Local Police" button are definitely contraindicated.

Properties of receivers

The object of our persuasive attempts is hardly a passive or inactive party. Not only is he actively thinking while we are attempting to influence him, the chances are very good that if he knows that an attempt will be made to persuade him, he will be preparing himself for the attempt. An experiment by Zajonc (1960) is most interesting. Zajonc reasoned that when we have knowledge that information will be forthcoming, we prepare ourselves for it. This state of preparation acts as a selective, filtering device for accepting some information, rejecting other information, organizing the information we are to receive, and so forth. By arranging a situation involving a "transmitter of information" and a person who was to be the "receiver of information," Zajonc demonstrated differences between the two roles. Transmitters tended to organize information in much more differentiated ways than did receivers. Moreover, transmitters paid far greater attention to detail. In addition, Zajonc's results showed that when one anticipates communicating with a person who holds a contrary position to one's own, one tends toward a much tighter organization of the material received and an increased specificity of subcomponent organization of the material.

A great deal of research has been directed at personality characteristics of the listener and his susceptibility to persuasive communications. Typical are those which attempt to relate level of self-esteem to persuasibility. From the results of some studies it would appear that low self-esteem is related to greater susceptibility to interpersonal persuasion and that high self-esteem is related to greater resistance. Cohen (1964) feels that this may be attributable to the fact that persons of low self-esteem are particularly sensitive to *external* pressures and stimuli. Persons of high self-esteem typically use psychological defenses of repression, avoidance, and denial; hence they are able to ignore disturbing and contradictory information from their environments and can therefore produce greater resistance to persuasion.

Unfortunately, we cannot leave the student with the impression that the effects of self-esteem upon persuasibility are known with any certainty. McGuire's review of this topic, as well as of other personality variables and their relationship to persuasibility, leaves one with the realization that there are far more puzzles than certainties (McGuire, 1968). In some studies, relationships are found while in others they are not. Some studies yield conclusions that are opposite to the expected: greatest influencability exists at moderate levels of self-esteem rather than at low or high levels. In any case, it is impossible in this small space to resolve the many puzzles and complexities in research that attempts to relate personality characteristics of receivers to their response to persuasive appeals.

Personality change and interpersonal communication

The belief that one person can bring about personality changes in another has given rise to a special area within psychology, that of *interpersonal psychotherapy*. Although this entire chapter has been concerned with the manner in which one person can influence the behavior of another, there is some benefit to considering briefly the more institutionalized forms of personality change. One of these, the *helping* relationship, has a long and distinguished career in psychology. In order to appreciate the many forms which the helping relationship can take, let us briefly compare and contrast three theorists, namely, Sigmund Freud, Carl Rogers, and Timothy Leary.

The classic psychoanalytic relationship. According to Freud, the helping relationship was an *unreal* and unnatural one. It was an unreal relationship because psychoanalytic theory required that the therapist's real beliefs, attitudes, opinions, and feelings should not be allowed to intrude upon the interaction between himself and his client. In classic psychoanalytic therapy, the therapist must take the role of a neutral *projection screen*. In effect, he is a mirror in which the patient "sees" the many infantile conflicts and unconscious motives that are thought to still dominate his life. In a successful analytic relationship, a *transference* develops. The patient literally transfers to his analyst the attitudes, emotions, and beliefs that he held toward significant adult figures in his early life. Once a transference develops, then the real work of analysis can begin. It is then that the therapist can proceed to make clear to the patient the origin of his conflicts by analyzing the transference which has developed. He does this by offering various *interpretations* of the patient's dreams, free associations, and feelings toward the analyst.

The student can now appreciate why the therapist in a classic psychoanalytic relationship must not let his own attitudes and behavior intrude. To the extent that the patient's behavior is actually influenced by the analyst, the transference picture is distorted. When this happens, the analyst does not know whether he is dealing with the *projections* of his patient or with very real reactions on the part of the patient toward the very real behavior and attitudes of the analyst. Because the analyst cannot be "genuine" in the interaction, one can readily see why it is an unreal and unnatural relationship. In some respects, it could be labeled a *pseudo-interaction,* that is, interaction in which one of the partners refuses to bring all of himself into the interaction and, moreover, persists in claiming that he has nothing to do with the behavior of the other person. In effect, the analyst is denying one of the most fundamental premises of human social interaction, that of *reciprocity* (the fact that the behavior of each of the participants to a human interchange both changes and is changed by the behavior of the other). Of course, within psychoanalytic circles this issue has been debated. There are those who insist that one cannot help but influence the other person with whom one is interacting and that analysts ought to recognize this fact and capitalize upon it rather than deny its existence.

Carl Rogers' views of a helping relationship. One cannot find a view of the helping relationship more in opposition to classic psychoanalysis than that of the American psychologist Carl Rogers. According to Rogers (1961), a helping relationship must be *very real* indeed. To withhold oneself as a person and to deal with the other person as an *object* does no good at all. The therapist, in Rogers' eyes, must be *genuine*. In discussing how a helping relationship can be brought about, Rogers poses the following questions:*

1. Can I let myself experience positive attitudes toward this other person—attitudes of warmth, caring, liking, interest, respect?
2. Can I be perceived as trustworthy, dependable, consistent?
3. Can I express myself to the other person unambiguously such that my messages are neither contradictory nor futile attempts at concealment and disguise?

Finally, Rogers sees the patient, not the therapist, at the center of the relationship. The therapist cannot *manipulate* his patient even if such manipulation is in the patient's "best interests." In contrast to the classic analyst, the therapist does not offer his own interpretations to the patient. Such interpretations, in effect, render the patient an *object of scrutiny* rather than a person. They are a threat to his own sense of selfhood. From Rogers' point of view, the therapist is truly a helper. His principal function is to provide a safe, warm, trusting relationship in which the client can explore himself with the aid of a sympathetic, nonpunitive, and accepting person, one who is adept in the complicated skills of interpersonal communication.

Tim Leary and games people play. Leary (1961), in contrast to both Freud and Rogers, presents still a third perspective. According to Leary, behavior is largely culturally determined. Culturally learned patterns of behavior are considered "game sequences" involving six factors: *roles, rules, goals, rituals, lan-*

---
*Rogers, C.: *On Becoming a Person*. Boston, Houghton Mifflin Company, 1961.

guage, and *values.* Leary states that personality change must be preceded by a change in the game-structured nature of personal and interpersonal "reality," and the change in the game structure must be preceded by a change in *consciousness.* The person must first become fully aware of the game structure of his life and go beyond it to the visionary experience—the nongame, mystic experience.

According to Leary, the most efficient way to achieve an altered state of consciousness is through chemicals, e.g., LSD, mescaline, and psilocybin. But one must understand that Leary does not advocate the use of chemicals when one is isolated from the interpersonal helping relationship. The therapist must do three things, according to Leary:

1. Provide a serious, supportive context for the consciousness expansion experience.
2. Set up an atmosphere in which insight can occur.
3. Join the subject in an "all-out collaborative" process of selecting and mastering new games.

Even though it is far too early to assess in any meaningful scientific way the consequences of psychedelic drug use in the service of personality change, it is ignorance bordering on primitive superstition to prevent serious workers from investigating the potential benefits of such chemicals and the social therapeutic procedures that accompany them. Instead of harassing those interested in the possible benefits to human beings from the use of psychedelic chemicals, those in appropriate governmental agencies should be fostering a climate in which such chemicals can be properly researched, intelligently used, and wisely controlled. As it stands now, ignorance, fear, and blind suppression has resulted in such extensive "underground" marketing and consumption of such chemicals under inadequate, uncontrolled, and personally hazardous conditions, that one can only marvel at yet another instance in which society has failed miserably to cope with its problems in a rational manner.

From these three examples of helping relationships—Freud's classic psychoanalysis, Carl Rogers' patient-centered therapy, and Leary's account of games, drugs, and visionary experiences—we see that the approaches to interpersonal helping relationships are varied indeed. An elaboration of still other points of view is precluded only by the lack of space. Psychotherapy, like love, is a many-splendored thing. The sophisticated consumer of psychological information should be well aware of this fact.

SUMMARY

In this chapter we have examined the important topic of interpersonal interaction. Our discussion has led us to consider the purposeful nature of interaction, the expected gains in interaction and how they are realized, and the tactics of interpersonal interaction. Our discussion of interpersonal influence involved a consideration of the bases from which social power is derived, behavior controlling strategies, and the nature of social learning. We have examined the nature of communication and social interaction, the development of communication and role-taking skills, the communication of expectancies, and finally, communication and interpersonal influence.

Although it was not possible to treat interaction in terms of all available perspectives and research findings, our subsequent treatment of the person in interaction in groups, organizations, and societies will lead us to examine other problems and other approaches in greater detail.

In this chapter we concentrated upon interpersonal interaction. Let us now shift our attention from the two-person interactive setting to settings involving greater numbers. Our first concern will be the person as a member of a group.

References

Allyn, J., and Festinger, L.: The effectiveness of unanticipated persuasive communications. J. Abnorm. Soc. Psychol., 62: 35, 1961.
Aronson, E., Turner, J., and Carlsmith, J. M.: Communicator credibility and communication discrepancy as determinants of opinion change. J. Abnorm. Soc. Psychol., 67: 31, 1963.
Bandura, A.: Vicarious processes: a case of no-trial learning. In Berkowitz, L. (ed.): *Advances in Experimental Social Psychology.* New York, Academic Press, Inc., 1966.
Bandura, A., and Walters, R. H.: *Social Learning and Personality Development.* New York, Holt, Rinehart, and Winston, 1963.
Berger, S. M.: Conditioning through vicarious instigation. Psychol. Rev., 69: 450, 1962.
Bernard, J.: The adjustment of married mates. In Christensen, H. T. (ed.): *Handbook of Marriage and the Family.* Chicago, Rand McNally & Co., 1964.
Berne, E.: *Games People Play.* New York, Grove Press, Inc., 1964.
Bettleheim, B.: Individual and mass behavior in extreme situations. J. Abnorm. Soc. Psychol., 38: 417, 1943.
Cohen, A. R.: *Attitude Change and Social Influence.* New York, Basic Books Inc., 1964.
Festinger, L.: A theory of social comparison processes. Human Relations, 7: 117, 1954.
Festinger, L., and Maccoby, N.: On resistance to persuasive communications. J. Abnorm. Soc. Psychol., 68: 359, 1964.

Festinger, L., Schachter, S., and Back, K.: *Social Pressures in Informal Groups.* New York, Harper & Row, 1950.
Flavell, J. H.: *The Developmental Psychology of Jean Piaget.* Princeton, D. Van Nostrand Co., Inc., 1963.
Flavell, J. H., Botkin, P. T., Fry, C. L., Wright, J. W., and Jarvis, P. E.: *The Development of Role-taking and Communication Skills in Children.* New York, J. Wiley & Sons, 1968.
French, J. R., and Raven, B.: The bases of social power. *In* Cartwright, D. (ed.): *Studies in Social Power.* Ann Arbor, University of Michigan Institute for Social Research, 1959.
French, J. R. P., Jr., and Snyder, R.: Leadership and interpersonal power. *In* Cartwright, D. (ed.): *Studies in Social Power.* Ann Arbor, University of Michigan Institute for Social Research, 1959.
Gerard, H., and Rabbie, J. M.: Fear and social comparison. J. Abnorm. Soc. Psychol., *62*: 586, 1961.
Greenspoon, J.: The reinforcing effects of two spoken sounds on the frequency of two responses. Amer. J. Psychol., *68*: 409, 1955.
Hovland, C. I., and Weiss, W.: The influence of source credibility on communication effectiveness. Public Opinion Quarterly, *15*: 635, 1951.
Jackson, D. D.: *The Etiology of Schizophrenia.* New York, Basic Books, Inc., 1960.
Jones, E.: *Ingratiation.* New York, Appleton-Century-Crofts, 1964.
Krauss, R. M., and Glucksberg, S.: Some aspects of verbal communication in children. Paper, American Psychological Association Convention, 1965.
Leary, T.: How to change behavior. *In* Bennis, et al. (eds.): *Interpersonal Dynamics.* Homewood, Ill., Dorsey Press, 1968.
Lovaas, O. I., Berberich, J. P., Perloff, B. F., and Schaeffer: Acquisition of imitative speech by schizophrenic children. Science, *151*: 705, 1966.
McGuire, W. J.: Personality and susceptibility to social influence. *In* Borgatta, E., and Lambert, W. W. (eds.): *Handbook of Personality Theory and Research.* Chicago, Rand McNally & Co., 1968.
Mead, G. H.: Language and the development of the self. *In* Newcomb, T. M., and Hartley, E. L. (eds.): *Readings in Social Psychology.* New York, Henry Holt, 1947.
Newcomb, T. M.: *The Acquaintance Process.* New York, Holt, Rinehart and Winston, 1961.
Piaget, J.: *The Language and Thought of the Child.* New York, Harcourt, Brace & World, Inc., 1926.
Piaget, J., and Inhelder, B.: *Le développement des quantités physiques chez l'enfant.* Neuchâtel, Switzerland, Delachaux & Niestle, 1962.
Priest, R. F., and Sawyer, J.: Proximity and peership: changing bases of interpersonal attraction (Abstract). Amer. Psychol., *20*: 551, 1965.
Raven, B. H., and French, J. R.: Group support, legitimate power, and social influence. J. Personality, *26*: 400, 1958.
Rogers, C.: *On Becoming a Person.* Boston, Houghton Mifflin Company, 1961.
Rosenthal, R., and Jacobson, L.: *Pygmalion in the Classroom.* New York, Holt, Rinehart and Winston, 1968.
Ross, S. A.: The effect of deviant and nondeviant models on the behavior of preschool children in a temptation situation. Unpublished doctoral dissertation, Stanford University, 1962.
Schachter, S.: *The Psychology of Affiliation.* Stanford, Stanford University Press, 1959.
Singer, R. D.: Verbal conditioning and generalization of prodemocratic responses. J. Abnorm. Soc. Psychol., *63*:43, 1961.
Spielberger, C. D.: The role of awareness in verbal conditioning. *In* Ericksen, C. W. (ed.): *Behavior and Awareness. A Symposium of Research and Interpretation.* Durham, Duke University Press, 1962.
Zajonc, R. B.: The process of cognitive tuning in communication. J. Abnorm. Soc. Psychol., *61*: 159, 1960.

CHAPTER

8

Groups and Organizations

Like everybody ought to be free to do their own thing. You know, like, nobody should lay their trip on anybody else. I don't want to lay my trip on anybody and I don't want anybody layin' their trip on me. If somebody wants to drop acid, well let them I say. If they want to smoke grass, well that's O.K. too. It's their heads they're messin' around with. Nobody has a right to tell them what to do with their own heads. Now, you want to know why I split the university. O.K. Like it was a bad scene . . . everybody trying to lay their trip on everybody else. I'm glad I'm out of it. Now I can do what I want, go where I want to and nobody is going to hassle me. Do you know where I can crash tonight?*

In truth, everybody ought to be free to "do their own thing." Unfortunately, as of 1970 no brilliant social theorist has shown convincingly how this might be done. Whether we like it or not, much of social reality is *social,* and although many of us might hunger after the completely private experience, it is difficult to see how one can escape the necessity of interacting with others in contexts ranging from small groups to large, modern organizations. Considering the many complex functions performed by persons in interaction with others, it is also difficult to see precisely how people would organize themselves to accomplish common purposes if each were left totally to his own devices and preferences. The very concept of social organization implies social processes such as communication among members, coordination of members' activities, and at least a minimal degree of conformity to objectives and accepted practices. Of course, much can be done in modern organizations to increase the amount of freedom of members, but this will sure-

---

*Interview with a transient youth, Southern California, 1969.

ly require enormous imagination, creativity, and scholarly effort. No amount of wishing will make it otherwise.

In actuality, the problem of increasing individual freedom in both group and organizational settings is an incredibly complex one. The vast majority of groups and organizations must operate under *very real constraints*, e.g., financial limitations, legal restrictions, political considerations, and so forth. Consider the current situation of the university in America. Rising student demands for self-determination must be met in a general situation characterized by *decreasing* financial support, increasing enrollments, unstable and often conflicting relationships between the inner university community and boards of regents or other governing bodies, decreased community support of the university, and faculty dissension.

A. S. Neill, the author of *Summerhill: A Radical Approach to Child Rearing*, was able to develop a school and a manner of education unequaled anywhere in the amount of freedom granted to learners. However, the claim by psychoanalyst Eric Fromm, in his foreword to Neill's book that "If it can happen once in Summerhill, it can happen everywhere—once the people are ready for it" is simply not true. Fromm apparently ignores the fact that it was necessary for Neill to found his "freedom" school in the English countryside in almost complete isolation from the rest of English society. A more sober interpretation of Neill's work is simply that much more can be done in certain types of educational institutions to increase the freedom of members. Certainly much more can be done to make the *school fit the child, the curriculum fit the student,* and *the classroom fit the learner.* However, given the many complex problems faced by most institutions of learning, it is difficult to see "total freedom" as anything other than an illusion—and a potentially hazardous one at that. Both individuals and institutions can be destroyed when members refuse to deal with social realities as they find them and persist in pursuing their private fictions regardless of the costs. But let us examine the matter more closely. Are constraints inherently bad?

The string quartet: a study in meaningful constraints

Within recent years, a variety of persons have railed against the "organization" or the "system" as the source of all discontent in their lives. For many, the very terms "organization" and "system" are sufficient to provoke a violent response. In many radical political groups, for example, a continuing tension exists between the recognition of the need for organizing and an almost fierce resistance to the establishment of such organization. Distrustful of authority and eager to prevent the loss of individuality, numerous persons view *any* organization as threatening. But surely it is not organization *per se* that is at issue but rather the *nature of social organization,* nor are constraints *per se* at issue but the *nature of constraints.*

As an example, consider the string quartet. This is one of the most highly organized and constrained groups of interacting individuals that one could imagine. Players must agree to recognize constraints involving meter, which consist of microdivisions of seconds. They must agree to constraints concerning variations in pitch that are almost undiscernible to the untrained ear. They must agree on very subtle distinctions in the interpretation of phrases, slight increases and decreases in volume, minor differences in tempo, and so forth. If constraints *per se* were the source of all human discontents, then we would expect the members of string quartets to be absolutely miserable! But, in fact, we find just the opposite as many a joyous amateur violist and cellist can readily testify. Much the same can be said of any other musical ensemble, such as blues bands, jazz groups, or rock bands. It is rather paradoxical to note that rock musicians, for example, characterized by their emphasis upon such things as freedom, spontaneity, and inner liberation, *recognize* and *obey* musical constraints that were characteristic of seventeenth and eighteenth century performance. For the most part, they have not yet caught up with nineteenth century innovations in the nature of musical constraints, much less those of the twentieth century. Beside such "wild" men of twentieth century music as Berg, Schoenberg, Cage, John Coltrane, and Ornette Coleman, the Beatles seem quite conservative.

However, we are not concerned here with essays on contemporary music, but our example should serve nicely to convince the student that neither constraints nor organization are inherently destructive of human beings. Under certain conditions, persons willingly accept constraints and organization, regard them as meaningful, and show positive rather than negative feelings about doing so. Our arguments should center upon *particular* constraints and their effects upon human beings rather than upon whether or not "total freedom," whatever that might mean, can be achieved. Similarly, we should concern ourselves with the many ways in which social organization can be achieved and the consequences of such variations in organization rather than manifest blind and unreasoning resistance to any and all forms of organized social activity.

Why study groups and organizations?

There are numerous reasons why the study of groups and organizations should be of particular interest to us. First of all, given the conditions of contemporary life, we can scarcely escape participation short of adopting the life style of the recluse. If we must participate in such social entities, knowledge of how they function is essential in order that we achieve satisfaction and a sense of well-being through participation.

Second, if one is interested in increasing one's own freedom as well as that of others in group and organizational contexts, one must first become aware of the many subtle and complex forces which operate to inhibit, control, and manipulate behavior in social contexts. Only by becoming aware of such forces can we begin to exercise control over them in our own interests as well as in the interests of those of the other persons with whom we interact.

Finally, it is clear from recent events in American society that much more attention must be paid to the design of organizational environments if human beings are to achieve fulfillment of their potentialities. We can ill afford schools that "turn kids off" rather than "turn them on" to learning and discovery. We can ill afford to perpetuate archaic organizational structures that invite attack by increasing numbers of dissatisfied, frustrated, and alienated persons. Obviously, the complex organization stands at the very center of modern societies. It is too precious a resource to be squandered in a host of increasingly violent confrontations between those who demand change and those who refuse to change.

The following discussion is in two parts. In the first section we will concern ourselves with the individual in interaction with others in the context of the group. In the latter section of the chapter, we will examine behavior in complex organizations.

THE PSYCHOLOGICAL STUDY OF GROUPS

Though we are often unaware of it, there are very real consequences of group membership. Many of our opinions, beliefs, attitudes, and feelings are derived from such memberships. When we aspire to membership in a particular group, that group is what is commonly referred to as a *reference* group. A reference group is one that possesses the capacity to set standards for our behavior, attitudes, and opinions. These standards, or *group norms*, are enforced through the group's control over desired social reinforcements such as prestige, recognition, and acceptance, as well as through various punishments such as social disapproval, and rejection.

Not only do reference groups serve a normative function by enforcing conformity to group standards, but they serve a *social comparison* function as well (see Chapter 7). The reference group provides its members with a "comparison point" against which they can evaluate themselves as well as others. Confronted with the discomforts of uncertainty as to what he should believe and how he should behave, the person can cope

Figure 21. Reference groups are an important source of political beliefs. (Photo by Cathy L. Jones.)

effectively with such uncertainty by using a reference group as the source of standards from which judgments and evaluations can be made.

In light of these two functions of reference groups, the normative function and the social comparison function, it is not surprising to discover that such groups can exercise considerable power over individual members' beliefs, opinions, attitudes, and actions. The social psychologist Theodore Newcomb demonstrated the importance of reference groups in a study of Bennington College girls in the 1930's. Bennington, at the time of Newcomb's investigation, was clearly a community of liberal political persuasion. Students who entered as freshmen conservatives more often than not matriculated as liberal seniors. In the college community at large, the possession of liberal attitudes was one strong factor associated with the achievement of individual prestige and recognition. Under these circumstances, it was not surprising that Newcomb found that for those girls for whom the larger college community comprised a reference group, considerable attitude change along the conservative-liberal dimension occurred. As one student remarked:

> It's very simple. I was so anxious to be accepted that I accepted the political complexion of the community here. I just couldn't stand out against the crowd unless I had many friends and strong support.*

It is clear from this example that groups in which one aspires to hold membership can come to possess great social control over one's beliefs, attitudes, and opinions. Even though Newcomb's study was conducted in the 1930's, it is obviously of relevance today. One strongly suspects that reference group theory has a great deal to say about the manner in which persons are recruited into radical political groups and social movement of all kinds in contemporary American society. The fact that such groups provide rewards for membership as well as standards for belief and action in a highly uncertain, complex, and confusing world cannot be underestimated.

Normative and informational influence in groups

Extending the work of Newcomb, Asch (1951) and Deutsch and Gerard (1955) have presented a clear distinction between

---

*From Newcomb, T. M.: Attitude development as a function of reference groups: the Bennington study. *In* Swanson, G. E., et al. (eds.): *Readings in Social Psychology.* New York, Holt, Rinehart and Winston, 1952, p. 273.

two types of social influence in groups. *Normative* social influence is influence directed at having the member behave in accordance with the expectations of another. Typically, such influence is accomplished through the occurrence of various effects or reinforcements, that is, if a group member conforms to the expectations of the group, positive effects are usually the result, e.g., group acceptance, reward, or recognition. One can also distinguish *informational* influence in contrast to normative influence. As we noted in Chapter 7, the individual may interact with others in order to gain information about the nature of reality, about self, and about others. Informational influence, then, is influence directed at getting the member to accept information about the nature of reality.

Deutsch and Gerard used a situation in which subjects were required to make judgments about the lengths of lines. These judgments were actually quite easy to make; however, they were made in a group context consisting of one "naive" subject (the true subject in the experiment) and three "stooges" who were in league with the experimenter. The "stooges" had been programmed by the experimenter to obviously overjudge line lengths but to show unanimity of opinion in doing so. Both the "naive" subject and the "stooges" were to publicly indicate their judgments.

Here, then, is the situation. A person finds himself in a situation in which the information from his senses, i.e., the perception of the length of a line, is in direct contradiction to the information he is receiving from his social surroundings i.e., from the unanimous majority. By varying a number of conditions of interaction, Deutsch and Gerard were able to show the following:

1. Even when a collection of individuals is best termed a mere "aggregate" of persons brought together randomly rather than a stable "group" in which members have had prior experience with one another, informational social influence is operative. Information influence can operate independently of normative influence. Considering our long socialization training in which we are taught dependence upon others for information about the nature of reality, it is not surprising that discrepancies between our own judgments and the opposing judgments of a majority, even in an aggregate of persons, can produce pressures toward modifying what we perceive to be unquestionably "correct."

2. When conditions of true group membership are fostered either through prior acquaintance or by creation of commitment to valued group goals, normative social influence is greatly increased and produces even greater changes in the individual's beliefs and opinions than does informational influence.

Although conformity to group opinion when such opinion is clearly incorrect is a clearly recognized fact, what is not often appreciated is simply that groups can be so structured as to discourage mindless conformity to the opinions of others. That is, just as the group can be used as an effective means of undermining the integrity of the individual, so can it be employed to encourage individuality. As Deutsch and Gerard so eloquently put it:

> Our findings... do, however, suggest that normative social influences can be utilized to buttress as well as to undermine individual integrity. In other words, normative social influence can be exerted to help make an individual be an individual and not merely a mirror or puppet of the group. Groups can demand of their members that they have self-respect, that they value their own experience, that they be capable of acting without slavish regard for popularity. Unless groups encourage their members to express their own, independent judgments, group consensus is likely to be an empty achievement. Group process which rests on the distortion of individual experience undermines its own potential for creativity and productiveness.*

Unfortunately, it appears to be the case that few persons have heeded these very wise words. Most typically, the group is employed precisely as a means of undermining individual integrity, of enforcing mindless conformity to group norms, and discouraging individual creativity. As we noted earlier in the instance of public school boards and their enforcement of dress and grooming codes, such efforts after mindless conformity are frequently built into the very fabric of organizations and institutions. As the dean of a major academic division in a large American university remarked to both dissident undergraduates and faculty members of a different mind, "If you don't like it here, then get out." Such blatant threats to conform may have suited the purposes of the dean and *his* organization but they obviously played havoc with the individual personal and scholarly growth of both undergraduates and faculty members of a

---

*From Deutsch, M., and Gerard, H. B.: A study of normative and informational social influences upon individual judgement. J. Abnorm. Soc. Psychol., 5: 636, 1955.

different persuasion. Obviously, such efforts after thought control have no place in a community of scholars.

Conditions that increase susceptibility to group influence

There are a host of factors which serve to increase the susceptibility of the person to group influences. In considering these, it may be helpful to place them within the context of an actual group. From extensive observations made by the author of a variety of self-help groups, numerous real life examples are readily available. In the following discussion, we will draw upon the author's intensive study of one such group, Alcoholics Anonymous, a voluntary self-help group that achieves remarkable success in the rehabilitation of problem drinkers.

Admission of personal incompetence. When a person believes that he personally can do little about his circumstances, that he is caught in a web of forces over which he can exercise no control, and that he is generally incompetent to cope with life's difficulties, his susceptibility to influence by forces *outside* of himself is markedly increased. This theme is common in Alcoholics Anonymous and, in fact, serves as the first formalized "step" on the road to recovery. The A.A. program consists of 12 recommended steps to recovery, the "first step" reading, "Admitted that I was powerless over alcohol, that my life had become unmanageable." A typical story one encounters with great regularity in A.A. is as follows:

> When I came here, I was down and out. I tried to control my drinking but I couldn't do it. There was nothing I could do. I bet I promised myself and others a million times that this drunk would be the last, that I was going to straighten up and go about my business sober only to find myself a week later roaring drunk. I tried everything—drinking beer only, drinking wine only, moving from one job to another, changing friends, moving from Cleveland to Pittsburgh, from Pittsburgh to Kansas, Kansas to California—you name it and I tried it. Nothing worked. *As long as I believed that I* could control my drinking, things went from bad to worse. But when I admitted that I was powerless over alcohol—powerless over anything, not just alcohol—just like that "first step" says, then things started to go all right. I began to listen to what you people here in A.A. said and damned if you weren't right all the time.

Here we have a perfect example of the effects of the admission of personal incompetence. This person admitted his inability to control his life as well as his patterns of drinking and, as a consequence, became susceptible to influence from other members in the A.A. program.

It is of more than passing interest to note that in American society generally the increasing complaint that persons are powerless over their own lives has been accompanied by intense recruitment into a host of novel social organizations, e.g., student revolutionary groups, black liberation groups, right-wing paramilitary groups, and communes. Furthermore, there is ample reason to suspect that such groups demand and extract from the individual what would otherwise be unreasonable conformity in perception of reality, beliefs, values, and actions. In short, it is reasonable to argue that what we have observed in the context of Alcoholics Anonymous is applicable to other persons in other groups. A sense of personal incompetence or

Figure 22. A sense of powerlessness over one's own life encourages recruitment into novel social organizations. (Photo by Cathy L. Jones.)

powerlessness in the face of complexity and uncertainty can motivate the person to seek membership and increase his susceptibility to influence from the group once membership has been achieved.

Willingness to accept influence from outside of self. When the person becomes willing to accept attempts to influence him, his susceptibility to influence increases accordingly. Negativistic and resistant attitudes constitute a major bulwark to group influence. To the extent that the person becomes willing to accept influence, sees such influence in his own best interests, and accepts those who are attempting to influence him, susceptibility to influence increases.

Expectations that conformity to group pressures will result in gains. Homans (1958) has presented an interesting analysis of group interaction in terms of an economic model of exchange. According to Homans, human beings in interaction with one another can be perceived as behaving in accord with "profit" maximizing and satisficing models (see Chapter 4). That is, the individual is faced with sets of alternative ways of behaving. Associated with each of these alternatives are a variety of "costs" as well as a variety of "rewards." For example, a person may choose to ignore a given social norm in order to achieve certain rewards, e.g., self-satisfaction in matters of dress. However, this alternative not only includes rewards for nonconformity, it also includes costs, e.g., disapproval by others whose opinions might be valued. To calculate the total profit that an individual accrues, one must calculate both the rewards and costs. Hence, profits equal rewards minus costs. One must remember that costs will not only include the direct negative outcomes of choosing a particular alternative, but will also include rewards which might have accrued if the person had chosen *other* alternatives.

Does it help to construe social interaction as Homans does in the context of classic economic theories of exchange? There is ample reason to believe that it does. In the context of the A.A. group, there is much discussion of what benefits the alcoholic will accrue if he chooses the alternative of sobriety rather than continued drinking. Each newcomer is assured that if he will but give up drinking, he too will come to share in the benefits of abstinence. Old-timers in A.A. stress the costs associated with drinking, e.g., marital difficulties, employment difficulties, and hassles with the law, and extol the rewards of sobriety, e.g., happiness, contentment, stable employment, marital success, self-respect, and so forth. Moreover, it is made quite clear that such benefits can be reaped through very little cost to the person, e.g., going to A.A. meetings, practicing the principles of the program, working the 12 steps of the program, and stopping drinking. In other words, an explicit exchange situation is established in which profits, costs, and rewards are clearly spelled out for the person. Each individual must decide for himself, then, if the costs of conformity to the group norms are worth the rewards gained from conformity and the rewards forgone as a consequence of giving up the alternative of a drinking career. With regard to the latter alternative, a commonly heard A.A. joke is explicitly economic: "Try our program for a few months and if you don't like it, we'll gladly refund your misery!"

In general, though, if a group member holds the expectancy that the profits associated with membership far outweigh the costs, it is likely that he will become more susceptible to influence from the group.

Perception of similarity between self and others. To the extent that a person *identifies* with a group, the influence potential of the group increases accordingly. The pursuit of common goals, agreement upon means to achieve such goals, and the perception that one shares a *common fate* with others are the essential ingredients. In addition, the extent to which the person sees himself as possessing a similar life history is a further factor contributing to the influence potential of a group. In short, the *cohesiveness* of a group is a further factor contributing to a group's potential for influencing a member. Back (1951) demonstrated that highly cohesive groups exert more influence over members than do less cohesive groups. Moreover, Back's findings suggested that the quality of cohesiveness can flow from a number of different bases, e.g., from high interpersonal attraction, high motivation for task success, and group prestige.

Many A.A. members stress the similarities between themselves and other members. Despite the fact that no evidence concerning the existence of an "alcoholic personality" has ever been produced, many members will persist in perpetuating a *stereotype* of such a personality complete with common character traits, motivations, beliefs, and values. Expressions of one's own uniqueness and individuality are frequently downgraded in favor of self-conceptions that stress similarity. Many an A.A.

member stresses the fact that when he was drinking, he used to think of himself as somehow different from others, but now sees himself much like everybody else in the program. Obviously, individuality is perceived as threatening by those who failed dismally at efforts after self-control. The hope lies in conformity and the "death of self," not in the celebration of self.

It is understandable, then, that despite the fact that group members may show vast individual differences in a host of characteristics, e.g., motivations, values, preferences, beliefs, and character traits, group pressures are exerted toward *denial* of such differences and toward the selective perception of similarity. This obvious distortion has instrumental value, however, in that it serves to increase cohesiveness and, hence, increases the ability of the group to influence its members.

Social reinforcements. As anybody who has ever received the applause of a group or suffered its disapproval most certainly knows, groups possess enormous potential for controlling members' behavior through the differential administration of rewards and punishments. In his intensely interesting discussion of the social psychology of social movements, Hans Toch (1965) illustrates the importance of social reinforcements in his portrayal of the self-help group TOPS (Taking Off Pounds Sensibly). TOPS was organized in 1948 by an obese woman and her physician around the principle that the will to lose weight could be effectively energized by competitive play. Toch's description of a typical TOPS chapter meeting is most interesting and, in the spirit of its founder, most amusing.

> The ceremony is conducted by the chapter Leader, the Weight Recorder, the Crying Towel Bearer, and the Piggy Bank Bearer. At the start of proceedings, the following dialogue ensues:
> *Leader:* Who pounds at our door?
> *Recorder:* Not who pounds. What pounds?
> *All:* Surplus pounds!
> *Leader:* Pounds Off!
>
> There follows a procession in the course of which members join hands and sing the following pledge:
> > The more we get together
> > Together, together—
> > The more we get together,
> > The slimmer we'll be.
> > For your loss is my loss;
> > And my loss is your loss;
> > The more we get together
> > The slimmer we'll be.

Names and weight statistics are then read off. Turtles are required to shed a symbolic tear for the Crying Towel Bearer. Pigs must deposit fines into the Piggy Bank, but are encouraged by the Piggy Bank Bearer with the words, "They'll all do better, so don't you fret." Meetings culminate with the crowning of the Queen (King, Princess, etc.), who has lost the most weight.*

The use of social reinforcements, such as fines for the backsliders and a "queenly" or "kingly" reward for those who conform most, i.e., lose the most weight, is open and above board in a group like TOPS. Moreover, these rewards are administered in a light-hearted context in the spirit of play. However, social reinforcements are not as visible in many group contexts. Rewards for conformity are often disguised in terms of rhetoric emphasizing more lofty purposes. Punishments are more subtle or often rationalized on other grounds. The radical young assistant professor, for example, whose appointment is terminated because his scholarly publications "lack depth" or, more vaguely, "fail to make a significant contribution" may be quite correct in the assumption that what was meant was that he "failed to conform."

Since many persons come to rely upon reference groups for a stable sense of identity, for self-esteem, and self-valuing, the use of group reinforcements to enforce conformity is a particularly insidious business. Considering the near tyranny that groups can exercise over insecure persons, one is best advised to look elsewhere for feelings of self-worth, a positive self-image, and a sense of identity. Being utterly dependent upon a group for these desirable qualities is particularly hazardous. One may embark on an endless search for approval and in doing so, sacrifice all individual integrity along the way. At the very least, persons should become aware of the potent effects of social reinforcements. Knowledge is the first step toward becoming capable of resisting group pressures toward blind conformity.

Of course, we do not mean to imply that social reinforcements are intrinsically bad, nor do we view them as the means through which manipulation of persons is inevitably accomplished. Certainly in self-help groups like TOPS and Alcoholics Anonymous, social reinforcements can lead to the maintenance of behaviors that are of value to the individual. Still, in the context of groups in general, one is cautioned not to treat such

---

*From *The Social Psychology of Social Movements* by Hans Toch, copyright 1965 by the Bobbs-Merrill Company, Inc., reprinted by permission of the publishers.

matters lightly. Group approval and rejection are powerful forces that can enforce conformity to the detriment of group members. It is good to be constantly aware of this fact when interacting in a group context—both because of what may be happening to oneself and because of what one may be doing to others.

Encouragement of antianalytical attitudes in members. The influence potential of groups increases when interaction takes place in an atmosphere in which analytical and intellectual attitudes toward the group itself are discouraged. Toch (1965) perceives an inevitable transition from initial commitment to dogmatism (closed-mindedness) in persons who join groups as a part of a larger social movement. This journey from initial commitment to a self-contained world that is highly resistant to information inconsistent with the purposes, values, and beliefs of group members is apparent in the socialization of people in groups such as the John Birch Society. It is also apparent in certain radical political groups of the far left in which contrary opinion is actively discouraged and more complex views of problems are dismissed as evidence of "liberalism." The author will never forget having addressed a disparate collection of radical persons only to be threatened with physical beating from a member of the Progressive Labor Party because the author had dared to question the accepted stereotype of a "police mind."

Commenting upon the development of close-mindedness and the worship of "sacred cows" among committed members of social movements, Toch (1965) has this to say:

> By providing them with like-minded fellow members, social movements convert their [members'] unstable individual beliefs into solid, authoritative norms. In turn, like-mindedness comes about because the members of the movement tend to acknowledge the authority of their ideology, their leaders, and their sacred literature. By holding these authorities in common, members come to hold beliefs in common. And their unanimity then becomes authoritative in its own right. This kind of circle creates a situation from which it is difficult to escape.*

Alcoholics Anonymous, for example, makes a strong informal pitch for the member to "utilize his program, not analyze it." Intellectual attitudes are often actively discouraged by members. Persons seeking to understand why the program seems to work are often told to stop analyzing and simply enjoy the

---
*Ibid., p. 137.

benefits of membership. Of course, this emphasis upon antiintellectuality and antianalytic attitudes sets up a situation in A.A. of maximal control over members' behaviors and attitudes. Since no one is in a position to say what it is about the program that is effective, new members must, in effect, "buy the whole program." That is, even if they wish to know what aspect of themselves they must change in order to achieve sobriety, they have no way of finding out. As old-time A.A. members caution newcomers, "If you are like me, then you might have to change everything. I had to get rid of *all* my old ideas." Moreover, newcomers to A.A are frequently reminded that half-efforts will get them nowhere. In this setting, fantastic influence can be exerted over the person. Nearly anything he is told *can* be an important factor in his achieving sobriety and other benefits of participation. On the other hand, it may not; but the person has no way of knowing which factors are important. Under these conditions, persons have changed their attitudes, motivations, beliefs about themselves and reality, religious convictions, job preferences, and so forth, in the search for the total change that is presumably necessary for the maintenance of sobriety.

The extent to which groups can foster antiintellectual attitudes in members that result in incredible distortions of reality is apparent in the work of Festinger, Riecken, and Schachter (1956) on an odd religious sect in the Midwest United States that had predicted the end of the world. Festinger, *et al.* were particularly fascinated by what the group members would do when the predicted "doomsday" did not occur as predicted. Would they disband? Would they regard their failure in prophecy as evidence of the incorrectness of their beliefs? Nothing of the kind occurred. In actuality, group members showed strong evidence of increased efforts to convince others of the wisdom of their beliefs. That is, they reacted to their failure by increasing their efforts to convert new members to their beliefs. As fascinating as these results might be, however, we must treat them with caution. Observations of two other "doomsday" groups did not show the same results of increased proselytizing of new members upon failure to predict the end of the world (Hardyck and Braden, 1962).

We do not have to search out odd religious sects, however, to discover examples of how antiintellectual attitudes are deliberately fostered in groups. The military slogan "Yours is not to question why, yours is but to do or die" is clearly reflective of the group interactional context that characterizes the combat infantry platoon. Similarly, the powerful authoritarian hierarchy of the Catholic Church is one which encourages conformity and actively discourages intellectual analysis of papal pronouncements. Faced with the threat of excommunication, the dissenting Catholic is often confronted with the choice of losing his faith or ignoring the integrity of his own intellect. That many Catholic intellectuals are finding this situation increasingly difficult to tolerate is evident in liberalization within the church as well as in increased dissent over recent papal pronouncements, e.g., the continuing position of the Church on birth control and world overpopulation.

These, then, are some of the more important factors associated with the increased ability of groups to exercise influence over their members. We have tried to illustrate the operation of these factors in real life groups, e.g., Alcoholics Anonymous, Take Off Pounds Sensibly, groups associated with social movements, and so-called "doomsday" groups. Although we have selected real life groups as interesting illustrations of general principles, the student should realize that considerable experimental laboratory work has also been devoted to the examination of these issues.

The significance of career choice

The selection of a career is important to the individual for many reasons other than the fact that it will bring him an income and work that interests him. Career choice is significant for the person because it sets the stage for group interactions that will have a great deal to do with what one comes to believe and value and how one acts. The person choosing a career in medicine, for example, will very likely come to hold attitudes and values that are quite different from those held by persons choosing a career in art. The interactional contexts that follow from the choice of medicine differ greatly from those contexts encountered by the budding young Picasso. Howard Becker (1963), a sociologist and jazz pianist himself, has written eloquently on the effects of career choice in a deviant occupational group, that of the jazz musician.

Becker's data consisted of careful observations of his fellow musicians in real life contexts. He traced such things as the development of attitudes toward using chemicals to get "high," attitudes toward spouses and family, and changing attitudes toward artistic integrity as a consequence of immersion in the career of jazz musician. For example, the neophyte jazz musician quickly learns that smoking grass is an accepted practice among older musicians with whom he works. It is, in fact, part of the role of jazz musician. From interaction with and observation of older musicians, the neophyte quickly learns how to smoke a "joint" and how to hold the smoke in his lungs before releasing it in order to derive maximal satisfaction. Most importantly, he learns what being high on marijuana is all about. For Becker, then, a heavy component of social learning is involved not only in learning the techniques of smoking marijuana but also in learning what to expect from it. Although Becker's observations were conducted upon what was then a "deviant" subculture, his results are clearly applicable to understanding the great significance of *peer influence* in the adoption of drug-use patterns of all kinds by increasing numbers of youths in American society. More importantly, it is probably true that much of what people think of as "drug effects" are more likely *social context* effects interacting with chemical alteration of the person.

Figure 23. Career choice can importantly influence what one comes to believe. (Photo by Cathy L. Jones.)

In any case, we can readily see from Becker's analysis of the career of the jazz musician that career choice will lead to specific interactional contexts in groups whose normative structures may differ greatly from those associated with another career choice. The student who chooses a career in sociology, for example, will be led into interactional contexts that are quite different from those encountered by the student who decides to major in business administration or physical education. The important point is simply that what we become is often determined by *what we have chosen to do*.

Groups and deviant behavior

When we realize that group membership can importantly affect opinions, beliefs, and values, it should come as no surprise to discover that groups can affect the occurrence of such things as delusions, hysterical reactions, panic, and delinquency.

Cases of *collective delusion* and *hysterical contagion* have been recorded in which large numbers of people developed what would otherwise be considered outright psychopathology. For example, in 1954 the city of Seattle, Washington, experienced a "strange outbreak" of mysterious pitting on the windshields of automobiles. By the time this particular delusion had run its course, emergency appeals had been made to the Governor of Washington and the President of the United States. Explanations of the causes of the windshield pitting ranged from meteoric dust to sandflea eggs hatching in the glass, but they particularly centered upon possible radioactive fallout from atmospheric tests of hydrogen weapons. People claimed to *see* pits in their windshields grow from tiny black specks into bubbles the size of a thumbnail. Over 3000 reports of such damage poured into Seattle police stations in a single evening!

Scientific examinations revealed that the pits were nothing more than particles formed by the improper combustion of bituminous coal, particles that were commonplace to Seattle for many years. As two sociologists who studied this particular collective delusion put it, it seems likely that for the first time people began to look *at* their windshields rather than *through* them (Medalia and Larsen, 1958).

More recently, Kerckhoff and Back (1969) reported upon a case of hysterical contagion among female workers in a factory. Although officials of the plant felt that an epidemic was in progress (possibly brought on by an insect arriving in a shipment of cloth from England), medical examiners could find nothing wrong with 62 hospitalized "victims" other than the fact that they seemed to be suffering from extreme anxiety. Kerckhoff and Back speculate about the factors associated with group transmission of hysteria. They feel that such contagion becomes possible when groups interact in an atmosphere of unresolved tensions. Tense and unhappy individuals seize upon any belief that will serve to "explain" the discomfort in the situation. Hence, when a belief concerning a particular source of threat is aroused, it is passed from one person to another much like the symptoms of physical disease are transmitted. It is this process of hysterical contagion that eventually spreads through a group, producing strange patterns of belief and symptoms. Of course, it is not clear why one individual responds to hysterical contagion and another does not. In Kerckhoff and Back's study it is of interest to note that women were far more susceptible—59 of the 62 "victims" were female.

The fact that groups can socialize members to all sorts of patterns of deviant behavior is now well-recognized. The normative structure of the urban *gang*, for example, is clearly quite different from that of the suburban middle-class Boy Scout troop. In the gang subculture, social reinforcements such as prestige, recognition, and respect are given to members whose attitudes, values, and actions are clearly at odds with those of the larger society. Among such groups, skills such as artfully "busting parking meters," rolling a drunk, conning a "mark," and so forth, are socially valued, and those who achieve competence in such skills are afforded considerable recognition and prestige from other group members. Considering the effects of membership in deviant groups, we see the practice of confining juvenile offenders along with more hardened adult criminal types in penal institutions as particularly deplorable. The results are usually further socialization in the values, attitudes, and skills of a criminal career rather than rehabilitation of the young offender.

Contagion effects are not limited to outbreaks of hysteria and delusion but occur in connection with mass rioting, violence, and crowd behavior generally. Social facilitation, imitation, lowering of inhibitions, and social transmission of emotionality are clearly involved in such outbreaks. The advent of television has facilitated the spread of such effects over large areas not directly involved with a particular incident. As a consequence, large scale rioting and violence throughout a very large portion of a nation becomes a real possibility. The effects of mass media coverage of urban rebellions throughout the United States is still being hotly debated among communications experts, media officers, and governmental officials. A study commissioned by the National Advisory Commission on Civil Disorders disclosed that in connection with the urban riots of the summer of 1967 a content analysis of a sample of 837 television sequences consisted of 494 calm, 262 "emotional," and 81 "normal" sequences. On a sheer statistical count, the researchers concluded that the media had not sensationalized the disturbances (National Advisory Council on Civil Disorders, 1968). Morris Janowitz (1969), however, correctly questions the appropriateness of such an interpretation as well as the validity of an analysis that simply shows that proportionately more calm scenes were displayed than emotional ones. Janowitz correctly perceives that a statistical difference of this nature is not very helpful in deciding whether televised contagion effects did or did not occur.

From studies of film-mediated aggression that have been conducted in psychology, however, it is quite clear that aggressive and violent scenes depicted on film can have significant consequences for observers. The probability of aggressive responses in observers is increased greatly after witnessing films in which aggression is clearly displayed. It would be most surprising if televised accounts of urban disorder had no effect whatsoever on observers.

Group conflict and its resolution

That conflict can occur both within groups and between groups is of course an obvious fact. Within groups, conflict can arise from disagreement over goals, means to attain such goals, differences over evaluations of individual members, arguments over the division of labor within the group, personality differences, and so forth. The sources of intragroup conflict are, of course, multiple. Conflict between groups can arise from culturally transmitted patterns of prejudice as exemplified in interracial conflict in America, competition, disagreements over distribution of resources such as those which occur in labor-management disputes, and in other sources as well.

Sherif and his colleagues (1961) have provided us with an example of how intergroup conflict can develop and how it can be reduced. These researchers deliberately created two groups of boys at a summer camp; each group subsequently developed norms of their own including hostility toward the other group. During the first five days of the experiment, neither group knew of the existence of the other. They used this period to develop high cohesiveness in their separate groups, and from each one, definite group structures emerged. Each of the groups had established normative standards, a recognized status structure, and a system of division of labor. Once these separate structures had developed, the experimenters deliberately involved the two groups in activities with one another designed to facilitate the development of conflict. The two groups, named the *Rattlers* and the *Eagles,* were brought into competitive sports complete with tournaments, record keeping, prizes, and so forth, and often under conditions of frustration deliberately created by the experimenters. In each case, care was taken to make it appear that the other group was the cause of the frustrations.

Under these conditions, it was not surprising that conflict soon developed between the Rattlers and the Eagles. Insults exchanged between members became common, and raids of one another's quarters, with stealing of prizes and disruption of

Figure 24. Two groups in conflict, the "Rattlers" and the "Eagles," cooperate in order to solve a common problem. *From* Experiments in Group Conflict by M. Sherif. Copyright © 1956 by Scientific American, Inc. All rights reserved.

beds, personal effects, and other things, were standard practice. One group burned the flag of the other.

After conflict had continued for a six-day period, the experimenters arranged for conflict resolution to take place. First, the boys were simply brought together in a variety of situations. This *increased exposure* did little, if anything, to reduce conflict; mere "integration" did not work. However, the experimenters arranged to create a situation of *perceived interdependence*, one in which it was obvious that the two groups would have to pool their resources in order to achieve a common goal. This was accomplished in several ways. First, the experimenters damaged the camp's water supply and made it appear that "vandals" had done it. Repair of the water supply could only be accomplished through cooperative effort on the part of the Rattlers and the Eagles. As the thirst of each group increased, such cooperative efforts were soon forthcoming. This was followed by another attempt to increase perceived interdependence. The boys were told that it would be possible to show a film that night but that sufficient monies were not available in the camp budget to do so. If they wished to see the film, the Rattlers and the Eagles would have to pool their resources. Each group contributed their funds and the film was shown to a gathering of Eagles and Rattlers. Then, finally, a long trip was planned in which the boys had to cooperate in such matters as tent pitching, meal preparation, and site clearing.

From this field study in the development and resolution of conflict we can conclude certain things about conflict resolution. First, once conflict has developed, increased exposure in and of itself is not sufficient to resolve conflict. The important issue seems to be what takes place during periods of increased exposure. If two groups can see that cooperation is in their best interests in achieving a mutually desired goal (the creation of the perception of interdependence), then the reduction of conflict becomes more probable.

Of course, other procedures exist through which conflict resolution can be achieved. The traditional practices of bargaining and negotiating can be brought into play. One must remember that in group situations, the commodities exchanged in bargaining need not be money or other material goods. Prestige, commitment to one goal rather than another, trade-offs on tactics to achieve goals, status, recognition, and so forth, can all enter into group bargaining situations as commodities to be exchanged.

In the process of committee work in a variety of contexts, the author became intrigued with the fact that *time* is often utilized as a commodity to be exchanged in conflict resolution. On one committee, two factions developed, both of which held substantially different ideas about the nature of the final product. They also differed on their perceptions concerning work flow, one group arguing that a preliminary report should be ready long before the other group thought it feasible or desirable. In this situation, the *substantive content* of the report was the principal issue. However, a secondary issue was the *time* at which various stages of the work should be completed. Unaware of what they were doing, the groups resolved their conflict by arranging trade-offs between time and content. One group offered the following: "If you guys will agree to the following general ideas in the report, then we will agree to setting the deadline for the preliminary report as of August instead of January." Interestingly enough, the opposing faction agreed! Questioning of faction members afterwards revealed that they had no idea that this was how the conflict was resolved. Most commented that they had finally gotten together on the issues; that is, compromise over content was at the focus of their attentions and they did not see that this was made possible by the trade-off between time and content.

Those responsible for the management of intergroup and intragroup conflict should be constantly aware of the fact that the situation can be elaborated greatly if one exercises one's imagination. It is precisely when groups appear completely "deadlocked" that one needs to find a different basis for proceeding, perhaps through creating "novel" commodities where none had previously existed, calling the groups' attentions to them, and arranging trade-offs that will bring satisfaction to both parties. In union-labor conflicts, the addition of so-called "fringe benefits" can frequently be used in precisely this fashion to tip the scales in "favor" of one or the other parties in the dispute.

Another factor important in reducing intergroup conflict is the maintenance of *communication*. It is unfortunately true that groups in conflict tend to stop communicating with one another. However, as in the instance of increased exposure, increased communication may intensify rather than reduce conflict. The husband and wife, for example, who agree that they must "sit down and have a long talk about their differences" may emerge from such a chat angrier and more frustrated than before! Once again, one must pay attention to the manner in which a social conflict resolution procedure is conducted. One very effective device for increasing the benefits of communication for either persons or groups in conflict is to arrange *explicit rules* under which such communication will be conducted. One such rule might simply be that each party must agree to act as if, for the moment, they had no *histories*. That is, the husband and wife in conflict must try communicating about present feelings and difficulties and attempt to exclude the past. It is unfortunate that people tend to possess different perceptions of the history of the development of a relationship and, as a consequence, attempts at communication frequently degenerate into squabbles over such things as who did what to whom, who was at fault in that instance, who said what, who behaved like an idiot, and so on and so forth. And, of course, little can be accomplished to resolve present tensions when the situation is further complicated by the tensions, frustrations, and hostilities arising over disagreements about *past* interaction. Even though tactics such as these concerning restricted rules of communication seemed to have worked admirably in the context of interpersonal conflict situations, it is, of course, another matter to generalize them to group conflict situations. Nonetheless, the important point has been made. Increasing communication between groups in conflict is, in and of itself, no assurance that conflict reduction will result. One must pay considerable attention to the conditions under which such increased communication is achieved.

Some generalizations emerging from group research

An enormous amount of research has been conducted upon groups within the past several decades. Although the findings are not often straightforward and unequivocal, it is possible to make some tentative generalizations. In considering these we will draw upon excellent summaries provided by McGrath and Altman (1966).

Group size. Although many people have definite feelings about the importance of group size, only a few consistent relationships appear to have accrued from the great number of studies on this variable. These are as follows:

1. Decreasing group size is associated with decreased emphasis upon the part of members that definite guidance and leadership are important.
2. Decreasing size is associated with decreasing attitude change among members.
3. Decreasing size is associated with increasing pride in accomplishment and perception of success on the part of members.
4. The general proposition that decreasing group size is associated with increased group effectiveness is not consistently supported. Systematic research on the effects of group size for many different types of subjects, groups, and tasks is definitely indicated.

Group composition. Even though it is commonly accepted that a group is much more than the mere sum of its parts, very little systematic research has been conducted on the problem of group compositions. It is difficult to generalize any proposition about the composition of a group. For some tasks and some variables it is quite possible that high similarity among members in such things as skill patterns, motivations, personality characteristics, and intelligence levels may be desirable. On the other hand, one can well imagine situations in which different but *complementary* patterns within a group would be preferable to highly similar patterns. If the task that a group is required to perform is a complex one requiring a mixture of complementary skills in the members, high similarity among members' skill patterns would not be as desirable as a diversity of skill patterns. In short, although it may very well be true that groups are much more than the sum of their parts and that interactions between and among such things as member characteristics, task requirements, and social context must be considered, little systematic research has been accomplished that sheds light on these complex interactions.

Attitudes of members. In general, it would appear that a variety of factors can affect the ways in which members regard the task of a group as well as the group situation itself. However, there is no clear evidence that members' attitudes are linked to their performance in groups. Despite the common-sense notions that poor morale and poor attitudes are associated with poor performance, the vast numbers of studies conducted on these variables do *not* support the common-sense notion. There is fairly clear evidence, however, that task and group attitudes can affect performance *indirectly* through increases in absenteeism, job turnover, and so forth, in industrial work group settings. Factors that favor the development of positive task and group attitudes are high social status within a group, member autonomy, cooperative group conditions, and the perception of success by members.

Authoritarian attitudes in members. One of the most frequently researched variables in small group research is the presence or absence of authoritarian attitudes among members. While authoritarian attitudes seem to be associated positively with status striving in a group and associated negatively with friendship and leadership choices of one group member by other group members, the results for this variable are generally confusing, inconsistent, and negative (in the sense that no relationship between it and other variables can be demonstrated).

Member position. In general, status and power tend to go together in a group; that is, those who have achieved high social or task status tend to exercise the power that accompanies these positions. Moreover, persons in groups who enjoy power as a function of position show more involvement in the group's efforts, greater commitment to the group, and greater satisfaction in group successes.

Interpersonal attraction in groups. It would appear that persons tend to like others in the group who hold similar beliefs and opinions, and, moreover, they are attracted to those who seem to have similar attitudes and orientations toward the group task. It would appear that there are consequences of interpersonal attraction within groups. High interpersonal attraction leads to greater communication, less defensive communication, greater attentiveness to others, and fewer communication difficulties. In addition, it seems that perceptions of both individual and group success are heightened by high interpersonal attraction. Quite simply, we are likely to regard those to whom we are attracted as doing a good job. In any case, we can see that attraction, communication, and perception of success are a set of *interdependent* variables. Increases in one variable will affect the others. People tend to like those with whom they have achieved success, tend to perceive their efforts as successful when attracted to one another, and they communicate more when attracted to one another.

Group leadership. When considering leadership, one must distinguish between a *designated* leader and an *effective* leader; these are not always the same. With regard to who emerges as a leader (designated leader), variables such as high status, skill level, and amount of training for the task at hand are important factors. However, a designated leader is not necessarily an effective one. It is here that the effort to distinguish between effective and noneffective leaders becomes far more complex and confusing. There is some evidence, however, that effective leaders are those who show a high frequency of problem definition and information seeking, high ego involvement in the activities of the group, and less reliance upon assumed similarity as an interpersonal perception strategy (see Chapter 7). However, along numerous other dimensions it has not proved possible to distinguish between effective and noneffective leaders.

Participation. The greater the extent to which a member perceives himself as participating in the decision-making of a group, the greater will be his commitment to action flowing from the decisions that are made. It is not always clear, however, precisely how participation will relate to group performance. Obviously, a point is reached at which participation becomes counterproductive. For example, members of a completely democratically run academic department, in which each is consulted about everything from buying paper clips to hiring new professors, might spend most of their time in committee meetings haggling over the number of erasers that each man should get!

Summary

In this portion of the chapter we have tried to show the student the important effects that group membership can have for the individual. We discussed the factors that augment the influence that groups can exercise over individuals and illustrated these in the functioning of "real life" groups, e.g., Alcoholics Anonymous, Take Off Pounds Sensibly, and groups associated with social movements. We illustrated the importance of career choice in a person's life, related the occurrence of deviant patterns of behavior to group membership, discussed group conflict and its resolution, and concluded our discussion with a brief survey of some generalizations from small group research. We shall now turn our attentions to the complex organization.

THE PERSON IN THE COMPLEX ORGANIZATION

In 1956, William H. Whyte presented his beliefs that a new "personality type" had appeared on the American scene. Moreover, this new personality brought with him a new ethic or system of values around which to order his life. Whyte named this new type the "organization man" and he referred to his ethic as the "social ethic." According to Whyte, the organization man not only worked in an organization, he *belonged* to it. In exchange for the security of the large organization, whether in business, government, education, or private foundation, the organization man permitted greater intrusions into his private life, more significant shaping of his aspirations and values by his work organization than ever before witnessed in American society. In contrast to the Protestant ethic of previous generations (an ethic characterized by hard work, thrift, individual effort, and competitive struggle), the organization man arranged his life around the social ethic (an ethic emphasizing such things as "belonging," "getting along with others," "fitting in," and "working well with others"). For Whyte, the progressive bureaucratization of work and the extension of organizational values into the private lives of persons signaled the end to traditional American values of rights to privacy, the importance of individual creativity, and individual striving for excellence.

Whyte never made particularly clear what factors gave rise to the organization man. He does, at one point, lay the blame upon the rise of the corporation in America. At another, he seems to indicate that it is the social ethic itself which has given rise to the organization man. But one is made a bit uncomfortable by these explanations. Upon careful examination, these explanations seem more "pseudo" than real and seem to be characterized by "circularity." That is, to say that one suddenly notices more bureaucrats running about as the numbers of bureaucracies proliferate is one of those "truisms" that really do not enlighten us in terms of explanatory power. And although it is perfectly permissible to define an organization man as one who holds a particular set of values, it is not permissible to then explain how he got that way by reason of these very same values. In doing so, we are in danger of confusing our definitions with *causal* statements. By treating the origin of his personality type in this manner, Whyte is in clear danger of finding precisely what he set out to find, or, to put it another way, he is in danger of "rediscovering" his original definitions.

Aside from the question whether or not it is meaningful to speak of an "organization man" and a "social ethic," it is clear that Whyte did put his finger squarely upon a problem of increasing concern to many persons, namely, the increasing *interdependence* of modern life and the dangers it portends for the values of individualism, rights to privacy, individual initiative, and creativity. But there are good reasons for such increased interdependence. As work organizations become more differentiated in response to increasingly complex tasks, technology, and specialized information, the need for greater communication, coordination, and collaboration among individuals becomes increasingly apparent. Consider, for example, the Apollo Space Program. The design and construction of the actual space vehicle required a staggering total of 500,000 parts and involved the coordinated efforts of several major companies and many widely separated subcontractors. Although a mission may involve only a handful of astronauts, literally thousands of people were engaged in a common endeavor to put the capsule into orbit around the moon and finally to place men on the surface of the moon.

Obviously, undertakings such as these require a cooperation, coordination, and collaboration never envisioned in the industrial work organization of America at the turn of the century. It is not surprising that the changing nature of the scientific information pool as well as the changing nature of both the product and the process of production have necessitated changes in the organization of human effort. In short, the reality of the scientific-technological revolution itself is a principal factor in the increased interdependence which characterizes modern organizations.

As it becomes apparent that no single discipline and no single individual researcher possess the capabilities to discover solutions to many pressing problems, it is not surprising to find many scientists turning to collaboration in interdisciplinary teams to seek answers to these complex problems. Solutions to problems such as air pollution may eventually yield to teams of specialists composed of ecologists, psychologists, political scientists, economists, engineers, and physicists. Such interdisciplinary efforts would be a natural outcome of the recognition of the fact that air pollution is not a problem consisting of only one dimension but one that involves ecological, psychological, political, economic, and engineering dimensions.

Given such realistic pressures toward collectivization of work, it is clear that the problem of increasing individual autonomy and freedom in organizations is an incredibly complex one. It involves far more than people and their ethics as Whyte would have us believe. If we are ever to learn how organizations can be designed to increase individual freedom, it is clear that we will have to take account of the changing nature of work and technology. We will have to examine the organization in the technological, economic, and sociopolitical environment in which we find it, and above all, we will have to learn a great deal more about organizations and how they function. Of course, these many factors are beyond the scope of our present discussion. In this brief space we can only hope to introduce the student to psychological inquiry in organizations.

Approaches to the Study of Organizations

The history of the study of behavior within organizations reveals that a number of approaches have been attempted. We can identify several schools of thought: scientific management, the so-called classic organizational theory, the human relations school, and the human potentialities theory. Let us consider each of these.

Scientific management

Frederick Taylor, an engineer by training who lived from 1856 to 1917, was one of the first persons to attempt a scientific approach to the study of behavior in organizations. Considering his engineering background, we are not surprised that Taylor became preoccupied with the problem of increasing the *efficiency* of the worker in the industrial organization. Taylor was convinced that there was one best method for doing a job that would be discovered after painstaking analysis of the job itself. Moreover, he felt that through careful *selection* coupled with intelligent *training*, job efficiency could be increased enormously.

An example of Taylor's approach is his application of a "best method" of bricklaying developed by Gilbreth, another scientific management worker (Taylor, 1911). From careful analysis of the movements of the bricklayer, Gilbreth devised an alternate way to lay bricks that he claimed was far superior to the means worked out by the bricklayer himself. According to Taylor, this method resulted in a reduction of movements by the bricklayer from eighteen to five and in a corresponding increase in efficiency reflected by an increase in output from 120 to 250 bricks per hour.

As we can see from this example of the work of the scientific management theorists, scant attention was paid to the worker as a *person*. In a very real sense, he was regarded as a "machine" much like the mechanical machines in a factory. The problem was not one of increasing his satisfaction, morale, and commitment to the organization, or to find ways in which the worker could fulfill himself through his work. The problem was purely one of efficiency.

Classic organization theory

Whereas scientific management theory treated the worker as though he were a "machine," classic organization theories, in a sense, pretended as though he did not exist. The central problem for the classic organization theorist was to develop a body of abstract principles concerning the best way to organize in order to get work done. For the classic organization theorist, the problem of organizational *structure* was uppermost, and by the term structure, he referred to a number of variables commonly thought of when people speak of organizations, e.g., the "chain of command," the "span of control," and so forth. Another way to appreciate what the classical theorist meant by structure is to think of the familiar "organization chart," a graphic means by which such things as the authority hierarchy, formal channels of communication, number of positions, and number of persons supervised in various positions are depicted. Figure 25 illustrates two different organizational charts, and hence two different formal organizational structures.

From Figure 25 we can see that considerable differences can exist in the ways formal organizations are structured. In structure *A*, a situation exists in which a single superior is responsible for eight subordinates. The superior can communicate with each subordinate, and they, in turn, can communicate with him. However, no provisions have been made for subordinates to communicate with one another. This might be a schematic representation of the structure of a highly authoritarian elementary school classroom, one in which the teacher and the individual student can communicate with each other. However, students are not permitted to communicate with one another.

In structure *B* we immediately note a greater complexity. In contrast to structure *A*, in which there is only one level of supervision, structure *B* shows three levels of supervision. In this instance we might think of a president of a university communicating with his vice-president who, in turn, communicates with three academic deans who, in turn, communicate with several professors.

The classic theorists then, in a sense, concerned themselves with finding the "best" ways to design organizational structures, taking into account such things as the authority hierarchy, the numbers of positions, and number of people supervised at each level. In a sense, their problem was one of "drawing the best organizational chart." As one student of organizations put it, classic theorists seemed to talk about "organizations without people" (Bennis, 1959). We can understand why this remark was made since it would appear that the many *individual differences* that people show in such things as values, motives, and intelligence were rarely considered by the classic theorists. It was almost as if such differences did not matter and that people were merely interchangeable slots. In viewing typical organizational charts, one certainly does not get the impression that the little circles represent struggling, breathing, flesh-and-blood *people*.

Despite the fact that many criticisms of the classic theorists have been made, an accumulating body of research suggests that they were not totally wrong in their preoccupations. While

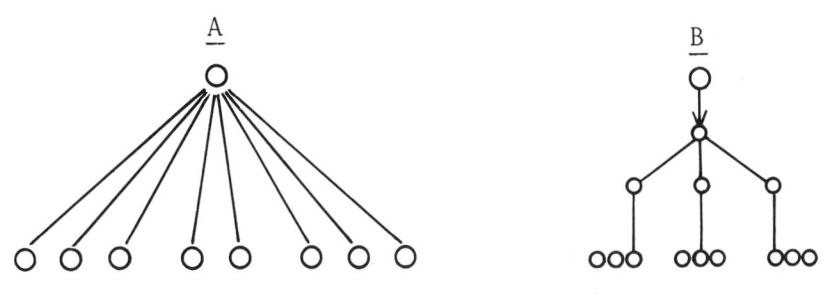

Figure 25. Two different formal organizational structures.

we must, of course, pay considerable attention to "people" variables in the study of organizations, we cannot neglect the structures in which they behave. Lyman Porter and Edward Lawler (1965), two organizational psychologists, have provided us with an excellent summary of the research on organizational structure, which we will now consider briefly.

Centralized versus decentralized structures. Within recent years, the cry for decentralized structures has been heard in a variety of contexts. Those dissatisfied with the highly centralized big-city school system seem convinced that "decentralization" will solve all their problems. University students attack the large, highly centralized university structure as the source of all their woes. The centralized corporate structure is seen as a factor in increasing worker unhappiness and alienation. Despite the fact that little research evidence exists, people seem convinced that decentralized structures are far superior to centralized structures. It is amusing to note that just a few years ago, in several contexts, the argument was just the reverse. For example, those interested in greater liberalization of public school education fought *against* the local control of schools. Without state control over education at the local level, it was feared that all of the ignorance and prejudice found in local power structures would operate to the detriment of the education of children, particularly minority group children.

It is obvious that many persons refuse or are unable to approach problems concerning the distribution of authority in a rational manner. The specter of a distant, powerful, centralized source of authority is so emotionally provocative that persons refuse to consider the possibility that *for certain purposes* a centralized structure may actually prove superior to a decentralized structure. With regard to education, it is most clear that numerous small independent school districts cannot possibly hope to possess the necessary resources for the purchase of complex educational equipment and materials. They possess neither the personnel nor the money to engage in significant and imaginative curriculum development, badly needed in-service training of teachers, and significant research into educational methods.

As Porter and Lawler point out, the research findings that do exist do not support the generalization that decentralized structures are superior to centralized structures. In general, the research indicates that there are no significant differences between centralized and decentralized structures for a number of variables, e.g., worker satisfaction, turnover rate, number of grievances, absenteeism, accident frequency, and accident severity. There is evidence to the effect that no generalization will ever be possible since it appears that the effects of centralization-decentralization are likely to vary as a consequence of the particular type of enterprise that one is engaged in. For some purposes, centralization is superior; for others, decentralization. We are best advised to avoid unreasoning, polemic debate in these matters and seek solutions in the realities of specific situations.

Organization shape: tall or flat. The shape of the organizational structure is revealed by its number of levels relative to its total size. For example, an organization of very large size with only two levels of supervision would be considered a "flat" organization. On the other hand, an organization of the same size but with fifteen levels of supervision would be considered a "tall" organization. In 1959 Worthy claimed to find in his studies of the Sears, Roebuck and Company that flat organizational structures with a maximum of decentralization tend to be associated with improved members' attitudes, greater individual responsibility, and more effective management. Curiously enough, Worthy did not present any data to back up his claims, but his study is widely cited as evidence for this proposition. Subsequent studies have not supported Worthy's claims, and in two particular studies, organizational shape had no demonstrable effect on employee satisfactions. From an unpublished study conducted by Porter and Siegel (cited in Porter and Lawler, 1965) it seems that one must consider the *size* of the organization as well as the shape. In companies having less than 5000 employees, flat structures were associated with greater managerial satisfaction, whereas in companies of over 5000 employees there were no differences between flat and tall structures. We should also note that one may have to consider organizational *level* as well since results may vary depending upon whether one is looking at employee attitudes or managerial attitudes.

Once again we are cautioned to avoid generalizations that seem meaningful but upon close examination leave much to be desired. Many people tend to react emotionally to complex organizational structures and consequently seem ready to believe the worst about them. Unfortunately, they do so in the absence of any clear-cut data that would serve as a basis for rational judgments.

Organizational size. The "big, impersonal" organization is frequently trotted out to explain every discomfort that anybody has ever experienced. Student turmoil is seen by many as a consequence of the large size of most contemporary universities. Worker dissatisfaction is seen as a direct consequence of the size of modern corporations. Once again the student is cautioned to treat such pseudo-explanations carefully. There is no clear evidence that the total size of an organization is a factor in member dissatisfaction. There is, in fact, sufficient evidence to suggest that pressures for conformity, for example, can take place in very small organizations as well as in very large ones. "Bigness" is an attribute that seems to invite fear, anger, and frustration. It is often the case that members use the "big" organization as a ready scapegoat for all their own *individual* difficulties. In many respects, the large organization in American society has become the scapegoat or whipping boy for many unhappy, frustrated, and dissatisfied people. Parents served this function before, but it now seems that the modern organization

Figure 26. The modern organization in conflict. Whether or not a communist should be permitted to teach arouses heated controversy on the campuses of the University of California. (Photo by Cathy L. Jones.)

has become the "garbage can" into which personal problems and "bad" feelings are dumped.

In considering size, one must take into account the size of subunits within an organization. This is probably a more critical factor than total size. What evidence exists indicates that increasing subunit size is associated with increasing worker dissatisfaction, decreasing group cohesiveness, and a host of worker difficulties, e.g., high job turnover, labor strife, and higher absenteeism. Rather than railing against "large, impersonal" organizations like Berkeley, students would be advised to concentrate their energies on attempting to devise plans through which an intelligent arrangement of small subunits could be devised.

Summary of research on structure. It should be clear to the student that questions concerning the "best" organizational structure will not be answered by emotional, unreasoning, and polemic attacks upon convenient stereotypes. Much careful *empirical* study of alternative structures in specific contexts is needed before intelligent decisions can be made. Clearly, structural variables are important to the individual in the organization. How best to deal with them is far from understood.

The human relations school

Whereas the classic theorists seemed to act as if organizations without people could be studied, the human relations school seems to act as if *people without organizations* could be studied. The human relations school neglected the structural properties of organizations to focus upon such things as member interpersonal relationships, superior-subordinate relations, motivations, values, feelings, and so forth. The focus upon human relations in organizations is generally attributed to the work of Elton Mayo and experiments conducted by his group at the Chicago Hawthorne Plant of Western Electric between 1927 and 1932. Mayo and his colleagues began their studies with the hope of establishing the effects of certain *physical* variables upon worker output. They were particularly interested in such things as the level of illumination under which work was conducted, humidity, and rest periods. Much to their surprise, work output increased under all conditions, even adverse conditions. Puzzled by these results, Mayo and his colleagues decided to look further into the situation. They simply concluded that *social factors* were far more important than physical factors in determining worker output. In one case, workers merely reacted positively to the attentions they received in being singled out as special subjects in research. From other observations it became obvious that work groups established *social norms* governing the rate at which any single worker could produce. In order to be accepted by the group, any single worker had to work at a rate deemed appropriate by group standards. Hence, it was the social norms of the group that determined rate of production and not such things as wage incentives. In the context of the group, one must not be a "rate buster" (over producer) or a "chiseler" (underproducer).

These inadvertant findings concerning the *informal social* structure of work groups and their importance for understanding worker behavior led to considerable preoccupation with human relations in organizations. Within recent years, researchers have turned their attentions to the ways in which interpersonal relationships in organizations can affect the total organizational enterprise. The *sensitivity training group* has become a standard method for increasing interpersonal competence, trust, and understanding in many organizational contexts. Through group interaction methods, members of organizations examine their fears, suspicions, and hostilities toward other members of the organization. It is claimed by many proponents of sensitivity training that such laboratories in interpersonal relationships not only improve individual and interpersonal feelings of well-being but also increase organizational effectiveness as well. Despite the enthusiasm of many proponents of sensitivity training, data verifying its effectiveness are difficult to come by. First of all, we need to realize that evaluation of such methods cannot be achieved by examining something as diverse as "sensitivity training." Obviously, such training can be conducted in a variety of different ways, in a variety of group interactional contexts, for a variety of purposes, and with persons of varying characteristics. Carefully conducted research that clarifies the effects of person, group, and context variables must be accomplished before a clear picture of the potentialities of sensitivity training can be fully appreciated.

Of course, we do not mean to imply that such research is not conducted at all, nor do we mean to question the reasonableness of the notion that interpersonal relationships in organizations are crucial matters. The work of Argyris (1962) and others (Stock, 1964) shows definite promise in this direction. However, we must not let the emphasis upon feelings, to the neglect of intellect, in the conduct of sensitivity training blind us to the fact that much careful *intellectual* analysis of such groups is in order. We need to know such things as the types of problems for which such groups are beneficial and the types for which they may actually prove detrimental. We need to know the organizational contexts in which they fit and those in which they do not. We need to know something about the various ways in which such groups can be conducted and the consequences of such variations.

Finally, it is important for those working with sensitivity training to recognize that interpersonal relations are imbedded in a larger organizational context which is, in turn, imbedded in a larger societal context. Many problems in interpersonal relationships in an organizational context may be associated with the *structure* of the organization and not with the fact that its members are unskilled in interpersonal relationships. For example, a communication structure which is so faulty that satisfying work within it is impossible may give rise to undesirable interpersonal relationships which no amount of sensitivity training can overcome. In this case, one must change the communication structure, *not* the ability of people to relate to one another. Similarly, many of the problems of complex organizations such as the modern American university will not be resolved by groups of students and faculty relating openly and honestly to one another (although that is obviously desirable and important). In order to produce improved faculty-student relationships, one might be forced to attempt to change not only such relationships but also the overall context in which such relationships occur, e.g., the reward structure of the university, the relationship of the university to the larger American society, and the relationship of the "internal" authority structure to the "external" authority structure.

Human potentialities theory

The human relations school was regarded with considerable suspicion by numerous critics. Their criticisms centered on the fact that human relations techniques gave the semblance rather than the substance of participation to the member of the organization. That is, many of the techniques of the human relations school seemed to be directed toward making the person in an organization "satisfied with his lot" rather than giving him a real voice in matters that concerned him. In effect, the decisions were still being made for the worker by higher authority. All that human relations techniques did was give management a potent means for manipulating the worker to cause him to feel happy about decisions made for him and, hence, to increase his efficiency. In a sense, these criticisms of the human relations school make it appear that this approach was really nothing more than a logical extension of Taylor's scientific management. However, instead of manipulating the movements of the worker to increase his efficiency, human relations theorists were manipulating his psyche. But, of course, these judgments by the critics of the work of the human relations theorists are far too harsh. It is obvious that the emphasis upon human relationships in organizations brought attention to bear on a host of neglected psychological and social factors. The human relations school is of undeniable historical importance in the gradual evolution of the worker, initially construed as a "machine" and later granted the right to seek such things as self-fulfillment in the organizational context.

In recent years, emphasis upon meaningful rather than pseudo-member *participation* has given rise to a school which, for want of a better title, we will label the "human potentialities school." The work of the organizational theorist Rensis Likert is characteristic of this position. In his book *The Human Organization*, Likert examines the effectiveness of four systems of management. System 1 is called an *exploitative-authoritative system* and is characterized by a rigid system of authority in which the organizational member is exploited in the interests of management. System 2 is a *benevolent-authoritative system*, one in which the orientation is still towards a rigid authority hierarchy but in which exploitation of the worker does not take place. System 3 is referred to as a *consultative system*, in which members are consulted about decisions but the power to make such decisions rests in the hands of management. System 4 is a *participative group system*, in which members share equally in decision-making power. From our discussion of approaches to organizational study, we can identify System 1 as the scientific management approach, System 2 as the bureaucracy or classic theory, System 3 as the human relations approach, and System 4 as the human potentialities approach. Likert claims to find the participative system (System 4) far superior to the other systems; that is, for a variety of indices, e.g., worker morale, productivity, and so on, participation through group decision-making concerning such things as goal setting and worker technique appeared to be superior to the other systems studied.

Once again, despite the almost fervid belief in the powers of participation evident today, the student is cautioned to weigh these and other claims carefully. A review of the findings on participation reveals that there is much that is not known with any great certainty (Golembiewski, 1965), and like any other variable in the study of organizations, inconsistent results are apparent. Of course, participation is a desirable value in American society, and naturally one should do all that he can to see that participation in organizational life is maximized. However, at the same time one must be aware that limits to the desirability of participation, for both the individual and the organization, may very well exist. First of all, it is perfectly clear that not all persons in organizational settings desire participation. There are many who would much rather have decisions made for them. Secondly, one must remember that the costs of participation are often high, both in terms of time and energy expended and in psychological costs as well, e.g., the frustration of long and often conflict-laden committee meetings, and the boredom of endless decisions over trivia. Third, one must remember that participation does not guarantee that one's ideas will be implemented. As many students who have recently gained the right to sit on faculty committees are now beginning to appreciate, mere participation does not automatically guarantee that one's ideas will be accepted. Often the distribution of power within a university is such that students may find themselves on faculty committees that never did have any power to change things. When we search for the elusive base of power within a complex organization like the university, we discover an obvious fact: power is not a fixed quantity residing in a particular place once and forever as organizational charts would have us believe. What the student is likely to find upon admittance into the politics of the university is simply that power is distributed among a host of shifting coalitions whose make-up may very well depend upon such things as a specific issue, the general political climate external to the university, and the state of internal politics at the time. In other words, increases in participation can clearly "boomerang." Once students have gained the rights of participation, they must acquire the knowledge, skills, and sophistication that go with *effective* participation. Otherwise, participation will come to appear either meaningless to the student or, in the worst possible light, as another attempt by the power structure to co-opt him, i.e., neutralize him by giving him a visible but essentially meaningless role in the establishment.

Assumptions about the individual and organizational theory

It is difficult, if not impossible, to develop a theory of social organization without first making certain assumptions about the *individual*. Douglas McGregor (1960), in his criticisms of classic theory of organizations, has exposed what he feels are the underlying beliefs about human beings imbedded in that theory. For McGregor, classic theory seemed to assume the following:

1. People inherently dislike work.
2. Because of their inherent dislike of work, people will not work unless they are coerced, controlled, directed, and threatened with punishments.
3. The average person prefers to be directed rather than left to his own devices, has little or no ambition, and above all else desires security.

According to McGregor, this particular body of assumptions about individuals led quite naturally to the development of classic theory. He felt, however, that it would be possible to develop a very different theory from an alternative set of assumptions, which were as follows:

1. Under the proper conditions, persons will welcome work and expend both mental and physical energy as naturally as they do in play.
2. Persons can exercise *self-direction* and *self-control*. Coercive pressures are not the only means by which people can be controlled and their activities directed.
3. The average person can be taught not only to accept responsibility but to value it and seek it out.
4. Within most organizations the imagination and ability necessary to solve most problems are present among *many* members at *all* levels of the organization, not only in those few at the top of the authority hierarchy.
5. Members' commitments to organizational objectives are less a function of coercive measures administered by authority than they are a function of various rewards associated with the achievement of objectives. The most important rewards are not monetary incentives but the fulfillment of ego and self-actualization needs.

Whether or not McGregor is correct about the assumptions that underlie classic theory, we must admit that he has posed a fascinating question. From McGregor's thoughts we can immediately sense the great relevance of psychology to the study of complex organizations. The important question is, "What set of assumptions about the person will lead to the most efficient, productive, and *human* organizations?" We think it reasonable to suppose that radically different organizations will emerge whether one holds the first or second set of assumptions mentioned earlier.

Psychology and the physical design of organizations

The physical spaces within which organizational work is performed are frequently designed without regard to the psychological characteristics of the people who will occupy the spaces. Most importantly, scant attention is paid to the *social requirements* of the organization as a physical entity. We continue to build universities, for example, on the basis of implicit theories of instruction that many people regard as outdated. Look at your own classroom. Chances are good that it has been designed with the notion that education is largely a matter of a one-way flow of information from an authority figure to a willing recipient. There is probably a lectern situated at the focus of attention in the front of the room. Seats are probably arranged in such a manner that they face directly to the front. In many instances, seats are bolted to the floor in this position, making it nearly impossible for all members of the learning situation to communicate easily with one another. In brief, most classroom spaces are designed around a model of education that is basically authoritarian.

In the design of the physical spaces within which organizational activities take place, we have consistently failed to appreciate the fact that physical design should *follow* the sociopsychological requirements of the space rather than *dictate* them. Given the fact that students can learn as readily from one another as they can from an authority figure, learning spaces could be designed to facilitate rather than inhibit this kind of learning. Not only do most learning spaces act to discourage student interaction, but they frequently act to discourage high professor-student interaction. Considering the nature of most physical arrangements in the modern university, it is clear that little is done to encourage professor-student interactions. In many cases, the only place that continued interaction between a professor and an interested body of students can continue to take place immediately following a particularly stimulating class session is *in a traffic flow area* directly outside the classroom. And as anybody who has ever tried to hold a group discussion in a hallway knows, it is difficult to hold an intelligent and fascinating discussion in the midst of what appears to be a veritable stampede of undergraduates.

In short, we should be always aware of the fact that physical space arrangements are intimately related to the social activities that can take place within them. The design of particular spaces reflects assumptions about the characteristics of persons who will occupy them as well as the nature of social activities that will take place in them. It is unfortunate that we persist in designing spaces that are out of step both with changing assumptions about persons and with the legitimacy of various kinds of social activity that could take place within them. That is, we fail to realize that buildings ought to be *social machines* that work *for* rather than *against* human social creatures.

It would, for example, be a fascinating classroom exercise to attempt to design a classroom space (and a university) by utilizing alternative theories of learning, differing conceptions of personality, and different models of social interaction and generating the many different spaces that flow from such differences in underlying concepts. Would one consistently end up with the modern university as it presently exists? One doubts that this would happen. We often persist in doing things in a given way simply because they have always been done that way. The search for alternatives is always an exciting way to realize that an extant social reality is not fixed, immutable, and in the "nature of things" but merely one of many possible social realities which we can *invent* if we will but use our imaginations.

The relevance of the psychological study of organizations

Within the very recent past, the problem of conflict within organizations has become a critical one in American society. Events on university campuses alone indicate that much more must be known about the conditions which foster conflict, the factors which maintain it, and the ways in which it can be reduced. Of course, conflict of severe proportions is not restricted to the American university. Recent teacher walkouts in the public schools indicate that the organizational structure of the schools as it currently exists does not permit an effective conflict resolution. Certainly, student discontent in the high schools is further evidence of the fact that public educational institutions need to devote considerable energy both to discovering ways to minimize conflict and to keeping it within healthy and constructive limits.

Surely, many of our problems stem from the fact that organizational changes have been terribly slow in coming. Crisis management seems more characteristic than effective and intelligent long-range planning and action. Unfortunately, as we have witnessed in American society, reliance upon crisis management techniques (wait until you have a critical problem before you try to solve it) has resulted in disastrous consequences. It is quite clear that we must develop methods that will permit continuous organizational change if serious conflict is to be avoided in the future. But it is equally clear that *effective* change will not be brought about in the superheated climates generated by the clash between those who refuse to change and those who demand change at any and all costs, including destruction of the organization itself.

The modern organization is a complex interdependent system. As such, we need all of our wits about us in order to understand how to make it do what we want it to do. Even the most well-intentioned individuals can bring about changes within the structure of a complex interdependent system which inadvertently make matters far worse rather than better. The changes demanded by many persons in the modern university, for example, may very well have the net effect of *increasing* organizational tyranny rather than reducing it. It is curious that many student demands have culminated in greater numbers of rules, procedures, committees, and levels of organization, than existed previously. In a sense, the bureaucratization of the university seems, in many instances, to be increased by the recent campus turmoil. Whether the bureaucrat's seat is occupied by the student, faculty member, or administrator seems hardly to make much difference if one's objective is to find ways to increase individual freedom within the context of the complex organization. In short, efforts after organizational change should involve far more than placing fresh actors in old seats. But it is here that the difficult and creative work remains to be done. Despite the sound and the fury, the problem remains unchanged: Can we discover ways in which social organization can be accomplished so as to meet the individual needs of persons and encourage the fulfillment of the potentialities of each? Before we can answer this question affirmatively, we shall have to know far more about modern organizations, the problems facing them, and the solutions available. Above all else, we shall need *imagination* as we have never needed it before.

SUMMARY

In this chapter, we have examined the individual in group interaction and the individual in the organization. We have considered ways in which group and organizational memberships can affect individual behavior. Our analysis led us to consider the factors that increase the susceptibility of the individual to group influences. We have considered both group and organizational conflict and the necessity for conflict reduction procedures. Our discussion of the individual and the organization centered on four major theories of organizational behavior. Finally, we considered the relevance of organizational study. As we have noted, the change of complicated, highly interdependent systems such as the modern organization requires careful analysis and much invention. Many of the problems of the modern organization in America will not yield to social thought grounded in current myths or stereotypes.

If our goal is to increase individual autonomy and freedom within both group and organizational contexts, it is obvious that we must come to know much more than is currently known. Above all, we must have the courage to resist conformity and, at the same time, to recognize the necessity for socially responsible cooperation. That, of course, is wisdom — something we rarely talk about in introductory psychology books.

References

Argyris, C.: *Interpersonal Competence and Organizational Effectiveness.* Homewood, Ill., Richard D. Irwin Inc., 1962.
Asch, S.: Effects of group pressure on the modification and distortion of judgment. *In* Geutzkow, H. (ed.): *Groups, Leadership and Men.* Pittsburgh, Carnegie Press Publishers, 1951.
Back, K. W.: Influence through social communication. J. Abnorm. Soc. Psychol., 46: 190, 1951.

Becker, H. S.: *Outsiders: Studies in the Sociology of Deviance*. Glencoe, The Free Press, 1963.
Bennis, W. G.: Leadership theory and administrative behavior: the problem and authority. Administrative Science Quarterly, *4*: 259, 1959.
Deutsch, M., and Gerard, H. B.: A study of normative and informational social influences upon individual judgment. J. Abnorm. Soc. Psychol., *5*: 629, 1955.
Festinger, L., Riecken, H. W., and Schachter, S.: *When Prophecy Fails*. Minneapolis, University of Minnesota Press, 1956.
Golembiewski, R.: Small groups and large organizations. *In* March, J. G. (ed.): *Handbook of Organizations*. Chicago, Rand McNally & Co., 1965.
Hardyck, J. A., and Braden, M.: Prophecy fails again: a report of a failure to replicate. J. Abnorm. Soc. Psychol., *65*: 136, 1962.
Homans, G. C.: Social behavior and exchange. Amer. J. Sociol., *63*: 597, 1958.
Janowitz, M.: Patterns of collective racial violence. *In Violence in America: Official Report to the National Commission on the Causes and Prevention of Violence*. New York, Signet Books, 1969.
Kelley, H. H.: Two functions of reference groups. *In* Proshansky, H., and Seidenberg, B. (eds.): *Basic Studies in Social Psychology*. New York, Holt, Rinehart and Winston, 1965.
Kerckhoff, A. C., and Back, K. W.: The bug. Psychology Today, June, 1969, pp. 46-50.
Likert, R.: *The Human Organization*. New York, McGraw-Hill Book Co., 1967.
McGrath, J. E., and Altman, I.: *Small Group Research*. New York, Holt, Rinehart and Winston, 1966.
McGregor, D.: *The Human Side of Enterprise*. New York, McGraw-Hill Book Company, 1960.
Medalia, N., and Larsen, O.: Diffusion and belief in collective delusion: the Seattle windshield pitting epidemic, Amer. Sociol. Rev., *23*: 180, 1958
National Advisory Council on Civil Disorders. 1968. p. 202.
Neill, A. S.: *Summerhill: A Radical Approach to Child Rearing*. New York, Hart Publishing Co., 1960.
Newcomb, T. M.: Attitude development as a function of reference groups: the Bennington study. *In* Swanson, G. E., Newcomb, T. M., and Hartley, E. L. (eds.): *Readings in Social Psychology*. New York, Holt, Rinehart and Winston, 1952.
Porter, L. W., and Lawler, E. E.: Properties of organization structure in relation to job attitudes and job behavior. Psychol. Bull., *64*: 23, 1965.
Sherif, M., Harvey, O. J., White, B. J., Hood, W. R., and Sherif, C.: *Intergroup Conflict and Cooperation*. Norman, University of Oklahoma Book Exchange, 1961.
Stock, D.: A survey of research on T-groups. *In* Bradford, I. P., Gibb, J. R., and Benne, K. D., (eds.): *T-Group Theory and Laboratory Method*. New York, John Wiley & Sons, 1964, p. 395.
Toch, H.: *The Social Psychology of Social Movements*. New York, Bobbs-Merrill Company, Inc., 1965.
Whyte, W. H.: *The Organization Man*. New York, Simon and Schuster, Inc., 1956.
Worthy, J. C.: *Big Business and Free Man*. New York, Harper & Row Publishers, Inc., 1959.

CHAPTER 9

The Psychological Study of Society

RIOTS IN ANYTOWN, U.S.A.
MAYOR REQUESTS NATIONAL GUARD

ANYTOWN, *July* 7. — The Mayor of this city entered a plea for help last night as violence and looting erupted in the mid-city section. Hundreds of blacks and a smaller number of whites roamed the streets, smashing shop windows, looting, burning business establishments, and destroying automobiles. Occasional sniper fire seriously hampered the efforts of firemen as fires blazed out of control. Millions of dollars in property damage occurred as a result of these fires. At least 25 persons were injured and 3 persons were reported killed. This, the most recent of a series of such disorders in our large urban centers, stunned the nation. The President asked the people to pray while the Governor of another state referred to the rioters as "mad dogs." Leaders of moderate civil rights groups expressed dismay at this most recent outbreak of disorder and violence; representatives of more militant groups did not. A commission of outstanding persons has been appointed to study this matter, and it is hoped that they will supply answers concerning the cause of the violence and make recommendations for the future.

THE RIOT COMMISSION REPORT

Chairman:
Mr. Gavel, distinguished Chairman of the Board of Generalized Motorics.

Members:
Dr. Sociology, Professor of Sociology
Dr. Psyche, Professor of Psychology
Chief Flame, Anytown Fire Department
Chief Law, Anytown Police Department
Dr. Econ, Professor of Economics
Dr. Planning, Professor of Urban Planning
General Arming, United States Army, Brigadier General
Mr. Wiretap, Head, Decentralized Intelligence
Mr. Power, Civil Rights leader
Mr. Nonviolence, Civil Rights leader

Chairman: Gentlemen, I have called you together here today to use your expert knowledge to see if we can determine the cause of these disturbances in our cities. I need not remind you of the gravity of the situation. Fires, looting, violence, millions of dollars in property losses, as well as lost lives and suffering. Gentlemen, the nation depends upon you. What is the cause of all this? What can be done? I call first upon Dr. Sociology.

Dr. Sociology: [In anger] This commission is a waste of time. We all know perfectly well the cause of this. Racial prejudice is a cancer eating away at the fabric of American society. These riots are a direct outcome of the absurd, brutal, and unjust treatment of the black man in American society for the past 275 years. Furthermore. . . .

Chief Law: [Interrupting Dr. Sociology] Mr. Chairman! Mr. Chairman! I object. I didn't come here to hear speeches. I came here in good faith to get at the cause of things.

Chairman: Please, gentlemen! We must have order in the commission room if not in the society! We have barely begun and already disorder has occurred. I must ask you to control your emotions. Chief Law, you seem to want a word on the subject.

Chief Law: Thank you, I do. In my opinion, these riots are caused by the failure of the police departments concerned to act quickly and efficiently at the very first sign of trouble. If we cracked down on those who would break the law and take matters into their own hands right away, these riots would not occur. Look at what happened in that other city. First, the police stood by and did not interfere with the looters. Then, after matters had gotten completely out of hand, they attempted to stop them. I say it was far too late. Quick, efficient action at the very beginning of trouble is necessary. Also, we need riot control legislation which will convince the potential rioter that he will pay dearly for breaking the law.

These, gentlemen, are my views on the cause of these riots: the lack of prompt and efficient police action at the very outset of trouble and the need for stiffer riot control legislation.

Dr. Psyche: If I may, Mr. Chairman, I must respond to Chief Law. [Chairman indicates approval] What you have said, Chief Law, makes some sense, but aren't you perhaps oversimplifying things? [Dr. Sociology nods his head in assent.] The cause of these riots isn't in police action or lack of it, but rather in other things. Look at it this way. Suppose you were a poor person, white or black, constantly exposed to the mass media communications of the good life in America. Watch your TV set any evening. What kinds of images are shown? Americans buying big, flashy automobiles, suburban women in beautiful kitchens in equally beautiful homes, endless pictures of brightly colored, expensive things, all available to the "typical" American family.

We are taught to *want* things, and this teaching is incessant, from the time we are children until the time we become adults. For many of us, we are able to work and get them. We have the educational background, the highly developed skills in an advanced technological society, and so forth, to demand the wages necessary to buy these things we have been taught to want. Unfortunately, for many of our citizens, this is not true. Although we are teaching them to *want things* as badly as we do, it is unhappily the case that because of many reasons, they are unable to get them legally. Gentlemen, it is, in my opinion, significant that the very first items to disappear when liquor stores were looted were the highest priced brands. Facts like these speak for themselves.

Dr. Flame: Mr. Chairman, if you please, I would like a word now. I'm not at all certain that I understand all that this gentleman has said. But, in any case, my business is fighting fires. You asked earlier what was the cause of all this — the millions of dollars of loss due to fires. I don't know the cause of some of these other things, but I certainly do know the cause of this property damage due to fire. Most certainly, the snipers hindered my men. However, there are other factors. For some time now the central city section has been a disgrace: overpopulated buildings, lax enforcement of the building codes, inferior materials, landlords who live in suburbia and never make a personal appearance on their property if they can help it, poor trash removal service, and so on. For some time now I have lived in constant dread of a major fire in the central city section. These conditions are deplorable. Clearly something must be done. After all, gentlemen, the best way to fight a fire is to prevent it. I have been waiting for an opportunity like this to express my views on the terrible conditions in the central city section. In my opinion, gentlemen, the cause of this great loss of property due to fire is attributable to our failure to correct the deplorable conditions that exist in this area of the city.

Dr. Planning: I wish to emphasize all that Chief Flame has said. And I wish to extend this line of thought, in a more general sense, as it pertains to the cause of these riots. It seems to me that these riots directly reflect the continued failure of urban administrations to recognize and deal effectively with certain problems. The fact that ghettos now exist in virtually all of our major cities is deplorable. Gentlemen, when did you last go to the central section of the city? Are you aware of the deplorable conditions that exist there — overcrowding, the absence of parks, greenbelts, and recreational facilities, and miserable substandard housing? Obviously, gentlemen, the cause of these riots lies squarely in the failure of urban administrations to plan effectively, provide adequate housing, and, in general, to provide a physical environment suitable for the human needs of human beings!

Dr. Sociology: Mr. Chairman, please excuse my earlier hasty remarks. I find it difficult to discuss these matters without a great deal of emotion. But let me try. Dr. Planning has talked about the physical attributes of ghetto life. Let me talk about the sociological aspects—Dr. Psyche will forgive me if I intrude on his territory. Imagine a child growing up in the ghetto of a large urban area. To what is he exposed? As we well know, the behavior of persons is greatly influenced by their social environments. And, in particular, the kinds of models, adults and persons of the same age, they see around them help to shape the kinds of persons they become. The young child is constantly exposed to social models who hold legitimate attitudes of anger, frustration, despair, and apathy toward the larger society of which they are supposed to be a part. An entirely different set of norms of conduct is learned in the ghetto than that learned in our "lily white" suburbs. Is it any wonder that the black child learns to hold cynical and hostile attitudes toward the white power structure! You will recall, gentlemen, that it was only a short time ago that the citizens of this fair state voted to amend our existing fair-housing laws so as to make them utterly worthless!

Mr. Law: Mr. Chairman, I object! This is hardly the place to discuss fair-housing legislation! We are here to discover the cause of the riots, not to question the feelings of the majority of people of this state. Furthermore, I . . . .

Dr. Sociology: I am sick and tired of being interrupted by Mr. Law. Why can't we discuss fair housing and the attitudes of the white power structure I feel it important and. . . .

Chairman [banging his gavel]: Gentlemen, gentlemen! Need I remind you again of the gravity of the situation!

Mr. Power: Burn, baby!

Chairman [striking his gavel repeatedly]: Enough, I say. Mr. Power, you will have your turn to speak. I insist, however, that talk like that be kept out of this discussion. Let's all be quiet, for heaven's sake, and hear what Mr. Wiretap has to say.

Mr. Wiretap: There is hardly any question in my mind but that these riots are part of a conspiracy, international in nature, designed to overthrow the government of this country. In our opinion, the so-called Civil Rights Movement has linked arms with the World-Wide Communist Party organization. My message is brief. The cause of these riots is a deliberate conspiracy.

Dr. Sociology: What evidence do you have for those statements?

Mr. Wiretap: I am not free to divulge that information.

Dr. Sociology: Just as I thought!

Mr. Power: Enough of this nonsense! Power is at the root of these riots, white power! White power that has kept the black man in slavery ever since he set foot on this soil. No longer will you have it your way! If the white power structure refuses to share its power with the black man, then it will have to suffer the consequences. You haven't seen anything yet. Looting, burning, and sniping are child's play. You, gentlemen, with your nice words! Words that don't mean a thing. It's power we need and power we will get. And we will get it in any way that we can. The cause of these riots is the unequal distribution of power between the white man and the black man.

Dr. Econ: Let's not forget the economic picture. Nobody has mentioned unemployment. We all know that unemployment among our central section population is very high. The picture is not encouraging. Consider the fact that the first person to be affected by job layoffs is the lower-class, unskilled or semiskilled worker. Studies of the automotive industry have shown that the first person to be laid off and the last one to be rehired is the lower-class Negro citizen. Gentlemen, we are facing the beginning of the automation revolution. What shall we do when more and more machines displace more and more men from their jobs? In my opinion, unemployment and its associated effects was the cause of these riots. These people want jobs. They cannot get them. They riot.

Dr. Arming: I'm an army man and I don't necessarily agree or disagree with all this talk. My job is to get a job done. I don't think this situation would have developed if the National Guard and local police departments had proper training and control equipment. These riots were caused by our failure to provide properly trained troops complete with the latest means of riot control techniques and materials available to them. We have chemicals that can quickly tranquilize large groups of citizens. Why don't we employ them? In my opinion, these riots are caused by the politician's refusal to pass legislation that would permit us to tranquilize large groups of persons through chemicals rapidly and efficiently. After all, tranquilizing agents are far more humane than bullets, bayonets, and clubs.

Mr. Nonviolence: I cannot agree with Mr. Power nor with General Arming. Violence begets violence. Talk about power, white or black, is not to my liking. It seems to me that human beings everywhere are confronted with a choice, and how we choose will determine our future. We must regain our lost sense of community. We must build a community in the true sense of that word. A community in which persons relate lovingly to one another and where violence, hatred, and injustice have no place. A community in which men regard one another as brothers rather than as inhuman objects. A community in which trust and goodwill prevail rather than suspicion and evil. This, gentlemen, is our choice. Shall we have community or chaos? The cause of these riots is simply that we have ghettos where communities should be.

Chairman: Thank you, gentlemen, for your thoughts on the matter. I must admit, I am more confused than when we started. What is the cause of these riots? Each of you presents a different view. Each view seems, in and of itself, deserving of further consideration. But how shall we choose? To those of you reading or listening to these words, how shall we choose? Who is right? What is the cause of these riots?

The perception of society and social issues

Our account of riots in "Anytown, U.S.A." and our description of the findings of the hypothetical "Riot Commission Report" is intended to be more than amusing. Hopefully it illustrates an important point, i.e., that multiple interpretations of complex societal events do exist. Each of us tends to elaborate a societal event in terms of our assumptions about society, our implicit values, occupational roles, implicit theories of personality, exotic beliefs about the factors which cause and control behavior, our expectations, and so forth. The fact that we do so is certainly not trivial. It is unfortunately the case that our efforts to effect *change* and *problem-solution* more often than not flow from our subjective elaborations of events rather than from adequate understanding and reliable information. There are those, for example, who are firmly convinced that the multifarious problems associated with over two hundred years of unjust and often brutal treatment of the black man in American society can be dealt with effectively simply by turning urban centers into military encampments. And as events surrounding the Chicago convention of the Democratic Party revealed, there are those who apparently feel that *all* political and social dissent and unrest should be dealt with in like manner.

Each of us appears to hold a naive theory of society, as each of us holds naive theories of personality as discussed in Chapter 6. Scratch any man deeply enough and you will find that he is not only an "expert" about human behavior, he also has a "social theory." As we shall see, these are often related. Each of us possesses a view of the society in which we find ourselves. These "frames of reference" are quite varied and range from simple and almost primitive systems of beliefs, values, and ethics to highly sophisticated and complex accounts of the relationships among individuals, organizations, and institutions. There are those who regard any questioning whatsoever of their government's goals, actions, and policies as unpatriotic and indeed "traitorous." The recent rash of automobile stickers boldly stating "America, love it or leave it" gives testimony to the almost childlike faith and blind emotional allegiance that some people demand of themselves and others. On the other hand, there are those who assert that the highest moral and patriotic service a man can give is precisely that of monitoring his government and dissenting publicly when its actions no longer conform to the ideals of the society.

In a pluralistic society such as the American society, it is small wonder that conflict is pervasive and continuous. As a people, we seem to construct our views of social "reality" from many different and often incompatible assumptions and values. We differ from one another in the extent to which we see one person as responsible for another, on what constitutes a "fair" redistribution of the goods of a society to its members, on the relative values of property rights versus human rights, and on the role of America in the affairs of other nations. We hold varied opinions on such matters as authority, sexuality, child-rearing, education, marriage, and religion; and our list could be extended indefinitely. As a nation, we seem more like a collection of nations ranging from the "underdeveloped" countries that characterize our ghettos to the sophisticated and economically affluent white, upper-middle-class suburbs.

As we have seen from the studies of Jessor and his colleagues (1968) on the plight of the Indian in Southwestern Colorado (see Chapter 1) and McClelland and his associates (1961) on achievement motivation and economic development (see Chapter 3), the psychologist has important contributions to make to the study of society. In this chapter, we will take up the psychological study of society. For the most part, our discussion will center on American society. Our focus on American society is more a recognition of the urgent crises that confront it rather than an expression of ethnocentrism on the author's part. In subsequent pages dealing with culture we will have the opportunity to examine other societies as well. We will first consider the important topic of racism in American society.

RACISM IN AMERICAN SOCIETY

One really did not need the official pronouncements of a Presidential Commission to realize that America is and has been a racist society. Any person who had taken the trouble to make even the most superficial examination of the black experience in America would have come to the same conclusion many years before this. The facts bearing out unequal educational opportunity, discrimination in housing and employment, unequal medical care, and unequal law enforcement have always

RACISM IN AMERICAN SOCIETY   329

been available. It is only recently that the American people and their elected officials have been willing to recognize their existence. In 1963, the author served as a school board member in a small elementary district in northern California. Concerned with the manner in which the black man had been portrayed in textbooks approved and adopted by the State of California, the Board of Education of this one small school district decided to analyze all of the textbooks for the fourth and eighth grades. To our astonishment, we discovered that the black man was not portrayed negatively in such books; he simply *did not exist.* As Gunnar Myrdal put it, he seemed to be an "invisible American." In book after book we searched pictures showing Americans on the streets, at amusement parks, at baseball games, in schools, in homes, subways, and crowds of all descriptions. In a sea of white faces, no one could a locate a single black face. Remember that this was 1963, not in the deep South but in California, and in textbooks approved and adopted by the California State Department of Education. Although over 50 letters protesting this situation were sent by our Board of Education to publishers

Figure 27. The inevitable response to American racism: militant black organization in the urban ghetto. (Photo by Gordon Cole.)

of school texts, not a single reply was received. In later investigations, we discovered that a major publisher of school texts had handled the situation quite efficiently by publishing an "integrated" textbook for marketing in California and a different version for marketing elsewhere. The only difference between the two editions was the addition of photographs of blacks in one and the continued absence of such photographs in the other. When we consider the probability of capturing at least one black face in a series of photographs such as those described above as well as the practice of publishing separate editions, one "white" and the other "black and white," it is an inescapable conclusion that the neglect of the black man was *deliberate,* not accidental.

While there are millions of Americans who still believe that the law is equally applied and equally administered, the facts are clearly to the contrary. At a recent symposium concerned with aspects of minority groups in American society, it was informative to note that when a police lieutenant from a community of moderate size in California was asked if, in his opinion, unequal enforcement of the law existed, he made no effort to refute the notion but launched immediately into explanations *as to why unequal enforcement existed.* In the lieutenant's opinion, inferior pay for police work results in selective recruitment of police officers who are poorly equipped for the increasingly complex and sensitive work of law enforcement.

But it is not necessary to rely upon anecdotal evidence and casual observation to document inequalities in American society. Recent statistics provided by Whitney Young (1969), the Executive Director of the Urban League, are most revealing.

Blacks and the opportunity structure

As Young points out, a variety of economic indicators show that the discrepancy between white and black is growing rather than diminishing. In 1950, for example, the median white family income was $3445 while the median black family income was $1869—a difference of $1576. By 1967 (after great reforms had supposedly taken place), this difference had reached $3379, with white and black median family incomes being $8318 and $4939 respectively. As Young correctly perceives, the fact that over half of all blacks live in urban centers while only a fourth of the whites are so located must also be taken into account when considering differences in income. Cities are areas of high cost of living. When we also realize that ghetto residents pay more for goods and services than more affluent citizens pay for identical goods and services in the suburbs, these differences are even more significant. In actuality, the typical black urban family must make ends meet on an income which is $4500 *less* than the income estimated by Federal Government necessary to maintain a moderate standard of living.

A further way of appreciating the black man's position in the *opportunity structure* of America (see Chapter 1) is to examine United States Census data on Negro vocational representation. Table 6 presents these data for the years 1940, 1956, and 1966.

Although gains have been made in certain categories, it is clear from these figures that the black man in America occupies a very low position in the opportunity structure, and to a black man in this situation there are very real consequences. Young reminds us that poverty is three times greater among blacks than among whites, that black high school graduates earn less than whites with a grade school education, that infant mortality rates for blacks are approximately double those for whites, that for blacks life expectancy is shorter, medical care and housing are necessarily inferior, legal assistance is difficult to obtain, credit is costly, and so forth. Considering these facts of life for the black man in America, is it any wonder that he is infuriated by whites who, enamored with the myth of equal opportunity in America, mouth such platitudes as "Well, if a man is willing to work hard enough, he can get what he wants in this country." One wonders if such comments apply equally to the black child in Mississippi who, because of a diet totally lacking protein, may be less capable of intellectual endeavor in adulthood than his

TABLE 6. U.S. Census Data Showing Percentages of Negro Vocational Representation

Occupation	1940	1956	1966
Professional and technical	3.7%	3.7%	5.9%
Managers, officials, proprietors	1.7	2.2	2.8
Clerical	1.2	3.8	6.3
Sales	1.2	1.8	3.1
Craftsmen and foremen	2.7	4.2	6.3
Semiskilled	5.8	11.3	12.9
Farmers and farm managers	15.2	8.5	6.1
Farm laborers and foremen	17.5	22.9	20.2

white counterpart across town where meat, fish, cheese and protein rich foods are matter-of-factly accepted as commonplace. Even more poignantly, do comments such as these apply to the black infant who, for lack of proper medical attention, diet, and other conditions necessary for proper growth, never reached the second year of life?

Ghetto social structure and the opportunity structure

Still another approach to understanding the position of the black man in the American opportunity structure is to consider the extent to which he has been invited to participate in the economy to which he contributes. Recent interest in so-called "black capitalism" reveals that despite efforts to the contrary by the Federal Government, the position of the black small business man is not an enviable one. As Nathan Glazer (1969) has pointed out, the numbers of self-employed black businessmen declined from 42,500 in 1950 to 32,500 in 1960. In New York, for example, only one out of a thousand blacks owns his own business while the corresponding figures for whites are one out of forty. In his recent book *Black Capitalism: Strategy for Business in the Ghetto,* Theodore Cross perceptively discusses the relationship of the ghetto social structure to the plight of the black businessman.

In his analysis of the possibilities of significant black capitalism, Cross finds that entrepreneurial activity in the ghetto will not increase until we understand certain facts about the ghetto economy and structure. First of all, one cannot think of the ghetto as a normal part of the American economic and social structure. As Cross makes clear, it is an isolated entity operating by its own rules and at tremendous expense. It is exceedingly doubtful that the typical white businessman could ever have achieved even a modest success working under the limitations of ghetto social structure. According to Cross, the ghetto operates to *prevent* the accumulation of capital rather than to encourage it. The availability of credit, risk capital, and abundant managerial skills is not characteristic of the ghetto. In many instances, because of inferior housing and safety conditions, fire insurance simply cannot be obtained. Bank loans are difficult, if not impossible, to obtain. As a consequence, ghetto credit systems are operated by far less than reputable persons who can demand and receive interest rates far in excess of those normally paid. Small businessmen cannot take advantage of the availability of discounts offered for buying in quantity. They must keep their inventories of goods low because of the dangers of looting or fire. Suspicion of other members of the ghetto can be a further complicating factor. A particularly poignant example is provided by the case of "Mr. Man's," a clothing store opened by a black businessman in Washington, D.C. with the aid of the Federal Government's Small Business Administration. "Mr. Man's" was in business only two days before a gang of young blacks were successful in breaking in and stealing almost the entire inventory of new clothing on display for the opening. The young men who looted "Mr. Man's" simply could not believe that a black man could achieve something like this on his own and for his own benefit. They were convinced he was serving "whitey" rather than his own interests.

Given these many adverse conditions which characterize ghetto economic structure, one wonders how many white businessmen who piously acclaim the virtues of a "free enterprise" system and the benefits of "competition" could survive. The ghetto social and economic structure breeds endless cycles of poverty from which escape is most improbable even for the most intelligent and highly motivated. To argue that the same principles that led to economic success for the small businessman in Beverly Hills, California, can be applied to Harlem, New York, seems as ethnocentric and foolish as attempting to export America's present economic system to every developing country of the world.

Education, unemployment, and the opportunity structure

When we realize that education is the keystone to success in a technologically centered society such as America, we can readily appreciate why black groups have pressured American universities for more liberal policies of admission and for special programs to insure that black students, once admitted, will succeed. Of blacks in metropolitan areas, only 7 per cent had completed college in 1960. By 1968, this figure had not changed appreciably. Employment opportunities show the same discrepancies. In 1968, unemployment dropped to 3.6 per cent in the United States, but black unemployment was approximately 7 per cent in general and rose to 9 per cent in the ghetto areas with *under*employment characterizing the situations of nearly half of all ghetto employees. Numerous studies have indicated that in the event of industry-wide layoffs it is the lower-class black who is first to be unemployed and the last to be rehired. Once again, the same dismal picture emerges with consideration of employment and education. One does need further documentation to understand that the black man in America must come a long way before it can be argued that he participates equally in the opportunity structure.

Psychological consequences of racism

In his recent book, *A Profile of the Negro American* (1964), Thomas Pettigrew, a social psychologist from Harvard University, has provided us with a comprehensive survey of the consequences of racism. Let us consider Pettigrew's thoughts with regard to a number of problems that the black man in America faces.

Self-identity and self-esteem. Commenting upon the work of Kenneth and Mamie Clark as well as on that of others, Pettigrew finds that studies of black self-identity and self-esteem

Figure 28. Black rural poverty in America. There is little joy for those outside the American opportunity structure. *From* Paul Barton (Black Star).

typically have yielded the conclusion that the black experience in America does not foster a strong sense of identity nor does it lead to acceptable levels of self-esteem. Quite early in life, black children sense the fact that they occupy an inferior status by virtue of their skin color alone. Until recently, little effort was made to permit young black children to see adult blacks performing socially desired and important roles. The black man in American mass media has typically been the "amusing but ignorant" clown, one who would tap dance at the drop of a saxophone and who never permitted himself any emotional expression other than a supercilious "giddiness." Where were our self-acclaimed watchdogs of public "morality" when the mass media engaged in the daily business of dehumanizing black human beings to the tune of cash registers and canned laughter? Unfortunately, "pornography," it seems, concerns only sexuality, not the deliberate distorting, falsifying, and dehumanizing of human beings.

It is small wonder that both black and white children become "racially" aware by the third year of life, that the black child frequently shows preferences for white dolls and white friends, and that both white and black children quickly learn to assign inferior roles, houses, clothing, and so forth, to black dolls. It does not take much imagination to see that the black experience in America can lead to profound problems in identity and chronically lowered self-esteem. However, it is clear that recent efforts from within and without the black community are doing much to alter these conditions. Slogans such as "Black is Beautiful" can be seen as part of a larger effort to correct the problems of confused identity and lowered self-esteem that have been visited upon blacks in a racist society. In the mass media the greater availability of blacks in socially acceptable roles is doing much to provide young boys and girls with appropriate role models with which to identify. That such efforts are working is evidenced by the greater acceptance on the part of many blacks of certain physical characteristics. The increased popularity of the "natural" hair style, Afro style clothing, and "soul food" stands as testimony that many American blacks will no longer look to white America for a confused and intolerable self-image and sense of identity. In increasingly greater numbers the black man in America is refusing to permit white America's racist images to control his behavior, shape his values, define his appearance, and determine his destiny.

Perception of the environment as threatening. As Pettigrew points out, studies indicate that the black child comes to perceive his environment as far more hostile and threatening than does the white child; and of course there is a realistic basis for such threat. It is simply that the black man in American society must contend with either an overtly or covertly hostile environment. He has faced discrimination in housing, employment, and education frequently enough to know that white America will not accept him openly and lovingly. Moreover, within his own community, he has had ample opportunity to observe the fact that threat can be expected in the form of not only greater criminal activity but *police* violence as well. Those who continue to doubt the fact that American police are quicker to use the gun or the club when the suspect is black rather than white have only to review the history of racial disturbances in America. For example, the Detroit race riots of 1943 resulted in the deaths of 15 blacks at the hands of police, but not a single white involved in the rioting died in this fashion. Of the 15 blacks slain by the Detroit police, only three had provided provocation by firing upon police officers. More recently, events surrounding black rebellions commencing in 1965 with the Watts rebellion provide ample evidence of the fact that in America police violence is more readily committed against the black man than the white. Although one might protest that surely the black man in civil disturbances, such as that one which occurred in Watts, provoked the police into violent action, he "got what was coming to him." In answer to this line of argument, one must remember that it is precisely in moments of crises that underlying attitudes of hatred are exposed and that concealed murderous impulses find expression. Robert Conot's recent book *Rivers of Blood, Years of Darkness* should be read by every white American who doubts that patterns of police protection can be anything other than what *he* personally experiences in *his* community. Conot's account of the Watts rebellion provides example after example of perfectly innocent blacks who died at the hands of overzealous, excited, and virtually uncontrolled police officers. Typical is the following account of the death of Aubrey Griffin:

> In the hour between 12:30 and 1:30 a.m. Monday morning, police received ten reports of shots having been fired.
> It was 1:30 a.m. when Pfc. John L. Freitas, stationed at the corner of Broadway and 93rd St., jumped, then flattened himself to the pavement as a

bullet skipped across the intersection. The round seemed to have come along 93rd St. from the direction of the freeway. The street was deserted, but Freitas could see one porch light on. . . .

Aubrey Gene Griffin, 38, and his wife, Rowena, were asleep in the bedroom of their home at 314 W. 93rd St. when they were awakened by a shot (apparently the one which frightened Pfc. Freitas). A native of Oklahoma, Aubrey Griffin had, for 10 years, been employed in a furniture factory. His wife worked in a laundry and dry cleaning establishment. They had two sons in the service, one of whom, Aubrey, Jr., an air force man, was home on leave and was sitting in the darkened front room watching the late show on television. They were the solid, middle-class American family of which the Negro community is so much in need.

Mrs. Griffin, hearing the shot, became frightened. Her husband, telling her to remain in the bedroom, put on his pants and told her he would go to see what had happened. Passing through the front room, he stepped out onto the porch, where he was illuminated by the light.*

Apparently Aubrey Griffin made a mistake no black man should make. He stood on his illuminated front porch during the height of a civil disturbance in an area where a shot of unknown origin had been fired. As he turned to go into his home, he could not have known that this simple action would bring elements of the National Guard, city police officers, and sheriff's deputies rushing to his home. Hardly had a warning been issued by the assembled law enforcement officers to "come out with your hands up," when a shot was fired followed by bursts of shotgun and revolver fire into the home. It is a wonder that Mrs. Griffin and her son were not killed. Aubrey Griffin was not so fortunate. His last words before he died, from a massive wound in the chest resulting from 11 shotgun pellets, were, "Mom, call the police, I've been shot." Little did Aubrey Griffin know that the police were already on hand.

But once again, you might say, "This was an emergency situation, people lose their heads, accidents happen," and so on and so forth. Remember the situation. An unarmed man, standing on his own porch under a light in the vicinity of a shot of unknown origin, was shot and killed by a small army of police officers. Without establishing guilt and without any knowledge whatsoever of who the occupants of the building might be, police officers poured shot after shot into the home of a private citizen. Suppose that, in addition to the three innocent persons who actually occupied the home, there were small

---

*From *Rivers of Blood, Years of Darkness* by Robert Conot. Copyright 1967 by Bantam Books, Inc.

babies and children. Suppose it were your home. Suppose that it happened in your community. If it did happen in your community, what would be done about it? In the case of Aubrey Griffin, nothing was done about it.

But to return to our argument. Is it any wonder that the black man comes to perceive his environment as threatening and hostile? At the time of the writing *Rivers of Blood, Years of Darkness,* there were 34 deaths attributable to the Watts rebellion. Since that time, in other disturbances in the ghettos of America, countless other deaths have occurred. Both black citizens and police officers have met violent deaths as a consequence of racism and its ramifications in American society. In addition to the fact that he has witnessed violence within his

Figure 29. The black man in America demands admittance to the university, the major gateway to the American opportunity structure. Can the university survive if it attempts to continue to meet the needs only of the affluent white American? (From *The Denver Post,* Dave Buresh, Staff Photographer.)

own community, the black American has watched as his leadership has been dealt with violently. Martin Luther King, Medgar Evers, and Malcolm X are but a few of those who have met violent deaths in their efforts toward black liberation. It is neither safe nor comforting to be a black man in a racist society.

Criminal behavior. The fact that crime rates for blacks are elevated is taken by white supremacists for evidence of the supposed biological inferiority of the Negro. A similar line of argument was raised concerning intelligence. The fact that the measured intelligence of any ethnic or racial group is demonstrably lower than another cannot be taken as evidence for "biological" inferiority of the one group and superiority of the other. Sufficient evidence has been accrued to establish the fact that intelligence test scores are importantly influenced by sociocultural factors. Although there is fairly clear evidence that both inherited and constitutional factors affect the development of intelligence, it is equally clear that one's early experiences, social surroundings, and cultural heritage are equally important. In Chapter 7, for example, we reviewed Rosenthal's work on teacher expectations and how these were related to gains in measured intelligence, particularly for minority group students. Although we will not take the time here, it would be a relatively easy matter to document the argument that *both* genetic and environmental factors contribute to measured intelligence.

When we turn to incidence figures for crime, however, the role of genetic factors is even less clear and the case for social factors much stronger. Although recent investigators (e.g., Montague, 1968) claim to have found a relationship between chromosomal constitution and criminal behavior, the data for genetic explanations of criminality are still far too sketchy and meager for such a hypothesis to be accepted. Moreover, even if it were to be demonstrated that criminals differ from noncriminals in chromosomal constitution, one must still show that such differences are related in a *causal* way to the occurrence of criminal behavior. Given the fact that our very definitions of criminal behavior are, in fact, *social* and that a wide variety of behaviors are subsumed under the rubric "criminal behavior," one can readily appreciate that it will not prove easy to devise a theory that neatly explains the manner in which chromosomes affect crime. Even more important to the problem of crime among American minority groups, no one to this writer's knowledge has yet established the fact that blacks differ from whites on the relevant chromosomal characteristics.

There are, however, a host of social factors associated with black crime rates that are obvious. First, from our discussion of the black man and the American opportunity structure we can readily appreciate that a greater percentage of blacks would find it necessary to resort to illegitimate means of achieving goal satisfaction. The student will recall that the American Indian in southwestern Colorado showed similar responses to his position outside the opportunity structure (see Chapter 1; Jessor, *et al.*, 1968). Second, from our discussions of the importance of social learning (see Chapter 7) the student should have a further basis for approaching crime incidence figures from a social perspective. Considering the social structure of the ghetto, it is clear that there the child will have a greater availability of deviant adult models to emulate and fewer models who show prosocial patterns of behavior. It is difficult, if not impossible, for the typical white American to appreciate the nature of ghetto social life and the patterns of behavior to which young children are exposed. When we also consider the fact that years of poverty have profoundly disorganized the black family unit in the ghetto, resulting in fatherless homes fitfully managed by a harassed and economically deprived mother, it is not difficult to see why crime statistics are elevated for black youth.

To these psychosocial factors, we must add psycholegal factors. As Pettigrew makes clear, there are many reasons why crime statistics for blacks are elevated beyond that which is accounted for by the reasons we have mentioned. Arrest data is contaminated by the fact that blacks are more subject to the misuse of police power than whites. Powerless before the abuse of authority, blacks have been arrested on the slightest suspicion, have been monitored more closely, and have been subjected to arrest procedures that would never occur in white communities, e.g., mass arrests or "roundups."

While conviction and commitment rates are definitely elevated for blacks, one must remember that many factors can contribute to these. In the American system of law, enormous prosecutorial discretion is available. For many offenses a district attorney can decide whether or not to prosecute. With regard to sentencing, judges possess considerable power to choose whether or not to grant parole or to levy fines rather than sentence imprisonment. It is precisely in these grey areas of discretion that we can expect the effects of prejudice and discrimination to operate most heavily. Finally, it is clear that the ability of a person to stand up to the law in American society is dependent upon his *ability to pay*. The legal services which more affluent citizens take for granted are simply unavailable to those of lesser means. Considering the complexities of the law, if you are ever hauled into court on a charge, resist the temptation to defend yourself. It is clear that criminal convictions frequently reflect income distribution rather than the actual commission of crimes.

In considering Negro crimes rates, one must not forget the further impact of the Civil Rights campaigns of the nineteen fifties and sixties. Arrests associated with civil rights activities as well as with other forms of protest surely contribute to the fact that crime rates for blacks are elevated beyond those of whites. In the Watts rebellion alone, a total of 3162 black adults and 514 juveniles were arrested.

Self-fulfilling prophecies. In Chapter 7, we discussed the importance of both self and interpersonal expectations in behavior control. We noted that the term *self-fulfilling* prophecies has been coined for those situations in which a *prediction* about the behavior of self or about another serves to insure the actual occurrence of the behavior. The role black American is particularly vulnerable to both individual and interpersonal self-fulfilling hypotheses. It is most tragic that many black Americans have never realized their potentials, victims that they are of the expectations of others or of their own *internalized* expectations. Expected to play the role of black man with all that it implies in a racist society, many black men learn to play the role only too well. In a series of studies by Katz and his colleagues (e.g., Katz and Benjamin, 1960; Katz and Cohen, 1962), black persons consistently downgraded their own capabilities when they perceived themselves in competition or in comparison with whites. Moreover, many blacks seem afflicted by a general sense of powerlessness. Since they have received much rejection despite their ability to perform adequately, many come to believe that there is no relationship between their own actions and the social reinforcements they desire. That is, they do not perceive themselves as being able to influence outcomes in many situations. In this sense they believe that their lives are controlled by "fate" rather than by actions they themselves might undertake. Using a personality test that measures the extent to which a person sees his actions and his reinforcements as somehow related to one another, Battle and Rotter (1963) and Lefcourt and Ladwig (1965) demonstrated that lower-class blacks scored lower than lower-class whites regarding the extent to which they perceived their own actions as affecting their outcomes.

Given these facts, it is reasonable to expect blacks to exhibit far less achievement motivation than whites. After all, why should a person struggle to achieve if the probabilities of obtaining of what he wants are very low and, moreover, if there is nothing he can do personally that will affect outcomes? From repeated failure experiences, many black children become fearful of failure and avoid the possibility of further failure at all costs. Refusal to compete and withdrawal from academic settings is, of course, one consequence of failure avoidant attitudes and negative self-fulfilling prophecies. With the appearance of self-fulfilling prophecies, the black child is caught in a "vicious cycle." He expects to fail and does so; this in turn leads to further expectations of failure, further failure, and so on. With regard to achievement motivation in blacks, studies agree upon very low need for achievement in the stories of southern rural black children (e.g., Mingione, 1965; Baughman and Dahlstrom, 1968).

Self-fulfilling prophecies can operate in situations besides those which are achievement oriented. Because a black has good reason to expect rejection from whites, he may enter into relationships with all whites sensitive to the slightest signs that rejection is forthcoming. And, of course, when one is searching for rejection, it is not difficult to find it in the behavior of another person.

Much of the difficulty in the relationships between the black community and the white police officer can be seen as a highly explosive and dangerous game in which mutual self-fulfilling hypotheses are validated. The police officer who expects trouble from blacks in making arrests is more likely to get it than the police officer who does not. Conversely, the black man who enters into all interactions with white police officers expecting violence is more likely to experience it than the one who does not. The problem, of course, is simply that it is becoming increasingly difficult to find blacks and police officers who do *not* expect "trouble" from one another. This hazardous situation of mutually negative self-fulfilling hypotheses demands that the potentially explosive situation that characterizes police-community relationships in the ghetto be given the most sensitive and skillful management available. Communities which continue to follow hard-line practices in which classic patterns of police work are followed to the neglect of enlightened community relations programs do so at their own risk.

Self-fulfilling hypotheses can operate in still other ways to the disadvantage of the black man in American society. Accustomed to rebuff and convinced that many reform programs and legitimate employment opportunities are further efforts by the white community to "dupe" them or to "entice" them only to reject them again, many blacks do not take advantage of such opportunities when they do present themselves.

In many respects the black role in America is concerned with a peculiar game of probabilities. Given his past, the probability of rejection and failure for the black man is quite high. Yet the black man, when assistance is finally offered, is expected to act as if such probabilities were, in actuality, quite low. In essence, he is asked to deny his past and pretend that history does not exist! It takes a supremely self-confident and capable person to commit himself to a course of action when the probabilities are not in his favor. The black experience in America does not encourage the growth and maintenance of such desired personal attributes.

Prescriptions for change

There are, of course, many lines of attack upon the problem of racism and its myriad consequences. Nothing short of an all-out effort by both public and private sectors of the society will suffice. Although it is clear that psychology will not be at the focus of many of these endeavors, it is equally clear that psychology has important contributions to make. With regard to education and cultural deprivation, for example, Kenneth Clark, in his recent book *Dark Ghetto,* makes the excellent point that we really do not know precisely how aspects of the social surroundings of the "disadvantaged" child interact with ability to learn in conventional learning situations. Rigorous studies of varying conditions of preschool learning are necessary before programs like Head Start can be brought to full fruition. Obviously, the hope for educationally disadvantaged children does not lie in simply getting them into school earlier than normal but upon *what one does with them* once they have achieved early placement.

In any case, it is apparent that programs like Head Start must be extended on a national basis throughout the early formative years of childhood development. The free nursery school and kindergarten should be a part of every local school district. Moreover, these should be centers for serious investigations into the causes of educational retardation in disadvantaged children as well as instructional centers. We should recognize that our problems here are not merely political and economic ones. Even if the funds necessary for a total effort to solve the problems of the educationally disadvantaged should miraculously appear, it is apparent that we simply do not know enough about the acquisition of cognitive, social, and personal skills in children in general, let alone disadvantaged children, to plan effective educational treatments. Many puzzles lie behind the rhetoric of "cultural disadvantage." Much careful scientific inquiry remains to be done. Unfortunately, as Bruno Bettleheim, the child psychiatrist, has put it, "Love is not enough."

Much the same thing could be said with regard to training programs in industry for the so-called "hard-core" unemployed. In such programs, as much attention must be directed to the acquisition of social and personality skills as to technical job skills if training is to lead to successful employment. Those responsible for training ghetto blacks must recognize that in many instances they will be dealing with people who have never participated in the social situation characterized by modern industrial work settings. The attitudes, values, expectations, and interpersonal skills of blacks are as important in designing both training and work situations as their ability to correctly assemble a complicated mechanism. Early efforts to train ghetto workers failed to account for the fact that such efforts were being directed at people from "another culture." As a consequence, difficulties which could have been avoided by informed and sociopsychologically sophisticated management were encountered.

In addition to intelligently conceived and expertly conducted educational and manpower training programs, there are, of course, a host of other lines of attack upon the problems of racism in which psychological analysis would be of benefit. With regard to police-community relationships within the ghetto, recruitment, selection, and training of police officers scheduled to work with minority citizens all need careful examination. Care must be taken to weed out those applicants for police training, as well as those already in the daily business of law enforcement, who for reasons of social attitudes or personality disturbance should not be working in close, sensitive relationships with people in general, let alone with minority persons. The problem here, of course, is simply that many police departments already are heavily staffed by persons from superiors on down who hold destructive social attitudes or personal attributes, or both, which are contraindicative of police work appropriate to the ghetto. In other words, inappropriate selection policies may, in many cases, prove to be a matter of official sanction rather than of incompetence or innocent bungling. One metropolitan police department known to the author held an official policy of selecting men high in "aggressiveness" for assignments to duties as patrolmen. Considering some of the more difficult aspects of the police officer's role, e.g., restraining hostile intoxicated persons, confronting armed criminals, and so forth, this particular department could not appreciate the fact that a *variety* of persons might be recruited for police work and that careful matching of persons to law enforcement situations through *assignment* would prove a possible solution. Hence, for example, one might deliberately recruit "passive, nonaggressive" persons for work with certain youth populations and "direct-aggressive" persons for work with other youth populations. Certainly, an officer who consistently approaches youth with "a chip on his shoulder" should be removed from duties which frequently bring him into contact with youth and reassigned to duties principally involving adults.

In addition to the alteration of policies of selection and recruitment of officers, much needs to be done in terms of on-the-job training. In working with ghetto residents police officers must frequently put on the lenses of the sociologist or the social psychologist in order to understand the social reality that confronts them in their day-to-day activities. Above all, police officers need to become aware of the fact that not all social protest is illegitimate, that human rights and property rights are of equal importance, that verbal insults are directed toward their role and not their person, and that there is a realistic basis for ghetto attitudes toward law enforcement officers generally. The police officer's role is a complicated and difficult one, and it is becoming more so every day. As such, it requires more, not less, extensive and sensitive preparation. Those aware of the complex problems facing the police officer in the ghetto will

346 THE PSYCHOLOGICAL STUDY OF SOCIETY

not be deceived by the recent rash of simplistic, irresponsible, and politically inspired "get tough" proposals. We are not involved in an infantile but murderous game of cops and robbers but in a struggle for the very survival of a nation.

In addition to modification of factors associated with law enforcement, other possible efforts to effect change are apparent. Considering their important role in maintaining stereotypes of the black man over the years in America, the mass media have a moral obligation to correct this situation by seeing that blacks appear before the American people in a variety of roles and a variety of contexts. That such efforts have been started in national television programming is now apparent. However, these beginnings must be elaborated and extended considerably. If we are serious in our efforts, there is no reason why regular messages counter to racially prejudiced values could not be presented on national television. With the aid of communications experts and psychologists knowledgeable in persuasive appeals and attitude change, such messages could be appropriately designed for maximum effect. But you might object that this is an improper use of both our communication

Figure 30. Racism and revolution. Can American society afford not to change? (Photo by Gordon Cole.)

media and the behavioral sciences. In answer to this one can only say (1) "Where were your objections when the mass media were used precisely in this fashion to the detriment of millions of American blacks?" and (2) "Such a program of national attitude change would not involve deception and manipulation but would constitute an open, rational, and potentially powerful attack on one of the most serious crises facing American society."

Finally, psychologists should turn their attention to the important problem of national priorities and the establishment of domestic policies. The intricate web of politics, economics, prejudice, and power, which permits the continued existence of the urban ghetto and the plight of the rural poor, should be constantly brought before the American people and exposed not only as shameless self-serving hypocrisy but also as criminal irresponsibility. The question is no longer are the American people and their elected representatives *capable* of solving the crises arising out of two centuries of racism? The relevant question now is do we *want* to? How we answer this question is crucial not only for the black man in American society but for all of us as well. It is difficult to see how America will function when its centers of commerce, communication, and culture are occupied by a large majority of deprived, angry, frustrated, and hostile blacks who perceive themselves as captives of an alien society rather than as equal participants. Where appeals to conscience have failed, it is just possible that appeals to *self-interest* may succeed. Despite their pious rhetoric concerning the "brotherhood of Man," many Americans are finally moved to action by appeals to self-interest. Once again, our capacity for hypocrisy would be amusing if it were not so hazardous.

Summary of racism in America

It is clear that our discussion of racism in American society has examined only a small segment of this vast and complex issue. Hopefully, however, our discussions of the opportunity structure of America and the ghetto and the psychological consequences of racism will alert the beginning student of psychology to the problems that lie here.

Our discussion has centered upon the problems of the black man in American society but could have included other minority groups as well. The discrimination practiced against the Mexican-American and the American Indian in our society is equally deserving of careful study by the student of social thought and behavior. But as we have seen in Chapter 1 (Jessor, *et al.*, 1968), the plight of the American Indian is in many respects similar to that of the ghetto black in America. And the Mexican-American faces many of the same struggles. It is not an enviable position to be outside the opportunity structure of an affluent nation such as the United States. As we have seen, there are very real consequences involving psychological, medical, educational, and social factors.

ALIENATION IN AMERICAN SOCIETY

As far back as the writings of early Greek philosophers we note a concern with the relationship of the individual to the larger social order. Plato's *Republic*, for example, was an early expression of the utopian vision. In this work, Plato grappled with the difficult problems involved in constructing a viable social order. Hobbes, Rousseau, Comte, Veblen, Thoreau, and Huxley are but a few of the many philosophers after Plato who concerned themselves precisely with the same problem. The sociological tradition, of course, has extended this line of thought by seeking formal expression of the relationship of individual behavior to the larger social structure. While many psychologists were busily pursuing theories of behavior and personality that involved events largely contained *inside* the person, sociologists such as Emile Durkheim (1947) and Robert K. Merton (1957) were exploring such things as crime, suicide, drug addiction, alcoholism, and delinquency in the context of the larger society. Durkheim, a French sociologist of unusual brilliance and originality, focused his attentions on the necessity for *division of labor* in complex societies and the possible consequences of various ways in which it might be accomplished. Simple societies, Durkheim argued, do not show great social differentiation. Characterized more by a single "collective conscience," based upon perceptions of similarity, common interests, and feelings, such societies neither require great division of labor nor encourage individuality. On the other hand, complex societies, such as modern industrial states, are characterized by extensive division of labor and the encouragement of individual differences among their members. When the nature of the division of labor in a society fails to produce sufficiently effective contacts between its members and when it fails to provide for adequate regulation of social relationships, a condition of *anomie* is thought to arise. Anomie can be thought of as a state of "normlessness," one in which little agreement as to social norms exists. The student should refer to our discussion of social norms and anomie in Chapter 1 in connection with the field study of the American Indian.

For Durkheim (1951), anomie was the answer to the puzzling fact that suicides increased not only during periods of economic depression but also during periods of *unusual prosperity*. Since sudden prosperity may result in large numbers of persons being thrown out of adjustment with their typical patterns of life, Durkheim reasoned that suicide might be the result. A man caught up by the rush of sudden prosperity might come to believe that anything would be possible and obtainable. Under such circumstances, there would be no limit to human desires. The breakdown of society's controls over desires and the destruction of socially approved norms and standards for behavior during periods of sudden prosperity give rise to anomie and set the stage for suicide.

While Durkheim sought an explanation for suicide in the concept of anomie, Merton (1957) sought to explain virtually all forms of deviant behavior by means of the concept. While Durkheim saw "normlessness" arising from the clash of individual aspirations and the breakdown of the regulatory function of previously held social norms, Merton held that the *social structure* of a society exerts definite pressure upon certain of its members to engage in nonconforming behavior. According to Merton, one must consider the stated *goals* or *values* of a society and the social *norms* that govern the *means* through which these can be realized. In other words, society defines what is desirable to strive for but it also defines the manner in which one should strive.

Merton saw anomie arising from still other sources:

1. Contradictory norms
2. Multiple values but no provisions for determining which are appropriate
3. Vague and ambiguous norms, insufficiently defined

One implication of Merton's analysis is simply that the values of a society "may help to produce behavior which is at odds with the mandates of the values themselves." Although this statement may sound paradoxical, its meaning is actually quite clear. As we have seen, in the case of the ghetto black, a person taught to value material goods but who is denied access to them by legitimate means may resort to illegitimate means of obtaining them. Moreover, in a pluralistic society like America, contradictions among professed values are characteristic. Hence, American youth are taught to value human life but are forced to value equally the taking of life. And, to take another example, American youth are taught to value cooperation with and obligation to their fellow man on the one hand and the contradictory values of competition and aggressive self-interest on the other.

According to Merton, the person may adapt to the pressures of the social structure in a variety of ways. Let us consider these briefly.

Conformity. The person may adapt to the social structure by conforming to both goals and socially approved means of attaining them.

Ritualism. The person may adapt to the pressures for upward mobility and the attainment of lofty goals by setting his level of aspiration considerably lower than the goals. He may, for example, downgrade high ambitions in favor of a bureaucratic position, playing it comfortably safe by conforming to society's dictates about acceptable *means* but denying the value of high achievement.

Rebellion. Adaptation can occur by rejection of the existing social structure and substitution of efforts to construct a new one in its place. This form of adaptation is clearly illustrated in the radical and revolutionary activity in the United States which has reached such an intense level of activity within recent years.

Retreatism. Equally familiar is the phenomenon of "dropping out." It is difficult to say which of the two adaptations, rebellion or retreatism, is more severely condemned by the larger society. On the one hand, the existing order actively resists change and regards those who advocate change as "dangerous," "traitorous," and "ungrateful." On the other hand, the nonproductive, nonstriving, nonsuccess oriented retreatist, using "illegitimate" means to attain his own personal goals, seems to equally infuriate those who find conformity to the values and means of the larger society a "legitimate" means of adaptation. The often brutal harassment directed against both "hippies" and "activists" alike in America society stands as mute testimony to the extent of this fury.

Innovation. Finally, the individual who accepts the goals of the society but is denied the means to achieve them may turn to "innovative" means such as delinquency and crime. In actuality, the use of civil disobedience in connection with both the Civil Rights Movement and the anti-war movement in the United States can be seen as adaptation by innovation. As Merton correctly perceived, although persecuted, the innovator is frequently the one who eventually succeeds in forcing the society to alter its structure in such a way that its institutionalized means are congruent with its values. We may persecute, harass, and even destroy our innovators, but history has a way of eventually recognizing their value when the names of their persecutors have long since been forgotten.

Of course, not all sociologists have fully accepted the thoughts of Durkheim and Merton. The history of the concept of anomie is filled with controversy. It is not our place here to settle a complicated argument in sociology, and the interested reader is referred to Clinard (1964) for a sound treatment of the subject. However, while most sociologists would question the *generality* of the concept of anomie as a "catch-all" explanation for a variety of forms of deviant behavior as presented by Merton, few would doubt the importance of discrepancies among goals and means, contradictory norms, ambiguous norms, and so forth. While it is obvious that deviant behaviors such as delinquency, drug addiction, crime, mental disorder, and suicide must be approached from a variety of levels of analysis, e.g., from the individual, interpersonal, and group levels, as well as from the perspective of many variables, it is clear that one cannot neglect "normlessness" and its consequences and expect to understand some forms of nonconforming behavior.

Rejection of American social structure and alienation

Whether we choose to call it "anomie" or "alienation," it is clear that America faces a crisis involving disaffected youths of increasingly greater numbers. In his book *Growing Up Absurd*, Paul Goodman perceptively commented:

> Nevertheless, we see groups of boys and young men disaffected from the dominant society. The young men are Angry and Beat. The boys are Juvenile

Delinquents. These groups are not small, and they will grow larger. Certainly they are suffering. Demonstrably they are not getting enough out of our wealth and civilization. They are not growing up to full capacity. They are failing to assimilate much of the culture. As was predictable, most of the authorities and all of the public spokesmen explain it by saying there has been a failure of socialization. They say that background conditions have interrupted socialization and must be improved. And, not enough effort has been made to guarantee belonging, there must be better bait or punishment.

But perhaps there has not been a failure of communication. *Perhaps the social message has been communicated clearly to the young men and is unacceptable.**

When we review the events of the nineteen sixties and realize that Goodman wrote these words in 1956, we are impressed with the accuracy of his predictions. Exacerbated by social turmoil over civil rights, the introduction of widely available drugs of all descriptions, and the Viet Nam War, the numbers of disaffected youth in America has grown as predicted by Goodman. It is no longer a matter of small numbers. A visit to Hollywood's Sunset Strip or San Francisco's Haight-Ashbury District will readily convince even the most skeptical. The increased numbers of run-away children, transitory youth of all ages, and "drop-outs" are everywhere apparent; and of course, the multitudes of protestors on our college and unversity campuses (and high schools as well) constitute even further evidence that increasingly larger numbers of youth no longer agree with or will tolerate the present direction that American society is taking.

For those who have difficulty appreciating the position of youth in American society today, we have produced a picture drawn by a 17 year old enrolled in a class for "problem" students in a southern California High School (Fig. 15). To quote an old saying, "One picture is worth a thousand words." The boy in conflict is obviously the artist himself. He has drawn what he described as "things coming in to myself" and "things going out." It is not accidental that the draft is symbolized so predominantly in his drawing. The message is loud and clear— his society wants him to Kill, Kill, Kill! Drugs will not help nor will his own attempts to live and to love. The inner struggle, he seems to be saying, will yield to violence. How can he do otherwise? "And what of a boy in conflict? He can only go one way, the draft!"

---

*From Goodman, P.: *Growing Up Absurd.* New York, Random House, 1956, p. 11.

Figure 31. Drawing by a 17 year old student enrolled in a class for "problem" students in a southern California high school.

The psychology of alienation

Although factors such as mental illness, incompetence, drug addiction, and alcoholism certainly contribute to the ranks of the alienated, one must not suppose that all alienated youth are simply those who cannot make it in American society. With regard to the alienated activist youth seeking to alter the social structure of America, a significant number of them have *chosen* to reject the larger social structure and for good reason, e.g., impatience with the snail's pace with which the society has moved toward civil rights, disagreement over United States' involvement in Viet Nam and American foreign policy generally, concern with the continued devastation of the ecosystem that sustains life of all kinds, including human life, and concern with the rise of American militarism. These focal concerns of the student activist movement can hardly be said to be expressions of deranged or incompetent minds! In point of fact, early studies of student activists at Berkeley and elsewhere repeatedly indicate that students of greater competence and idealism are more attracted to such movements than students in general.

Although there are undoubtedly personality factors that affect recruitment into the role of "activist student," it simply will not do to "psychologize" away protest as some have attempted to do as indicative of "trouble with authority figures," "unconscious hostility toward parental surrogates," and so on. We must recognize that the problems outlined above are in and of themselves problems of critical significance for American society, and amateur psychoanalytic clichés will not suffice. Moreover, it is perfectly obvious that student radicals have "trouble with authority figures"; they would not be "sitting in" in the chancellor's office if they did not! Redundant and circular *descriptions* of the behavior we are seeking to understand do not suffice as *causal* statements. Obviously, students have the right to protest the nature of the social structure in which they find themselves. It simply will not do to deny the reality of their complaints by dismissing them with the taint of psychopathology.

Psychological difficulties are more evident in the uncommitted, alienated youth who seeks adaptation through retreatism rather than rebellion. However, even in this instance one must not suppose that all youth who have adapted through more passive means are incapable of "making it" in the larger society. Some persons *choose* an alienated life style characterized by the search for novel aesthetic and perceptual experiences, either with or without the assistance of drugs, and are not driven to such a style by "underlying psychopathology." Many of these youths have consciously rejected the American emphasis upon achievement, success striving, and marriage, as well as the larger social structure in which these operate, and are searching for fresh alternatives.

Perhaps the most comprehensive study of uncommitted and alienated youth in American society has been conducted by the Harvard University psychologist Kenneth Keniston (1967). Working intensively with small numbers of alienated students over a three year span, Keniston was able to formulate a number of interesting hypotheses regarding the alienated student as well as the society. Keniston chose to use the clinical case method (see Chapter 1). From repeated interviews, observations under controlled conditions, and psychological tests, information derived from approximately 200 hours of psychological study per student was amassed. Clearly, in terms of intensive study of the person, one would be hard pressed to find a more diligent worker than Keniston.

For Keniston, the alienated college age person is one who seems caught in late adolescence. The characteristic pattern is a refusal to assume conventional adulthood and all that it implies. The alienated young person prefers to dwell in the psychological *present*, he prefers immediate *experiencing* to analytical understanding, shows clear evidence of *fragmentation of identity*, and an almost mystical search for *oneness* or *fusion* with others. According to Keniston, the psychological defense mechanisms of repression and denial (see Chapter 4) are two of the most common adaptive mechanisms in American society. But the alienated, in their search for "awareness" and "genuine" confrontation with both their inner worlds and their external worlds, have undermined the usefulness of these mechanisms. That is, in their search for self-awareness and in their openness to experience, alienated youth have succeeded all too well in ridding themselves of the necessity to repress or deny experiences that others in the society could not tolerate. As a consequence, alienated youth do not undergo the extreme socialization process common to others in the society. There is a failure of *acculturation*.

Keniston has stated that alienated youth

> ... view adult men as broken, damaged, and hypocritical, adult women as possessive, controlling, and destructive to men, and adult competition and rivalry as damaging to the competitor. Their own abruptly discontinuous development has allowed them little opportunity to abandon gradually their longing for dependency, total union, and fusion, and these longings make the impersonal and cold world of adulthood seem more forbidding in contrast. They bring from childhood a deep reservoir of potential anger at both parents, which in later life is easily displaceable onto the "conventional adult world." All of these factors predispose these young men to repudiate adult-

hood by rejecting what they see as the dominant values, roles, and institutions of their society.*

Keniston is quick to add that these young men came by their alienation "honestly." As have many other theorists of deviant behavior, Keniston lays the blame on the parents of these young men who are described as, in reality, "poor parents to their sons." He goes on to describe the parents of alienated youth as follows:

> The mothers sought from them satisfactions that they should have found with their husbands or not at all; they bound their children to them with heavy ties of guilt and dependency. The fathers were seldom adequate fathers; they were largely absent from their son's psychological development, and they suggested through deed and word that their sons should not become like them. Furthermore, both parents were disappointed and frustrated in their marriages and lives.†

The alienated life style, Keniston feels, is not so much a criticism of the parent by the child, but rather a means by which the child manages to *excuse* the failures of his parents. It is not so much the parents who have failed; it is the society that has failed the parents. In this fashion, the alienated youth displaces blame from his parents onto the larger society which he perceives as destructive and dehumanizing to human beings.

In addition to focusing upon the alienated person, Keniston attempts to place him within the context of an "alienated society." Thus, Keniston's thoughts on the origins of alienation are *psychosocial* rather than derived purely from individual psychology. The psychological factors discussed previously *predispose* the person to an alienated life style. The conditions of life in modern American society are the further determinants necessary for the appearance of alienation in a given person. The argument sounds much like that advanced for certain diseases. The fact that two persons may both smoke heavily but only one falls victim to cancer is sometimes explained by saying that the victim was predisposed to cancer while the other was not. Presumably some genetic or other factor is present in the victim but not in the nonvictim. With regard to alienation, then, the life experiences of the person as he matures, particularly his relationship with his parents and his parents' relationships with one another, may predispose him to an alienated life style.

---

*From Keniston, K.: *The Uncommitted: Alienated Youth in American Society.* New York, Dell Publishing Co., 1967, p. 200.
†Ibid., p. 201.

However, the societal conditions which foster alienation must be present before it will be manifested.

According to Keniston, the accelerated rate of change, the advent of technological values, the fragmentation of work, the destruction of community, the undue emphasis upon cognitive processes to the neglect of feeling, and the conflicted family torn by contradictory expectations are some of the factors in American society that contribute to the alienated life style in those so predisposed.

In evaluating Keniston's ideas it is important to bear in mind that he employed the clinical method with all the strengths and weaknesses inherent in that approach (see Chapter 1). Even though we are provided with exhaustive observations of subjects, we must remember that Keniston's sample was only 12 persons. Moreover, while Keniston assures us that these 12 persons were cases of extreme alienation, he does not provide information as to how they were selected. Hence, we cannot be certain that subjects were selected for study precisely because they showed those attributes which the research claims to have subsequently *discovered* as characteristics of extremely alienated persons. A further criticism centers about Keniston's use of *comparison subjects*, i.e., nonalienated subjects. Although we are told that a nonalienated group was also selected for study, we are not given appropriate comparison data. Hence, for example, we do not know if the parental factors thought to be associated with alienated youth are *characteristics of parents in general* or confined to those of alienated youth. Finally, it is unfair to condemn the parents of alienated youth as being "poor parents" as Keniston has done. One must remember that Keniston did *not* study such parents directly. He studied the *perceptions* and *recollections* of parents by his subjects. Given the fact that his sample was an extreme one, the possibility of distortion of parental characteristics and behaviors is clearly present. As a consequence, Keniston cannot speak as he does about the supposed "objective" and "real" nature of parental shortcomings; he can only speak of the "subjective" perceptions of his subjects.

Despite these shortcomings, Keniston has succeeded in describing rather fully the ways in which alienated youth look at their developmental histories, themselves, their parents, and their society. These are valuable observations in and of themselves. However, we must recognize that we cannot generalize from these findings, that considerable uncertainty exists as to whether these findings are true of alienated youth in particular or true of nonalienated youth as well, and most importantly, that even if many of these factors do exist in the lives of alienated youth, it has not been demonstrated that they are related in any *causal* fashion with the development of an alienated life style. Once again, one must be on guard against confusing correlated attributes with causal factors, an ever-present danger in the clinical method. We would not, for example, conclude that simply because alienated youth might show a greater frequency of red hair that red hair is somehow causally linked with the development of an alienated life style.

Life in the kibbutz: an interesting contrast to American society

In relatively recent years, American psychologists have been attracted to fascinating experiments in social living being conducted in Israel. Based entirely upon cooperation rather than competition, the Israeli kibbutz is a community based microsociety in which collective economic production and collective child-rearing are practiced. Predominantly agricultural, the kibbutz system is one of community-owned property collectively acquired rather than individually owned property acquired through individual enterprise. At present, there are more than 200 kibbutzim in Israel.

There is good reason for psychologists to be attracted by the Israeli kibbutz as an intriguing topic of study. Leslie and Karen Rabkin (1969) characterize the typical kibbutz member in this manner: "The kibbutznik is a healthy, intelligent, generous, somewhat shy but warm human being, rooted in his community and in the larger Israeli society." The widespread and increasing alienation of youth in American society is in interesting contrast to the youth of the kibbutz.

In effect, the kibbutz is a thoroughly planned community with a consistent and thoroughly planned program of socialization. Consider the description of the kibbutz studied by the Rabkins. From earliest infancy (three days after birth), the child is assigned to the care of persons other than the parents (Fig. 16). Although the mother may actively participate in the feeding of the child and in other activities associated with its care, by the ninth month, she is visiting the child for only brief periods, since she is occupied with her work elsewhere in the kibbutz. From the nursery the child progresses to the "toddlers house," in which, in an atmosphere of warmth, affection, and permissiveness, he learns to interact with peers and experiences the difficult childhood challenges of toilet training, feeding, and dressing. From here, the child progresses though an educational system designed to give him a sense of belongingness, of being rooted in a community with other human beings. In elementary school there are no grades and no examinations, students call the teacher by her first name, and passing is automatic. The curriculum is centered about various projects, e.g., transportation projects in which children study, build models, and ride on various forms of transportation. By the time the child graduates from high school, he will have participated in the kibbutz economy by working portions of each school day. Throughout his years of education, he is considered a member of the "children's society," a microcosm of the adult kibbutz

Figure 32. Kibbutz infants being attended to in a collective nursery. *From* Psychology Today. Children of the Kibbutz, Rabkin, K. & Rabkin, L. Y. September, 1969.)

society. The children's society participates in the planning of the curriculum, social programs, and the disciplining of its members.

By increasing the dependency of the child upon others in the community, the kibbutz system clearly avoids many of the evils that are associated with exclusive patterns of dependency that characterize the family in American society, as well as love relationships generally in American society. We are taught early in childhood that there is really only one person who can meet our needs—mother. Later on, we are expected to transfer this narrow dependency relationship to one other woman—the wife. In the kibbutz no single person is expected to assume total responsibility for another. The integrating concept is *community* rather than the isolated two-person or family relationship.

What can we say of the kibbutz? As results indicate, a society based upon community and cooperation can result in happy, warm adults who are deeply committed to one another and to the larger society in which they are imbedded. But we must remember that probably no societal arrangement can *satisfy everything*. Despite the persistence of the utopian image, it is probably true that one must choose what one wants and then attempt to maximize that goal while neglecting other potentially valuable outcomes. Whether the kibbutz can foster uniqueness and individual creativity as well as cooperation and a stable sense of identity and community remains to be seen. Some individuals may be entirely willing to pay the prices (personal and social) associated with societies characterized by great differentiation, competition, and the encouragement of individuality. Of course, the real question concerns the *level* of prices we are willing to pay. At a specific point does one become willing to forgo individuality in favor of community? At what point does a society conclude that it can no longer afford the consequences of extreme social differentiation? Unfortunately, we do not know the answers to these questions. Perhaps none exist.

PSYCHOLOGY AND THE ECOLOGICAL CRISIS

The planet earth can be likened to a vast spaceship traveling through time and space. Just as the spaceship is a complex of highly interdependent components designed to sustain life, so is the planet earth. As we have become increasingly aware, the earth is a vast system composed of highly interdependent systems within systems in which life is nurtured and sustained. The science of *ecology* deals precisely with these many subtle and often neglected relationships between living creatures and their environments. It is not a comfortable position to be an ecologist in the world as of 1970; one does not have the luxury of ignorance. For as the ecologist knows with almost complete certainty, unless current attitudes toward the physical environment change and unless drastic changes in the uses and abuses of technology take place *immediately*, the earth and everything on it are doomed. It may, in fact, be already too late.

But what does psychology have to do with ecology? As we shall see, a great deal.

Human values and ecological catastrophe

Picture America as it appeared at the end of the eighteenth century and throughout much of the nineteenth century. As far as the eye could see there was abundance. The rivers teemed with fish. The skies were clear. Clean, fresh water was readily available. The forests were filled with wildlife. Vast stretches of land invited exploration, settlement, and cultivation. It was here that an enterprising man could surely get ahead. Intelligence, hard work, and capital investment were all that were required. A conservationist would have been laughed at in this atmosphere of great abundance. There was little reason to fear that human beings would ever exhaust the vast treasures that America offered.

It was in this setting of frontier America that stable values were developing. "Let each man strive in his best interests to maximize his own benefits, and the result will be in the interests of all" became a fundamental dictum. Although such a principle seemed selfish, there was a certain reasonableness to it. That is, it seemed that through the virtues of "rugged individualism," the operation of a competitive system, and the pursuit of individual benefits to the neglect of the welfare of others, progress would be made that would benefit all of the citizens of the nation. The more modern version of this principle of "selfishness" finds expression in the motive of profit maximization of classic economics. Quite simply, the firm is seen as behaving rationally when it attempts to maximize its profits and minimize its costs. In the competitive struggle for survival in an economy such as America's, this principle is more typically applied as "seek the short-term gain and to hell with the long-range consequences," especially if such long-range consequences do not directly threaten the survival of the individual firm or current management. A general manager who must choose between the survival of his firm (and of his position) and the larger interests of the society would very likely choose in favor of the former. From one perspective, it is perfectly rational behavior to seek the short-term advantage and neglect the long-range consequences for the larger society. What rational man would deliberately choose alternatives that would raise the probability of short-term failure? From another perspective, what appears to be rational for the individual is nothing short of *collective* insanity.

While appropriate to America in its formative years, the accepted strategy of sacrificing long-term social benefits in the interests of short-term profit maximization is no longer an in-

Figure 33. Detergent scum mars an otherwise beautiful pond. (Photo by Gordon Cole.)

telligent and rational way for men to conduct their affairs. Is it reasonable for men to continue to attempt to maximize their own satisfactions while such behavior is rapidly turning the earth into a dead planet? Consider the behavior of a large chemical concern in the business of making and selling an insecticide. Even though the company is aware of the fact that this particular insecticide is not only ineffective against the insect for which it is intended but under certain conditions may *actually increase* the pest population, they continue to market the insecticide to farmers. They cover for themselves nicely by stating in their advertisements that if a rapid build-up of the pest population should occur *because of migration*, increases in the recommended dosage will quickly bring them under control (Ehrlich, 1969). Is this rational behavior? Is this socially responsible behavior?

Obviously, the science of ecology must take into account more than the complex relationships that characterize the physical world. It must also contend with human beings, their values that were formed in a world which no longer exists, their ignorance about the manner in which they have dangerously tinkered with the complex balance of forces that sustain life, as well as their vastly increased ability to play havoc with Earth through the instruments of technological advance.

Not only must we contend with short-term profit seeking on a national level, it is clear that we must now also consider it on an international level. Foreign policies of all nations of the world that increase their positions of advantage and decrease the probability of survival of the earth are clearly a one-way road to disaster. If, for example, the United States were to compete with Soviet Russia for the control of the underdeveloped nations of the world and if such competition would take the form of aid and development programs that would maximize short-term gains for these nations at the expense of the ecological well-being of the earth, what good would such aid be? Suppose that Russia, in the service of establishing good relations (i.e., read "setting up the conditions for favorable trade"), shipped massive amounts of pesticides to a given underdeveloped country. Such pesticides might very well, in the short run, permit that country to increase its agricultural output and, as a consequence, look favorably upon Russia. But what about the consequences in the long run, not only for that country but the earth as a whole?

Although this might appear quite fantastic, it is not at all unreasonable to argue that competition among nations results in each nation choosing those domestic and foreign policy alternatives that maximize their own advantage in the short run to the neglect of the long run and the common good of men everywhere. The effects of such international policies are nowhere more apparent than in the social psychology and politics of weapons research. That both the United States and Russia undertook atmospheric testing of nuclear weapons without full understanding of their grave consequences amounts to criminal negligence on the parts of both nations. The effects of excessive radiation on the human body are now well recognized. However, despite the fact that evidence linking nuclear tests in Nevada to an increase in death rates by leukemia in New York State in 1953 exists, and despite the fact that a storm of controversy has erupted among radiation physicists about the long-term genetic implications for yet unborn babies, plans for continued *underground* testing of nuclear weapons are still extant. At the time of this writing, plans have been announced for underground tests of the Spartan warhead, a long-range interceptor for the American ABM system. (The ABM system itself constitutes an incredible demonstration of the failure of conventional politics to squarely confront the realities of ecological disaster.) While ignorance may have partially explained the failure of the political system to deal with the problem of atmospheric testing in the fifties, this excuse is no longer believable in 1970. Will we make the same mistakes with regard to the so-called "peaceful" development of nuclear systems and add the very real threat of radiation pollution to the parade of other ecological horrors that now confront us?

What we must come to realize is simply that values that were forged in yesteryear are no longer appropriate to a changed world. Whether human beings can continue to survive by pursuing their own interests to the neglect of the common good, both within their own nations and in their relationships with other nations, appears questionable. We must build new values on the premise that we are all now a highly interdependent people, not only nation by nation, but throughout the world. While it may strike many Americans as absolutely heretical, we must begin to experiment in earnest with both domestic and foreign policies based upon *cooperation* rather than competition.

At the very least, we must somehow devise means in which

individual, corporate, and governmental decision-makers find a place in their decision-making models for aesthetic, social, and ecological factors as well as for monetary costs. In short, decision-makers must begin, as messy as it may appear for their elegant equations based upon monetary and equipment constraints, to calculate *human ecological* costs. Despite opinion to the contrary, a decision-making model, regardless of how elegant its mathematical properties might be, is *not* a rational model when it excludes the enormous costs that will eventually be paid in terms of the destruction of Earth and its multitude of life forms, including human beings.

At the governmental level perhaps this could be encouraged by large government incentives to corporations that do take into account human and ecological variables or at least attempt to find ways in which such variables can be brought into the very focus of decision-making. We have subsidized many wealthy land holders to do nothing but sit on their vast lands for years. We might very well begin to subsidize large

Figure 34. Ecological diaster off the coast of Santa Barbara, California, in 1969. The costs of drilling oil in the Santa Barbara Channel include far more than the operating expenses of oil companies. (United Press International Photo.)

corporations that take a serious interest in clean air, clean water, and the multiple problems associated with pollution. Are we willing to pay taxes for fresh air? Are large corporations willing to forgo some portion of their profits for this?

But, of course, extensive changes in *political attitudes* must occur before such programs can become more than token programs at the federal level. What is needed is a massive program for the reshaping of attitudes towards the physical world as well as for a massive educational program in which the true nature of the ecological catastrophes confronting modern man are explicated. But, of course, such solutions require time. Even this is no longer an "abundant" resource in the race against eco-catastrophe. Also, it is not altogether clear what a massive program of reeducation concerning the physical world and the crises that confront us would accomplish. It is difficult to believe that those who wield power in the multifarious decision-making contexts of business, government, the military, and in domestic and foreign policy-making situations are *unaware* of the dangerous game they are playing. Obviously, they operate under very real political and economic constraints, and it is because of these that their decision-making continues to show evidence of seeking short-term gain in their own interests rather than in the interests of the larger community of man in which they are imbedded.

In the complex relations that characterize the relationship of human beings to their physical surroundings, we must recognize that there will be no easy solutions. However, we must also recognize that solutions to the ecological crisis will not appear unless we consider it in the total context of psychological values and attitudes, political ideologies, domestic and foreign policies, motivations of both individual and corporate decision-makers, and economic constraints. The *social* ecology and the *biological* ecology of the earth are intimately related. They are, in fact, *the total ecosystem* which we call Earth. We must recognize that a politically motivated decision made in Moscow or Washington may very well reverberate far beyond the political system. It may, in fact, be one further step towards a dead ocean.

The Multi-dimensional Nature of Ecological Problems

In our preceding discussion of ecological catastrophe we concentrated upon three factors: human values, motivations, and ignorance of the complex interdependent life systems on the planet earth. The student must realize, however, that far more than these are involved in the numerous problems involved in air and water pollution, forest and wildlife conservation, and urban environments. Ecological problems are complex mixtures of economic, technological, and political factors. Take, for example, the problem of extensive use of DDT as a preferred pesticide. A shift to a less dangerous but possibly less efficient pesticide might very well result in an ecologically desirable outcome. At the same time, however, the economic effect might very well result in higher food pricing. Higher food costs would further contribute to the widening gap between the affluent and the poor in American society. In order to insure adequate diets for millions of Americans who find it impossible to obtain adequate nutrition even at present prices, meaningful federal food programs would have to be instituted. This, of course, would place considerable stress upon the American political system and also necessitate considerable attitude change on the part of many Americans opposed to any increased federal welfare spending. In this example concerning pesticide control, one can readily appreciate the interdependence of the technological, economic, and political systems.

Ecological problems are not restricted to the United States but are world-wide. Virtually every major city of the world is beset with the same set of problems. Ecological problems are characteristic of nations with widely differing social, political, and economic systems. As a consequence, it cannot be maintained that ecological catastrophe is exclusively associated with any single political-economic system. Both the "Free World" and the "Communist World" are plagued by smog and water pollution. The fact of world-wide ecological problems does suggest, however, that no single country has evolved an adequate system of social organization to cope with the underlying causes of ecological catastrophe. Uncontrolled technological development and the failure to evolve planning systems of considerable scope, coupled with the rapid increase in world population, have led quite naturally to the current dilemmas confronting human beings everywhere.

It is impossible in any discussion of ecological catastrophe to ignore the underlying issue of uncontrolled population growth. Let us consider this matter in greater detail.

Population and the necessity for changes in human values

It is ironic that while scientific and technological advances continue to be made to extend and maintain life forms, sheer *abundance* of living creatures should be one of the most critical problems confronting modern man. The population problem staggers the imagination. It is simply incredible to contemplate the fact that if drastic measures are not undertaken *immediately*, the population of the world will have increased from its present level of 3000 million to 25,000 million by the year 2250—just 280 years into the future. Although a current growth rate of 2 per cent per year may not sound like much, one can gain an appreciation of its significance by considering the following: If the current growth rate in the world's population had existed since the time of Christ, there would be 20,000,000 people for every person now living. It has been estimated that this would amount to approximately 100 people per square foot (Taylor, 1968). Obviously, the present situation simply cannot continue. As the report of the U.S. National Academy of Sciences concluded, "Either the birth rate must go down, or the death rate must go up."

If we can generalize from the results of animal studies, the consequences of intolerable population increase are formidable indeed. Calhoun (1962) deliberately created conditions of overcrowding in rat colonies and observed the consequences, which were disastrous indeed! The *social organization* of the colony showed radical change with concomitant breakdown in the behavior of the animals. Bizarre courtship patterns developed, sexual deviations were apparent, and a host of other behavioral abnormalities including "cannibalism" appeared. The infant mortality rate soared as high as 96 per cent; premature births of litters were common and inadequate patterns of mothering in the female rats were quite apparent.

Population biologists have recently become aware of the effects of overcrowding upon *stress*-mediated diseases and death. The size of the adrenal glands increases under periods of prolonged stress. Investigations of a massive "die-off" among deer populations on St. James Island off the coast of Virginia revealed the presence of adrenal abnormalities in *every* deer studied. Although the deer population had increased drastically, there were still abundant food supplies on the island.

More than sufficient quantities of foliage were apparent and, moreover, the dead deer showed no evidence whatsoever of having undergone death by starvation. Their coats were rich and sleek and the carcasses heavily laden with fat. These observations are hard to square with the commonly accepted hypothesis that increases in population will automatically produce scarcity of food, which will automatically result in a lowering of the population. One must search for a different answer in the case of the massive "die-off" of deer on St. James Island.

One possible explanation concerns the effects of overpopulation upon social organization. It would appear that social organization, at least in lower creatures, is dependent upon proper *spacing* between and among animals. Territoriality has long been observed in animals. Lions, for example, will supposedly not attack unless a stranger intrudes upon "their" territorial space. It is commonly observed in both man and lower animals that those who occupy positions of high status in an authority hierarchy are frequently afforded more space. The chief baboon, for example, occupies a position in the center of the troop into which no juvenile dares enter. The corporate executive is given a suite of offices in which to stretch his legs while the office secretary is customarily given a space of approximately five feet by five feet in which to conduct her business.

It would appear, then, that social organization is intimately related to the way in which available space is distributed among creatures who are to occupy it. In the case of the deer on St. James Island, it is highly probable that as population increased, frequent violations of territorial restriction occurred. These violations may have led to the increased stresses attendant upon close physical proximity of other animals, increased contact, fighting, threat, and so forth. We know that adrenal activity is stimulated by social interaction, especially by the challenge of attack and the need for self-defensive counterattack. Given the unmistakenly clear evidence of severe adrenal abnormalities in the dead deer, the conclusion that the animals died of *stress-mediated* disorder is most tempting. Furthermore, it is reasonable to conjecture that the stress occurred as a function of social disorganization, which in turn occurred as a function of severe alterations in the spacing of animals.

Of course, whether such findings can be generalized to human beings is another matter. Nonetheless, there is some evidence that overcrowding of human beings should be taken seriously. Population density has been associated repeatedly with high rates of both juvenile and adult crime (Schmitt, 1957). Moreover, Wechsler (1961) has reported a positive association between the rate of community growth and the frequency of both serious depression and suicide. There are, of course, many other alternative explanations for these findings. However, we should note that they are at least consistent with the hypothesis that overcrowding can be associated with the occurrence of deviant behavior in human beings.

In addition to the fact that overcrowding may very well have serious psychological and sociopsychological implications for persons, there are still other ways in which the population problem can be construed as a psychological one. If the population increase continues on its present course, it is quite obvious that human beings will have to learn to live with great curtailment of individual freedoms. Vast numbers of people cannot be left free to go where they wish, when they wish, and in whatever manner they wish. Fantastically effective organization and planning will prove absolutely necessary. Such extreme efforts to obtain order are clearly at odds with the emerging values of "self-realization," "freedom," "spontaneity," and "lack of inhibitions." The demands of the larger society and the pursuits of the individual will be plunged into enormous conflict. If population continues to increase, then we will be forced to change our individual values and to become far more acceptant of an all-pervasive authority in our lives — not a pleasant thing to contemplate.

If restriction of our freedoms is to be avoided, we must face squarely the necessity for *other* types of attitude and value changes. People must come to regard child-bearing and child-rearing as not absolutely necessary for individual happiness and self-fulfillment. This, of course, may be particularly difficult for females. Socialized to believe that marriage and children are essential ingredients of the successful female, many girls place an almost fanatical emphasis upon their rights to bear children. As one of my female students raged when I discussed the necessity for either voluntary or coercive measures to halt the growth of the population, "Who the hell are you to tell me that I can't have children?" If she could become so angry with a mere college professor, one who, in fact, had no power to control whether or not she had children, how might she react to an official act of Congress stipulating that henceforth no female whose maiden name begins with A through M is permitted to bear children in the United States of America!

It is possible that couples would learn to value the cooperative raising of children. In other words, values associated with the *exclusive* love relationship of the child to a single set of parents within a single family eventually have to be altered. The sharing of *a* child among as many as four or five young families might prove a workable solution if enough effort were devoted to studying how this might be done in the best interests of the child. After all, considering the current high divorce and remarriage rates, this is already being done to a certain extent. The probability that a child will have more than one set of parents, at least in California, is quite high indeed.

While various *individual* approaches emphasizing voluntary solutions to the problem could be encouraged, e.g., voluntary practice of birth control, it seems very clear that no amount of individual education and encouragement of voluntary effort will suffice. As difficult as it may be for many Americans to accept, actions by the Federal Government will almost certainly be necessary if disastrous consequences are to be avoided. We may have to alter our values in the sense that we become willing to accept a decision made by the government as to who may bear children and who may not, restrictions on the numbers of children that are permitted to be born to any couple, and so forth. But, of course, considerable ideological change must take place among the American people before such a solution becomes politically feasible. It is unfortunate that we tend toward "crisis" solutions of our problems. When things become unbearable, then we become willing to search for solutions. With the population crisis, however, it is most conceivable that we have already passed that point. When the majority of Americans, as well as the members of other societies, become willing to accept the fact that governmental intervention is absolutely necessary, the point of "no return" will have long since passed by.

The scientific-technological information environment

As science and technology continue to generate information that reaches far beyond the capacities of both individuals and societies to assimilate it, we can expect further crises and further necessity for changes in human attitudes and values. What shall we think of *death,* for example, when it becomes possible to sustain life indefinitely by such procedures as organ transplants and freezing of persons in states of clinical death? Who will choose to die when it becomes possible to live far beyond any current reasonable estimate of life expectancy? Considering the enormous population problem that confronts us now, it is obvious that people cannot be permitted to finance "parts" privately in order to go on living. But who will decide who is to live and who is to die? If this appears fantastic, remember that in the case of kidney disease, the limited availability of life sustaining equipment has already required the formation of special hospital boards who make precisely these decisions. But we can see that our very attitudes toward death must change. We must evolve life philosophies in which aging and death are an integral part of the human experience rather than a terrifying, strange, and tragic occurrence. Otherwise, who would choose to die?

Indeed, our very concepts of what it is to be "human" will face severe tests, and not in the very distant future. What shall we think of the values of the individual and of the uniqueness of personality when it becomes possible to transplant the brain of one man into the body of another? Where is the person—or *who* is the person seems a more appropriate question. Will we cling desperately to our fragile conceptions of what it means to be "human" or will the rush of events force upon us, against our will, utterly strange and foreign concepts of the person?

Finally, as more and more weapons of total destruction become available, will we have evolved the necessary political and social attitudes for world survival? Unfortunately, the gap between technological know-how and the sociopolitical system appears to be growing wider. As it has been remarked, in the light of our current social attitudes, values, and political immaturity, we are like children playing in a nuclear playground. In the face of eco-catastrophe, many of us cling to social, political, and economic philosophies and values that were appropriate to the eighteenth century. The alarm has been sounded. Will we climb into the ring to fight for our right to be wrong? Is it important to think clearly and deeply? Nature is not going to give us much more than a first round.

SUMMARY

In this chapter we have concentrated upon the psychological study of society and for the most part, American society. Moreover, we have devoted our attentions to three major crises that confront this society, namely *racism, alienation,* and the coming *eco-catastrophe.* Of course, none of these problems is unique to American society; they are world-wide. As we have seen, the psychologist has important contributions to make to understanding these complex problems. Perhaps one of the more important contributions that the psychologist can make is to analyze how persons attempt to solve complex problems that involve social systems. Typically, we approach our problems with the belief that there is a cause and that this cause can be pinpointed rather accurately. Our description of "Riots in Anytown" illustrated this tendency. If we are to make progress toward the solution of complex system problems, we must discard simple cause and effect models. We must begin to think in terms of *systems and their complex interconnections.*

Instead of asking, "What is the cause of a complex social event such as American racism?" we must learn to pose fundamentally different questions. These might be something like the following:

1. Can I describe rather accurately the system in which this event is located?
2. Can I specify the interconnections among component systems within the system in such a way that I will know with some degree of accuracy what changing one aspect of it will do to other aspects?
3. Where in this complex system is it most profitable for me to intervene in order to *change* that which needs changing and still prevent other aspects of the system from changing in undesirable directions?

By approaching complex social events in this manner, it is conceivable that we might confront the uncertainties and complexities of current social, political, and economic reality rather than the comforting certainties of our own naive theories of society.

References

Battle, E. S., and Rotter, J. B.: Children's feelings of personal control as related to social class and ethnic group. J. Personality, *31*: 482, 1963.
Baughman, E. E., and Dahlstrom, W. G.: *Negro and White Children: A Psychological Study in the Rural South*. New York, Academic Press Inc., 1968.
Calhoun, J. B.: Population density and social pathology. Scientific American, *206*: 139, 1962.
Clark, K.: Dark Ghetto: *Dilemmas of Social Power*. New York, Harper and Row Publishers, Inc., 1965.
Clinard, M. B. (ed.): *Anomie and Deviant Behavior*. New York, The Free Press, 1964.
Conot, R.: *Rivers of Blood, Years of Darkness*. New York, Bantam Books, 1967.
Cross, T. L.: *Black Capitalism: Strategy for Business in the Ghetto*. Atheneum Publishers, 1969.
Durkheim, E.: *The Division of Labor in Society*. (Translated by G. Simpson) New York, The Free Press, 1947.
Durkheim, E.: *Suicide*. (Translated by G. Simpson) New York, The Free Press, 1951.
Ehrlich, P.: Eco-catastrophe! Ramparts, September, 1969.
Glazer, N.: The missing bootstrap, Saturday Review, August, 1969.
Goodman, P.: *Growing Up Absurd*. New York, Random House, 1956.
Jessor, R., Graves, T., Hanson, R., and Jessor, S.: *Society, Personality, and Deviant Behavior: A Study of a Tri-ethnic Community*. New York, Holt, Rinehart, and Winston, 1968.
Katz, I., and Benjamin, L.: Effects of white authoritarianism in biracial work groups. J. Abnorm. Soc. Psychol., *61*: 448, 1960.
Katz, I., and Cohen, M.: The effects of training Negroes upon cooperative problem solving in biracial teams. J. Abnorm. Soc. Psychol., *64*: 319, 1962.
Keniston, K.: *The Uncommitted: Alienated Youth in American Society*. New York Dell Publishing Co., 1967.
Lefcourt, H. M., and Ladwig, G. W.: The American negro: A problem in expectancies. J. Pers. Soc. Psychol., *1*: 377, 1965.
McClelland, D. C.: *The Achieving Society*. Princeton, D. Van Nostrand Co., Inc., 1961.
Merton, R. K.: *Social Theory and Social Structure*. New York, The Free Press, 1957.
Mingione, A. D.: Need for achievement in Negro and white children. J. Cons. Psychol., *29*: 108, 1965.
Montagu, A.: Chromosomes and crime. Psychology Today, October, 1968, pp. 42–49.
Pettigrew, T. F.: *A Profile of the American Negro*. Princeton, D. Van Nostrand Co., Inc., 1964.
Rabkin, L. Y., and Rabkin, K.: Children of the kibbutz, Psychology Today, September, 1969, pp. 40–48.
Schmitt, R.: Density, delinquency, and crime in Honolulu. Sociology and Social Research, *41*: 274, 1957.
Taylor, G. R.: *The Biological Time Bomb*. New York, World Publishing Co., 1968.
Wechsler, H.: Community growth, depressive disorders, and suicide. Amer. J. Sociol., *67*: 9, 1961.
Young, Whitney M.: *Beyond Racism*. New York, McGraw-Hill Book Co., 1969.

CHAPTER

10

Culture and the Person

From our previous discussions of the many contexts of human interaction, we are led to the inescapable conclusion that human beings do not dwell in social vacuums, that they possess social environments, and that these produce remarkably enduring and pervasive effects upon both thought and behavior. Commencing with efforts to understand the individual, our discussion has gradually broadened to include ever-widening contexts within which we view human thought and behavior. Having considered human beings in interpersonal, group, organizational, and societal contexts, we have arrived finally at the broadest perspective possible, the perspective of culture. As we shall see, the psychological study of culture, more than any other similar study, convinces one that much that a person comes to "know," value, and believe, as well as many of his characteristic forms of behavior, is determined by his *point of appearance in history and his place of appearance.* Obviously, a child born in the early part of the 1950's in Laguna Beach, California, will come to view the world quite differently than one born several centuries earlier, or later, in Mexico City, Nigeria, Turkey, Micronesia, or Pakistan. A person can readily appreciate the meaning of this simply by imagining what he would be like had he been born into an Australian aboriginal family. Or suppose he had been born into a family in ancient Greece or that he were to be born into the twenty-first century, twenty-fifth century or even the year 10,000! While fascinating in and of themselves, such idle speculations about time and space should readily convince one that much of what we regard as self-initiated and self-directed thought and behavior is largely

375

delusional. Our thinking takes place within the context of rules of which we are largely unaware but that have been part of our intellectual heritage for centuries. The languages that we use to make reality coherent, to construe ourselves and others, and that permit thought to take place can be traced back through time to many peoples of whom we know relatively little. The actions that we consider so appropriate, so inherently "correct," so "given," similarly can be placed within the broader context of the culture into which we have been born.

Engaged in what appears as a frantic effort after novelty, contemporary Americans seem to be an *ahistorical* people. The youthful preoccupation with the present, with what is "happening *now*," can be seen not so much as a radical departure in life style from their elders as it is a further extension of American values and attitudes. It is ironic that much of the recent talk of a "generation gap" disguises the fact that, in the broader context of traditional American values, many of these differences are more apparent than real. We have already noted, for example, that the fact that youth and their parents appear to be divided over the choice of a chemical, marijuana versus alcohol, hardly seems a basis for concluding that they are pursuing different life styles. The use of chemicals as a means of coping with life problems, altering views of reality, and altering oneself is and has been so deeply imbedded in the American belief and value structure that one can scarcely grasp the reasons for the horror expressed by adults that their children might use *chemicals* to achieve certain purposes. Much of the preoccupation of youth in America with "emotional liberation," "spontaneity," and "freedom of emotional expression" seems less an expression of the desire to develop a range of subtle feeling states and sensitive emotional experiences than it does a preference for *activation* and high intensity experiences. Tsujioka and Cattell (1965a, 1965b), for example, found consistent differences when comparing Japanese students to American students. Whereas the American students scored very high on personality tests measuring preferred level of excitement or activation, Japanese students scored high on "feeling" and "emotional sensitivity." The similarity of the long session at the discotheque to the dance marathon of the 1930's in terms of sheer energy expenditure is much too striking to conclude that people are searching for more radically different activities in this form of amusement now than they were forty years ago. Americans have long been suckers for indoor sports characterized by the search for pure intensity that has no meaning other than itself, and the fact that contemporary youth in America seem conflicted over authority is hardly a factor that separates them from their elders. The history of American society provides ample evidence that conflictual attitudes toward authority have been characteristic of Americans long before students began challenging the legitimacy of the "power structure." Moreover, the current wave of anti-intellectuality among many American youth can hardly be considered alien to a society in which the pejorative term "egghead" was freely applied to those who seemed out of step with "common sense," "down-to-earth," "no-nonsense" pragmatism.

It is not so much that American youth and their elders are separated by values, ideals, and preferences. It is more a matter that youth seem insistent upon giving expression to these commonly shared values in their lives—by *acting* upon them, not merely verbalizing them, and it is here, of course, that generational problems occur. It is one thing to hold anti-war attitudes and values; everybody is for "Peace." But it is quite another thing to act upon these values, i.e., to burn a draft card, refuse induction, attempt to interfere with the transportation of military units, or flee the country.

We do not mean to imply that no differences exist among youth and their elders in American society. That would of course be an impossible position to defend. However, our point is simply that a combination of factors exists that prevents many Americans from perceiving the broader cultural context which renders many of their values, beliefs, and actions common rather than unique. Certainly, the *ahistorical* attitudes of many Americans prevent them from seeing the similarities between themselves and those who have lived before them. The incessant search for novelty and the profits that accrue to those who are successful in this search are clearly dependent upon the willingness of both the individual and the society to *deny* that present products have any resemblance to past products. Whereas the American seems intent upon building a present and future on the presumably rusting remains of the discards of the past, the Japanese, for example, make every effort to provide continuity by assimilating new products into an ever-expanding cultural heritage.

In addition to the ahistoricism of Americans, we can point to our celebration of the individual as still another factor which produces cultural "blindness." From the elementary school years on, even though conformity is demanded, we are socialized heavily in the values of "individual differences," respect for such differences, and encouragement of them. Although there is, of course, nothing objectionable in valuing individuality, we should be aware that our intense glorification of the individual, of his rights and freedoms, is very likely an important factor in the apparent inability of many Americans to perceive similarities between themselves and others who share their common cultural heritage.

It is precisely for these reasons that the study of other cultures is of considerable potential value for the student. Without the benefit of comparison and contrast with other cultures, it is difficult for a person to come to see himself and his relation to the broader cultural context in which he is imbedded. It is most reasonable to suppose that we can often learn more about ourselves not by focusing upon ourselves but by focusing upon others. Someone was supposed to have once remarked, "The universe is so difficult to understand since there seems to be only one of it." In this rather humorous remark, we sense a strong element of truth. Much of what we call "understanding" consists largely of information concerning contrast and similarity. We see the implications of theory X when we are able to contrast it with a radically different theory Y. The real significance of a given life style only becomes apparent when we can anchor it among a number of different life styles. Similarly, the extent to which we are bounded by our culture only becomes apparent when we examine cultures other than our own. This, then, is one reason why the study of other cultures is of vital importance to any person seeking to understand the origins of his thought and behavior and the factors which maintain them. There are also other reasons for studying other cultures. Let us examine these briefly.

The relevance of cross-cultural study and psychological inquiry

If we were to ask a particular psychologist why he performed an experiment involving college age females from the freshman class of the University of Wisconsin, he would probably say something like the following: "Well, isn't it obvious? I'm trying to find out something about *human behavior*." Notice that the psychologist said that he hopes to discover something about *human behavior*. He did not say he wished to find out how the typical University of Wisconsin freshman woman behaved as of September 25, 1970. We assume that the psychologist is interested in general laws of behavior, laws that have universal generality; that is, laws that transcend time and space.

Suppose, however, that we asked the psychologist, "How long have you been studying University of Wisconsin female freshmen in the interests of finding out something about human behavior?" Further, suppose that he said, "Well, this is my fifty-seventh experiment and I've been at it ever since I got out of graduate school twenty years ago. During this time, I've learned an awful lot about human behavior." Now, if you are as *culture-bound* as this hypothetical psychologist, you might very well say something like, "Gee, that's impressive, I'll bet you *have* learned a lot about human behavior." But if you have been fortunate enough to have traveled beyond the boundaries of Madison, Wisconsin, and remember images of Japanese geishas, Delhi housewives, Ceylonese school children, Eskimo mothers, Buddhist priests, Kenyan hunters, and other diverse human types, you are likely to say something like, "Gee, that's impressive, I'll bet you have learned a lot about *Wisconsin female freshmen*."

It is at this point that our discussion of the problem of the generality of psychological inquiry presented in Chapter 2 should become extremely meaningful. One should very well ask how it is that a psychologist who has studied nothing but University of Wisconsin freshmen women for twenty years can pretend to make statements about human behavior in general. Psychologists are not immune to the effects of culture. They spin their theories, gather their observations, and draw their subjects from within a given cultural context. That cultural factors limit the extent to which their findings can be claimed universal surely cannot be denied. The very thought of the psychologist, the hypotheses he investigates, and the findings he expects are surely as much a product of cultural conditioning as the clothes he wears to class, the foods he prefers, and the kind of transportation he uses. Moreover, the institution in which he conducts his research and the subjects upon which he conducts it are as much a part of the culture as he is. As we have seen in the work of Orne, Rosenthal, Milgram, and others, the psychological experiment is a social interaction situation which has much in common with other interactive situations; and there is good reason to believe that not only persons but also their contexts of interaction are influenced by culture.

Of course, psychologists are not unaware of the importance of cross-cultural study. Within recent years, increasing efforts to establish the generality of findings in American laboratories have been apparent. However, it is now quite obvious that an enormous number of cross-cultural studies must be completed before we can speak confidently of a psychology of human behavior.

It is clear, then, that cross-cultural study is one of the means through which the psychologist can establish the universality of his findings. Let us examine other important values of such study.

Testing hypotheses through cross-cultural study. For many aspects of human thought and behavior it is clearly impossible to arrange the conditions necessary for study. If, for example, one were to believe that a given method of child-rearing is likely to result in severe mental illness in adulthood, one could not have mothers deliberately raise children in this fashion to see what would happen, nor could one manipulate a national economy in order to see if changes in social behavior would result. For these and many other questions it is obvious that the psychologist himself cannot vary the conditions that would provide answers. However, he can take advantage of variations that occur naturally, i.e., cross-cultural variations.

An interesting example of how cross-cultural research can be used to test hypotheses is provided by early but fascinating work by anthropologists concerned with the universality of Freud's psychoanalytic theory. Malinowski (1927), for example, while studying Trobriand Islanders (off the coast of New Guinea), came to the conclusion that the Oedipus complex (see Chapter 4) was not universal. According to Malinowski, much of the hostility that boys in western societies direct toward their fathers grows from the fact that the father is the disciplinarian in the family. Since the father acts in an inhibiting and frustration-producing manner for the child, one does not need to postulate sexual rivalry between the father and son to explain hostile attitudes on the son's part. In the society of the Trobriand Islanders, the mother's brother is the disciplinarian in the family. Hence, even though there was ample evidence to suggest that the Trobrian child was fully aware of the sexual relationship between mother and father, Malinowski failed to find hostility directed toward the father. The aggressions of the sons were directed at the mother's brother, the disciplinarian of the family. Father-son relationships among the Trobriand Islanders were characterized by much mutual respect, affection, and cooperation, rather than the tensions associated with such things as sexual jealousy, rivalry, and "castration anxiety." Moreover, Malinowski discovered that sexual guilt among Trobriand Island boys involved not the mother but the sister.

Whether or not Malinowski's results are characteristic of matrilineal societies in general is open to question. One would have to provide contrasts among a number of societies to discover whether or not the father-son relationship found among Trobriand Islanders is generally found in matrilineal societies. At least one investigator (Roheim, 1950) has claimed to have found results on Normanby Island, one quite near the Trobriand Islands, that contradict Malinowski's findings. Of course, it is impossible to draw firm conclusions as to Malinowski's hypothesis concerning aggression and discipline from this study alone. In order to evaluate his belief that aggression is directed toward the disciplinarian of the family, we would need to have before us information concerning the nature of discipline and aggression from a number of societies.

In any event, from Malinowski's observations we have good reason to question the universality of the Oedipus complex. Although Freud asserted that it was an inevitable occurrence in the life of the male child, one has reason to believe that it may be more the outcome of varying social factors rather than biological factors and hence that it is nonuniversal.

Discovery of attractive alternatives through cross-cultural study. For many persons cross-cultural study is interesting because it provides fascinating insights into the "peculiar" patterns of behavior of so-called "primitive" peoples. One supposedly studies people from other cultures not because one can learn something of value from them but because they are "odd," "peculiar," "strange," and "primitive." The student should realize that attitudes like these more often than not emerge from the assumption that one's own culture is superior to all others—a questionable assumption indeed. The belief in the superiority of one's own culture is referred to as *ethnocentrism*. This quality in human beings was noted as far back as 450 B.C. by the Greek philosopher Herodotus, who, in the course of his travels, concluded the following:

If one were to offer men to choose out of all the customs in the world such as seemed to them best, they would examine the whole number, and end by preferring their own; so convinced are they that their own usages far surpass those of all others.*

But surely one of the great values in studying other cultures is precisely that one may very well uncover attractive alternatives to one's own culture. The great cultural diversity of peoples throughout the world can be considered as a vast treasury of naturalistic social experiments involving a host of considerations. Consider the manner in which societies treat death. All societies must establish ways in which the death of members is handled. The corpse must be disposed of, provisions must be made for the relatives of the deceased, opportunities for the expression of grief must be created, and arrangements must exist to help the grieving pick up their lives again and return to the problems of the living. In American society, death is anything but a community affair. It is, in fact, the occasion for a lot of money to be made. Elaborate floral arrangements, expensive coffins, and grave sites that will be given "perpetual care" (at a price of course) make death one of the worst bargains that you or I will ever get in America. Of course, there are powerful lobbies and special interest groups who will do their best to insure that this situation does not change by the time you and I are shopping (or more correctly, somebody is shopping for us). Aside from these crass commercial considerations, we are more struck by the social implications of death in American society, particularly for the widow of the deceased. For the most part, the widow in America must endure the death of her husband alone. Of course, there is the brief period of social support at the time of the funeral and shortly thereafter, but the widow, particularly the elderly one, knows that this will quickly pass and will be followed by the long and almost unbearable loneliness that will likely haunt her remaining years. But, of course, this situation is not unique to American society but is found in other "advanced" societies as well.

Consider how death is handled, however, in a so-called "primitive" society. David Mandelbaum (1965) has provided us with a fascinating study of the social management of death among the Kotas of South India. Like many "primitive" peo-

---

*From Blakeney, E. H.: The History of Herodotus. (Translated by G. Rawlinson.) London, Everyman's Library, 1910, Vol. 1, p. 89.

ples, the Kotas have two funeral ceremonies. The first funeral is called the "green funeral" and takes place shortly after death. It is at this time that the body is cremated, after which a bit of skull bone is taken from the ashes and retained for the second funeral, the "dry funeral." The "dry funeral" takes place once a year, or once every two years, and is the occasion for the community to gather together to observe *all* the deaths that have occurred in the village over a period of time.

By holding two ceremonies, the Kotas recognize the importance of both the *religious* and *social* requirements of the management of death in a society. The long interval between the "green" and "dry" funerals makes it possible for the society to manage the death of its members in an adequate fashion. Rather than endure a discrete and abrupt end to life, the deceased is gradually moved from the status of "living" to the status of "dead." In the period between the "green" and "dry" funerals, the deceased is accorded all the respects of a living person. His goods and properties are respected. If his wife should become pregnant in this period, the child will bear his name and in all respects will be considered his.

The "dry funeral" consists of four main acts. The first week is devoted to observance of strict mourning taboos by bereaving kinsmen of the deceased. The dead are memorialized one by one. The second act commences with a procession to the cremation grounds. A second cremation involving the bones of the deceased, personal ornaments, and other goods is conducted. The bereaved and other participants stay the night at the cremation grounds. The third act begins with the first morning star. Dancing and feasting take place. Ritual acts designed to bring widows and widowers back into the social life of the village take place. At nightfall, a pot is smashed, and this is the occasion for the people to "turn their backs on the dead" and run back to the village "toward life" and normal social relationships. The reentry of the widows and widowers into the normal life of the village is encouraged by the requirement that they have sexual relationships, preferably with a sibling of the deceased. The "dry" ceremony ends after several days of singing and dancing.

In their complex treatment of death, the Kotas manage several important functions. First, the social order is reaffirmed with cohesion of the family and kinship system demonstrated. Second, the ceremony provides the widow or widower with an opportunity to realize once again his sense of belonging in a larger social structure, namely the community. Finally, important individual psychological functions are managed. Arrangements are made for the expression of grief and for the gradual and socially approved means by which the bereaved can be returned to full participation in the community.

The student might well ask himself which of the two is the more "primitive"—the "American way of death" or death as managed by the Kota people of South India. Obviously, there is much that the receptive person can learn from the study of so-called "primitive" peoples.

As we have seen, then, there are good reasons why cross-cultural study is of enormous value. First, it is obvious that a science of social thought and behavior cannot be established upon the basis of exhaustive observations within a single society. Second, the natural variations extant among world cultures provides one with a ready-made laboratory for testing hypotheses. Finally, the study of other peoples and other cultures may lead to the discovery of attractive social arrangements that are far superior to one's own.

Some generalizations in the study of culture and the person

Pelto (1965) has provided us with some useful generalizations concerning the study of the person in the broad context of culture. Let us consider these briefly.

1. *Culture is much more than a superficial overlay of customs. It is an all-pervasive way of life which significantly influences belief, perception of reality, values, emotions, and actions.*

Doob (1964, 1965) has argued, for example, that culture may influence such basic things as the way information is stored by the person. Doob studied the extent to which eidetic imagery occurred among two African societies. An eidetic image is a vivid and highly detailed memory image which, in Western societies, is found much more frequently among children than adults. In contrast to Western societies where verbal means of memory storage are characteristic, Doob discovered in the two African societies a great reliance upon eidetic imagery as the means by which information is stored.

Beliefs in witchcraft and magic have, of course, long been recognized as characteristic of persons from various societies.

Bowen's remarkable "novel" *Return to Laughter* provides us with a fascinating description of magical thought in a West African tribe—as well as the difficulties experienced by an American anthropologist in her first encounter with the incredible web of tribal life in conjunction with the power of magical thought and witchcraft. In attempting to explain the nature of vaccination, Bowen found herself inadvertently convincing others of the tribe that she possessed miraculous powers. The following interchange between herself and a boy of the village is indicative not only of the beliefs of the people she studied but the extent to which these beliefs challenged every belief Bowen had held dear:

> "It is our medicine (vaccination)," I told him, "to protect you from water."
>
> "That is possible," Rogo said politely. "It is not important." He came to the point. "It is you, my mother, who will protect me from the water. You have told everyone that water was brought to you when you were a child. Even at Nder's they know it. I knew you had a strong heart," his voice held admiration, "but I didn't know you could pour water over others. Now everyone will be afraid of you, and we, your children, will be safe under your protection."
>
> I had been talking about vaccination. People had interpreted what I said in terms of witchcraft. From my words they understood that as a small child my parents had first exposed me to smallpox and then taught me the black art of causing it in others. I had branded myself a witch and a braggart. Humor and perspective lost, I, like Yabo, turned for refuge to an inner and contemptuous superiority over this foolish world. Let them fear me. It has its uses. As long as my work was not impeded, I didn't care. I was past laughter.*

But, of course, within the total context of a particular society magical beliefs have an undeniable logic. Malinowski (1948) was perhaps the first to show relationships between feelings of incompetence in the face of uncertainty and the development of magical thought. In the face of highly uncertain activities, e.g., ocean sailing, warfare, and hunting, it seems reasonable to suppose that people would resort to magical beliefs and practices as a means by which otherwise unbearable anxiety could be managed and contained.

Nadel (1952), in his studies of West African tribes, showed that accusations of witchcraft tend to be directed against those perceived as the most anxiety-provoking persons in the tribe. More recently, Swanson (1960) has demonstrated a relationship

---

*From Bowen, E. S.: *Return to Laughter: An Anthropological Novel.* New York, Doubleday and Company, Inc., 1964, p. 250.

TABLE 7. Relationship of Witchcraft Beliefs to Presence of Legitimated Social Controls*

Prevalence of Witchcraft	Societies with Legitimate Controls	Societies without Legitimate Controls
High	1	17
Intermediate	14	7
Low	9	1

*Adapted from Swanson, G.E.: *The Birth of the Gods.* Ann Arbor, University of Michigan Press, 1960, p. 147.

between the absence of legitimated social controls and the presence of witchcraft. Swanson's work was truly impressive in that he examined a sample of fifty societies. Table 7 presents his findings.

But one need not travel to far-off, exotic places to discover magical thought and practices. The "rabbit's foot," superstitious practices of all kinds, and belief in magical powers of all kinds are evident in complex, modern societies as well. Competitive sports in America are particularly susceptible to the development of magical thought. Certain big-league baseball players are reputed to be enormously superstitious, as exemplified by one who refused to change his socks while in the middle of a hitting streak and another who eats only a particular food before a game.

It is interesting to apply Malinowski's findings concerning uncertainty, anxiety, and magical thought to the current outbreak of interest in astrology, magic, and novel belief systems among many people in contemporary America. Many people today complain of a general sense of "helplessness," of incompetence and powerlessness in the face of almost overwhelming complexity and uncertainty. Under these conditions, we would expect to find a turning away from scientific, rational modes of orienting oneself to the world to prescientific orientations.

In Alcoholics Anonymous, for example, there is more than ample evidence to suggest that in persons who have experienced the ultimate in powerlessness over their own lives, beliefs in "powers greater than oneself" are readily fostered. Certainly, many sudden religious conversions share the same motivational base. That belief in magical powers can result from feelings of helplessness and powerlessness seems entirely reasonable. But one must not scoff at such beliefs. It cannot be denied that dramatic *positive* changes can take place within the lives of persons as a consequence of the adoption of this or that exotic belief concerning benevolent supernatural forces. Literally thousands of reformed alcoholics lead sober, productive, serene, and happy lives by orienting their beliefs around the assumption of a benevolent power greater than themselves. Much the same can be said of persons committed to other spiritual and religious views of life. In a purely pragmatic sense, exotic beliefs are extremely useful even if their *truth value* remains in question.

Still another example of the pervasive effects of culture upon the person is Ghei's study of the differences in need profiles between American undergraduates and University of Delhi undergraduates (Ghei, 1966). On need for autonomy, for example, Americans clearly scored higher than their Indian counterparts. Ghei concludes that in the United States the qualities of initiative, independence, and individualism are reinforced from early childhood, whereas deference is reinforced in India. Indian children are described as prevented from going out unaccompanied, from speaking freely in front of adults, and from disagreeing with their fathers.

In these three examples, then, we gain some appreciation for the generalization that culture is much more than a superficial overlay of customs. We have seen how culture can enter into such things as memory storage, belief systems, and the patterning of human needs.

2. *Culture is best construed as a complex, interdependent system, one in which the alteration of one component can result in alteration of others.* Virtually every major theorist of culture has commented upon the necessity of viewing it as an interdependent system. Thus, for example, social organization is associated with the techniques involved in food gathering. Male dominance is found in societies emphasizing animal husbandry. In hunting and foraging societies, child-rearing practices seem to be far more permissive than in agricultural societies. Even the typical games of a culture seem to be associated with both social organization and techniques of food gathering. Games involving strategy are found in societies with a differentiated, hierarchical social structure, whereas games involving physical skill and prowess are found in societies characterized by low levels of social and technological differentiation, e.g., simple hunting and foraging societies (Roberts, Arth, and Bush, 1959).

Relationships between technology and social organization are readily apparent in examples of change. When steel axes were introduced into an Australian aboriginal society, changes in the distribution of power resulted. Previously, the tools of the society had been very scarce stone axes that served as status symbols and were held primarily by the elders; but the introduction of numerous and highly efficient steel axes upset the power distribution. Young men and women who gained access to efficient high-status tools were given the means to shake off the subservient position they had held vis-à-vis their elders prior to the introduction of the steel axes (Sharp, 1952). Of course, as we indicated in Chapter 8, the effects of technological change are not confined to simpler societies. There is every reason to believe that major changes in the modern work organization in America have come about primarily because of changes in the means, processes, and products of production. Similarly, we noted that technological and scientific changes have important implications for value change and change in social organization generally in advanced technological societies. It is reasonable that increasing automation, for example, will bring with it the necessity for changes in values, work orientation, achievement motivation, career aspiration, and political ideology.

One must not underemphasize the importance of viewing culture as a dynamic system of interrelated parts. Patterns of work, play, family organization, technology, child-rearing, social organization, and individual beliefs, values, and motivations are intricately bound to one another, often in complex and poorly understood ways.

3. *Despite the fact that the behavior of members of other cultures may appear strange to us, understanding of another cultural system enables us to see the coherence and logical quality of behavior within that cultural system.* We frequently attempt to understand the behavior of persons from another culture while viewing it in isolation from its cultural context. It is typically the case that people tend to view any behavioral fragment from another culture through the lenses of their own cultural experiences. Under these circumstances, it is, of course, not surprising that many of the beliefs, practices, and actions of persons from another culture appear "odd," "bizarre," and "peculiar." This is precisely the problem faced by the inquisitive anthropologist investigating patterns of behavior in a culture other than his

own. The very categories and constructs he uses may be inappropriate to the culture he seeks to understand. In cross-cultural psychological testing, for example, one is never sure even with careful language translation that one is tapping "real" cultural differences. It is not only that translation of test materials is a touchy business, but persons from a different culture may react quite differently to the mere fact of being tested, to the form of questions, and to habitual ways of approaching a given task. These problems are readily indicated by work conducted by Dennis with a psychological test called the "Draw a Person Test."

Dennis (1960) had Bedouin Arabs draw the human figure, a technique used in personality analysis in the United States. Although the evidence for the validity of this procedure even within the cultural context of the United States is primarily negative (Swenson, 1957), there are many people who persist in believing that human figure drawings are indicative of stable personality characteristics. In any case, Dennis was surprised to note that Bedouins drew strikingly small human figures in relation to the size of the paper. While such small drawings are often said to be indicative of "personality constriction" or "inhibition," the overt and actual behavior of the Bedouins was hardly in accord with such a picture. If anything, they are expansive, uninhibited, and socially aggressive! However, when Dennis viewed these findings within the larger cultural context of the Bedouins, their significance became immediately apparent. Bedouin visual art is generally meager and largely confined to nonrepresentational decorative objects, small in size and impoverished in detail.

With regard to the supposed inability of so-called "primitive" peoples to engage in logical thought, Pospisil (1963) has provided us with an extremely fascinating account of a stone age people who, within a few years of their contact with the civilized world, showed very sophisticated thought. An old man of the region came to Pospisil and expressed much puzzlement about the apparent inconsistencies in the ways of the white man. He had ample evidence of the technological achievements of the white man as witnessed by airplanes flying over the region, medicines, guns, and so forth. But he was puzzled by how such technological ability could exist side by side with what he regarded as logical inconsistencies in the religious convictions of the white man. As he asked Pospisil:

How can you think that a man can sin and can have a free will, and at the same time believe that your God is omnipotent, and that he created the world and determined all the happenings? If he determined all that happens, and (therefore) also the bad deeds, how can a man be held responsible? Why, if he is omnipotent, did the Creator have to change himself into a man and allow himself to be killed (crucified) when it would have been enough for him just to order men to behave.*

In this case, the situation is dramatically reversed with the "primitive" man questioning the "primitive" logic of those from a supposedly more advanced civilization.

HUMAN PERSONALITY IN CULTURE

In her studies of the Balinese, Margaret Mead (1946) came to the conclusion that the very basis of Western motivational striving, i.e., goal-oriented behavior, might not be characteristic of all peoples. Much of what Westerners regard as "rational" behavior is behavior in the service of achieving some goal, attaining an objective, or serving some purpose. It is a curious fact that in the author's classes on personality, one of the most difficult concepts for students to grasp is nongoal-oriented behavior. For American college students, it would appear that all behavior is "purposeful" in the sense that it can be referred to some *end state* which the actor is attempting to bring about. This emphasis upon means-ends relationships is so deeply ingrained in Western thought that it is difficult, if not impossible, for some persons to imagine that some behaviors may not be the means to anything at all. Perhaps we are so socialized in the values of competence as a means to achieve something other than itself that we find noninstrumental views of one's own behavior and of that of others not only unthinkable but even a bit frightening. As one student in my class put it, "You mean that a lot of what I do is 'purposeless'?" For this student, referring to her behavior, or some part of it, as noninstrumental was equivalent to saying that it possessed no *meaning*. It is understandable how she could be led to this conclusion. Our language itself is structured so as to make it difficult to think about noninstrumental behavior. The opposite of "purpose" is "purposelessness." One term connotes "meaning" and "significance" while the other connotes lack of meaning and insignificance.

---

*From Pospisil, L.: *Kapauku Papuans of West New Guinea.* New York, Holt, Rinehart and Winston, 1963, p. 85.

Moreover, in an achievement-oriented society, very few acts can come to possess value in and of themselves. Meaning is not inherent in action but in the direction of action. One does not learn to play music because of the intrinsic value of making music but because competence in music may lead to the attainment of particular goals, e.g., money, prestige, or recognition. And, of course, as long as a person construes his own behavior and the behavior of others in these terms, it is not surprising to find that external reinforcements associated with goal attainment have undeniable effects upon behavior. We do not mean to imply that reinforcement affects behavior *only* because people *think* that it should. There is enough evidence from animal studies concerning the effects of reinforcement to render that position clearly untenable. However, we would be willing to defend the position that because of a cultural context that emphasizes means-end relationships, a far greater number of varying kinds of behavior become dependent upon external reinforcement for their maintenance than would be apparent in a culture that did not emphasize such relationships. Quite simply, in a culture in which acts are viewed as instrumental to goal attainment for which rewards are given, persons will come to accept such a sequence as "natural." Moreover, they might very well come to look upon various acts not as valuable in and of themselves, but as merely steps to the attainment of objectives and hence to the rewards which they expect as a consequence.

In any case, Mead's observations of the Balinese renders the culture-boundedness of means-ends relationships a distinct possibility. The Balinese do not see their behavior as imbedded in means-ends relationships. According to Mead, they see their behavior "either as an infinite continuum leading nowhere, or else as separate atomic pieces." But, of course, it is possible, as Child (1968) points out, that Mead's observations of the Balinese may simply reflect the fact that Mead's way of "talking about things" and the Balinese way of "talking about things" are so dissimilar that Mead has failed to see instrumental behavior when it actually exists. If this were the case, one would have to turn to nonverbal methods of study, e.g., the experiment, to see whether or not differences between Balinese orientation and Western orientation do actually exist. Would studies of instrumental learning hold for the Balinese as they do for Americans? Even if they did, how would we interpret such findings? The fact that Balinese might show evidence of learning in instrumental learning situations would tell us that they were capable of learning under such situations. It would not tell us anything about their *preferred* orientation to the world.

In any case, our discussion of the possible culture-boundedness of a relationship as basic to one's orientation to the world should alert the student to the fact that culture and personality are intimately related. It is conceivable that the very concept of motivation, or at least extrinsic motivation, is, in large measure, an expression of cultural values rather than a statement about the immutable nature of things. To state our hypothesis more accurately, the importance one attaches to extrinsic motivation as a determinant of behavior may reflect one's cultural biases. Hence, the very concepts we employ in building a *naive theory of personality* (see Chapter 6) may reflect our cultural surroundings. But let us move on. To what extent is human personality shaped by cultural context?

Group character versus modal personality

In attempting to understand the effects of culture upon personality, it is useful to draw a distinction between two concepts, namely *group character* and *modal personality* (Wallace, 1961; Child, 1968). When a description of the character of a group of persons is *inferred* from a study of the cultural system in which they are imbedded, one is dealing with a description of group character. On the other hand, when descriptions are based upon *direct* study of representative samples of individuals drawn from a particular culture, these are referred to as descriptions of modal personality. On the basis of our observations of American society, for example, we may be tempted to conclude that the typical American is preoccupied with competition and social approval. This *inference* based upon American values is, in effect, a stereotype of group character. To discover the extent to which this particular group character actually corresponds to the modal personality of individuals within American society we would have no recourse but to draw samples of individuals from the society and compare them with samples drawn from other societies. In actuality, research of this nature has been accomplished (Turner, 1960).

Turner investigated the extent to which the American group character matched the modal personality by drawing samples of college students from both the United States and England. Whereas the American group character centers on competition and striving for social success, the English group character does not. On tests of these variables, Turner was unable to find over-all differences between his total American samples and his total English samples. Although there was appreciable variation between and among schools within each group of samples, over-all differences were not obtained. Turner concluded that "surface" cultural differences in competitiveness and striving to be accepted apparently do not alter the "private preoccupations" of individuals when highly similar economic and social structures exist for both societies. In other words, Turner concludes that even though differences in expression of values exist at the cultural level, the economic and social institutions of the two societies are similar enough to produce similar behaviors at the individual level. Certainly, from Turner's results one must be cautious about accepting stereotypes of group character in the absence of data concerning modal personality of the individual.

From Turner's work we can conclude that discrepancies between group character and modal personality can occur. That this should be the case is not surprising. Not all individuals share equally in the cultures in which they are immersed. In the culture in which considerable freedom is permitted in certain areas of functioning we would expect consistently large differences between group character and modal personality. That is, personality differences become more apparent when such differences are permitted to be expressed.

Even though we can identify situations in which discrepancies between group character and modal personality exist, we can also point to examples where they match, i.e., examples in which the national stereotype seems to fit the modal personality. Grinder and McMichael (1963), for example, correctly predicted differences between the behavior of children of American origin and children of Samoan origin from knowledge of group character. Grinder and McMichael reasoned that in American society children are socialized in ways that are likely to result in internalized guilt as the means by which social control is effected. On the other hand, Samoan culture is supposedly a "shaming" culture, one dependent upon the administration of external sanctions entirely to produce control over behavior. When children of these differing cultural backgrounds were tested on both a personality test and a situational test in which temptation to cheat was present, clear differences were obtained. American children made more mention of guilt and guilt-related themes in their stories and showed less evidence of willingness to cheat when conditions favored successful cheating.

For particular personality traits, very good agreement between group character and modal personality has been obtained. One of the more clear-cut findings emerges from the study of authoritarianism in cross-cultural comparisons. Both Germany and the Arab societies of the Middle East have long been considered culturally authoritarian. On measures of tendency toward authoritarian attitudes, German and Arab students consistently score higher than do comparable samples of American students (Cohn and Carsch, 1954; Melikian, 1959). In terms of authoritarian attitudes, Arab students far exceed both German and American college students.

From these and many other studies we can conclude that group character may be a *useful source of hypotheses* concerning modal personality. However, in the absence of data on samples of individuals representative of the culture, one is best advised to treat group character descriptions with caution.

Cross-cultural studies of child-rearing practices

Perhaps the most effective means by which culture is transmitted is through the relationship between parent and child. Through direct instruction, social learning, and reinforcement learning the child is socialized into the customs of the culture into which he is born. It is perfectly reasonable to suppose that childhood training practices will bear some relationship to adult personality characteristics.

Perhaps one of the most interesting attempts to relate childhood training practices to adult personality is the work of Whiting and Child (1962). Using both Freudian theory and learning theory, Whiting and Child reasoned that relationships between the severity of training in oral matters, e.g., feeding practices, breast feeding, and weaning, and adult personality might be obtained. In particular, they felt that early weaning or harsh weaning of the child would result in anxiety about oral activities. They further reasoned that this anxiety over oral matters would find expression in explanations of illness. In societies in which early or harsh weaning was typically practiced, explanations of illness would take oral forms, i.e., eating "tainted" food, eating poisoned food, or eating the wrong kinds of food. In a comparison study involving 39 societies, the relationship was confirmed. Whiting and Child's findings are presented in Table 8.

Still other studies of childhood socialization concern the relationship between patterns of child-rearing and subsequent attitudes toward supernaturals, or gods. Spiro and D'Andrade (1958) discovered that in societies where infants are indulged, people tend to believe that the behavior of the gods can be controlled by the behavior of the people. Work by Lambert, Triandis, and Wolf (1959) found harsh parental treatment of

Figure 35. This young Gusii of Kenya must show unflinching bravery during circumcision rites. The older men have led him to believe that he would be speared if he should cry or try to run away. *From* LeVine, R. A.: Africa. *In* Hsu, F. L. K. (ed.): *Psychological Anthropology: Approaches to Culture and Personality.* Homewood, Ill., Dorsey Press, 1961.

TABLE 8. Relationship Between Oral Socialization of Anxiety and Oral Explanations of Illness*

	Societies with Oral Explanations Absent	Societies with Oral Explanations Present
	A	B
Societies Above Average (median) on Oral Socialization Anxiety	Lapps Chamorro Samoans	Marquesans Lesu Dobuans Masai Baiga Lepcha Kwoma Maori Thonga Pukapukans Alorese Trobrianders Chagga Kwakiutl Navaho Manus Dahomeans
	C	D
Societies Below Average (median) on Oral Socialization Anxiety	Arapesh Balinese Hopi Tanala Paiute Chenchu Teton Papago Flathead Venda Warrau Wogeo Ontong-Javanese	Chiricahua Comanche Siriono Bena Slave Kurtatchi

*From Whiting, J. W. M., and Child, I. L.: *Child Training and Personality.* New Haven, Yale University Press, 1962, p. 156.

infants to be associated with beliefs that the gods were far more aggressive than benevolent toward human beings. A third study by Whiting (1959) provided further consistency by showing that in societies in which the treatment of infants is indulgent, people tend not to fear ghosts. From these three studies, one is tempted to conclude that attitudes toward supernaturals is determined by projection of attitudes toward parental figures. If one's parents are pleasant and indulgent, then he will view supernaturals in that way. However, if one's parents are harsh and punitive, one will perceive supernaturals as similarly harsh and punitive.

A more recent study by Scofield and Sun (1960) attempted to relate differences in child-rearing practices to differences in modal personality in Americans and Chinese. Information about child-rearing practices was gathered by having Chinese college students who recently arrived in America write descriptions of child-rearing practices in their own homes. From these Scofield and Sun concluded that Chinese practices were far more severe than American middle-class practices. Chinese practices were judged as less accepting of aggression and sexuality, less tolerant of independence, and highly moral in comparison with American middle-class practices. On tests of personality, Chinese students were found to have traits associated with greater emotional withdrawal, shyness, insecurity, introversion, suspicion, sensitivity, and aloofness.

Cross-cultural studies of parent-child relationships show consistent findings, and father-son relationships appear particularly important for a number of variables. Work by Mussen, Young, Gaddini, and Morante (1963) seems to clearly indicate that affectionate father-son relationships importantly affect the development of identification of the child with the father. Moreover, identification with the father is further associated with the child's adoption of appropriate sex-role behaviors (i.e., he acts as a boy should in terms of cultural expectations), the development of moral attitudes, and good social adjustment in general.

In studies of Caribbean people, Mischel (1961) found evidence that the mere presence of a father in the home is associated with the child's ability to delay his gratifications. When children were asked to choose between small immediate rewards or large delayed rewards, children from homes in which the father was present more often chose to wait for the larger delayed reward than to take the immediate small reward. Hence, one concludes that the presence or absence of the father is one factor affecting ability to tolerate delay in gratification.

Sechrest and Wallace (1967), commenting on the work of Bulatao, a Filipino psychologist, concluded that "split-level" personalities can appear in cultural settings undergoing rapid cultural change. In the Philippines, values associated with modern, urban Western values exist along with traditional Filipino values. The result is that in their efforts to deal with two often conflicting value systems, Filipinos end up with a so-called "split-level" personality. On one level they adhere to Western values, but on another level traditional Filipino values compete. It is possible that a primacy effect operates with strong emotional conditioning attached to early learning of traditional values in the home and Western values learned later on a more formal and verbal level.

Sechrest and Wallace supply the following amusing example of the consequences of a split value system:

> Filipino students undoubtedly cheat for the same reasons as other students, but a good bit of importance is attached in the Philippines to making a good impression on others and thus gaining status and recognition. But to the consternation of just about everyone, cheating was found to be the most common in ethics classes! The students were being taught the value of honesty, but when that value came into conflict with a more traditional value, the traditional value ruled.*

These examples, then, illustrate the importance of child-rearing practices in the consideration of the cultural transmission of modal personality characteristics. The student should, of course, realize that we have barely scratched the surface of the enormous body of literature on cross-cultural patterns of child-rearing. However, it was not our purpose to survey this body of literature but to give the student a beginning appreciation of the fascinating work that has been done and remains to be done in this area.

Some cautions in interpreting cross-cultural studies of child-rearing

While it would appear that simple and direct relationships between child-rearing practices and modal adult personality exist, it is important for the student to realize that the situation is far more complex than we have pictured it. Consider the Kaska Indians of northern British Columbia and Alaska.

Among the Kaska, patterns of child-rearing are thought to be associated with the development of an adult personality style of emotional isolation. The Kaska people are said to show a "strong desire to maintain aloofness from emotional experience and emotional involvement as well as a tendency to suppress all feeling" (Honigmann, 1961). This characteristic of the Kaska adult is thought to be related to inconsistent treatment of the child by its mother. During the first two years of life, the Kaska baby receives much maternal attention, warmth, and affection. However, as the child grows older, at about the second or third year, the mother gradually withdraws emotionally from the child and becomes less patient and indulgent. Honigmann feels

---

*From Sechrest, L. B., and Wallace, J.: *Psychology and Human Problems.* Columbus. Charles Merrill, 1967, p. 563.

that under these circumstances the child may make an "unconscious decision" never again to invest in a strong emotional relationship with others.

As intuitively appealing as Honigmann's explanation for emotional aloofness in the Kaska may be, we must treat it with caution. First of all, it is difficult, if not impossible, to test the assertion that the Kaska child makes an "unconscious decision" never again to invest in emotional relationships. Perhaps a simpler explanation could be drawn in terms of *social learning processes*. Given the fact that Kaska adults generally show this pattern of behavior, one could argue that the mere fact that the child is exposed each day of his life to adult models who display an attitude of emotional aloofness is sufficient to explain his adoption of the pattern. Second, as Sechrest and Wallace (1967) point out, any given event in the life of the child must be considered in its total cultural context. That patterns of initial indulgence followed by emotional withdrawal in the mother

Figure 36. This Kaska Indian child already shows in her facial features the emotional aloofness of the Kaska. She not only imitates the mother in the manner in which she carries her doll but perhaps in emotional expression as well. *From* Honigmann, J. J.: North America. *In* Hsu, F. L. K. (ed.): *Psychological Anthropology: Approaches to Culture and Personality.* Homewood, Ill., Dorsey Press, 1961.

need not lead to an adult personality of emotional aloofness is apparent in the Maori people of New Zealand. Despite the fact that Maori children are indulged early in their lives and then left largely to fend for themselves as far as further emotional development is concerned, the Maori people are described as generous, cooperative, and friendly (Beaglehole and Beaglehole, 1946).

The fact that the total cultural context must be considered is evident in studies of child development conducted within the United States. The evidence for *consistency* between childhood personality and adult personality is quite meager. In fact, one is almost tempted to conclude that in a society such as the United States, in which one is provided with many varied life experiences during both developmental and adult years, there is far more *inconsistency* than consistency in personality over long periods of time. Tuddenham (1959) studied adolescents and then restudied them in their early or middle adult years. The resulting correlations for 53 personality characteristics were so low as to render prediction of adult characteristics from adolescent characteristics impossible. A similar conclusion is reached in work by Rohrer and Edmonson (1960), who were largely unsuccessful in predicting adult characteristics from adolescent characteristics in Negro Americans.

The effects of cultural context upon the stability of certain characteristics is clearly evident in the work of Kagan and Moss (1962), who studied twenty-one males and females on four occasions in childhood and again when the children had reached twenty years of age. The continuity of certain personality characteristics was clearly dependent upon their congruence with cultural sex-role differentiations. That is, patterns of behavior clearly linked with traditional expectations for either male or female sex-role differentiations showed continuity. For example, we would expect males and females to differ in such attributes as passivity, dependence, aggression, and sexuality. Continuity for these characteristics was more stable than for other characteristics for which clear cultural expectations are not held. In general, however, the magnitude of the correlations between childhood characteristics and adult characteristics obtained in Kagan and Moss's study leads one to suspect that far more *change* than consistency can be expected in the development of personality, at least in American society.

In approaching the various findings that emerge from

cross-cultural studies of child-rearing practices and adult personality, it is important to bear in mind that it is highly unlikely that straightforward relationships can be expected. In the case in which a society provides diverse and rich developmental experiences, we would expect weak or nonexistent relationships between early experience and later experience. Even in cases in which relationships do appear in less complex cultures, one must be cautious in interpreting such findings. Child-rearing practices may be but one aspect of a host of other related variables that combine, often in poorly understood ways, to determine modal adult personality. Hence, to make inferences such as the Kaska child "unconsciously decides never again to invest in emotional relationships" as a consequence of inconsistent parental indulgence is particularly hazardous in explaining modal personality. There are many other features of Kaska culture, including the nonavailability of adult models who exhibit patterns of emotional style other than aloofness, that could explain adoption of modal personality style by the child.

In any event, the apparent difficulties in attempting to predict adult characteristics from childhood and adolescent characteristics in American society should caution one against any simple explanation of the effects of *early experience* on later behavior. Despite the fact that animal studies consistently show such effects, studies of human beings in fairly complex cultural contexts do not indicate a strong primacy effect of early experience. This fact suggests that in order to understand behavior, we may have to place far more emphasis upon an analysis of the person's *contemporary* social situation than upon his childhood. In the case of cross-cultural studies showing relationships between child-rearing practices and adult behavior, it is conceivable that such practices are imbedded in a total cultural context consistent with them. Hence, one must examine the contemporary cultural context for factors which *maintain* patterns of behavior initiated in early childhood. It is not reasonable to suppose that *no* subsequent pattern of experiences can modify tendencies established in early childhood. There is ample reason to believe that personality change can occur throughout the life of the person and that it is rarely fixed once and for all in early childhood. In examining the many justifications that persons offer for their behavior in American society, one is often tempted to believe that childhood experiences continue to be determinants of adult behavior largely because many people tend to *think* that they are. Moreover, for some the "tyranny" of early experience and especially the "shortcomings" of parents undoubtedly serve as convenient explanations for present deficiencies.

Factors affecting child-rearing

Varying child-rearing practices do not arise in a cultural vacuum. Examination of the larger cultural context in which they are imbedded indicates that child-rearing practices are in turn related to such factors as the physical environment and the economic system. For example, Barry, Child, and Bacon (1959) classified societies by their means of food gathering. They reasoned that vast differences exist in the types of social pressures generated between societies dependent upon animal husbandry and societies dependent upon hunting, fishing, and trapping. In a society sustained by animal husbandry, discipline, cooperation, and obedience are all necessary patterns of behavior both within the family and within the larger society. A hunting society, on the other hand, may result in considerable individual effort and, hence, less dependence upon others. Classifying societies as to their central means of food gathering, Barry, Child, and Bacon sought relationships between their classification system and the degree to which parents exerted pressures for compliance and conformity upon their children. As we can see from Table 9, clear relationships emerge.

In a recent study, Minturn and Lambert (1964) examined factors associated with different patterns of mothering in Mexico, India, Africa, Okinawa, New England, United States, and

TABLE 9. Relationship Between Food Gathering Practice and Pressure for Compliance*

Type of Economy	Percentage above median on compliance pressure	Number of societies
Animal husbandry	83%	24
Agriculture only	93	15
Agriculture, hunting, and fishing	33	18
Hunting and fishing	14	22

*Reproduced by permission of the American Antropological Association from American Antropologist, Vol. 61, No. 1, Yr. 59.

the Philippines. They discovered that maternal warmth was clearly associated with the relative *privacy* of living quarters. The least warm mothers were found in Mexico and India, both of which are characterized by "courtyard" or "semicourtyard" types of living arrangements, i.e., ones in which the mother and child relationship is most public. On the other hand, African and Filipino mothers who dwell in separate houses that are partially enclosed were intermediate in warmth. Okinawan mothers, who enjoyed even greater privacy, were the warmest of all. The possibility that the relationship is not strictly linear is suggested by the fact that New England mothers enjoyed the greatest privacy of all but ranked only fourth in maternal warmth.

While the exact relationship may be in doubt, it appears that living arrangements are related to maternal warmth. But why should this be the case? Minturn and Lambert reasoned that mothers in "close and crowded quarters" may control their emotional expressiveness to avoid quarrels between the children and their cousins and between themselves and their sisters-in-law.

Another finding from this study showed clearly that the degree to which the mother tolerated aggression directed toward her as well as the degree to which she herself behaved aggressively toward the child was related to the extent to which she participated in the economy in order to make contributions to the subsistence of the family. Mothers who performed work other than child-care and home management in order to meet the needs of the family were much more likely to be aggressive toward their children and to be intolerant of aggression directed toward themselves by the children. Apparently, this finding is not explained simply on the basis that working mothers are more impatient with their children or require them to perform more duties in the home. Minturn and Lambert speculated that mothers who achieve higher status by making economic contributions "emphasize" and "enforce" their high status in the family by refusing to tolerate child defiance.

From these studies, then, we can readily appreciate how pressures arising from features such as the type of economy, patterns of living arrangements, and economic well-being of the family unit can give rise to specific patterns of child-rearing. Of course, all of these are intimately related to the physical ecology of a people. A hunting subsistence economy can only arise in a

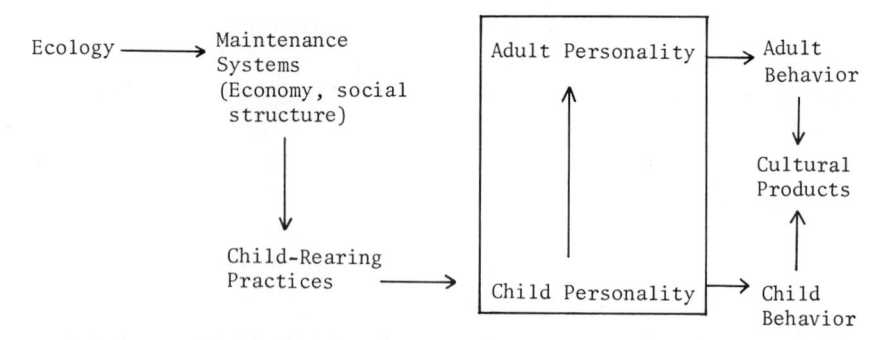

```
Ecology ──▶ Maintenance          Adult Personality ──▶ Adult
            Systems                      ▲                Behavior
            (Economy, social             │                  │
             structure)                  │                  ▼
                │                        │              Cultural
                │                        │              Products
                ▼                        │                  ▲
            Child-Rearing                │                  │
            Practices      ──────▶ Child Personality ──▶ Child
                                                          Behavior
```

Figure 37. Relationships among the components of a cultural system. *Adapted from* Whiting, J. W. M.: Sorcery, sin and the superego: A cross-cultural study of some mechanisms of social control. *In* Nebraska Symposium on Motivation. Lincoln, Neb., University of Nebraska Press, 1963, p. 5.

region of abundant game. Open courtyard living arrangements are encouraged by both economic and climatic factors. Working mothers are fostered in societies where the nature of work is appropriate and where economic well-being of the family is dependent upon the mothers' participation in the economy. These many complex relationships are best grasped in a schematic representation. In Figure 37 we see the relationships between the ecological system and the social system.

From Whiting's conceptual scheme for approaching a cultural system, we are reminded of the intimate relationships between the physical ecology and the social ecology of a region (see Chapter 9). In essence, then, the ecology of a people can give rise to particular types of subsistence economies which in turn can affect practices of child-rearing that can lead to different modal personalities.

Language, thought, and personality

The fact that languages vary across different societies is an important consideration in understanding cultural differences. There is ample reason to believe that the very nature of thought and, hence, the ways in which reality is experienced are influenced by language. The work of Benjamin Whorf (1960) is most intimately associated with the subtle connections between language, culture, and personality. It is amusing to note that Whorf was not led to his ideas about the link between language and behavior as an anthropologist or psychologist working among exotic peoples but as an investigator for a fire insurance company. It apparently took Whorf's considerable ingenuity and imaginativeness to note that many fires were caused not only by physical conditions as physical conditions but by the *linguistic meaning* which people attached to such conditions. For example, Whorf noted that around gasoline storage drums, great care is exercised, e.g., smoking is restricted and lighting of matches is prohibited. However, around "empty" gasoline drums behavior is different, i.e., there is little effort to control smoking, lighting of matches, or discarding of cigarette butts. In truth, the "empty" gasoline drums may constitute the more dangerous situation since they may very well contain highly explosive vapors. As Whorf points out, "Physically, the situation is hazardous, but the linguistic analysis according to regular analogy must employ the word 'empty,' which inevitably suggests lack of hazard." From examples such as these, Whorf concluded that the *linguistic meaning* which persons attached to various situations and actions was frequently involved in the development of costly and destructive fires.

Fortunately for the study of psychology and culture, Whorf did not confine his investigations to those in the service of fire insurance companies. He extended his ideas to include an exhaustive study of the Hopi Indian culture and the ways in which the Hopi language differs from European languages. In a fascinating study, Whorf showed that formal aspects of the language of the Hopi Indian could be related to the manner in which he experiences and represents *time*. Moreover, certain characteristic patterns of behavior of the Hopi could be related to his conceptions of time. In this manner, Whorf elegantly linked linguistic structure to thought and behavior.

In European languages time is represented as a linear succession of events with the aid of three tenses, namely past, present, and future. For the Hopi, time is not represented as a linear succession nor do words corresponding to the three tenses exist. As Whorf so neatly puts it,

> To the Hopi, for whom time is not a motion but a "getting later" of everything that has ever been done, unvarying repetition is not wasted but accumulated. It is storing up an invisible change that holds over into later events. As we have seen, it is as if the return of the day were felt as the

return of the same person, a little older but with all the impresses of yesterday, not as "another day," i.e., like an entirely different person.*

Given such remarkably differing ways of talking about and experiencing time, it is not surprising to find considerable difference between Hopi behavior and the behavior of persons using other linguistic representations. It is curious to reflect upon the fact that one can only come to feel guilty about "wasting time" when time is construed as a linear succession of events. For the Hopi, nothing that one does can be construed as "wasting time"—one cannot use up time when everything that ever was is simply "getting later"!

Of course, as we have pointed out in our discussions of naive personality theory and naive theory of society, language may be an important determinant of the ways in which both personal and social reality is known and experienced. The languages of the psychologist and the layman differ, and it is often these differences which lead each to construe social reality quite differently. Much the same can be said of any group of persons who specialize in the use of some article. Conklin (1954) reports that the Hanunoo tribesmen in the Philippines distinguish a total of 92 different varieties of "rice." The Nuer people of Africa, for whom cattle are an integral part of their subsistence economy, have literally thousands of terms in their vocabulary pertaining to cattle (Evans-Pritchard, 1940). Similarly, the Eskimo can distinguish among a far greater number of varieties of snow than can people living in different climates. Obviously, in matters of rice, cattle and snow, the respective perceptions of reality of the Hanunoo, Nuers, and Eskimos must differ enormously from those of the average American who can distinguish "white" and "brown" rice, "dairy" and "range" cattle, and "wet" and "dry" snow!

In considering language and personality, we are impressed with the many possible ways in which the meanings that we attach to events affect how we behave toward them. It would be surprising indeed if such meanings were not significantly shaped by the language through which we struggle to represent events. In order to appreciate the significance of Whorf's hypotheses concerning language, culture, and behavior, the

---

From Whorf, B. L.: The relation of habitual thought and behavior to language. *In* Spier, L., et al. (eds.): *Language, Culture and Personality.* Salt Lake City, University of Utah Press, 1960, p. 87.

student should consider them in light of material presented previously in Chapter 6 concerning interpersonal constructs, language, and interpersonal knowing. Much of what we think we "know" about ourselves and others is intimately related to how events are represented.

Culture and deviant behavior

It is possible from cross-cultural study to develop some understanding of the factors leading to deviant behavior. For example, Bacon, Barry, and Child (1965) found that with regard to alcohol usage, societies that exert strong pressure for achievement upon children but offer little opportunity for the satisfaction of adult dependency needs show a high frequency of drunkenness. Bacon, Child, and Barry (1963) found that criminal behavior varies with the opportunities for the child to have intimate contact with his father.

Societies differ greatly in the manner in which hostile-aggressive behaviors are managed. From these natural variations, it is possible to gain some understanding of the factors which encourage excessive hostility. It is possible, for example, that when individuals are prevented from expression of aggression in even its mildest forms, they fail to learn what might be termed a "graded series of aggressive behaviors" useful in coping with life's inevitable frustrations, heartaches, and disappointments. A "graded series of aggressive behaviors" means that each individual can be conceived as possessing a number of possible responses to frustration, anger, undesirable situations, and so forth. These responses range from very mild responses like, "I wish you wouldn't keep after me so, dear," to intermediate responses like, "If you don't stop talking that way, I'll haul off and sock you," to highly aggressive-hostile responses such as knifing, shooting, beating, or strangling another person. A person with a graded series of aggressive responses can use responses of lower intensity to warn others that he is "in no mood" to tolerate certain things, to save face in an argument, or even to "bully" a person whom he perceives as weaker than himself. However, when such responses are not possible, situations can frequently escalate to the point where a response of very serious magnitude can occur. Oftentimes excessive indulgence in alcohol will lower inhibitions against performing a hostile or even murderous impulse in a person in whom milder forms of aggression do not exist. It is possible, for example, that a person may possess no aggressive responses other than a high intensity "rage" response. Because he is incapable of warning others with low intensity aggressive responses, situations may escalate to the point where a severe response is almost appropriate.

That something like this may occur is evident from cross-cultural studies of the management of aggression. The Kaska Indians, for example, view hostility and anger quite negatively. Normally, individuals will go out of their way to avoid expression of aggression, yet drunken rages are reported as common occurrences among the Kaska. Sechrest (1966) reports that hostile aggression is strongly suppressed in the Philippines and that considerable effort is maintained to restrain children from both fighting and the expression of hostility through verbal abuse. Curiously enough, Filipinos, who are known for their "kindness," may murder in a sudden rage. Moreover, violence including murder is not uncommon in the course of drunken brawls in the Philippines. On the other hand, Whiting (1941) reports that the Kwoma people of New Guinea encourage much expression of hostility. However, though there is much evidence of intermediate hostility among the Kwoma in controlled hand-to-hand fights and other types of fighting, hostility rarely mounts to dangerous proportions.

We might conclude from these studies that in societies in which people are encouraged to utilize and to learn to utilize aggressive tactics of mild and intermediate strengths, expressed hostility will tend to stabilize around these levels of intensity. However, in societies in which this type of learning is not permitted and mild and intermediate expression of hostility is not encouraged, outbursts of excessive hostility may be a paradoxical consequence.

It is curious to note that "mass murderers" in American society are almost invariably described as "nice," "well-behaved" and "quiet" boys who never hurt anyone. Recently in a study of youthful murderers, Megargee (1964) has reported that prior to their committing a particularly violent and vicious murder, they showed evidence of far greater control of themselves than did youths convicted of other types of crimes.

Culture and mental disorder

It has long been suspected that cultural factors may very well be associated with the incidence, form, and symptoms associated with severe mental disorder. But, of course, considering the many complex problems associated with demonstrating these effects, it is difficult to establish the cultural factors involved in mental disorder clearly and unambiguously. First, there is the recurrent problem of lack of comparability in definitions of mental disorder. An act or pattern of behavior in one culture may signify totally different things in another culture. Given the fact that it is often difficult to obtain agreement between and among experts drawn from the *same* culture as to the presence or absence, nature, and formal diagnosis of mental disorder, it is not surprising to find that cross-cultural judgments are even more difficult to make.

Second, there is the persistent problem of separating cultural effects from genetic factors and biological factors generally, e.g., differences in diet, ingestion of differing chemicals, and so forth. For example, there is a form of psychosis called *pibloktoq* that occurs among the polar Eskimo people of northern Greenland (Fig. 21). The course of this disorder is as follows (Wallace, 1961):

1. Mild irritability and signs of withdrawal.
2. Wild excitement characterized by tearing off of clothing, smashing of furniture, and obscene shouting. Typically, the person leaves his shelter and races off across the tundra diving into snowbanks or climbing on icebergs.
3. The excitement, which may last for a period of several minutes to a half-hour, culminates in a stuporous sleep of 10 to 12 hours' duration.
4. Upon awakening, there is amnesia of what has happened, and the person resumes his normal business. Some people have repeated attacks; others have no more than a single attack.

Noting the similarity of the pibloktoq attack to Freud's account of hysteria, several writers have attempted to provide a psychoanalytic interpretation of it. Gussow (1960), for example, interprets the flight of the victim, a basically insecure person seeking love and reassurance, as a "seductive maneuver" or an invitation to be pursued. According to Gussow, the attack is little more than an expression of "basic Eskimo personality." It is, of course, difficult to see how Gussow determined what he claims to know about the underlying motivational basis for the attack.

Figure 38. An attack of Arctic pibloktoq. The woman has collapsed in a snow bank after racing wildly from her home. Courtesy of the American Museum of Natural History.

A different psychological explanation has been provided by Parker (1962), who argues that the Eskimo shaman is a powerful model. His characteristic histrionic and dramatic behavior may provide the people with a model of behavior when stress reaches intolerable limits.

Wallace (1961) takes a different line altogether. He notes that the high arctic environment does not provide the Eskimo with year round adequate supplies of calcium. Low levels of ionized calcium in the blood can produce a disorder called tetany which is in many respects highly similar to the cognitive and emotional disorganization of the pibloktoq attack.

Although it is not possible to choose among these alternative explanations of pibloktoq among the arctic Eskimos, we can readily appreciate the fact that psychocultural explanations cannot be accepted until plausible dietary differences are ruled out as a possible cause.

Aside from dietary deficiencies, the possibility of genetic inbreeding among small isolated cultural groups is a further difficulty in separating psychocultural explanations from psychobiological explanations.

Given these cautions in attempting to understand possible relationships between culture and mental disorder, there is sufficient reason to consider them as at least plausible explanations of mental disorders. As we have seen, cultures differ enormously in the extent to which they experience stress, the ways in which stress management is encouraged, and in a variety of ways of raising children, punishing deviants, and so forth. Hence, it is plausible that these factors may foster the development of mental disorder. Among certain peoples such as the Dobuans of New Guinea one can find "paranoia" (delusional thought, extreme suspicion) elevated to an institutionalized "life style." Among the Dobuans, magical thought is normative; crops will not grow without magical incantations, deaths are attributable to witchcraft, sexual desire depends upon love-magic, and economic transactions are thought to be dependent upon magic. The Dobuans are an intensely suspicious lot who evoke much hostility and counterhostility among themselves. Bad luck, a death in the family, and so on, are thought to be deliberately willed by other persons, and revenge murders are commonplace. But, of course, in the context of Dobuan society such behaviors are not deviant.

It is almost certainly true that the *nature and content of symptoms* are influenced by culture. As Sechrest and Wallace (1967) point out, visual hallucinations are much more common among Filipino patients than among American patients. In cultures where *residual* beliefs about witchcraft and sorcery are still in evidence, the symptoms of patients in mental hospitals are likely to reflect continued preoccupation with such beliefs. In contrast, in societies such as the United States, where residual beliefs of this kind are largely absent, the delusions of mental hospital patients are likely to center on the government, persecution by the FBI, or communists who plan to take over the country.

Marvin K. Opler (1957) has demonstrated that patterns of schizophrenia (a serious mental disorder) vary depending upon the cultural background of the patient. Opler examined Irish and Italian schizophrenic patients and concluded that Irish patients were inclined to develop elaborate and fixed delusions in which paranoid ideas concerning remarkable personal power or persecution were in evidence. Italians, on the other hand, expressed their difficulties in terms of violent swings of mood, hysterical laughter, and destructive outbursts. Curiously enough, while homosexuality is thought to be characteristic of schizophrenics, Opler found no evidence for overt homosexuality in his Irish sample, but 20 of the 27 Italian patients had become overtly homosexual. Opler attributed these differences to the fact that interest in sexuality is suppressed in Irish culture, whereas among the Italians frank and open interest in sexual matters is encouraged. Virtually all of the Irish patients tormented themselves with preoccupations of guilt over sex while none of the Italian patients were so inclined. Opler felt that these differences in the *expression* of the same illness, schizophrenia, were traceable to the differing family experiences and stress experiences of the Irish and the Italian patient.

Finally, it would appear that both the form and frequency of mental disorder varies from culture to culture. In the United States, the ratio of schizophrenics to manic-depressives (a disorder characterized by extreme variances of mood, elation, and depression) is about 3:1. On the other hand, it is reported to be 10:1 in the Philippines, 1:1 in some cultures, and in still others the ratio is reversed, showing a greater number of manic-depressives than schizophrenics. In terms of over-all frequency of mental disorder, Lin (1953), in reviewing a number of studies, reports that incidence figures vary from culture to culture. However, the precise meaning of such variation is, as we have pointed out above, difficult to interpret. Whether such differences reflect lack of comparability in definition, methods of data collection, dietary factors, genetic factors, or true psychocultural variation is not known with any degree of certainty.

SUMMARY

As we have seen, then, the individual can scarcely escape the pervasive and enduring effects of culture upon his thought, values, beliefs, and behaviors. We have examined the necessity of carrying out investigations in more than a single culture if psychology is to arrive at general laws of human thought and behavior. There is, in fact, ample reason to suspect that the very thought of the psychologist, the methods he employs, and the behavior of his subjects all can reflect cultural conditioning and hence cannot be generalized beyond a single culture.

From studies of child-rearing and the cultural context in which such training is conducted we have come to the conclusion that the serious student of social thought and behavior must come to think in terms of a cultural system composed of interdependent parts that interact with the physical ecology of the person.

With this discussion of culture and the person our present study of *Psychology: A Social Science* is completed. We began by examining the methods of inquiry used by the psychologist in the study of social thought and behavior. From our discussions of problems of inquiry in psychology as a social science it should be clear that both the layman and the inquisitive scientist must come to grips with the same problems of knowing. In the course of showing the relevance of psychological inquiry across a number of *levels of analysis*, we have seen that the psychologist has important contributions to make to the study of the individual, interpersonal interaction, group and organizational behavior, society, and culture. We have tried to examine substantive questions of clear relevance wherever possible. In this spirit, our discussion turned toward such matters as racism in America, violence, alienation, and ecological catastrophe. In addition, we examined some individual matters of importance, e.g., the self-concept, interpersonal tactics and defenses, social motives, and so forth.

If, in the course of his readings, the student has come to the conclusion that much of what he thinks he "knows" about human social thought and behavior requires reexamination, that is very good. But if he desires to know more and has gained a good idea of how to go about achieving this goal, that is very good indeed. It is, in fact, far more than any teacher should ask.

References

Bacon, M. K., Barry, H., and Child, I. L.: A cross-cultural study of drinking: II. Relations to other features of culture. Quart. J. Stud. Alcohol, 1965, pp. 29–48.

Bacon, M. K., Child, I. L., and Barry, H.: A cross-cultural study of correlates of crime. J. Abnorm. Soc. Psychol., 66: 291, 1963.

Barry, H. A., Child, I. L., and Bacon, M. K.: Relation of child training to subsistence economy. Amer. Anthro., 61, 1959.

Beaglehole, E., and Beaglehole, P.: *Some Modern Maoris.* Auckland, Whitcombe and Tombs, 1946.

Blakeney, E. H.: *The History of Herodotus.* (Translated by G. Rawlinson) London, Everyman's Library, Vol. 1, 1910.

Bowen, E. S.: *Return to Laughter*: An Anthropological Novel. New York, Doubleday and Company, Inc., 1964.

Child, I. L.: Personality in culture. *In* Borgatta, E. F., and Lambert, W. W. (eds.): *Handbook of Personality Theory and Research.* Chicago, Rand McNally & Co., 1968.
Cohn, T. S., and Carsch, H.: Administration of the F scale to a sample of Germans. J. Abnorm. Soc. Psychol., 49: 471, 1954.
Conklin, H. C.: The relation of the Hanunoo culture to the plant world. Unpublished doctoral dissertation, Yale University, 1954.
Dennis, W.: The human figure drawings of Bedouins. J. Soc. Psychol., 52: 209, 1960.
Doob, L. W.: Eidetic imagery among the Ibo. Ethnology, 3: 357, 1964.
Doob, L. W.: Exploring eidetic imagery among the Kamba of central Kenya. J. Soc. Psychol., 67: 3, 1965.
Evans-Pritchard, E. E.: *The Nuer.* Oxford, Clarendon Press, 1940.
Ghei, S. N.: A cross-cultural study of need profiles. J. Pers. Soc. Psychol., 3: 580, 1966.
Grinder, R. E., and McMichael, R. E.: Cultural influence on conscience development: resistance to temptation and guilt among Samoans and American Caucasians. J. Abnorm. Soc. Psychol., 66: 503, 1963.
Gussow, Z.: Pibloktoq (hysteria) among the Polar Eskimo: an ethnopsychiatric study. *In* Muensterberger, W. (ed.): *Psychoanalysis and the Social Sciences.* New York, International Universities Press, 1960.
Honigmann, J. J.: North America. *In* Hsu, L. K. F. (ed.): *Psychological Anthropology.* Homewood, Ill., Dorsey Press, 1961.
Kagan, J., and Moss, H. A.: *Birth to Maturity: A Study in Psychological Development.* New York, John Wiley & Sons, 1962.
Lambert, W. W., Triandis, L., and Wolfe, M.: Some correlates of beliefs in malevolence and benevolence of supernatural beings: A cross-cultural study. J. Abnorm. Soc. Psychol., 58, 1959.
Lin, T. Y.: A study of the incidence of mental disorder in Chinese and other cultures. Psychiatry, 16: 313, 1953.
Magargee, E. I.: Undercontrol and overcontrol in assaultive and homicidal adolescents. Unpublished doctoral dissertation, University of California, Berkeley, 1964.
Malinowski, B.: *Sex and Repression in Savage Society.* London, Kegan Paul, 1927.
Malinowski, B.: *Magic, Science, and Religion.* New York, The Free Press of Glencoe, 1948.
Mandelbaum, D. G.: Social uses of funeral rites. *In* Feifel, H. (ed.): *The Meaning of Death,* New York, McGraw-Hill Book Co., 1965.
Mead, M.: Research on primitive children. *In* L. Carmichael (ed.): *Manual of Child Psychology.* New York, John Wiley & Sons, Inc., 1946.
Melikian, L. H.: Authoritarianism and its correlates in the Egyptian culture and in the United States. J. Soc. Issues, 15 (No. 3): 58, 1959.
Minturn, L., and Lambert, W. W.: *Mothers of Six Cultures.* New York, John Wiley & Sons, Inc., 1964.
Mischel, W.: Father-absence and delay of gratification: cross-cultural comparisons. J. Abnorm. Soc. Psychol., 63: 116, 1961.
Mussen, P. H., Young, H. B., Gaddini, R., and Morante, L.: The influence of father-son relationships on adolescent personality and attitudes. J. Child Psychol. Psychiat., 4: 31, 1963.
Nadel, S. F.: Witchcraft in four African Societies: an essay in comparison. Amer. Anthro., 54: 18, 1952.
Opler, M. K.: Schizophrenia and culture. Scientific American, August, 1957.
Parker, S.: Eskimo psychopathology in the context of Eskimo personality and culture. Amer. Anthro., 64: 79, 1962.
Pelto, P. J.: *The Study of Anthropology.* Columbus, Charles Merrill, 1965.
Pospisil, L.: *Kapauku Papuans of West New Guinea.* New York, Holt, Rinehart and Winston, 1963.
Roberts, J. M., Arth, M. J., and Bush, R. R.: Games in culture. Amer. Anthro., 61: 597, 1959.
Roheim, G.: *Psychoanalysis and Anthropology.* New York, International Universities Press, 1950.
Rohrer, J. H., and Edmonson, M. S.: *The Eighth Generation.* New York, Harper and Row Publishers, Inc., 1960.
Schofield, R. W., and Sun, Chin-Wan.: A comparative study of the differential effect

upon personality of Chinese and American child training practices. J. Soc. Psychol., *52*: 221, 1960.
Sechrest, L. B.: Patterns of homicide in the Philippines and the United States. Unpublished paper, Northwestern University, 1966.
Sechrest, L. B., and Wallace, J.: *Psychology and Human Problems.* Columbus, Charles Merrill, 1967.
Sharp, L.: Steel axes for stone age Australians. *In* Spicer, E. H. (ed.): *Human Problems in Technological Change.* New York, Russell Sage Foundation, 1952.
Spiro, M. E., and D'Andrade, R. G.: A cross-cultural study of some supernatural beliefs. Amer. Anthro., *60*: 456, 1958.
Swanson, G. E.: *The Birth of the Gods.* Ann Arbor, University of Michigan Press, 1960.
Swenson, C. H.: Empirical evaluations of human figure drawings. Psychol. Bull., *54*: 431, 1957.
Tsujioka, B., and Cattell, R. B.: A cross-cultural comparison of second-stratum questionnaire personality factor structures — anxiety and extraversion — in America and Japan. J. Soc. Psychol., *65*: 205, 1965a.
Tsujioka, B., and Cattell, R. B.: Constancy and difference in personality structure and mean profile, in the questionnaire medium, from applying the 16 P.F. Test in America and Japan. Brit. J. Soc. Clin. Psychol. *4*: 287, 1965b.
Tuddenham, R. D.: Constancy of personality ratings over two decades. Genet. Psychol. Monogr., *60*: 3, 1959.
Turner, R. H.: Preoccupation with competitiveness and social acceptance among American and English students. Sociometry, *23*: 307, 1960.
Wallace, A. F. C.: Mental illness, biology, and culture. *In* Hsu, F. L. K. (ed.): *Psychological Anthropology.* Homewood, Ill., Dorsey Press, 1961.
Wallace, A. F. C.: *Culture and Personality.* New York, Random House, 1961.
Whiting, B. (Ed.): *Six Cultures: Studies of Child Rearing.* New York, Riley, 1963.
Whiting, J. W. M.: *Becoming A Kwoma.* New Haven, Yale University Press, 1941.
Whiting, J. W. M.: Sorcery, sin and the superego: a cross-cultural study of some mechanisms of social control. *In* Nebraska Symposium on Motivation, University of Nebraska Press, 1959, pp. 174–195.
Whiting, J. W. M., and Child, I. L.: *Child Training and Personality.* New Haven, Yale University Press, 1962.
Whorf, B. L.: The relation of habitual thought and behavior to language. *In* Spier, L., Hallowell, A. I., and Newman, S. S. (eds.): *Language Culture and Personality.* Salt Lake City, University of Utah press, 1960. (Originally published, Menasha, Wisconsin: Sapir Memorial Publication Fund.)

INDEX OF NAMES

Alexander, H. M., 104, 137
Allard, M., 205, 229
Allen, G. E., 32, 55
Allport, G., 123, 137
Allyn, J., 264, 273
Altman, I., 299–302, 321
Argyris, C., 312, 320
Aristotle, 161
Aronson, E., 114, 137, 268, 273
Arth, M. J., 387, 414
Asch, S. E., 201–202, 229, 280, 320
Atkinson, J. W., 78–79, 89, 147–150, 186

Bachrach, A. J., 134, 137
Back, K. W., 232, 274, 286, 293–294, 320, 321
Bacon, M. K., 402, 407, 413
Bain, H. M., 20, 30
Baker, J. W., 32, 55
Bandura, A., 162, 186, 252–253, 255, 273
Barker, R., 39–41, 45, 55
Barron, F., 8, 30
Barry, H., 402, 407, 413
Battle, E. S., 342, 374
Baughman, E. E., 342, 374
Bavelas, A., 66, 88, 262
Beaglehole, E., 400, 413
Beaglehole, P., 400, 413
Becker, H., 291–293, 321
Benjamin, L., 341, 374
Bennis, W. G., 307, 321
Bentham, J., 119
Berberich, J. P., 245, 274
Berger, S. M., 255, 273
Berkowitz, L., 162–164, 186
Bernard, J., 241–243, 273
Berne, E., 238–240, 273
Bettleheim, B., 248–249, 273, 344
Bevan, W., 218, 229
Bieri, J., 205, 229

Birney, R. C., 144, 146, 149, 186
Blacke, R. R., 20, 30
Blakeney, E. H., 382, 413
Botkin, P. T., 260, 274
Bowen, E. S., 385, 413
Bower, J. L., 120, 137
Braden, M., 290, 321
Breland, K., 51, 55
Breland, M., 51, 55
Broverman, D. M., 144, 186
Bruner, J., 178, 186
Bush, R. R., 387, 414
Butler, R. A., 104, 137
Byrne, D., 181, 186

Calhoun, J. B., 368, 374
Calvin, J., 81–82, 88
Campbell, D. T., 42, 55
Cannon, W. B., 107, 137
Carlsmith, J. M., 113–114, 137, 268, 273
Carlson, E. R., 205, 229
Carsch, H., 394, 414
Cattell, R. B., 376, 415
Chapanis, A., 114, 137
Chapanis, N. P., 114, 137
Child, I. L., 391, 392, 394, 396, 402, 407, 413, 414, 415
Chodorkoff, B., 183, 186
Christie, R., 151, 156–158, 186
Clark, J., 177, 186
Clark, K., 334, 343, 374
Clark, M., 334
Cleckley, H. M., 5, 30
Clinard, M. B., 351, 374
Cline, V. B., 218, 229
Cohen, A. R., 267, 269, 274
Cohen, K. J., 22, 23, 30
Cohen, M., 341, 374
Cohn, T. S., 394, 414
Cole, D., 144, 186

417

INDEX OF NAMES

Commager, H. S., 33
Conklin, H. C., 406, 414
Conot, R., 336-338, 374
Coopersmith, S., 59-63, 88, 168, 182, 186
Cronbach, L. J., 217, 229
Cross, T. L., 332-333, 374
Crowne, D. P., 125-126, 137
Cummings, E. E., 190
Cyert, R. M., 22, 23, 30

Dahlstrom, W. G., 342, 374
D'Andrade, R. G., 79, 89, 395, 415
Darwin, C., 91
Davies, J. C., 165-167, 186
deCharms, R., 198, 229
Dekker, E., 133, 137
Dembo, T., 39-41, 45, 55
Dennis, W., 389, 414
Deutsch, M., 280-282, 321
Dollard, J., 101-104, 137
Domhoff, W., 154-156, 186
Doob, L. W., 384, 414
Dukes, W. F., 218, 229
Durkheim, E., 348-349, 374

Edmonson, M. S., 400, 414
Ehrlich, P., 363, 374
Ericksen, C., 178, 186
Erwin, W. J., 134, 137
Evans-Pritchard, E. E., 406, 414
Evers, M., 339

Feld, S., 78-79, 89
Festinger, L., 113-114, 137, 232, 233, 264, 265, 273, 274, 290, 321
Flavell, J. H., 259-260, 274
Fowler, R. G., 19-20, 30
Freedman, J. L., 114, 137
French, J. R. P., 244-252, 257, 274
Freud, S., 53, 93-100, 176, 179, 180, 270, 380-381
Friar, J. T., 221-222, 229
Fromm, E., 276
Fry, C. L., 260, 274

Gaddini, R., 397, 414
Geis, F., 151, 156-158, 186
Gerard, H., 235-236, 274, 280-282, 321
Ghei, S. N., 387, 414
Glazer, N., 332, 374

Glucksberg, S., 259-260, 274
Golembiewski, R., 315, 321
Goodman, P., 351-352, 374
Graves, T., 14-19, 30, 328, 374
Greenspoon, J., 244, 274
Griffin, A., 336-337
Grinder, R. E., 393-394, 414
Groen, J., 133, 137
Gurin, G., 78-79, 89
Gussow, Z., 409, 414

Haire, M., 211, 229
Hall, E. T., 220, 229
Hall, G. S., 173
Hampton, D., 83-88, 89
Hanson, R., 14-19, 30, 328, 374
Hardyck, C. D., 221, 229
Hardyck, J. A., 290, 321
Harlow, H. F., 104, 105, 137
Harlow, M. K., 104, 137
Harvey, O. J., 295-297, 321
Hatch, R. S., 217-218, 229
Hebb, D. O., 4, 30
Hecock, D. S., 20, 30
Heider, F., 114-115, 137
Heilbroner, R., 70, 89
Hernandez-Peon, R., 217, 229
Herodotus, 381-382
Heron, W., 105, 137
Hill, H., 168, 187
Hill, K. T., 170, 186
Homans, G. C., 285-321
Honigmann, J. J., 398-399, 414
Hood, W. R., 295-297, 321
Hovland, C. I., 10-14, 30
Hsu, F. L. K., 395, 399
Hull, C., 101
Hunt, J., 175

Inhelder, B., 258, 274

Jackson, D. D., 265-266, 274
Jacobs, S., 144, 186
Jacobson, I., 262-263, 274
James, W., 91
Janowitz, M., 295, 321
Jarvis, P. E., 260, 274
Jessor, R., 14-19, 30, 328, 374
Jessor, S., 14-19, 30, 328, 374
Jones, E. E., 196-198, 229, 240-241, 274
Jordan, E. J., 144, 186
Jourard, S. M., 182, 186
Jouvet, M., 217, 229

INDEX OF NAMES

Kagan, J., 400, 414
Kahn, R. L., 129, 137
Katz, I., 341, 374
Kelley, G. A., 110–112, 137, 204–205, 222
Kelley, H. H., 202, 229
Keniston, K., 355–358, 374
Kenny, D. T., 162, 186
Kerckhoff, A. C., 293–294, 321
King, M. L., 339
Kish, G. B., 105, 137
Kogan, N., 168–170, 187
Krasner, L., 134
Krauss, R. M., 259–260, 274

Ladwig, G. W., 342, 374
Laird, C., 22, 30
Lambert, W. W., 395–396, 402, 403, 414
Larsen, O., 293, 321
Lasswell, H., 152–156, 186
Lawler, E. E., 308–311, 321
Lazarus, R. S., 179–180, 186
Leary, T., 271–272, 274
Leavitt, H. J., 67, 89
Lefcourt, H. M., 342, 374
Lefkowitz, M., 20, 30
Leventhal, M., 205, 229
LeVine, R. A., 395
Levinger, G., 177, 186
Lewin, K., 39–41, 45, 55
Likert, R., 314–315, 321
Lin, T. Y., 412, 414
Lorenz, K., 161–162, 186
Lorge, I., 27, 30
Lovas, O. I., 245, 274
Lowe, M. C., 168, 186
Luce, R. D., 25, 30

Maccoby, N., 265, 273
Maher, B., 176, 186
Malcolm X., 339
Malinowski, B., 380, 381, 385–386, 414
Mandelbaum, D., 382–384, 414
March, J. G., 23, 30
Marlow, D., 125–126, 137
Maslow, A., 108, 138
Matkom, A., 203–204, 229
Mayo, E., 311–312
McClearn, G. E., 104, 137
McClelland, D. C., 71–82, 89, 141–150, 328, 374
McDougall, W., 91–92, 138
McGinnies, E., 178, 186
McGrath, J. F., 299–302, 321
McGregor, D., 316–317, 321
McGuire, W., 117, 138, 269, 274
McKeachie, W. J., 219, 229

McMichael, R. E., 393–394, 414
Mead, G. H., 257, 274
Mead, M., 390–392, 414
Medalia, N., 293, 321
Megargee, E. I., 408, 414
Mehrabian, A., 220–223, 229
Melikian, L. H., 394, 414
Merritt, C. B., 19–20, 30
Merton, R. K., 348–351, 374
Meyer, D. R., 104, 137
Milgram, S., 43, 55, 63–65, 89
Mill, J. S., 119
Miller, N., 101–104, 137, 174–176, 186
Mills, C. W., 156
Mingione, A. D., 342, 374
Minturn, L., 402–403, 414
Mischel, W., 397, 414
Mohr, J. P., 134, 137
Montague, A., 339, 374
Montgomery, K. C., 105, 138
Morante, L., 397, 414
Morgenstern, O., 25, 31
Moss, H. A., 400, 414
Mouton, J. S., 20, 30
Mulder, M., 68, 89
Murray, H., 107–108, 138
Mussen, P. H., 397, 414

Nadel, S. F., 385, 414
Neill, A. S., 276, 321
Newcomb, T., 117, 138, 232, 274, 280, 321

Opler, M. K., 411–412, 414
Orne, M. T., 43, 55
Osgood, C., 116–117, 138

Parker, S., 410, 414
Pastore, N., 226, 229
Pavlov, I., 132–133
Pelto, P. J., 384, 414
Perloff, B. F., 245, 274
Pettigrew, T., 334–336, 339, 374
Phillips, I., 144, 186
Piaget, J., 258–259, 274
Pierce, J., 178, 186
Porter, L. W., 308–311, 321
Pospisil, L., 389–390, 414
Postman, L., 178, 186
Priest, R. F., 232, 274

Quinn, R. P., 129, 137

INDEX OF NAMES

Rabbie, J. M., 235–236, 274
Rabkin, K., 358–359, 374
Rabkin, L., 358–359, 374
Raiffa, H., 25, 30
Raven, B., 244–252, 257, 274
Razan, G., 134, 138
Remy, R. M., 182, 186
Ricks, D. F., 183–185, 187
Riecken, H. W., 290, 321
Roberts, J. M., 387, 414
Rogers, C. R., 125, 138, 271, 274
Roheim, G., 381, 414
Rohrer, J. H., 400, 414
Rosen, B. C., 79, 89
Rosenberg, M. J., 115–116, 117, 138, 168, 186
Rosenthal, R., 46, 55, 262–263, 274, 339
Ross, S. A., 255, 274
Rotter, J. B., 342, 374

Sarason, S. B., 170, 186
Sarbin, T. R., 131, 138, 221, 229
Sawyer, H. G., 20, 30
Sawyer, J., 232, 274
Schachter, S., 232, 234–235, 274, 290, 321
Schaeffer, B., 245, 274
Scherrer, H., 217, 229
Schmidtt, R., 370, 374
Schofield, R. W., 396–397, 414
Schwartz, R., 42, 55
Sechrest, L. B., 20, 31, 42, 55, 173, 180, 187, 397–398, 399, 408, 411, 415
Secord, P. F., 218, 229
Shakespeare, W., 219
Sharp, L., 388, 415
Shaw, G. B., 227–228, 229
Shaw, M. E., 27, 28, 31, 67, 68, 89
Sherif, C., 295–297, 321
Sherif, M., 295–297, 321
Simon, H., 121–123, 138
Singer, R. D., 245, 274
Skinner, B. F., 135, 138, 252–253, 274
Snoek, D. J., 129, 137
Soelberg, P., 23, 30, 123, 138
Solomon, H., 27, 30
Snyder, R., 252, 274
Spence, J. T., 171–172, 187
Spielberger, C. D., 244, 274
Spiro, M. E., 395, 415
Stock, D., 312, 321
Sudnow, D., 5–6, 31
Suinn, R. M., 168, 182, 187
Summer, C., 83–88, 89
Sun, C., 396–397, 414
Swanson, G. E., 385–386, 415
Swenson, C. H., 389, 415

Tannenbaum, P., 117, 138
Taylor, F. T., 305–306

Taylor, G. R., 368, 374
Thibaut, J. W., 196–198, 229
Thigpen, C. H., 5, 30
Thomas, E. J., 128, 138
Toch, H., 287–289, 321
Tolman, E., 52
Triandis, L., 395–396, 414
Tsujioka, B., 376, 415
Tuddenham, R. D., 400, 415
Turner, J., 268, 273
Turner, R. H., 392–393, 415
Tyhurst, J. S., 217, 229

Ullman, L. P., 134

Vannoy, J. S., 205, 229
Veroff, J., 78–79, 89
Von Neumann, J., 25, 31

Walker, D., 160–161, 187
Wallace, A. F. C., 392, 409–410, 415
Wallace, J., 131, 138, 173, 180, 187, 397–398, 399, 411, 415
Wallach, M. A., 168–170, 187
Walster, E., 225–226, 229
Walters, R. H., 162, 186
Watson, J. B., 92
Webb, E., 42, 55
Webber, R., 83–88, 89
Weber, M., 72, 73, 89
Wechsler, H., 370, 374
Weiss, W., 10–14, 30
Welsh, G. S., 8, 30
Wesman, A. E., 183–185, 187
White, B. J., 295–297, 321
Whiting, B., 415
Whiting, J. W. M., 394, 395, 396, 404, 408, 415
Whorf, B. L., 404–406, 415
Whyte, W. H., 303–305, 321
Wiley, R. C., 124, 126, 138
Winterbottom, M., 75, 89
Wolf, M., 395–396, 414
Wolfe, D. M., 129, 137
Wolpe, J., 133, 138
Worthy, J. C., 309, 321
Wright, J. W., 260, 274
Wundt, W., 4

Young, H. B., 397, 414
Young, W., 330–331, 374

Zajonc, R. B., 268–269, 274
Zubok, B., 144, 186

INDEX OF SUBJECTS

Ability to judge others, individual differences in, 217–218
Achievement, anxiety and, 170
 need for, 141–150
Achievement motivation, parental expectations and, 74–75
Affiliation, social comparisons and, 233–237
 uncertainty and, 233–237
African societies, 384–386
Aggression, catharsis and, 161–162
 displacement of, 164
 frustration and, 164
Ahistorical attitudes, of Americans, 376
Alcohol, ethnic groups and, 15
Alcoholic personality, 286
Alcoholics Anonymous, antiintellectual attitudes and, 289–290
 expectations of gain and, 285–286
 group influence and, 283–291
 identification and, 248
 magical powers and, 386–387
Alcoholism, drive reduction theory and, 103
Alienation, adolescent values and, 355
 failure of acculturation and, 355
 perceptions of parents and, 355–356
 protest and, 352
 psychology of, 353–358
 social structure and, 351–353
American group character, 392–394
American Indian(s), normative structure of, 16–18
 opportunity structure and, 16
 social control structure and, 18
American values, antiintellectualism and, 377
 generation gap and, 376–378
Anal character, 98
Anal stage, 96
Anomie, deviant behavior and, 17
 goal attainment and, 349
 normlessness and, 349

Antiintellectual attitudes, doomsday groups and, 290
 group influence and, 289–291
 social movements and, 289
Antiintellectualism, American values and, 377
Anxiety, achievement and, 170
 creativity and, 168–170
 curiosity and, 170–171
 defense and, 178
 drive theory and, 171–172
 generalization and, 172–173
 guilt and, 168
 learning and, 171–174
 magical thought and, 385–387
 school achievement and, 170
 self-esteem and, 167–168
 sensation seeking and, 170–171
Apparent movement, 194
Apparent personality, 203–204
Approach gradient, 174–176
Approval seeking, 125–126
Arab modal personality, 394
Arousal, attention and, 217
 interpersonal perception and, 216–217
 neurological blocking and, 217
 optimal level of, 106
Arousal theory, 106
Aspiration, level of, 121
Assumed similarity, 209
Attitude change, balance theory and, 114–116
 dissonance and, 113–114
 prejudice and, 115–116
Attitudes, ahistorical, of Americans, 376
 antiintellectual. See *Antiintellectual attitudes*.
 authoritarian, in groups, 301
 child rearing and, 394–398
 credibility of communicator and, 10–14
 political, and ecological crisis, 366–367
 sleeper effect and, 13–14
 toward death, 372

421

INDEX OF SUBJECTS

Attraction, in groups, 301
Authoritarian attitudes, in groups, 301
Authoritarianism, Arab, 394
  German, 394
Authority, obedience to, 63–66
Avoidance gradient, 174–176

Balance theory, 114–116
Balinese, 390–392
Bedouin Arabs, draw a person test and, 389
Behavior. See under adjective, as, *Defensive*, *Deviant*.
Behavioral models, 253
Benevolent-authoritative system, 314
Bennington College Study, 280
Black power, 151–152
Blacks, crime and, 339–341
  education of, 331
  health and medical care and, 331
  income and, 330–331
  opportunity structure and, 330–332
  unemployment and education and, 333–334
Bounded rationality, 121

Career choice, group interaction and, 291–293
  marijuana and, 291–293
Castration anxiety, 97
Categorization, 209
Catharsis, 161–162
Causal genetic set, 197
Causality, locus of, 224–225
Centralized structures, vs. decentralized structures, 308
Character, anal, 98
  genital, 98
  oral, 97
  phallic, 98
Chicago Democratic Convention, 158–161, 327
Child, concrete operational, 258
  preoperational, 258
Child-rearing, American vs. Chinese, 396–397
  attitudes toward supernatural and, 395–396
  courtyard living and, 403–404
  factors affecting, 402–404
  father-son relationship in, 397
  relation to food gathering, 402–403
Choice theory, 118–123
Classic conditioning, vicarious, 255–257
Classic organization theory, 306
Cognitive complexity-simplicity, generality of, 205–206

Cognitive complexity-simplicity (*Continued*)
  interpersonal perception and, 204–206
  reinforcement and, 205
Cognitive-informational theories, 109–127
Cognitive strain, interpersonal perception and, 191–193
Collective delusion, 293–294
Communication, conflict resolution and, 298–299
  credibility and, 267–268
  development of skills and, 258–261
  double-bind, 265–266
  egocentric, 258–260
  expectancies and, 261–263
  explicit vs. implicit conclusions and, 266–267
  incidental, 264
  influence and, 263–273
  one-sided vs. two-sided, 267
  organizational structure and, 83
  primacy vs. recency in, 267
  psychotherapy and, 269–273
  public commitment and, 267
  role-taking skills and, 260–261
  transmitters and receivers in, 268–269
Communication networks, 66–69
Communication structure, intermittent and inadequate, 86
  stress waves and, 86–87
  unidirectional patterns, 84–85
  unpredictable patterns, 85–86
Communicator, credibility of, 267–268
Competence, role theory and, 128–129, 131
Competition, ecological crisis and, 364
Computers, simulation and, 21
Concrete operational child, 258
Conditional reflex, 132
Conditional response theory, classical conditioning and, 132
  instrumental learning and, 134–136
Conditioning, asthma and, 135
  awareness and, 133
  classic vicarious, 255–257
  fear and, 133
  operant, 135–136
  psychotherapy and, 133
Conflict, among values, 397–398
  approach-approach, 174
  approach-avoidance, 174–176
  double approach-avoidance, 174
Conflict, group, 295–299
  organizational structure and, 84, 129–130
  social role, 129
  temporal gradients of, 176
Conflict resolution, bargaining and, 297–299
  communication and, 298–299
  increased exposure and, 297

Conflict resolution (*Continued*)
　perceived interdependence and, 297
　time-substance trade-off and, 298
Conformity, 281–282
　opinion, 240
　social structure and, 350
　status and, 20
Congruity, interpersonal description and, 200–201
Congruity-incongruity theory, 116–117
Connotative meaning, 116
Consciousness, drugs and, 271–272
Consistency, balance and, 114–116
　congruity and, 116–117
　dissonance and, 113–114
Constancy, 194
Constraints, social organizations and, 276–278
Constructive alternativism, 110
Constructs, 111
Consultative system, 314
Courtyard living, child-rearing and, 402–403
Creativity, anxiety and, 168–170
　preference for complexity and, 7–8
Credibility, of communicator, 267–268
Crime, among blacks, 339–341
　overpopulation and, 370
Cross-cultural study, relevance of, 378–381
　testing hypotheses of, 380–381
Cuban missile crisis, 154–155
Culturally disadvantaged, 343–344
Culture, generalization about, 384–390
　mental disorder and, 409–412
Curiosity, anxiety and, 170–171

Death, attitudes toward, 372
　in American society, 382
　hospital management of, 5–6
　in Kota society, 382–384
Decentralized structures, vs. centralized structures, 308
Decision-making structure, communication nets and, 68
Defense, anxiety and, 178
　perceptual, 177–180
　　defense mechanisms and, 179–180
Defense mechanisms
　denial, 96
　fixation, 95
　identification, 95
　projection, 95
　regression, 95
　repression, 97
Defensive behavior
　repression, 177
　sublimation, 94
Delay of gratification, 397

Deliberate misperception, 214–215
Delusion, collective, 293–294
Denial, 96, 179–180
　perceptual defense and, 179–180
Denotative meaning, 116
Dependency, drunkenness and, 407
Detroit race riots, 336
Deviant behavior, anomie and, 17
　cross cultural study and, 407–412
　group interaction and, 294
　normative structure and, 16–18
　opportunity structure and, 16
　organizational, and social systems, 83–88
　parental, and self-esteem, 182–183
　social control structure and, 18–19
　social-cultural system and, 15
Dietary deficiency, mental disorder and, 409–410
Differential accuracy, 218
Discriminative stimulus, 135
Dissonance theory, 113–114
Distance, interpersonal, 221
Division of labor, 348
Dobuans, paranoid thinking in, 411
Doomsday groups, antiintellectual attitudes in, 290
Double-bind communication, 265–266
Draw A Person Test, Bedouin Arabs and, 389
Drive doctrine, 100
Drive reduction, reinforcement and, 101
Drive reduction theory, alcoholism and, 103
　drug use and, 103
　learning and, 100–106
　reinforcement and, 101
Drives, learned, 100
　primary, 100
　secondary, 100
Drugs, use of, and drive reduction theory, 103
　and social learning, 254

Early experience, effects of, 400–402
Ecological crisis, multidimensional nature of, 366–367
　political attitudes and, 366–367
　profit maximization and, 361–363
　values and, 361–364
Ecology, human values and, 361–366
　relation to social ecology, 403–404
Economic development, and Protestantism, 73–74
Egocentric communication, 258–260
Eidetic imagery, 384
Elicited responses, 135
Emitted responses, 135

INDEX OF SUBJECTS

Empirical theory, 121
Energy theories, 90–109
English group character, 392–394
Environment, scientific-technological, 371–372
Eskimo personality, mental disorder and, 409–410
Eskimos, 406
Ethic, Protestant, 303
 social, 303
Ethnocentrism, 381–382
Event matching, 121
Expectancy, failure and, 147–148
 success and, 147–148
Expectancies, communication of, 261–263
 teacher and, 261–263
Expectations, experimenter bias and, 46
 failure in blacks and, 341–342
 group influence and, 285–286
 intelligence quotients and, 261–263
 interpersonal perception and, 207–208
 role theory and, 128–129
 violence and, 165–167
Expected gain, social interaction and, 237–238
Expected value, 119–120
Expert power, intelligence and, 252
Exploitive-authoritarian systems, 314
Extinction, 135
Eye contact, interpersonal perception and, 219–220

Failure, motivation to avoid, 147–148
 negative incentive value and, 148
 self-concept and, 126
 subjective probability of, 148
Fait accompli, as marital tactic, 242
Father absence, effects of, 397
Father-son relationship, identification and, 397
Filipinos, 397–398
 hallucinations in, 411
 hostility in, 408
Fixation, 95
Flattery, 240
Freedom, in organizations, 275–278
Free enterprise, ghetto social structure and, 332–333
Friendship choice, 232
Frustration, aggression and, 164
 regression and, 39, 41

Game(s), 238–240
 culture and, 387
 nonzero-sum, 26

Game(s) (*Continued*)
 prisoner's dilemma, 25
 zero-sum, 26
Generality, across operations, 50–51
 across situations, 49–50
 across subjects, 49
 temporal, 51, 68
 truth and, 51–53
Generalization, anxiety and, 172–173
Generation gap, 376–378
Genital character, 98
Genital stage, 97
German modal personality, 394
Ghetto social structure, 332–333
Goal-oriented behavior, the Balinese and, 390–392
Goals, attainment of, and anomie, 349
 by illegitimate means, 15–16
 interpersonal perception and, 195–198
Gradient, of approach, 174–176
 of avoidance, 174–176
Graffiti, 20
Gratification, delay of, 397
Griffin, Aubrey, case of, 336–338
Group character, 392
 American, 392–394
 English, 392–394
Group conflict, 295–299
Group influence, antiintellectual attitudes and, 289–291
 expectations of gain and, 285–286
 identification and, 286–287
 personal incompetence and, 283
 powerlessness and, 283–285
 social reinforcement and, 287–289
 willingness and, 285
Group interaction, deviant behavior and, 294
 problem-solving and, 27
Group research, 299–302
Groups, attraction in, 301
 reference, 279–280
 size of, 299
Guilt, anxiety and, 168
 social control and, 393–394

Hallucinations, in Filipinos, 411
Hanunoo tribesmen, 406
Hawthorne studies, 311–312
Higher-order needs, 108
Hippies, 212–214
Homeostasis, 107
Homosexuality, in schizophrenia, 412
Honesty, 19
Hopi Indians, language of, 405–406
 time concepts of, 405–406
Hostility, 158–167
 catharsis and, 161–162

INDEX OF SUBJECTS

Hostility (*Continued*)
 in Filipinos, 408
 in Kaska Indians, 408
 in Kwomas, 408
 in mass murderers, 408
Human potentialities, participation and, 313–316
 theory of, 313–316
Human relations, 311–313
Hypothesis testing, cross-cultural, 380–381
Hysterical contagion, 293–294

Ideal self, 181
Identification, father-son relationship in, 397
 group influence and, 286–287
 referent power and, 248–249
 with aggressor, 248–249
Identity, racism and, 334–335
Illness, oral socialization and, 394–395
Incidental communication, 264
Individuals, assumptions about, 316–317
 organization theory and, 316–317
Inference, 34–38
 interpersonal perception and, 195
Inferential sets, 196–198
Influence, communication and, 257–273
 group. See *Group influence.*
 interpersonal, 243–257
Informal social structure, 312
Information overload, interpersonal perception and, 191–193
Information processing, interpersonal perception and, 190–193
Information reduction strategies
 assumed similarity, 209
 behavioral tests, 215–216
 categorization, 209
 deliberate context variation, 215
 deliberate misperception, 214–215
 generalizing attributes of behavior, 209–210
 role perception, 210–211
 stereotyping, 211–214
Information-seeking, social comparisons and, 232–236
Informational influence, 280–282
Innovation, social structure and, 351
Inquiry, scientific. See *Scientific inquiry.*
Insecticides, ecological crisis and, 363–367
Instinct, 34
 death, 93
 life, 93
Instinct theory, 93
Intelligence quotient, expectation and, 261–263
Intentionality, 225–226
Interaction, group. See *Group interaction.*

Interpersonal distance, 221
Interpersonal perception, ability to judge by, 217–218
 cognitive complexity and, 204–206
 context and, 223–228
 distance and, 220–221
 emotion and, 216–217
 eye contact and, 219–220
 facial features and, 222–223
 goals and, 195–198
 information overload and, 191–193
 information processing and, 190–193
 language and, 198–204
 naive personality theories and, 202–204
 observation and, 195
 physical characteristics and, 218–219
 postural cues and, 221–222
 strategies of, 208–216
 temporal focusing and, 206–208
 vocalization and, 222–223
Interpersonal tactics, ingratiation by, 240–241
 people's games and, 238–240
Interpersonal description, 200–201
Intuition, 189
Irish, schizophrenia in, 411–412
Italians, schizophrenia in, 411–412

Jazz musicians, marijuana use and, 291–292
John Birch Society, 289
Justifiability, 226

Kaska Indians, 398–399
 hostility in, 408
Khan, Genghis, 153
Kibbutz, life in, 358–360
Kotas, 382–384
Kwomas, hostility in, 408

Language, ambiguity and, 22
 interpersonal perception and, 198–204
 of Hopi Indians, 405–406
 thought and, 404–407
 trait inference and, 201–202
Latency period, 97
Law enforcement, racism and, 330
Leadership, 301–302
Learned drives, 100
Learning, anxiety and, 171–174
 classic conditioning and, 132–134
 cultural disadvantages and, 343–344
 instrumental learning and, 134–136
 secondary drives and, 100
 social, 252–257
 teacher expectations and, 261–263

426 INDEX OF SUBJECTS

Legitimate power, elections and, 250
Level of aspiration, 121
Locus of causality, 224–225
LSD, interpersonal influence and, 272

Machiavellianism, 156–158
Magic, anxiety and, 386–387
　helplessness and, 386–387
Manic-depressive psychosis, 412
Manpower training programs, for blacks, 344
Maori people, 400
Marijuana, drive reduction theory and, 103
　use of, and jazz musicians, 291–292
　and peer influence, 292
　and social learning, 254
Mass murderers, hostility in, 408
Maximizing, 121–122
Means-ends relationships, in Balinese culture, 390–392
Media, racism and, 346–347
Mental disorder, dietary deficiency and, 409–410
Methods of inquiry
　clinical, 4–6
　correlational, 7–8
　field study, 14–19
　games, 25–26
　laboratory experiments, 8–14
　mathematical models, 26–28
　quasi-experiments, 19–21
　simulation, 21–26
Mexican-Americans, teacher expectations and, 263
Misperception, deliberate, 214–215
Modal personality, 392
　of Arabs, 394
Models, behavioral, 253
　mathematical, 26–28
　simulation, 21
Mood variability, self-ideal discrepancy and, 184
Motivation, to avoid failure, 147–148
Multiple personality, 5

Naive instinct theory, 91–93
Naive personality theories, 202–204
Naive theory of society, 327
Nazi revolution, 165
Need for achievement, and Protestantism, 72–73
　economic development and, 70–82
　reliability of measurement, 146
　risk-taking and, 147–149
　scholastic achievement and, 143–145
　Thematic Apperception Test and, 142–143

Need for achievement (*Continued*)
　validity of measurement of, 143–146
Need theories, 106–109
Needs, higher-order, 108
　of Indians vs. Americans, 387
Neurotic paradox, 119
Normative influence, 280–282
Normative theory, 121
Norms, 279–280
　alienation and, 348
　ambiguous, 349
　contradictory, 349
Novel belief systems, uncertainty and, 386
Novelty, American values and, 377
Nuclear weapons, ecological crisis and, 364
Nuer people, 406

Obedience, authority and, 63–66
Observation, 34–38
　interpersonal perception and, 195
Observation, 34–38
Oedipus conflict, 96, 99
　cross-cultural study of, 380–381
Operant conditioning, 135–136
Opinion conformity, 240
Opportunity structure, blacks and, 330–332
　of the ghetto, 332–333
Optimal level of arousal, 106
Oral character, 97
Oral socialization, 394–395
Oral stage, 94–96
Organization man, 303–305
Organization theory, assumptions about individuals and, 316–317
Organizational behavior, social systems and, 83–88
Organizational change, 318–320
Organizational structure, centralized vs. decentralized, 308–309
　classic theory and, 306–311
　interpersonal conflict and, 83–88
　psychological stress and, 83–88
　size, 310–311
　tall vs. flat, 309
Organizational study, value of, 278
Organizations, freedom in, 275–278
　physical design of, 317–318
　shape of, 309
　size of, 310–311
Overpopulation, crime and, 370
　social organization and, 368–369
　social pathology and, 368

Parental behaviors, self-esteem and, 182–183

INDEX OF SUBJECTS

Participation, human potentialities and, 313–316
  in groups, 302
Participative group systems, 314
Peer influence, marijuana use and, 292
Perceived self, 181
Perceived size, 194
Perception, interpersonal. See *Interpersonal perception.*
  of social issues, 327
Perceptual defense, accuracy of self-perception and, 183
  defense mechanisms and, 179–180
  denial and, 179–180
  repression and, 179
Perceptual vigilance, 178
Personal construct theory, 110–112
Personality, childhood to adult, 398–402
  modal, of Arabs, 394
  of eskimos, and mental disorder, 409–410
  politics and, 152–156
Phallic character, 98
Phallic stage, 96–97
Pibloktoq, 409–410
Police, selection of, 344–345
Police training, 344–345
Police violence, Chicago Democratic Convention and, 158–161
  Watts rebellion and, 336–338
Political attitudes, ecological crisis and, 366–367
Politics, personality and, 152–156
  radical, 151
Population, governmental control of, 370–371
  human values and, 368–371
Posture, interpersonal perception and, 221–222
Power, 150–156
  bases of, 244–252
  black, 151
  coercive, 246–247
  expert, 251–252
  legitimate, 249–250
  motivation to, 152–156
  referent, 247–249
  reward, 244–246
  status and, 301
Power elite, 155–156
Powerlessness, black achievement and, 341–342
  group influence and, 283–285
  magic and, 385–387
  susceptibility to influence and, 283–285
Power-seeking, deprivation and, 152–154
  inherited advantage and, 154–156
  self-esteem and, 153–154
Prediction, 35–38
Preoperational child, 258

Prescriptive theory, 121
Primacy, vs. recency, 267
Primary drives, 100
Primitive people, logical thought and, 389–390
Principle of association, 132
Probability, subjective, 120
Problem-solving, 27
Profit maximization, ecological crisis and, 361–363
Progressive Labor Party, 289
Projection, 95
  psychoanalysis and, 270
Propinquity, 232
Protestant ethic, 303
Protestantism, economic development and, 73–74
Psychosexual development, adult personality and, 97–98
  anal stage in, 96
  genital stage in, 97
  libido and, 94
  oral stage in, 94–96
  phallic stage in, 96–97
Pseudo-participation, human relations and, 313–314
Psychoanalysis, 270
Psychosexual stages. See *Psychosexual development.*
Psychotherapy, communication and, 269–273
  conditioning and, 133

Rebellion, social structure and, 350
Racism, identity and, 334–335
  school textbooks and, 329–330
  self-esteem and, 334–335
  threat and, 336–339
  unequal law enforcement and, 330
Recency, vs. primacy, 267
Reciprocity, interpersonal perception and, 227–228
Reference groups, 279–280
  social comparisons and, 280
Regression, 95
Reinforcement, 135
  cognitive complexity and, 205
  drive reduction and, 101
Repression, 94, 97, 177–179
Repressors, 178–179, 181
Response hierarchies, 171
Responses, elicited, 135
  emitted, 135
Responsibility, 226
Retreatism, social structure and, 350
Revolution, rising expectations and, 165–167
Riot Commission, report of, 322–327

INDEX OF SUBJECTS

Riots, urban, 294–295
Risk-taking, expectancy for failure and, 146–147
  expectancy for success and, 147–148
  need for achievement and, 147–149
Ritualism, social structure and, 350
Role Construct Repertory Test, 111
Role perception, 210–211
Role-taking, aptitude for, 131
  skill for, 131, 260
Role theory, ambiguity and, 130
  competence and, 128–129
  conflict and, 129
  discontinuity and, 130
  expectations and, 128–129
  overload and, 130

Sampling, generality and, 49
  situations and, 48
  subjects and, 48
  tasks and, 48
Satisficing, 121–122
Schizophrenia, cross cultural, 412
  double-bind communication and, 265–266
  homosexuality and, 412
  in Irish, 411–412
  in Italians, 411–412
  metabolism of epinephrine and, 9
School achievement, achievement motivation and, 143–145
Scientific inquiry, alternative explanations and, 38
  uncertainty and, 39–49
Scientific management, 305
Scientific-technological environment, 371–372
Secondary drives, 100
Selection of police, 344–345
Self-acceptance, mood fluctuation and, 183–184
Self-actualization, 108, 125, 127
Self-concept, approval seeking and, 125–126
  ideal self and, 181
  perceived self and, 181
  positive regard and, 125
  self-ideal discrepancy and, 181, 184
  success and failure and, 126
  unconditional positive regard and, 125
Self-concept theory, 123–127
Self-esteem, anxiety and, 167–168
  creativity and, 59–63
  intelligence and, 61–62
  parental attitudes and, 182–183
  persuasibility and, 269
  power seeking and, 152–154
  racism and, 334–335

Self-fulfilling prophecy, 261–263
Self-fulfilling prophecies, black failure and, 341–342
  police-ghetto relations and, 342–343
Self-ideal discrepancy, adjustment and, 181, 184
  mood variability and, 183–184
Self-insight, adjustment and, 127
Self-presentation, 240
Semantic differential, 116
Sensation-seeking, anxiety and, 170–171
Sensitivity training, 312–313
Sensitizers, 178–179, 181
Simulation, computers and, 21
  descriptive, 23
  general hypotheses and, 23
  man-machine systems and, 24
  RAND air defense, 24
  social system design and, 23
  training and, 24
Situation-matching set, 197
Social comparisons, affiliation and, 233–237
  information seeking and, 232–236
  reference groups and, 280
Social-cultural system, deviant behavior and, 15
Social ethic, 303
Social learning, conditioned emotional responses and, 255–256
  delinquent behavior and, 254
  drug use and, 254
  in Kaska Indians, 398–399
  marijuana use and, 292
  racial prejudice and, 255–256
Social motives, achievement and, 141–150
  hostility and aggression and, 158–167
  machiavellianism and, 156–158
  manipulation and, 150–158
  measurement and, 141–146
  power and, 150–156
Social movements, 289
Social norms, reference groups and, 280
Social reinforcement, Alcoholics Anonymous and, 288
  awareness and, 245
  group influence and, 287–289
  of allergic symptoms, 246
  of antiauthoritarian attitudes, 245
  operant conditioning and, 244–245
  punishment and, 246–247
  TOPS and, 287–289
  unwitting, 245–246
Social structure. See *Structure, social*.
Social systems, organizational behavior and, 83–88
Socialization, Samoan vs. American, 392–394
Split-level personality, 397–398
Stereotype accuracy, 218

INDEX OF SUBJECTS 429

Stereotyping, 192-193, 211-214
  of alcoholic personality, 286
  of blacks, 212, 214
  of hippies, 212-214
Status, conformity and, 20
  power and, 301
Stimulus, discriminative, 135
Stimulus seeking, 105
Strategic promise, 242
Strategic threat, 242
Strategies, for interpersonal perception, 208-216
Stress-mediated disease, overpopulation and, 368-369
Stress waves, communication structure and, 86-87
Structure, social, ghetto, 332-333
    informal, 312
    rebellion and, 350
    retreatism and, 350
    ritualism and, 350
Structures, centralized, vs. decentralized, 308
Students for a Democratic Society (SDS), 151
Subjective probability, 120
Sublimation, 94
Success, incentive value and, 147
  self-concept and, 126
  subjective probability of, 147
Suicide, 349
System, benevolent-authoritative, 314
  exploitive-authoritarian, 314
  participative group, 314

Tachistoscope, 177
Tactics, ingratiation, 240-241
  interpersonal, 238-243
  machiavellian, 156-158
  marital, 241-243
  vs. defenses, 180
Tactile comfort, 104
Television, racism and, 346-347
  urban riots and, 294-295
Temporal focusing, interpersonal perception and, 206-208
Testing, of hypotheses, 380-381
Thematic Apperception Test, achievement motivation and, 142-143
Time, group bargaining and, 298-299
  in Hopi culture, 405-406
TOPS, 287-289

Transference, 270
Trobriand islanders, 380-381

Uncertainty, affiliation and, 233-237
  experimenter effects and, 44-45
  incomplete experimental design and, 40
  intervening variables and, 41
  magic and, 385
  maturation and, 42
  observer bias and, 40
  reactivity of measurement and, 42
  response biases and, 44
  sampling and, 47
  social comparisons and, 233-237
  uncontrolled subject changes and, 41
Urban riots, 294-295
Utility-maximization, 119-123

Values, American, 376-378
  antiintellectualism and, 377
  generation gap and, 376-378
  conflict among, 397-398
  ecological crisis and, 361-364
  population and, 368-371
  split-level personality and, 397-398
  technological change and, 371-372
Value-maintenance set, 196
Vicarious Classical Conditioning, 255-257
Violence, at Democratic National Convention, 158-161
  effects of witnessing, 162-163
  fire arms control and, 163-164
  hostile stimuli and, 163-164
  inhibition to, 166-167
  justified, 163-164
  police, 336-338
  revolutionary, 165-167
  rising expectations and, 165-167
  snowballing effect of, 163-164
  television contagion and, 294-295
  television programming and, 162-163
Vocalizations, interpersonal perception and, 222-223
Voter choice, ballot position and, 20

Watts rebellion, 336
Witchcraft, 384-386
Word association, 177